Also by Richard Norton Smith

THOMAS E. DEWEY AND HIS TIMES
AN UNCOMMON MAN: *The Triumph of Herbert Hoover*

Richard Norton Smith

THE HARVARD CENTURY

The Making of
a University to a Nation

SIMON AND SCHUSTER

NEW YORK

Copyright © 1986 by Richard Norton Smith
All rights reserved
including the right of reproduction
in whole or in part in any form
Published by Simon and Schuster
A Division of Simon & Schuster, Inc.
Simon & Schuster Building
Rockefeller Center
1230 Avenue of the Americas
New York, New York 10020
SIMON AND SCHUSTER and colophon
are registered trademarks of Simon & Schuster, Inc.
Designed by Edith Fowler
Manufactured in the United States of America

10 9 8 7 6 5 4 3 2 1

Library of Congress Cataloging in Publication Data

Smith, Richard Norton, date.
  The Harvard century.

  Bibliography: p.
  Includes index.
    1. Harvard University—Presidents—Biography.
I. Title.
LD2136.S64 1986   378'.111 [B] 86-6769
ISBN 0-671-46035-8

Grateful acknowledgment is tendered the following:
    Harvard University Archives, for permission to quote from the A. Lawrence Lowell
Papers.
    Mr. Theodore Conant, for permission to quote from the personal papers of James
Bryant Conant.
    Interviews with W. E. B. Du Bois, Arthur Page, Ralph Lowell, Claude Fuess, William Laurence, Roger Baldwin, copyright © 1972; Norman Ramsay, copyright © 1980;
used by permission of the Trustees of Columbia University in the City of New York.
    Interview with Mary I. Bunting, by permission of the Arthur and Elizabeth Schlesinger Library, in cooperation with the Columbia University Oral History Collection.
    Interview with Paul H. Buck in the Columbia University Oral History Collection,
used by permission of Mrs. Paul H. Buck.
    Interview with William Cowley in the Columbia University Oral History Collection, used by permission of the William Cowley estate.

To LAURA J. CONNOLLY,
who guided my steps to Harvard,
and JAMES STROCK,
who encouraged me to write about what I found there,
these pages are dedicated with affectionate thanks.

It is not learning but the spirit of service that will give a college place in the public annals of the nation. . . . We dare not keep aloof and closet ourselves while a nation comes to its maturity. The days of glad expansion are gone, our life grows tense and difficult, our resource for the future lies in careful thought, prudence, and a wise economy; and the school must be the nation.

—WOODROW WILSON

To accomplish its mission Harvard must be a truly national university.

—JAMES BRYANT CONANT

Contents

PROLOGUE

The Country and the College

A republic within the Republic, a church that cuts across the churches, a class drawn from all classes.

—BERNARD DE VOTO'S
definition of Harvard

1986 MARKS the 350th anniversary of Harvard College, and of higher education in America. Those who gather in Harvard's Tercentenary Theatre this September will carry on in the tradition of John Adams, who long ago informed his radical cousin Sam, "Boston town meetings and our Harvard College have set the universe in motion." As it has throughout its own considerably shorter history, the rest of America will pay attention. For now, as in Adams's day, Harvard remains a symbol of excellence, a synonym for elitism, and an inviting target in a land whose twin ideals are achievement and egalitarianism.

However venerable, this latest milestone by itself would hardly seem to justify yet another volume to add to the hundreds composed over the years, describing, interpreting, assailing, or defending an institution that claims six American Presidents, thirty Nobel laureates, two dozen Pulitzer Prize winners, over two hundred Rhodes Scholars, and numerous Supreme Court justices, congressmen, Cabinet officers, governors, ambassadors, pundits, publicans, and bond salesmen. Still, since Samuel Eliot Morison published his monumental survey of the colonial college half a century ago, there has been no comprehensive attempt made to carry Harvard's story to the present day. Nor has there been a volume that tried to place

11

Harvard in its national context or explain how the country and the college grew as uneasy allies and frequent antagonists. Their love-hate relationship reveals much about our attitudes toward scholarship versus citizenship and the value of culture in a world that demands expertise. In a search for civilized pluralism and for tolerance of what Willa Cather called "the noisy push of the present," they have come to reflect one another more than either suspects.

It would be difficult to exaggerate the importance of the nation's oldest academy. When H. L. Mencken compiled his famous dictionary of Americanisms, he found space for three references to Harvard, though none for Yale. As late as the 1930s, the University did not recruit professors; it issued a "call" to eminent scholars. And why not? Harvard held itself to be the epicenter of American education. It had invented the case study method of legal and business instruction. It had pioneered in American history and political economy, city planning and preventive medicine.

Modern Harvard can lay claim to discoveries in DNA and about hybrid corn, blood banks, birth control pills. From a Cambridge lab came the first primitive forerunner of computerized intelligence (it was a fifty-foot "mechanical brain" used mostly by the U.S. Navy, with only Christmas and New Year's Day off). Other Cambridge classrooms have produced such writers as Thomas Wolfe, John Dos Passos, Norman Mailer, and John Updike, poets with as wide a range as T. S. Eliot and Ogden Nash, musicians from Virgil Thomson to Cole Porter, and thespians Thornton Wilder, Robert Sherwood, Jack Lemmon, and Peter Sellers.

The faculty in their robes and mortarboards who fill the Yard this autumn of 1986 to celebrate 350 years can look over their shoulders at both Frederick Jackson Turner and Timothy Leary. Their illustrious predecessors have awakened or disciplined the curiosity of undergraduates from Cotton Mather to Alger Hiss.

Secretary of State George Marshall journeyed to Harvard's commencement in the Spring of 1947 to unveil the European rescue operation that bears his name. Thirty years later, Aleksandr Solzhenitsyn mounted that platform to scold the West for moral and spiritual apathy. Asked by reporters why he had chosen Harvard, Solzhenitsyn replied, "Harvard is Harvard."[1]

The same institution has served as foil for rebelling youth and resentful presidents. Lyndon Johnson said he would never get credit for anything he achieved in foreign affairs because he had not gone to Harvard. Richard Nixon made snide references to the school to his Cabinet, four of whose members held Harvard degrees.[2]

Under John Kennedy, the University sometimes imagined itself to be the fourth branch of government, an impression JFK did little to dispel. Consider his 1961 encounter with Nathan Pusey, then president of his alma mater. The two men met in the shadow of Kennedy's tense summit confrontation with Nikita Khrushchev that June. Their conversation soon turned to the demands on the American presidency, and how they had grown since the office had been filled a generation earlier by another Harvard man. As Kennedy put it, "Well Nate, when Franklin had this job . . . he didn't have all these world problems. He had only to cope with poverty in the United States. But look what I've got." The description revealed much about an era filled with hubris—individual, institutional, and finally, national.[3]

A few years ago, a brash undergraduate on his way to being a brash, single-term congressman from Long Island wrote a book entitled *Harvard Hates America*. William F. Buckley Jr. said the title was the best thing about John Le Boutellier's slender volume. But as an eye-catching phrase, it expressed perfectly the distrust many outside Cambridge harbored for ivory towers and social engineers.

Inside the Harvard community, most of the attacks were launched by Le Boutellier's contemporaries on the left. Such critics regarded the University as an integral link in a ruling structure which justified foreign wars, oppressed Cambridge's downtrodden, or simply stifled the individuality William James had in mind when denouncing "the curse of bigness" and defining Harvard's undisciplinables as her proudest product.

Colorful as they may be, these examples represent merely a first draft of history. My own intention is admittedly more audacious: an attempt to trace the process by which a provincial academy, flavored by regional and religious pride, threw off its Puritan chrysalis and declared itself America's de facto national university. The reader is hereby put on notice that while 1986 may technically be Harvard's 350th anniversary, it is a much younger institution that draws attention from the world over. Until the Civil War, Harvard was little more than an academy of manners for Boston's gentry. Reflecting modest ambitions and the ideals of literary New England, it was content to supply liberal arts grounding to ministers and magistrates.

Then came the age of expansion dominated and personified by Harvard President Charles William Eliot. It was Eliot, a plain man in a plush age, who unmortgaged Harvard from her past, severed her Yankee roots, and began her transformation into an instrument of national purpose. What followed forms the heart of this narrative. It also explains why Harvard demands interpretation from a fresh perspective.

From Eliot's manifest destiny to the corporate management of President Derek Bok, the last century of Harvard's evolution reflects the development of American society in surprising ways. This is nowhere truer than in our definitions of authority, the establishment of goals, and the fashioning of leadership capable of realizing a common agenda. Empire has yielded to Commonwealth. Those who dwelt comfortably atop Eliot's Olympus have made way for other leaders. While America has been governed by twenty-three presidents since the Civil War, Harvard's destinies in the same period have been entrusted to just five men. Their trials and triumphs, in an office which the *New York Herald Tribune,* as late as 1937, labeled the most important in the land, combine to make this both institutional biography and an examination of leadership's shift away from yesterday's heroic model. By inviting the outside world to enter Harvard's cloister, Eliot and his successors ensured that it would one day level the University's walls.

Thinkers and Doers

*Another light was kindled at Newtown in the
Bay Colony in 1636. But the spark that touched
it off came from a lamp of learning first lighted
by the ancient Greeks, tended by the Church
through the Dark Ages, blown white and high
in the medieval universities, and handed down
to us in direct line through Paris, Oxford, and
Cambridge.*
                              —SAMUEL ELIOT MORISON

WHEN MORISON wrote his magnificent multivolume history to coincide
with Harvard's last big birthday party in 1936, he described a picturesque
child of the Reformation, a merry ensemble of oddballs and savants, student rebels and professorial freethinkers. He took proud note of early
Harvard's unique freedom from statutory oaths of any kind. Learned
adversaries would later question his interpretation of colonial Harvard's
stated reason for being: "to advance Learning and perpetuate it to Posterity; dreading to leave an illiterate Ministry to the Churches." Was
America's first college designed to be a liberal arts school, or a thinking
man's seminary?[1]

It was, in fact, the offspring of a sixteenth-century revolution gone
awry. Luther hadn't intended his uprising against Rome to spawn democracy. Yet the individualizing faith of Protestantism could not be contained. Neither could the curiosity of New England's early inhabitants.
And so there grew up a Puritan paradox of individual conscience and
theocratic orthodoxy.

The tradition that made education a vassal of the state, a custom as old as the first universities of Bologna and Paris, traveled to the New World intact. It had a place among the Great and General Court of Massachusetts Bay when that distinguished body convened on the afternoon of October 28, 1636, under the guidance of a twenty-three-year-old governor named Harry Vane. The day's agenda included measures to restrict the sale of lace for garments, reimburse George Munnings five pounds "in regard for the loss of his eye in the voyage to Block Island," and provide for selection of Boston's newest purveyor of arms and munitions. Before the legislators adjourned, they also awarded four hundred pounds toward construction of "a schoale or colledge . . . the next Court to appoint where and what building."

The seaside village of Marblehead offered three hundred acres for the college, but to no avail; the new establishment was sited in a one-acre lot surrounded by cowfields in the settlement of Newtown (which soon changed its name to Cambridge, in recognition of the British academy from which the colony drew much of its ruling class). "It pleased God to stir up the heart of one Mr. Harvard (a godly gentleman, and a lover of learning, there living amongst us)," noted a 1643 pamphlet entitled *New England's First Fruits,* "to give the one half of his estate (about 1700 pounds) towards the erecting of a college, and all his library; after him another gave 300 pounds; others after them cast in more, and the public hand of the State added the rest."

The college opened for business in the fall of 1638. It barely survived its first master, the rascally Nathaniel Eaton, who beat students with a walnut cudgel "big enough to have killed a horse," while his wife economized by rationing student beer and, if her accusers are to be believed, mixing goat dung in the hasty pudding. Not long after, Eaton fled to Virginia, a place, according to his biographer, "where immorality was less rare than excommunication."

Having been shuttered for a year, Harvard got a second chance with the arrival of Henry Dunster, at thirty-three the first and youngest of all her presidents. The institution that greeted him in the fall of 1640 was a puny thing. Dunster's first freshman class numbered four members. With civil war racking the mother country, New England received few immigrants to swell their ranks. Dunster pressed ahead anyway, instituting a three-year course in the Liberal Arts, the Three Philosophies, and the Learned Tongues. He turned aside the advice of Governor John Winthrop to dispense with the collegiate style of instruction and accommodation, and opened the "Old College" within two years, secured Harvard's first scholarship funds (one hundred pounds, donated by Lady Anne

[Radcliffe] Mowlson), and was pleased to accept patronage from the General Court, which diverted tolls from the Boston-Charlestown ferry to the support of the college.

In 1650, Dunster obtained a royal charter from King Charles II. Henceforth, Harvard would be governed by the Corporation, consisting of the president, the treasurer, and five fellows, self-perpetuating in their membership. The oldest such body in the western world, the new council played Lords to an older Commons, the Board of Overseers, which in its original form included state officers and orthodox clergy. Later, the Overseers swelled to as many as sixty-five members, among whom were Beacon Hill legislators eager to detect and expose Harvard's elitist ways. (Not for another two centuries would alumni win the right to choose their own Overseers, and to populate the board with Cabots, Lowells, Coolidges, Lees, and other nobles from Boston's codfish aristocracy. Massachusetts law still prohibits the president of Harvard from residing outside Cambridge.)

From the first, Corporation and Overseers battled over theology and politics. Early Overseers took exception to classroom use of *The Imitation of Christ* by Thomas à Kempis, "a Popish Minister." They joined forces with the General Court in 1654 to force Dunster from office because of his persistent and publicly stated liberality on the subject of infant baptism. Students might focus their energies on a curriculum that stressed Logic and Rhetoric, Greek and Hebrew, Ethics and Metaphysics, but the State House crowd paid more attention to presidential orthodoxy. Dunster's successor, Charles Chauncey, was directed to remain silent regarding his belief in total immersion. Nor was he permitted to advocate nighttime celebration of the Lord's Supper.[2]

Still, no amount of official displeasure could squelch heresy. Under Dunster and Chauncey, seventeenth-century Harvard opened its doors to Copernican theory, in clear contradiction of Scripture and more than a hundred years in advance of European universities, whose scholars' tongues had been tied by the Spanish Inquisition. While Oxford and Cambridge remained sectarian institutions as late as 1860, Harvard by 1701 had so offended conservative thought that President Increase Mather, having belatedly realized that tutors to whom he had entrusted most of the college's affairs were far less orthodox than he, felt compelled to leave his post and throw his support to forces of reaction who assembled at New Haven to form a new, more pious academy. Thus Harvard, the first college in the American colonies, became a colonizing power, instituting Yale.[3]

Visitors to the Yard at Commencement time were horrified by the godless debates. "Nothing said in Latin is a lie," retorted students. All the while, Harvard continued in bondage to the state, which paid its president (in part by levying a tax of one peck of grain on each New England family), dictated its Overseers, and set aside a forest in central Massachusetts as part of the college's dowry.[4]

Increase Mather's successor, the eighth man to hold the presidency, was another minister, Samuel Willard of Boston's Old South Church. But the Mathers were not about to see their hold on Harvard broken. Increase's son, Cotton, led a campaign after Willard's death in 1707 against the presidential candidacy of John Leverett. Leverett's offense? He was a layman. This appalled Mather. "To make a lawyer, and one who never affected the study of divinity, a president for a College of Divines," he argued, "will be a very preposterous thing, a thing without precedent." Mather's own aspirations to the presidency were as obvious as his credentials were impressive. Among his over 350 titles was *Magnalia Christi Americana,* whose 1702 publication introduced the Old World to Harvard, in the spirit of its author's bold assertion: "I WRITE the *Wonders* of the CHRISTIAN RELIGION, flying from the Deprivations of *Europe,* to the *American Strand.*"[5]

Mather received the news of Leverett's election with something close to despair. Governance of the college, he noted, might as well have been handed over to the Bishop of London. Leverett, the grandson of one colonial governor and the friend and colleague of others, was too friendly to the Anglicans for Mather, who declared war with his pen upon the new regime. Harvard responded in kind, withholding an honorary degree from America's greatest scholar. In 1718, a disenchanted Mather proposed that the rival institution chartered in 1701 as the Collegiate School of Connecticut be renamed for Eli Yale, a London diamond merchant and former president of the East India Company whom he had persuaded to make a large financial contribution to the fledgling academy. By then, his own College of Divines was showing more devotion to card-playing and horse races than to theological discourse and mandatory chapel.[6]

As the share of Harvard graduates who entered the ministry plummeted, Leverett dropped the practice of referring to graduating seniors as Sons of the Prophets; henceforth, they were Sons of Harvard. He offered a newly relaxed atmosphere to his intellectual family, friendly to the scientific rationalism of Enlightenment thought. But he could do little to stem continued antagonism between Harvard and many of those who paid its bills. From their perch atop the social ladder the Mathers looked on in disgust. At the same time, that irreverent firebrand sixteen-year-old

Benjamin Franklin lambasted the place as a sinkhole of indolence and misplaced pride.

> *The knowing sons of Harvard we revere,*
> *And in their just Defense will still appear;*
> *But every idle fop who there commences,*
> *Shall never claim Dominion o'er our Senses . . .*
> *We judge not of their knowledge by their Air,*
> *Nor think the wisest Heads have curled Hair.*[7]

With Leverett's death in 1725, the Corporation elevated one of its own, the Reverend Benjamin Wadsworth, to the presidency. A compromise choice, Wadsworth was elected as much to placate state officials as to advance Leverett's cautious reforms of the curriculum. He managed both, adding new courses in mathematics and natural philosophy, inviting instruction in French from an outside tutor, supervising astronomical observations made through the college's first telescope, and easing strained relations between the governing boards and Boston.

Wadsworth deserved the new presidential residence voted him, along with an orchard fertilized by the contents of a nearby privy. Less justifiable were the student shenanigans which made his decade in office a torturous experience, as youths dissatisfied with bland cuisine slipped outside the Yard to steal turkeys or geese to roast later in their drafty chambers.

The old ways of the Puritan fathers were fading in Massachusetts, as the Corporation learned for itself when it chose a successor to Wadsworth. The orthodox Calvinism officially enshrined by John Winthrop's generation was under challenge from milder creeds. In a preview of a much sharper split which would roil nineteenth-century Harvard, the college turned in 1737 to Edward Holyoke, a forty-eight-year-old resident of Marblehead, a layman like Leverett and a liberal who was, in the words of an admirer, "too much of a gentleman, and of too catholic a temper, to cram his principles down another man's throat."

To undergraduates, their new leader was known as "Guts," a quality he displayed during the 1740 visit to Harvard of the English itinerant preacher George Whitefield. Whitefield, embarked upon an evangelistic tour of America, decried the sad state of religion before fifteen thousand on Boston Common and then crossed the river to Cambridge. There he found the Overseers and the Corporation again at loggerheads. While the senior body welcomed Whitefield to Harvard, President Holyoke and his cabinet had no trouble in containing their enthusiasm. Neither, it would seem, did most of the student body. The Great Awakening might stir the rest of New England to its soul, but Harvardians persisted in celebrating November 5 as usual, toasting the memory of Guy Fawkes and his thwarted attempt to blow up the British Parliament.

When Whitefield returned next, he was quietly disinvited to preach in the college pulpit. Not for the first time, there was talk among legislators in Boston of a state-imposed loyalty oath for the irreverent Sons of Harvard. As President Holyoke fended off such assaults, he also stepped up the pace of educational reform. Reading lists were overhauled. Tutors were assigned to instruct individual specialties, instead of attaching themselves to an entire class. Public debates were instituted. The president supported the country's first physics lab. He also lent his blessing to a faculty member who attracted more than passing attention for his revolutionary theory that earthquakes, such as the one that destroyed Lisbon in 1755, were natural phenomena and not signs of heavenly rage.

The curriculum in colonial Harvard was a balanced one. Future patriots like John Hancock and Sam Adams studied Plutarch and Cicero as well as John Locke and volumes that offered insight into Whiggish politics. In 1758, John Adams took the affirmative position in a debate on the question, "Is Civil Government Necessary for Men?"

Adams's college played a patriotic part in the drama of Revolution. Eight Harvard men signed the Declaration of Independence. George Washington received his command of the Continental Army on Cambridge Common, along with an honorary degree. Sixteen hundred soldiers were quartered in the college buildings, while the roof of Harvard Hall was mined for half a ton of lead, later fashioned into bullets to be shot off at Saratoga and Brandywine.

The scholars themselves removed to the town of Concord for the war's duration, only to return with their reputations enhanced. "You are now among . . . Legislators and Heroes, Ambassadors and Generals," John Adams wrote his namesake son in 1786. "I mean among Persons who will live to Act in all these Characters." Two years later, a French visitor took note that Montesquieu and Racine were part of a library numbering thirteen thousand volumes. Others commented favorably on the Harvard uniform of blue-gray coats, plus an elaborate hierarchy of black gowns and cuff buttons setting freshman apart from senior.[8]

Still, rebellion was never far away. John Quincy Adams's own son was ringleader of one revolt, a protest against student fare which led the boy's palsied grandfather, America's second president, to demand the return of flogging in place of such milder punishments as rustication.

Even more controversial than moldy butter on student tables was the place of religion in the governing boards and classrooms. For some time a dispute had been brewing between those who clung to Calvinist dogma and others for whom Harvard's original objective, a literate ministry, had been superseded by events. The issue came to a head in 1803, when the Hollis chair of divinity fell vacant and laymen on the Corporation fell afoul of President Joseph Willard. Thoroughly committed to the faith of his fathers, he would sooner cut off his hand, declared Willard, "than lift it up for an Armenian Professor."

To such pillars of the old regime, the times were trying. Eliphalet Pearson, Hancock Professor of Hebrew and the man who briefly succeeded Willard after his friend's death in 1804, made careful note of a series of outrages committed against the established order: snowballs tossed at a praying tutor, whistling in chapel, a breakfast interrupted by teacups and knives sailing across the table. Hardly less offensive was the behavior of the students' elders, including the governing boards who, having selected a Unitarian named Henry Ware to fill the Hollis chair, proceeded to consolidate the new creed's hold within twelve months by installing in Willard's place another liberal, mathematics instructor Samuel Webber.

Not long after, the religious Old Guard took their leave, withdrawing to found the Andover Theological Seminary, and Harvard declared herself a Unitarian stronghold. At the same time, she remained a Federalist fortress, contemptuous of the democratic politics of Thomas Jefferson, resentful of Jacobin France, devoted to government by the well-bred and well-read. When the War of 1812 depressed New England's maritime economy, Harvard conferred an honorary degree on the old Federalist Harrison Gray Otis, an uncompromising foe of the war who had encouraged and then attended a convention at Hartford, Connecticut, called to consider New England's secession from the Union.[9]

Little wonder, then, that Jeffersonian journals like the *New England Patriot* boosted sales through unremitting assaults on the irreligious, unpatriotic college at Cambridge, or that Daniel Webster was forced to come to the school's defense when Massachusetts convened a constitutional convention in 1820 and Harvard was threatened with loss of its special status as Massachusetts' de facto university, written into the state constitution of 1780 at John Adams's behest.

By then, however, Harvard had inaugurated another new president, John Kirkland, whose primary allegiance was to education rather than political agitation. It was Kirkland's singular accomplishment that under his leadership Harvard became a university in fact as well as name. During the eighteen years of his presidency, separate divinity and law schools were added, and handsome new buildings were erected, including Charles

Bulfinch's masterpiece, University Hall. A number of endowed chairs were created in place of the old tutorial method of instruction and the influence of German research methods began to make itself felt on the classroom. About the same time, a handful of restless scholars set off on independent excursions to Europe. Having met Goethe at Weimar and experienced a heady skepticism even among theologians paid by the State; having sampled the German elective system, under which young men could design their own curriculum, youthful instructors such as Edward Everett and George Ticknor returned home to sing of the glories of Old World education. Everett left for politics, but Ticknor and others, aided by another student rebellion in 1823, campaigned tirelessly for reforms on the German model.

They got little of what they wanted, however. Kirkland's Harvard passed up the chance to revolutionize American education. Instead, the governing boards cautiously embraced a few minor changes. Ticknor himself concentrated on overhauling the department of modern languages. He stayed on as its chairman until 1843, before giving way to Henry Wadsworth Longfellow, who yielded his own place to James Russell Lowell.

In the classroom as in the waterside mills and newly capitalized industries of Yankee New England, it was a time of creative tension. Bostonians pointed with pride at their new bridge spanning the pestilential Charles River, among the world's longest and a marvel of nineteenth-century engineering. The same citizenry were meanwhile building a cultural atmosphere broad enough to span a continent.

Ralph Waldo Emerson proudly proclaimed that "Boston commands the attention as the town which was appointed in the destiny of nations to lead the civilization of North America."

In the sunburst of intellectual, literary, and political genius that earned for nineteenth-century Boston the title Athens of America, no one shone more brightly than Emerson. The apostle of self-reliance was also a child of Unitarian liberalism. The true scholar, according to this scholarship student of the class of 1821, "must embrace solitude as a bride . . . expel companions; set your habits to a life of solitude; then will the faculties rise fair and full within, like forest trees and field flowers . . . think alone, and all places are friendly and sacred."

Henry Thoreau followed his Concord neighbor to Cambridge, where the hermit of Walden first studied natural history and the rational universe. For such youths, these were golden years, Harvard's most productive since the first classes had assembled in Newtown. The difference now lay in the absence of theological constraint. Freed from Calvinist orthodoxy, allowed to pursue their own interests regardless of official doctrine, Harvard students in the age of Emerson and Thoreau reveled in the lonely, often cranky eminence of individual achievement.[10]

One of the reasons for this lay in a faculty steeped in similar values, eminent instructors who combined their classroom work with independent research. Under their benevolent light, Harvard nurtured the seedcorn of its nineteenth-century greatness: such luminaries as historians George Bancroft, Francis Prescott, and Francis Parkman (who conceived his epic account of North America before the Revolution as a Harvard sophomore), legal scholar Joseph Story, scientist Asa Gray, and humanist Henry Wadsworth Longfellow (whose auditors included Charles Sumner, later to combine literary and political careers to an extent unprecedented in American annals). Beginning around 1820, the school served as a laboratory for America's most creative intellects. In July 1838, Emerson came to the divinity school to pronounce his condemnation of religious formalism, which touched off angry denunciations of apostasy even from the school's own faculty. A year before, the sage of Concord, invited to address the Phi Beta Kappa exercises at his alma mater, had risen to the occasion memorably with "The American Scholar," his homeland's intellectual declaration of independence and another in a crowded procession of firsts which made Unitarian Harvard a jewel in the young nation's crown of culture. Local reaction was divided between those who thrilled to the implications of Emerson's "Man Thinking," and others frankly baffled by the transcendental message.

Boston provided in the first half of the nineteenth century a worthy setting for such jabs at the status quo. As Harvard under Kirkland and his successor, Josiah Quincy, attained her full flowering, so the city of which Quincy was three times mayor opened the nation's first public high school and free library, perused the *North American Review* and *Atlantic Monthly,* gathered at the Old Corner Book Store to eavesdrop on Hawthorne and Whittier, pioneered in the use of ether on the operating table, and introduced abolitionism on the public platform. In 1843, Dorothea Dix appealed to the Massachusetts legislature to relieve the forlorn condition of the state's insane asylums. Labor's advocates cheered when Chief Justice Lemuel Shaw overruled Boston's municipal court and declared unconstitutional laws restraining trade unions.

No longer hermetically sealed as before, the university across the Charles River welcomed William Ellery Channing's Unitarian creed, which entrusted Reason and Conscience, rather than Scripture, with authority for the ultimate determination of "truth." Boston and Harvard drew still closer together, much to the annoyance of Democrats, Congregationalists, and Berkshire farmers descended from Daniel Shays's rebels.

The English traveler Harriet Martineau paid a visit to Cambridge in 1838. While acknowledging Harvard's roster of past services, the vigorously democratic Miss Martineau detected an unmistakable scent of decline. Its source wasn't hard to fathom.

> The politics of the managers of Harvard University [she wrote] are opposed to those of the great body of the American people. She is the aristocratic college of the United States. . . . The best friends of Harvard believe that it is not by additional contrivances that her prosperity can be restored; but by such a renovation of the whole scheme of her management as shall bring her once more into accordance with the wants of the majority, the spirit of the country and of the time.[11]

John Quincy Adams held differently. Even as Miss Martineau criticized Harvard's pretensions, the former president took umbrage of another sort. Then an Overseer, Adams refused to attend a ceremony awarding an honorary degree to his nemesis and White House successor, Andrew Jackson. He could not bear to see the school of his youth, he wrote sourly, "confer her highest literary honor upon a barbarian who could not write a sentence of grammar and hardly could spell his own name."[12]

As Harvard's prestige grew, so did her vulnerability. Throughout the years just before the American Civil War, officeholders in Boston seized on the University's lack of popularity among rural voters to further their own ambitions. The legislature criticized the school for failing to make young men "better farmers, mechanics, or merchants." The college had lost the sympathy of the people, according to an 1853 report authored by a rising young politician named George S. Boutwell. "The people," as defined by Boutwell, were mostly his fellow Democrats, and others in the western part of the state who were put off by the commercial interests holding sway from Essex County to Buzzards Bay. Such Harvard-baiting played a role in Boutwell's subsequent election as governor.

After Josiah Quincy, the University seemed to go into a stall. A series of weak presidents did nothing to counteract official displeasure. "When I asked to come to this university," declared President Edward Everett, fresh from a stint as Ambassador to the Court of St. James's, "I supposed I was to be at the head of the largest and most famous institution in America. I have been disappointed. I find myself the submaster of an ill-disciplined school." Everett discovered his first official responsibility was to attend to a new pew rug in chapel. In the months that followed, he was frequently called upon to referee disputes involving the propriety of blue swallowtail coats, and hooligans tossing chestnuts at Professor Ware in mid-lecture. While Everett administered petty discipline (at least until he left early in 1849, later to become Millard Fillmore's Secretary of State in 1852), Harvard surrendered its place as the largest college in the country. By 1860, it had fallen behind such rivals as Amherst and Union. Emerson took a seat on the Board of Overseers, but the college failed to produce new philosophers or poets of his caliber. Still tied to the state government, Harvard on the eve of the Civil War relied on socially correct conduct as much as classroom performance in awarding its degrees.[13]

Henry Adams was not far off the mark in recalling the place as experienced by his class of 1858.

> Harvard College [Adams recalled], as far as it educated at all, was a mild and liberal school, which sent young men into the world with all they needed to make respectable citizens, and something of what they wanted to make useful ones. . . . The Unitarian clergy had given to the College a character of moderation, balance, judgment, restraint, what the French called *mesure;* excellent traits, which the College attained with singular success. . . . In effect, the school created a type but not a will. Four years of Harvard College, if successful, resulted in an autobiographical blank, a mind on which only a watermark had been stamped.[14]

Adams later estimated that the work of his four undergraduate years might easily have been compressed into four months. He dredged up from memory two or three Greek plays, a smattering of free-trade theories, a bit of chemistry. Nothing of Marx or Comte. He did remember with pleasure a series of lectures conducted by geologist Louis Agassiz, who illumined brilliantly the glacial period and in so doing, outstripped the rest of Adams's education altogether. Harvard had taught him little, he concluded, "but it left the mind open, free from bias, ignorant of facts, but docile. The graduate had few strong prejudices. He knew little, but his mind remained supple, ready to receive knowledge."[15]

On an 1861 visit the English novelist Anthony Trollope was surprised to find that Harvard had no final examinations, as in his own land, no degrees conferring special honor, no "firsts," and no "senior opts." As Trollope saw it, Harvard was content to offer more diversified schooling, minus "that old-fashioned, time-honoured, delicious, medieval life which lends so much grace and beauty to our colleges." It lacked as well butteries and battals, common rooms and porter's lodges. Any festive entertainment was to be reported immediately to the president, and wine and spiritous liquors were strictly forbidden. "It is not a picturesque system, this," said Trollope, "but it has its advantages."[16]

Then came Fort Sumter. As the factions separated, neither Harvard nor America was ever to be the same again. In the next few years, alumni won the right to choose their own Overseers, a reform which did much to sever the suffocating relationship of Harvard Yard to Beacon Hill. Equally important, the war paved the way for nationalization, centralization, standardization. In his first inaugural address, Lincoln spoke of "the mystic chords of Union." His sentiment was soon transmitted across the land. As James MacGregor Burns wrote, the war homogenized a crazy-quilt society of college students and factory workers. It was a geography lesson "in which men from Maine occupied islands off Texas, men from Florida marched through the fields of Pennsylvania, men from New Orleans discovered snow and snowballs. The war was a regional exchange in which accents, attitudes, habits collided, coexisted, even coalesced."[17]

In the years before Sumter, Harvard had attracted young men from Savannah and Pittsburgh. By 1869, however, Boston's reputation as Hub of the Universe was starting to fray. This presented the University with a challenge, and an opportunity. If Harvard clung too closely to the old girl's skirts, and to its own past, however glorious, if it shirked involvement in a society both energetic and vulgar, it might easily succumb to dilettantism. It would in any event forgo any claim to leadership more dynamic than the prestige bestowed by antiquity. Up until this time, Harvard's national reputation had rested largely on her august origins and the careers of such celebrated graduates as Emerson, the Adamses, and Sumner, plus faculty giants like Ticknor, Agassiz, and Longfellow. Her presidency had been filled by men of some renown, but they had been too occupied with internal discipline and financial struggle to devote much time or energy to the external world.

A Harvard struggling to be both contemporary and useful would require a leader of imagination, someone equipped with Concord's Transcendental breadth and Wall Street's fiduciary drive. Could Boston produce such a man? And if she could, would the University pay him heed? How those questions were answered would go a long way toward determining Harvard's place in postwar America. Most of all, they would decide whether the school of Dunster, Leverett, and Kirkland could become a truly national university.

CHAPTER ONE

The Soil and the Seed

Every true man is a cause, a country, and an age; requires infinite spaces and numbers and time to fully accomplish his design; and posterity seems to follow his steps as a train of clients.

—RALPH WALDO EMERSON

The American university has not yet grown out of the soil. It must grow from seed. It cannot be transplanted from England, France or Germany. . . . The American university will be the outgrowth of American social and political habits. The American college is an institution without a parallel; the university will be equally original.

—CHARLES WILLIAM ELIOT

FEW MEN better embodied Emerson's dictum that an institution is the lengthened shadow of one man than Charles William Eliot. No one did more to establish higher education in general, and Harvard in particular, as an accomplice to American greatness. For forty years, this Yankee mandarin, "New England's topmost oak," embodied a cause, a country, and an age. Canonized as the patron saint of mass, democratic learning, before he died in 1926, Eliot was known to millions of admiring countrymen as "First Citizen of the Republic," a title Theodore Roosevelt first bestowed on him. He was also "adviser at large to the American people on things in general," a popular oracle, a republican hero.

> If the people of the United States have any special destiny, [Eliot contended] any peculiar function in the world, it is to try and work out, under extraordinarily favorable conditions, the problems of free institutions for a heterogeneous, rich, multitudinous population, spread out over a vast territory. We indeed want to breed scholars, artists, poets, historians, novelists, engineers, physicians, jurists, theologians and orators, but first of all, we want to breed a race of independent, self-reliant free men, capable of helping, guiding and governing themselves.[1]

To Eliot, as to Emerson, self-reliance was the heart and soul of the American experiment. Yet in the post-Civil War era of nascent monopolies and sanctioned greed, an individualism once picturesque had turned predatory. With the coming of affluence, unevenly distributed, classes took shape, cities became patchwork quilts of inequality, and a money-hungry land demanded specialists: engineers to build bridges, geologists to wrest mineral wealth from the earth's crust, social scientists to gauge the human cost of such dizzying advances, psychologists to probe hidden motives, legislators and administrators equipped to marry expertise to majority rule.

"The university must accommodate itself promptly to significant changes in the character of the people for whom it exists," claimed Eliot. It was the first sign of a rage to be relevant. Neither Harvard nor America ever threw it off. In presiding over the transformation of Harvard from a sectarian college, Eliot withstood hot blasts of dissent from traditionalists who disagreed with his campaigns to eliminate Greek as an entrance requirement, abolish obligatory chapel, and prevent raises in tuition that would inhibit his primary objective of achieving "a college of broad democratic resort."

In the age of Herbert Spencer and Charles Darwin, Eliot's Harvard came to reflect the needs of a contradictory people, both creative and acquisitive. Eliot himself was a kind of human crossroads, an intersection of the old American impulses toward having and being. As an educational reformer, he reflected his countrymen's reflexive optimism, their lack of a deeply rooted culture, their preference for individual philanthropy over government largesse. As a scholar, he argued the case for Science, the secular religion then pressing for equal status with Aristotle and Plutarch. Just as certain of ultimate success as Voltaire's Dr. Pangloss or the railroad magnates who endowed a host of rival universities during the Gilded

Age, Eliot evolved from being a disciple of Emerson, a classical nine-teenth-century liberal distrustful of government intervention in the name of safer travel and more reliable currency, to become in his own words an advocate of "democratic collectivism." Along the way, he changed Harvard's focus. Henceforth, it would reflect the creed he had chiseled into one of the high brick walls which came to encircle the Yard halfway through his long reign:

> Enter to grow in wisdom;
> Depart to serve thy country and thy kind

"We seek to train doers," he explained of the new, intensely practical Harvard, "achievers, men whose successful careers are much subservient to the public good. We are not interested here in producing languid observers of the world, mere spectators in the game of life, or fastidious critics of other men's labors."[2]

To Eliot's critics—and they were vociferous—classical learning died a violent death in Victorian America, and the murder weapon was sticky with his fingerprints. Eliot took no notice. If called upon to define the spirit of his University, he liked to say, he would fall back on the single word, Service. His favorite motto was borrowed from Edward Everett Hale:

> Look up and not down;
> Look forward and not back;
> Look out and not in;
> And lend a hand.

Eliot's service was to catch the energy of his times and distill it, fashioning a distinctly American institution. Borrowing equally from the old British model, with its emphasis on character formation, and the aggressively secular German research university, the founder of modern Harvard did not see himself as a revolutionary. In his inaugural address, he said that the community owed schooling only to an elite, "to those who, having the capacity, prove by hard work that they also have the necessary perseverance and endurance." At the same time, he said nothing about either bloodlines or bank accounts as tickets of admission to this intellectual Valhalla. Harvard men belonged to a natural aristocracy. Of that Eliot was certain. But it was Jefferson's brethren of talent and virtue, not the old New England junto of Federalist politics and pulpit connections.

By instituting an elective system of instruction, Eliot changed Harvard's emphasis from humanist breadth to specialized, useful knowledge.

In his devotion to science, he delivered the first bulletin of an affliction which would lead his descendants to proclaim the death of God. For him, as for most Americans, the past was a foreign land, rarely visited. "Sam," he once remarked to his son, "I can't seem to get interested in heaven. I want to know what's to happen to the World Court."[3]

Like the nation he advised and the university he remade, Eliot was accused by rivals of a superiority complex. It ran in his blood. "Eliza," his mother demanded of a friend, "do you kneel down in church and call yourself a miserable sinner? Neither I nor any member of my family will ever do *that!*" True to her forecast, her son displayed his own slightly starchy humor when a student came knocking on his door at two o'clock one morning. He had just had a dream, the boy told Eliot, in which he'd been informed that the president was prepared to accept Jesus Christ as his Savior. Surprised and amused by this, the friend to whom Eliot told the story pressed to know his response.

"I said to him that he must have been misinformed."[4]

Beneath the stoic's mask, Eliot was on intimate terms with tragedy. Born into a prominent Beacon Hill family in March 1834, Charles was disqualified from a normal childhood by a large, unsightly splotch discoloring the right side of his face. As a youth, he was taunted by North End bullies for being different; as an old man, he was mocked by opponents as "a birthmark on legs." In papers found at the time of his death were several sheets drawn up in response to Eliot's own inquiry: "What possessions or acquisitions in college life lead to success in afterlife?" There followed some predictable maxims about self-discipline and scholarly application. Then came a paragraph as close to self-revelation as this sphinxlike Yankee would ever come: "Reticent, reserved, not many acquaintances, but a few intimate friends," he prescribed. "Belonging to no societies, perhaps. Carrying in his face his character so plainly to be seen there by the most casual observer, that nobody ever makes to him a dishonorable proposal."[5]

Disfigured by nature, detached by inclination, young Charles was a born individualist; he liked nothing better than to withdraw from the company of other boys, burying himself in Dickens and Scott's Waverley novels which lined the shelves of his parents' comfortable library. Twice each Sunday, he went to King's Chapel, where his father was a high priest in the Unitarian Sanhedrin that dominated Boston's politics, commerce, and culture.

Samuel Eliot served his native city as mayor and as congressman. When the economic panic of the late 1850s struck home, the officeholder was left with little more than his dignity. He gave his son some practical lessons in woodworking and carpentry and sent him to Harvard College, which under President Edward Everett was little more than a backyard institute dispensing Latin verbs and corporal punishment. During the regime of Everett's predecessor, Jared Sparks, Harvard had turned its back on Josiah Quincy's brief flirtation with elective courses. It had left John Kirkland's graduate schools of law and medicine to languish. Frustrated in his attempt to graft German research methods onto the undemanding church school preferred by the Unitarian clergy, George Ticknor had departed for greener pastures.

As a student, Charles Eliot turned his attention to the twice-daily prayers mandated in the college. Attendance at Sunday services and instruction in natural and revealed religion were also required. Charles's class was offered only one course in English literature, an introduction to Chaucer (whom the youth disliked for his crudities). Although faculty councils included some of America's most distinguished scientists, they enjoyed only sporadic contact with pupils for whom recitations formed the core of instructional offerings. Not one scientific laboratory was open to undergraduates, nor could books be withdrawn from Harvard's impressive central library.

Charles himself managed to elude the straitjacket of prescribed courses long enough to pursue training in mathematics instead of ancient Greek. In a rare dispensation, he was allowed into the lab of Professor Josiah Cooke, where he gained a rudimentary knowledge of chemical science. He was among the lucky few, like George Herbert Palmer, who later became William James's partner in Harvard's famed "philosophical menagerie" of the late nineteenth century. Palmer recalled his own undergraduate education as a shop window filled with obsolescent goods. So he had put his spare time to good use, devouring Tennyson and Mill, rubbing up against the strange doctrines of Bentham and the forbidden heresies of Comte. This was self-education at its purest, embraced by exceptional boys like Eliot, the scarred son of the Beacon Hill Establishment who would compensate for being different by developing his mind and perfecting his character.[6]

Harvard's future president never forgot a story told by the Corporation's Francis B. Crowninshield, who described Harvard's early austerity by recalling how, as a youth, he had pinned an extra slice of steak to his college dinner table with a fork, to be collected at a later meal. Intellectual nourishment was just as unpredictable. William James remembered a student of the era whose complaint revealed much about Harvard's limited fare. "I can't understand your philosophy," he told James long after graduation. "When I studied philosophy, I could understand it. We used to commit it to memory."[7]

Eliot's classmates were ranged on a geographical scale whose narrowness matched their academic exposure. Two-thirds of the class of 1853 were from Massachusetts. Graduating second from the top, Charles appraised himself near the close of his college career as, "a stiff, pokerish, glum, unattractive young man." Torn between commerce and chemistry, in looking around for a future career, Eliot was both pious and shrewd. "Man glorifies God, 1st by being useful," he wrote his mother in March 1854, "2nd by being happy. . . . A successful teacher is a useful citizen."

That fall, he was back at Harvard as a tutor in mathematics, one of thirteen faculty members assembled under the new president, James Walker. The students called him "Old Man Eliot" and pegged their instructor as a cold fish. But Walker took an instant liking to the grave young man, whose voice suggested to Oliver Wendell Holmes the decorum of a house with a corpse in it. Most of all, Walker appreciated the tutor's practical knack for getting things done. He entrusted Eliot with overseeing construction work on a new chapel, and the task of drawing up an agenda for faculty meetings. He responded with fatherly approval to his protégé's campaigns for gas lights in student dormitories, instruction inside scientific labs, and an end to the traditional practice of having graduating seniors take oral examinations before the Overseers.

Walker himself was a man of limited imagination. When Eliot once complained of insufficient room to write at the faculty table, the president agreed with him that a replacement would be useful. Unfortunately, Walker went on, a more spacious table would cost money and Harvard had none to spend on amenities.

Other restrictions similarly chafed. Eliot found parietal rules "disagreeable to shirk and disagreeable to do." He pressed President Walker to divide classrooms into sections, in order to encourage competition and the individual thirst for knowledge so much a part of his own emotionally stunted nature. Once he managed to escape deadening routines long enough to lead a trigonometry class on a surveying tour of the Yard. Looking for other outlets for his bounding energies, he joined a boat club, and when Harvard rowers without uniforms faced the better-heeled crews of rival colleges, he and a friend went out and purchased crimson handkerchiefs to set them apart and give the University an identifying color. In his spare time, the chemist also worked on a textbook, which modestly advanced his career among the test tubes.[8]

In October 1858, Eliot married the daughter of a Unitarian minister and went to live in a brick duplex on Cambridge's Kirkland Street. Its other half was occupied by his parents, refugees from depressed Boston. The Corporation soon after invited him to take charge of the Lawrence Scientific Laboratory. His appointment as assistant professor, Harvard's first, was not renewed at the end of five years. Instead, the college enlisted the services of Wolcott Gibbs, an older, more experienced chemist, and Eliot fell victim to the up or out syndrome. Undaunted, he took his young family to Europe to study the effects of Old World education and reinforce their sense of New World superiority. With the Civil War raging, the family checked out of a London hotel that flew the rebel stars and bars.[9]

Eliot the nineetenth-century liberal held views that would shock his warmest admirers of today. When he noted throngs of French women in the churches, kissing altars and crossing themselves with holy water, he commented, "They don't lead good lives, but they have the sweetest associations with their Church." During a moment of intense feeling he wrote, "I hate Catholicism as I do poison. Nasty smells are not cheerful, and all Rome stinks." Later asked to define the single most important quality for a successful college president, he replied without hesitation, "The capacity to inflict pain." He kept one young scholar off his faculty owing to a wife who was, as he put it, "a she-devil," criticized another for his "sappy manner," attacked the portraitist Romney for immortalizing Lady Hamilton—in Eliot's opinion little more than a hussy—and wished the defeated South to be treated as a conquered province. For good measure, Eliot insisted that "the scab and strikebreaker is a good type of citizen" and stoutly opposed intermarriage between black and white, German and Italian, French and Jew.[10]

As guest speaker at the 150th anniversary of the University of Pennsylvania, his tribute to its founder was equivocal. To be sure, said Eliot, Benjamin Franklin combined personal ability with a vigorous patriotism. Yet he could never be regarded as a truly great man since he had more than once violated the moral laws of Christian civilization. Such remarks inspired the *Harvard Crimson* to take a look at the president's flat-top derby and nearsighted gravitas and proclaim him "Bunker Hill on wheels."

What Eliot lacked in charm, he made up in character, as craggy and unyielding as the stony fingers that jutted into the Atlantic near his Maine summer retreat. His was a practical intelligence, and in postwar America that was a highly valuable commodity. Eliot returned home in 1865 to a land whose guns had fallen silent, but whose industries were noisily expanding. That fall, he joined the faculty at the newly established Massachusetts Institute of Technology. Not long after, when Columbia's F. A. P. Barnard released a report showing a relative decline in college atten-

dance in America, Eliot became more intrigued than ever by the possibilities of a revived elective system at Harvard.

In 1868, alumni newly freed of restraints imposed by the legislature
in Boston elected Eliot to Harvard's Board of Overseers. That fall, he
stunned the educational community with two articles in *The Atlantic
Monthly* expressing views he conceded were "rather novel in eastern
Massachusetts." Here was his prescription for a "New Education" to help
form and inform the national mind. The United States was rapidly developing, he argued. Its appetite for engineers, architects, and chemists would
no doubt be matched by its need of thoughtful men and civilizing scholarship. In the spirit of educational pioneer Horace Mann, who insisted
the reading of fiction was inimical to scientific attainment, Eliot urged
separate technical schools for those of purely vocational instincts. Yet he
also proposed the happy coexistence of liberal arts and practical studies.

Quoting Ezra Cornell ("I would found an institution in which anyone may study anything"), he also had kind words for Yale, which since
1861 had bestowed America's first Ph.D.'s. In his writings, he called for
a system both relevant and lively, "based chiefly upon the pure and applied sciences, the living European languages, and mathematics."

In Eliot's New Education, each student ought to be able to arrange
his personal course of study. "There is no uniform boy," he insisted, with
a certainty traceable to his own solitary campaign for self-knowledge. He
castigated universities for recruiting their presidents from clerical ranks.
And without intending to do so, he tossed his hat into the ring to succeed
Harvard's retiring president Thomas Hill.[11]

In March 1869, the same Corporation which six years earlier had
been content to let him go, asked him back. At the time, his personal life
was in turmoil: his wife was dying, and he'd lost one of his children to
illness. Harvard's Overseers openly rebelled against the Corporation's
choice. Traditionalists, aghast at Eliot's *Atlantic Monthly* argument that
classical studies were no guarantee of gentlemanly conduct, proposed another candidate. Informed of Francis Parkman's personal opposition to
his candidacy, Eliot said that he agreed with the historian's own choice.
What's more, he said, being all too aware of the frustrations that accompanied it, he didn't want the job. Parkman was converted on the spot. So,
eventually, were the Overseers.

Ralph Waldo Emerson was one of the visiting committee of Overseers bearing news of his election to a bemused Eliot. "What *are* they going to say or do?" the victor asked himself. "Pat me on the head, doubt-
less, and say 'good boy'—'Vision and strength'—that is well said—that is
exactly what is needed. Take 'care of your stomach and reserve yourself

for good days to come.' " Although there were many good days to come in Eliot's presidency, grief and surprises also lay ahead. For years, Eliot referred to the balky Overseers as "Her Majesty's Opposition." His own diadem wobbled from time to time in the face of criticism monotonous as the call of a whippoorwill.

But the new president set out full of plans and resolved to be patient. Like a general addressing his troops on the eve of battle, Eliot chose his words carefully. "This University recognizes no real antagonism between literature and science," he declared in his inaugural address, "and consents to no such narrow alternatives as mathematics or classics, science or metaphysics. We would have them all, and at their best."

For those who would confuse popular democracy with profound leadership, however, Eliot had a caveat. "We are accustomed to seeing men leap from farm or shop to courtroom or pulpit," he said, "and we half believe that common men can safely use the seven league boots of genius." Harvard would serve, he made clear, but according to its own missionary standards. It would civilize parsons' sons and train a ruling class. But first, vowed Eliot, it would develop the habit of excelling.

I was never lonely; I always had a fight on my hands.

—CHARLES WILLIAM ELIOT

1869 IS AS GOOD a year as any from which to date the birth of modern America. That year, Ulysses Grant became president of a nation in the throes of political reconstruction and economic renewal. As new wealth was taken from the ground or baked in steaming factories, its concentration or denial fed new animosities and demands from those left on the social outskirts. The Knights of Labor came into being in 1869. The same year witnessed the birth of Susan B. Anthony's feminist movement, and the National Convention of Colored Men, led by the ex-slave Frederick Douglass. The country was beginning to think of itself as a cohesive organism, and Harvard struggled to catch up. Under Eliot, the University redefined its mission with the nation in mind. Hereafter, it would supply what America needed (according to its own lights, of course) and it would reflect, however imprecisely, what America wanted to believe about herself.

One of America's most cherished beliefs concerned the inevitable march toward human perfectability which the classroom guaranteed. Just a few years before, in 1862, Americans had averted their eyes from the battlefield long enough to embrace the idea of making higher education available to the common man by establishing colleges of the practical arts in each state. This concept, the brainchild of a Vermont storekeeper named Justin Morrill, led to a sort of Homestead Act for higher education. Henceforth, the federal government would donate to each state acreage from the public lands, and the proceeds from their sale would be invested in establishing state-run colleges "to teach such branches of learning as are related to agriculture and the mechanical arts . . . in order to promote the liberal and practical education of the industrial classes in the several pursuits and professions of life."

Soon, a number of states founded their own "land-grant" universities, or added "A and M" units to existing ones. Princeton made room for an engineering department while Eliot at Harvard was emboldened to abolish that pillar of traditional schooling, Greek, as an entrance requirement. As higher education became more widely available, the number of degree candidates rose from 52,000 pupils in 1870 to nearly a quarter-million by the end of the century. Supporters of democratized, practical education expressed hostility to ivory towers and ivy-covered walls. "Almighty God was not mistaken," declared one friend of the land-grant college, "when he put the first man in the garden instead of the academy, and made his own son a carpenter instead of a rabbi."[12]

All of this was in keeping with society's worship of William James's bitch-goddess Success. "In the past," according to Frederick W. Taylor, whose ideas of impersonal scientific management laid the foundation for Harvard's school of business administration, "the man has been first; in the future the system must be first." "Taylorization," as his system came to be known, with its emphasis on mass production as measured by the stopwatch, was a hymn to the efficient life, sung by consulting engineers and marketing specialists. Sociologist Thorstein Veblen spoke for many who celebrated the advent of Technocracy, and dismissed the study of Latin as an expendable frill.

Eliot meanwhile contributed his own prestige to the professionalization of American education. As the old college receded, like a ship on the horizon, its replacement contained far more of the outside world's stress on practical skills. Even as controversy swirled around his blueprint for reform, millions of people likened Eliot to an Old Testament prophet, calling on his fellow academics to repent their monastic disdain for the real world. Most of all, he clung to a grandiose vision of Harvard as the naturally selected guardian for all of American education, and much of American culture. He had not been elected to serve as clerk to the Corporation, he announced before taking office. Neither did he have any intention of repeating Everett's travail as headmaster to a gang of unruly boys.

"It's good to be in good things at their beginning," he liked to say. As yet, however, few saw what he saw. In 1869 the institution was a university in name only. To James Bryce, it seemed "a struggling college, with uncertain relations to learning and research." No department had a dean; none issued so much as an annual report. Any graduate with a B.A. who managed to sustain "a good moral character" for three years following commencement, and was willing to meet the asking price of five dollars, could purchase a Master of Arts degree to adorn his office wall or dignify his library. At the law school, diplomas were little more than certificates of residence. The medical school required no college training for admission; it routinely handed out the license to cure or kill after a year of desultory studies. William James's final examination consisted of a single question put to him by Oliver Wendell Holmes. "If you can answer that," Holmes informed the successful applicant, "you can answer anything! Now tell me about your family and how things are at home."

Eliot's domain also included a divinity school ("three mystics, three skeptics, and three dyspeptics"), supervised by the least denominational of denominations, and a handful of graduate students ("shirkers and stragglers," in the president's words), who attended the Lawrence Scientific School. Everywhere, instruction revolved around oral recitations, supplemented by a few lectures. Stingy with lab work and student-teacher contact, the whole place operated under an impoverishment far less romantic than the one Eliot in his inaugural address called "of inestimable worth in this money-getting nation."

Eliot appeared to Van Wyck Brooks as "a Channing Unitarian of the Boston-Puritan-Roman type, serene as Cato, cheerful as a boy . . . marked by a passion for the practical and a singular grandeur of nature." He would need all these qualities and more, if Harvard were to reach the summit he envisioned. No one who heard his inaugural address could entertain doubt about Harvard's future course. "The notion that education consists in the authoritative inculcation of what the teacher deems true may be logical and appropriate in a convent, or a seminary for priests, but it is intolerable in universities and public schools."[13]

Beginning briskly with a tuition increase and the first installment of an alumni subscription fund, the president in his first year was able to hire five new professors and pad his faculty's salaries. Touching off a series of explosives, he abolished Bloody Monday, with its sanctioned terrorizing of freshmen by sophomores, slashed the winter vacation from six weeks to two, converted the Rank List into a measure of intellectual achievement rather than classroom conduct, summoned his Corporation to meetings at a dizzying rate, and banished privies from the Yard. Enlarging the college catalog, Eliot made certain it appeared on popular magazine racks. He advertised on the cover of *Harper's*. He also expanded the University's real estate holdings, made elocution an optional study, freed seniors of all prescribed studies, and secured Henry Adams and Charles Eliot Norton for a faculty that doubled within the first of his four decades at the helm.[14]

Deadwood must be cleared before new growth can begin. Within twelve months of his election, Eliot had pruned away much of old Harvard. For those in search of a pattern, there was the new president's bold assertion that an open mind, trained to skeptical investigation, was preferable to complacency of any kind. Seeking out kindred spirits, Eliot asked Emerson, William Dean Howells, and John Fiske, disciple of Spencerian evolution and a controversial advocate of science as theology, to deliver University Lectures. The *New York World* questioned some of the "astonishing changes" suggested by the presence in Cambridge of a freethinker like Fiske. When Eliot called for the creation of a Graduate School of Arts and Sciences in 1872, faculty members forgot to be grateful for their fattened pay envelopes—not to mention their previously unheard-of sabbatical leaves and pensions. To those who protested that there were insufficient resources to establish such a school and who foresaw a weakening of undergraduate education, Eliot had a ready response. "It will strengthen the College. As long as the main duty of the faculty is to teach boys, professors need never pursue their subjects beyond a certain point. With graduate students to teach, they will regard their subjects as infinite, and will keep up that constant investigation which is necessary for the best teaching."

At that moment, it dawned on his listeners that Eliot had meant what he said about fashioning a thoroughly American university, free of government controls and divorced from churchly influence. He was turning the place over like a flapjack, according to Dr. Oliver Wendell Holmes. "King Log has made way for King Stork," judged the Autocrat of the Breakfast Table in April 1870. This followed a stormy session of the medical faculty, at which an eminent physician had protested that doctors are born, not made, and demanded to know why an institution accustomed to leadership for eighty years was suddenly being ordered to re-invent itself. "We have a new president," Eliot told him.[15]

The new president prevailed, but it took years for the medical school to recover from the defection of students unwilling to test themselves against stiffened entrance requirements and extended course loads.

A similar conservatism prevailed at the law school, whose course catalog hadn't changed by so much as a sentence in twenty years, and whose three-man faculty offered drab lectures while maintaining private practices on the side. Theoretically, student reading would fill the gaps. But with no grades and no progressive curriculum, the training students bought for their hundred-dollar tuition fee differed little from that available in a country lawyer's office.

Then Eliot thought back to a student acquaintance of his, a highly intelligent young man so poor he had stoked fires to earn his keep. He tracked Christopher Columbus Langdell to New York, where others in his law firm thought him a queer fellow indeed. Langdell lived in his office, slept on a cot behind a screen, and was tolerated at all because of his superior brainpower. He was just the sort of unorthodox teacher whom Eliot envisioned at Harvard. The president set out to woo Langdell, who not only became dean of a reorganized law school, but also gave up his own practice in time to fashion the case study method, a radical innovation that changed the face of legal education in America.

Undeterred by protest, Eliot filled slot after slot with prodigies like thirty-two-year-old Charles Sprague Sargent, chosen to oversee the new Arnold Arboretum. Sargent had never published a scientific paper, but he nurtured the Arboretum to global prestige. For the Harvard Observatory, Eliot selected an amateur astronomer the same age as Sargent. Edward C. Pickering stayed on the job forty-two years, winning two gold medals from the Royal Astronomical Society and scholarly praise for his work in spectroscopy and stellar photometry. Eliot's librarian devised a stack system that Pope Pius XI duplicated in the Vatican.[16]

In 1887, the president offered a place in his history department to Charles Gross, a brilliant medievalist who had taken his degree at Gottingen and followed it up with an additional four years' work in Britain. Gross, a Jew, had been unable to find an academic position in his native United States, and was about to return to his father's clothing store in upstate New York when Eliot's invitation arrived. In the event, Gross remained in Cambridge for many years, lending distinction to his department and spreading Harvard's reputation as a haven for scholars of diverse nationality and temperament.[17]

Eliot's new instructors shared a penchant for empirical methods, a distaste for fixed principles, and an uncommon tolerance of heresy. As Langdell's case studies freed the law to follow sociological paths, so Oliver Wendell Holmes Junior, who taught constitutional law and jurisprudence, challenged legal precedent in his classic work, *The Common Law*. Long before the native humorist Mr. Dooley revealed that Supreme Court justices read election returns like anyone else, future Justice Holmes suggested that intuition, prevailing morality, and judicial prejudice all played their part in determining the rules by which men should be governed. "The life of the law has not been logic," he declared, "it has been experience." Harvard philosopher Charles Peirce seconded Holmes's case for pragmatic thought in an 1878 issue of *Popular Science Monthly*. As Holmes de-emphasized precedent, so Peirce downgraded belief itself. Action counted for more than speculative thought, he asserted, and practical action most of all.[18]

Eliot picked up on the theme, ordering philosopher George Santayana to teach facts instead of ideas. "I might have replied that the only facts in philosophy," wrote a nonplused Santayana, "were historical facts, namely, the fact that people had or had had ideas." Santayana's relations with the University were already strained by his preference for undergraduate teaching over specified research. He judged Eliot's Harvard both democratic and superficial. "College, and all that occupied the time and mind of the College, and seemed to the College an end in itself, seemed to President Eliot only a means. The end was service in the world of business." John Jay Chapman went further. Appalled at the sight of the Harvard president arm in arm with J. P. Morgan at a medical school dedication, the literateur accused Eliot of pulling down the columns of the temple. "Eliot in his financial rhapsodies drew golden tears down Pluto's cheek," wrote Chapman bitterly, "and he built his college. The music was crude; it was not Apollo's lyre; it was the hurdy-gurdy of pig iron and the stockyards. To this music rose the walls of Harvard, and of all our colleges."[19]

There was an element of bitter truth to this. For in Eliot's wake came other intellectual innovators, eager to transform the sectarian school and red brick cloister. Andrew White of Cornell was one. "Stagnant as a Spanish convent," he pronounced the traditional college, "self-satisfied as a Bourbon duchy." William Rainey Harper of the new University of Chicago was another. Traditions could be established at Chicago, it was claimed, by two-thirds vote of the faculty, a distinguished body lured from Yale and other eastern institutions by such novelties as major and minor studies and a four-year curriculum divided between junior college and more advanced scholarship. James Garfield, onetime classics professor at Williams, took exception to the emerging academy: the ideal college, he insisted, was composed of Mark Hopkins on one end of a log and a student on the other. But although Garfield might summon electoral majorities, his instructional views proved as fashionable as the periwig.

"The old education simply trained the mind," declared railroad magnate Chauncey Depew at the opening of the Drexel Institute of Art, Science, and Industry in 1892. "The new trains the mind, the muscles, and the sense. The old education gave the intellectual a vast mass of information useful in the library and useless in the shop." Endowed by plutocrats like John D. Rockefeller, Andrew Carnegie, Leland Stanford, and James Duke, Depew's vision outraged antiquarians of John Jay Chapman's stripe, for whom Eliot was less prophet than turncoat. Humanists of the Chapman school did not reckon with the practical spirit of the age, nor the explosive ingenuity of basement labs, backyard forges—and college classrooms. To maintain the leading position for which Eliot had cast his University, something had to be jettisoned. A new kind of energy had to be harnessed, entirely different from if not hostile to the piety of earlier days. As the student body and faculty grew to mirror the diversity of an expanding population, Harvard could no longer afford dogmatism. The search for useful truth supplanted preservation of revealed truth.

Eliot pressed ahead. (He had help: the senior member of the Corporation that chose him remained until he was ninety-three. Earlier retirement might have doomed the great experiment, and cut short Eliot's presidency.) "Can you fight?" he asked one recent addition to his faculty. Yes, the man replied, he thought he could. "Can you fight when you are in the minority?" Eliot demanded. Indeed, said the professor, he had done so on more than one occasion. "Can you fight when everybody is against you," persisted Eliot, "when not one man is ready to lend you support?" The newcomer was prepared to try. "Then you need have no fear. But if you have convictions it will sometimes be necessary."[20]

One of the president's strongest convictions had always been the elective system. Such a system, he maintained, gave play to natural preferences and inborn aptitudes. In this, it mirrored Eliot's own singular education. More than that, however, electives would also raise the standing of both the natural and the physical sciences. They would further new avenues of inquiry, strengthen existing departments, and draw students and teachers closer together in a genuine community of shared interests.

By any conventional measurement, Eliot's success was overwhelming. A catalog listing 32 professors and 73 courses in 1870 had grown forty years later to include 169 instructors teaching over 400 courses. Those who wished to sample classes in Old Iranian and Comparative Osteology could do so. By 1894, only a single course in English composition was required of any undergraduate, and Harvard men could nail down a degree with no grade higher than a C. Even so, each year's freshman class typically surrendered a fifth or more of its membership before summer break.[21]

Early in his presidency, a delegation of eight other college presidents beseeched the Corporation to repudiate Eliot and retain Greek as an entrance requirement. But Eliot dug in his heels, and carried the day. Before long, Cambridge's politically active were carrying placards declaring their loyalty to Hard Money and Soft Electives. The president of Bryn Mawr suggested that credit might soon be given for ladder work in the gymnaisum, or swimming in a tank. "Why not one's morning bath?" Eliot and Princeton's James McCosh debated electives before New York's Nineteenth-Century Club. With his Calvinist fear of unbridled freedom and suspicion of egalitarian arrangements, McCosh attacked what he called "dilettanti courses." Eliot's vaunted freedom, he said, was nothing more than a bid for student popularity. More pointedly, McCosh, who believed the alternative to compulsory attendance in the classroom was to have freshmen off duck hunting, noted that few great poems, scientific discoveries, or works of philosophical insight had emerged from modern Cambridge.

Even within his own camp, Eliot was accused of offering academic laissez-faire. His response was typical. To be sure, he acknowledged, electives would little benefit "careless, lazy, indifferent boys." But then, "it really does not make much difference what these unawakened minds dawdle with." It was the curious minds the elective system benefited. At last encouraged to pursue their own interests, permitted to take books out of the library, and discover that modern learning could hold its own with ancient theory, grateful undergraduates roused envy at sister institutions.[22]

Amid the sharp divisions of the 1890s, Edward Page, a dissatisfied Yale alumnus, noted in *The Nation* that Harvard offered far greater variety of instruction than his own alma mater. In Cambridge, classes in political economy were conducted by a professor, an assistant professor, and an instructor. At Yale, a single man performed all those functions, meanwhile doubling as professor of social science. "It is apparent," Page concluded, "that something more is offered at Harvard than a merely superficial knowledge of a subject which few men have the time to pursue in afterlife."[23]

As Eliot fattened the course catalog, he shrank the student rulebook from forty pages to five, demonstrating his belief in liberty and self-governance. Before the end of his first decade, Harvard men were no longer forbidden to visit Boston theaters or required to attend college chapel, and smoking was tolerated in the Yard. He ordered proctors to remain indoors when bonfires broke out, reasoning shrewdly that mischief-makers would soon tire of rebellion if authority seemed indifferent. In still other ways did Eliot make Harvard attractive to the serious student. He installed a letter system of grading, gave vigorous backing to college athletics, and exposed undergraduates to memorable teachers such as Barrett Wendell on drama, Albert B. Hart on American history, Frank Taussig on economics, and Nathanial Shaler on geology.

If, as McCosh insisted, the elective system was a bid for popularity, it rubbed off on the institution and not the president. Asked to identify what attracted them to Cambridge in the first place, most who answered an 1889 survey cited Harvard's historic status as America's first college, the quality of instruction, and what one respondent called "the spirit of a universal learning and development, as distinguished from the intent and temper of a sectarian college." No one mentioned Eliot himself.

It isn't hard to fathom. Saints can be tiresome, Olympians pompous. Eliot's faculty liked to imitate his portentous tones, investing the latest forecast of clear skies or unseasonably hot weather with the familiar sonorous timbre. Asked if the president had a sense of humor, one of his deans replied, "He has, but it's unreliable." John Jay Chapman, thinking that Eliot recoiled instinctively from human contact, always made a point of seizing his hand and pumping it vigorously. Once a prominent visitor who was to breakfast with the president was set upon by pranksters who assured him that Eliot regularly sat down to dine in formal wear. Displaying a sensitivity for which few gave him credit, the president outsmarted his tormentors. Spotting his guest coming down Quincy Street in elaborate formal regalia, Eliot sprinted upstairs in time to don his own tuxedo. He would have no one embarrassed on his account.[24]

"His heart was his dominating characteristic," wrote Nicholas Murray Butler, "but he never let people know it." Perhaps, like Coriolanus, he simply would not show his wounds. One man still living in Cambridge recalls the sight of Harvard's chief executive towering before his neighbor's door, silently offering up the remains of a vast ice cream dessert that had been confected for an official dinner. Although his own salary was five thousand dollars a year, Eliot was sympathetic to those for whom academic life was a financial trial.[25]

He hid his compassion behind a chilly countenance. He once left a room after rejecting the pleadings of parents whose son had been expelled because he didn't wish them to see the tears streaking his face. When a friend surprised by a yellow flag of quarantine flying from the president's house inquired who in the Eliot family was ill, it turned out no one was; the president had taken in an undergraduate whose family was too distant to offer care. Thereafter, Eliot nursed the boy back to health with his own hands.

For all this, he refused to court popularity. When football swept the land and the Greek ideal of competition threatened to degenerate into a Roman circus, Harvard's president remarked that "A game that needs to be watched is not fit for genuine sportsmen. It is hard to find trustworthy watchers." He denounced "tyrannical public opinion—partly ignorant, partly barbarous."

Henry Cabot Lodge took exception. Football, claimed the self-professed Scholar in Politics, was part of the price that English-speaking peoples must pay for being world conquerors. The debate escalated. "Continuous, pumped cheering during good and bad playing alike is absolutely unnatural," countered Eliot. What's more, it had no relation to the contests of real life. A spate of injuries inspired him twice to attempt to ban the sport, a drastic move averted only when Theodore Roosevelt called a White House conference of college athletic directors in 1905. TR, it was rumored, had called Mr. Eliot a mollycoddle.[26]

Eliot had his revenge; he suspended crew members caught rifling books from a library days before the annual regatta with Yale. The White House sent an executive appeal for leniency but the president was unmoved. His correspondent might be President of the United States, but *he* was president of Harvard University. "One must never do scurvy things in the supposed interest or for the pleasure of others." The team won anyway, no doubt confirming Eliot's faith in the Unitarian Fatherhood of God, Brotherhood of Man, and Neighborhood of Boston.[27]

TR publicly praised Eliot as First Citizen of the Republic, but his relations with him were at best warily correct. This was due partly to differing styles: Roosevelt confided to his friend Owen Wister after attending one Harvard reunion that he felt like a bulldog that had strayed into a Cambridge symposium of perfectly clean, white Persian cats. Part stemmed from political differences. Eliot the anti-imperialist judged TR the jingoist "a degenerate son of Harvard." The younger man was then prompted to complain to Cabot Lodge, "If we ever come to nothing as a nation, it will be because of the teaching of Carl Schurz, President Eliot, the *Evening Post* and futile sentimentalists of the international arbitration type" who had succeeded in eating away what Roosevelt called "the great fighting features of our race."[28]

Most of all, these two pillars of Victorian America differed in tone and temperament. As President of the United States, TR arrived in Cambridge for his twenty-fifth class reunion, his Secretary of War in tow. "Taft's a brick! Taft's a brick!" he repeated to anyone who would listen. That morning, Roosevelt entered the Eliot residence, flung his clothes violently across the bed, and slapped a pistol in the drawer. A little later, he careened down the stairs. When Eliot invited him to breakfast, Roosevelt replied that he had already promised to break bread with Episcopal Bishop William Lawrence, "and, good gracious [clapping his right hand to his side], I've forgotten my gun!" While the guest retrieved his firearm, Eliot reflected on the Massachusetts statute forbidding him to carry it at all. "A very lawless mind!" judged the educator of the politician.[29]

> *Universities are among the most permanent of human institutions. They outlast particular forms of government, and even the legal and industrial institutions in which they seem to be embedded. Harvard University already illustrates this transcendent vitality.*
> —CHARLES WILLIAM ELIOT,
>   *on Harvard's 250th anniversary, 1886*

FOR HER bicentennial observance in 1836, a thousand alumni had gathered to hear the first performance of the newly composed anthem "Fair Harvard," before attending a dinner which lasted over six hours and included forty toasts (with "principally light wines"). By 1886, Eliot's Harvard had gained a global stature and internal tensions to match. Delegates from Cambridge, Edinburgh, and Heidelberg listened to James Russell Lowell declaim about "poor puppets, jerked by unseen wires, after our little hour of strut and rave." But Lowell discerned significance in the work and the workers around him.

> *Ah, there is something here*
> *Unfathomed by the cynics' sneer*
> *Something that leaps life's narrow bars*
> *To claim its birthright with the hosts of heaven.*

To the same audience, the Holmes family dramatized the split between old and new Harvard. Oliver Wendell Senior, of whom it was said that he spoke for an age unable to distinguish between an idea and an epigram, offended Princeton's president with his light verse. Oliver Wendell Junior issued a call for passionate specialists in the Eliot mold, on the grounds that "civilized men who are nothing else are a little apt to think that they cannot breathe the American atmosphere." Others used the occasion to acknowledge Eliot's transformation of the place, and its implications for the rest of the educational community. The comment of one Johns Hopkins scientist was typical: "We measure everything today by the standard of Harvard."

Eliot had no higher authority in Washington observing his actions for their compliance to federal mandate. Congress had created an office of Commissioner of Education in 1867, but its budget was miserly and its functions largely restricted to the collection of statistics. More important was the broad consensus under which Eliot's Harvard showed the way for others. Its faculty was diverse and by the end of Eliot's tenure its student body included representation from nearly every state and more than a dozen foreign countries.

In Cambridge, as in neighboring Boston, age, social position, and local pride served as bonding agents for an otherwise fragmented culture. George Santayana exaggerated only slightly when he described his employer as "the Seminary and Academy for the inner circle of Bostonians." Bliss Perry, who left *The Atlantic Monthly* at Eliot's invitation to join Harvard's faculty, thought Brattle Street as secure as the close of an English cathedral, "an island in the stream of new and alien races swarming into Greater Boston."[30]

The future black nationalist W. E. B. Dubois was one such alien. He arrived at Harvard from Fisk University in the autumn of 1885. Dubois stayed with a black family from Nova Scotia and boarded at the Foxcroft Club, where you could eat for thirty-five cents a day, and prevailing standards forbade wine, beer, and tobacco. Barrett Wendell read the young man's compositions to his class. But southern students objected to sitting at Dubois's side, he was turned down by the Glee Club, and on Class Day he was mistaken for a waiter. (Even Eliot, whose racial views were enlightened, was quick to reassure the Southern Club that while Harvard would do its duty by the Negro, should his numbers swell to such a point "as to impede the progress of the College," limitations would be imposed.)[31]

Eliot's faculty operated within a culturally rarefied atmosphere. Gentlemen wore silk hats when making formal calls. They reinforced their social position in such bastions of Yankeedom as the Somerset or Emerson's old Saturday Club. A detectable scent of self-importance hung over these academic watering holes, where scholarship was a product of leisure and religion more impulse than theology. After testifying to the useful biographical data to be found in *Who's Who in America,* Bliss Perry was asked, if one were seeking information on the prominent, "wouldn't the Harvard Quinquennial Catalogue answer every purpose?"[32]

Eliot's faculty appreciated intellectual variety more than social contrast. In proposing his ideal department of philosophy, William James went so far as to urge a kind of cerebral anarchy.

> If our students now could begin really to understand what [Josiah] Royce means with his voluntaristic-pluralistic monism, what [Hugo] Munsterberg means with his dualistic scientific-ism and platonism, what [George] Santayana means by his pessimistic platonism . . . what I mean by my cross plural-ism, what you mean by ethereal idealism, that these are so many religions, ways of fronting life, and worth fighting for, we should have a genuine philosophic universe at Harvard. The best condition of it would be an open conflict and rivalry of diverse systems. . . . The world might ring with the struggle, if we devoted ourselves exclusively to belaboring each other.

The conflict of ideas was not to be confused with a basic clash of values. Those who, a hundred years later, held that Harvard hated America could not have known the circling of wagons that characterized the college in the final years of the nineteenth century. Then it beckoned to those escaping what Barrett Wendell called "the wilds of Ohio." Wendell himself deplored the American Revolution and the divorce from Britain's ruling class that followed. Santayana boasted, "We poets at Harvard never read anything written in America except for our own compositions." The same philosopher declared a preference for a world run by cardinals and engineers. Boston had no room for anything American, claimed Henry Adams. Before forsaking the New World for the soothing vespers of Chartres and Mont Saint Michel, Adams gave the back of his hand to Emily Dickinson, Stephen Crane, and Winslow Homer.[33]

Others stayed on, even though they shared Adams's feelings. Mrs. Jack Gardner welcomed aesthetes to her Italianate palace in Boston's Back Bay. Some of her admirers joined the city's flourishing Anglo-Catholic movement or royalist cults. Across the river, Irving Babbitt preached the refined glories of ancient Sanskrit, while dismissing French as a cheap substitute for Latin. There was the waspish anti-Semite George Lyman Kittredge, who was said to Fletcherize Shakespeare's plays, so thoroughly did he digest their content for undergraduates to whom he was barely civil. When Kittredge slipped off the stage one afternoon in mid-lecture, he announced from the floor that for the first time in his life, he found himself at his students' level.

Most appalled by his immediate surroundings was Charles Eliot Norton, whom Eliot had entrusted with a new fine arts department. In America, Norton claimed, even the shadows were vulgar. Once, after addressing his audience as gentlemen, Norton quickly corrected himself, "As I speak these words the realization comes over me that no one here has even seen a gentleman."

Although more varied than these instructors, Harvard students were almost as clannish. Eliot's laissez-faire accepted inequalities as it tolerated snobbishness. Twelve hundred men were on board, lining up to take their meals at Memorial Hall, a gloomy brick pile put up to honor Harvard's war dead. Several hundred more were obliged to work at least part-time to finance their education. The affluent minority, on the other hand, turned their attention to dinners at Marliave's in Boston, beer and rabbit at Charlie Wirth's, roadhouses, and polo ponies.

Disdain for scholarly exertion was prevalent, especially among the socially prominent and leading opinion-makers. "We deem it narrowminded to excel," wrote one of Theodore Roosevelt's classmates,

> *We call the man fanatic who applies*
> *His life to one grand purpose till he dies.*
> *Enthusiasm sees one side, one fact;*
> *We try to see all sides, but do not act.*
> *. . . We long to sit with newspapers unfurled,*
> *Indifferent spectators of the world.*[34]

The *Harvard Crimson* (briefly dubbed the *Magenta*) professed indifference to all but social niceties. "That Harvard students have brought the art of dressing to the greatest perfection attainable on this side of the Atlantic is an unquestionable fact," the paper declared early in Eliot's presidency. Then it offered some typically precious advice to the newcomer. It was commonly supposed of the Harvard man "that if he develops his muscles, if he subscribes to athletic enterprises and the College papers, if he occasionally attends recitations, and if he professes a healthy antipathy to frigid religious exercises at frigid hours of the most frigid winter mornings, he has done enough. In other universities, he very probably has; but in Harvard the case is otherwise." Strong, liberal, and learned as their alma mater might be, said the *Crimson*, "her greatest glory lies in the faultless folds of her classic garments." An acerbic laundry list of sartorial do's and don'ts contained scorn for "grotesque gold pins embellished . . . with Greek letters . . . bad hats, seedy coats, and pepper and salt trousers." For the Harvard man to achieve true style, the editors continued, "he must be as Britannic as possible." One should talk much and loudly about prices, while avoiding formerly desirable black frocks. Why? "The Jews have got hold of them of late; they have become rather tigerish, and blue, reaching fully to the knee."

A final word of advice to aspiring gentlemen: "No one ever thinks of paying his tailor out of his allowance. The correct thing is to let the bill run, and not pay it at all—payment encourages impudence; but if the tradesman grows clamorous and threatens jail, all you have to do is to plead minority, and let your parents and guardians settle the matter at their convenience."[35]

John Marquand, who would later immortalize the likes of George Apley and H. M. Pulham, had his first encounter with the Harvard product as a child. He had gone to the Square to buy himself a sarsaparilla, had lost his way, and was directed to a nearby soda fountain by a grave youth in tweed knickerbockers and Norfolk jacket, smoking a stem briar pipe. Inside, Marquand overheard two college boys discussing the high price of banana splits. As one put it, "I do not think in all my life I'll have to bother about fifteen cents, because I'll always have it."[36]

Disregarding evidence of student self-indulgence, Eliot clung to his own form of indifference. "One could wish that the University did not offer the same contrast between the rich man's mode of life and the poor man's that the outer world offers," he sighed, "but it does, and it is not certain that the presence of this contrast is unwholesome or injurious. In this respect, as in many others, the University is an epitome of the modern world."

Although Eliot staunchly opposed construction of additional student dormitories (a new infirmary and Union were both inspired and paid for by wealthy alumni) and ignored the growing division between well-heeled clubmen and those who were struggling to assimilate themselves into such an exotic culture, his curriculum reforms and his admissions policy were opening Harvard to a broader, more socially conscious student body. Noblesse oblige began to take its first tentative steps toward political involvement. "Our man of leisure must learn as his first lesson that with him leisure should mean work," Theodore Roosevelt told a packed Sever Hall in 1889. "You are out of place in American politics . . . until in opposing or backing a man, it simply never occurs to you to think of anything but his capacity, integrity, and courage."

A decade passed and another Roosevelt arrived, a privileged youth from the Hudson Valley and Endicott Peabody's Groton. Sarah Roosevelt's boy Franklin dined in style on Mt. Auburn Street. Evenings he left his four-room suite at Westmorely Court to play billiards at Sanborne with friends from St. Paul's and Pomfret. But he also raised funds for women and children of South Africa's war-ravaged Boers. He joined the college Republican Club, and tramped eight miles of local pavement carrying a torch for William McKinley and his distant cousin Teddy.

(Later, he questioned TR's intervention in a nationwide coal strike; to young FDR, it was symptomatic of the president's regrettable tendency "to make the executive power stronger than the House of Congress.")

FDR's academic achievements were unspectacular. They included a warm defense of Alexander Hamilton's role in securing New York's adoption of the Constitution—without even passing reference to the Federalist Papers. "It is not so much brilliance as effort that is appreciated here," he wrote. Disappointed over failure to make Porcellian, Harvard's most prestigious finishing club, Franklin bounced back as librarian of the Fly. Fly members were not noted for their social consciousness. According to local legend, clubsters liked nothing better than to heat copper pennies to a near-molten state, then toss them out of their windows onto Cambridge's icy streets, where tattered urchins were sure to pick them up out of necessity or greed. Yet FDR was unlike the "rich young fashionables" recalled by his contemporary Oswald Garrison Villard, boys from Newport or Fifth Avenue who showed no interest in world affairs, much preferring idleness on Mt. Auburn's Gold Coast to sampling the rich menu of Eliot's electives.[37]

Along with others of his class, Roosevelt was slowly awakening to the world beyond. Conscience led him to continue his work with the Groton Missionary Society and to join the Harvard Social Service Society. As editor of the *Crimson* during his last two years, Franklin mingled passionate appeals for support of the football squad with challenges to the Corporation to replace rickety wooden fire escapes on aging dormitories and narrow boardwalks laid across the Yard's muddy expanse. Others began to emulate him, their preoccupation with amusement yielding to an interest in the labor movement, women's rights, foreign controversies, and local injustices. As an undergraduate, Roger Baldwin, who went on to found the American Civil Liberties Union, pledged his troth to Edward Everett Hale's Lend-a-Hand-Society. Four hundred Harvard men became volunteer social workers, gave entertainments in poorhouses, and conducted clothing drives for Booker T. Washington's Tuskegee Institute. Hundreds more flocked to Francis Peabody's course, "Ethics of the Social Questions," popularly known as "Peabo's drainage, drunkenness, and divorces."[38]

Radical sentiments were as yet far removed from mainstream thinking. When Jack London signed a Cambridge guest book "Yours for the revolution," he inspired a prompt reply. "There ain't going to be any Revolution," scribbled the next lecturer. Nor were alumni any more favorably inclined toward London and his ilk. After donating $100,000 for Soldier's Field, Boston Symphony patron Henry Higginson was frank in asserting his motives. "How else are we to save our country if not by education in all ways and on all sides?" he demanded. "Democracy has got fast hold of the world, and *will* rule. Let us see that she does it more wisely and more humanely than the kings and nobles have done. Our chance is *now*—before the country is full and the struggle for bread becomes intense and bitter. Educate, and save ourselves and our families and our money from mobs!"[39]

Higginson's credo was the rallying cry for a university whose sense of entitlement grew as fast as its course catalog. By now, Eliot's reforms were taking hold in the divinity, law, and medical schools. There were new departments of fine arts, architecture, and forestry. Twenty-seven young women crowded into four rooms at 6 Appian Way, which after 1894 bore the name of Anne Radcliffe, Lady Mowlson. In a quarter-century the Harvard faculty had tripled in size; the teacher-student ratio declined to one to eight. Increasing numbers from outside New England were attracted by new museums and lecture halls, or by courses in Egyptology, Celtic literature, and anthropology. In 1897, Lawrence Lowell became Harvard's first full-time instructor in government. Boylston Hall housed one of the world's foremost chemical research labs. Greek dramas were performed in Sanders Theater, and the economics department was enriched by scholars lured from Cornell and Wisconsin, Michigan and California. The New Education of 1869 had become a yardstick with which to measure every college in the land.

As the 400th anniversary of Columbus's discovery of America approached, patriotic Americans wished to proclaim their country's coming of age. What better way than to throw a party, a sprawling world's fair, surpassing in size and grandeur anything yet glimpsed on foreign soil? Innovative as the first Ferris Wheel and crass as Little Egypt, the World's Columbian Exposition of 1893 was a striking metaphor of a nation in development. With its thin veneer of Greece and Rome, its 150 plaster palaces painted white to resemble marble, and its strong emphasis on the mechanical genius of a tinkering race, the fair drew thirty million visitors. Surrounding the Court of Honor and its towering stature of Columbus were inscriptions from the Bible, and from Lincoln. But most came from the epigrammatic pen of Charles Eliot.

Among the hundreds of exhibits from over seventy different countries displaying the wonders of the time was an impressive collection from Harvard, America's foremost educational institution. In the south gallery of the world's largest building, sprawling over forty-five hundred square feet, Harvard's display combined charts, graphs, laboratory specimens, and photographs from the college Camera Club to tell the story of modern-day Cambridge. No attempt was made to attract a crowd with historical relics, reported the *Harvard Graduates' Magazine*. In spite of a crimson banner bearing the date 1636, "it is to recent achievements, to its fitness to cope with present problems, and its foresight in preparing for the future, that the University commands the attention of the student in search of training, the teacher in search of methods, and the expert in search of accurate knowledge. . . ."

Harvard's exhibit told a practical tale. One chart measured the University's growth over the previous fifty years. Another traced the steady rise in endowment. A third showed ever-increasing gifts to Alma Mater, while a fourth followed annual expenditures from less than $100,000 in the 1850s to more than ten times as much under President Eliot. Colored maps compared the fair-site with Harvard's campus: the fair covered 600 acres, the University owned 57 acres more. Indeed, Eliot's Harvard might be likened to a sort of academic exposition, its floor space nearly equal to that in the fair's Mechanical Arts Building, its physical plant as splendid as anything devised by Stanford White or Richard Morris Hunt. For proof, there were large photos of student dormitories, including Hastings Hall, "a stately building, the destined home of generation upon generation of students, netting to the University an unrestricted income of about $14,000 a year."

Next to busts of Longfellow, Ticknor, and Lowell, a placard announced the availability of endowed professorships. Cases filled with the work of law school professors rubbed shoulders with pictures of generous benefactors. The Astronomical Observatory featured patrons of its own. There was apparatus from the physics department, agates from Mineralogy, glass flowers from Botany, and the proud advertisement of 203 new compounds devised by Harvard chemists.

"Numbers do not constitute a university," Eliot once wrote, "and no money can make it before its time." To the millions of fair-goers who viewed the exhibit of President Eliot's educational miracle that summer, it was apparent that Harvard's time had come.[40]

Having remade Harvard, Eliot could now turn his attention to the rest of America.

An admirer once likened him to the Puritan statue on Cambridge Common, "alone in the cold and dark, in the wet and dry, always calm and patient, without bitterness waiting for each new opportunity for human service." With the same sublime confidence that smothered two generations of opposition within his own realm at Harvard, Eliot interrupted his puritanical solitude to address one national issue after another. At first, he restricted his admonishings to education. Whatever else might divide them, he and Princeton's McCosh agreed on the futility of land-grant colleges. To support any additional funding for such schools, Eliot maintained, would "array class against class, and sect against sect."[41]

In an uncharacteristically bitter retort to the friends of public education, Harvard's president drew a careful distinction between state support of his own institute and that accorded the behemoths of the middle west and the Pacific coast. Harvard students paid "a very fair tuition fee," while "it was reserved for the present generation in our Western States to insidiously teach communism under the guise of free tuition in State colleges."[42]

In opposing plans for a national university at Washington, he was no less critical. The idea was too European for his tastes. On the Continent, said Eliot, government responsibility was axiomatic. The French lexicon didn't even include a word for public spirit, "for the reason that the sentiment is unknown to them." Subsidizing railroads or steamship companies was bad enough; to abandon what Eliot called "the old Massachusetts method" of local control and private oversight would invite "the military, despotic organization of public instruction which prevails in Prussia." Of course, the president failed to mention that preserving the status quo would leave newer schools at a financial disadvantage, and hasten Harvard's development as a de facto national university.

Over time, Eliot achieved more by stratagem than by blunt disavowal. For instance, after a bill was introduced in the Massachusetts legislature to establish a one-year teacher's academy in Boston, he announced Harvard's intention to provide similar training. A separate graduate school was rejected, but summer courses were devised for secondary teachers in the sciences, and faculty appointments were made in "the history and art of teaching." At the same time, Eliot also showed interest in Cambridge's public school system, encouraging his faculty to write new textbooks and course guides for use in the public classroom.

Throughout America, universal education was at last coming into its own. Public libraries and adult education courses proliferated, as the progressive educational theories of John Dewey became widely accepted. The classroom, Dewey boldly declared in *The School and Society,* was the cradle of a civilization more "worthy, lovely, and harmonious." In 1870, barely 80,000 students attended U.S. high schools, little more than the ranks of private preparatory schools would admit, and a tiny fraction of the nearly seven million enrolled in all of public education. By the end of the century, however, the number of students in U.S. high schools had grown to a million. In the half-century from 1870 to 1920, per-capita expenditures on public instruction rose from $1.64 to $9.80.

In education as in economics, the trickle-down theory prevailed. A few years after having been named president of Harvard, Eliot had become active in the National Educational Association, then a conservative body. (After a wave of railroad strikes the NEA's president claimed credit for having averted a domestic version of the French Commune. Violence might have been prevented altogether, he went on, if only workers had been taught "to think as well as to toil.") Early in his presidency, Eliot had called for a general reform of college admissions standards. Specifically, he proposed entrance ages lowered from nineteen to eighteen, more and better high schools, the introduction of algebra and other secondary school subjects into the upper grades of public instruction, and less emphasis on grammar. In 1892, the NEA created the famous Committee of Ten, with Eliot in the chair, to study improving public secondary schools. With a budget of $2,500 for its groundbreaking work, the committee proposed to narrow the gap between popular education and the walled enclave of advanced study. Henceforth, secondary schools were to open their doors and invigorate their curricula. Such schools would be forerunners of the comprehensive high school of the twentieth century, a reform closely linked with another Harvard president, James Bryant Conant.

Eliot wished to eliminate the caste-consciousness of secondary education, to recognize both the potential and the usefulness of noncollege careers, and to implant in each mind the seeds of intellectual longing. His motives were not purely altruistic. By first upgrading high school courses, he could then justify the death of Greek and Latin entrance requirements at Harvard. Both were steps in the right direction, toward a school steeped in his own priorities: English, French, German, mathematics, chemistry, physics, American history. What was good for Harvard turned out to have profound implications for the rest of society.

Hard upon the Committee of Ten came Eliot's proposal for a College Entrance Examination Board to unify entrance requirements and fashion common rules of measuring academic potential. The Board was instituted in 1900, and only several years later did Harvard's faculty accept the new order. But Eliot had achieved another breakthrough. As usual, others traveled comfortably in his footsteps.

A few clung to old passions, soon to harden into firm prejudices. John Jay Chapman was one.

> Bend down and look into the peephole of this man's mind
> [he wrote]. The whole world looks like a toy village lighted
> by Arctic moonlight. . . . Here is Education running around
> on its little track, and here is Art. Poetry is thought of—a dainty
> tin wreath lies on the little shrine. Humanity is spelt with large

letters and taxes are explained like clockwork. Marriage and happiness are understood. How simple, how excellently planned are all thy works. O Arctic Village! shallow common sense—faith in machines—easy optimism—dogma of progress—wishful forgetting that there is always night and madness and mystery to contend with, coexisting with daylight and science and universal literacy.[43]

Chapman may have been indelicate, but he was not inaccurate. When Eliot boldly predicted coming restrictions on armaments, an international court with a police force to carry out its edicts, and what he called "the compelled appeal to public opinion before war," it was difficult to know on what he based his confidence. He was no less convinced of the virtues of daily walks and the economical uses of veal loaf. A similar taste for big buildings and substantial fund drives led him to fill Harvard Yard with structures as out of place as a Mayan temple in a Georgian square. He denounced King David as a scoundrel, the pitcher's balk as an outrage, and (although he tolerated Radcliffe) women's education as a threat both to femininity and physical health.

In his inaugural address, Eliot had said that however important the position of Harvard's president, "it must not be forgotten that he is emphatically a constitutional executive. It is his character and his judgment which are of importance, not his opinions." This did not prevent Eliot from sharing his views with the rest of America. He proposed a third political party in 1884, argued long and eloquently for civil service reform, and raised his voice against restricted immigration.

One week before William McKinley asked Congress to declare war on Spain in April of 1898, Eliot's name headed a list of eighty-six Harvard professors who opposed the fighting. As war fever swept the nation, spurred on by reports of Spanish atrocities in the bright yellow journals of William Randolph Hearst, William James was another Harvard luminary who took exception to the flagwaving. A bulwark of the Anti-Imperial League, James ended one lecture with the solemn order, "Don't yelp with the pack!"

Much later, James, who sourly assessed most of his own country as "white trash," struck the bloody but unbowed stance that reminded one colleague of Ireland's members of Parliament. "One better man *shall* show the way," James asserted, "and we *shall* follow." Charles Eliot Norton, one of the best of men in his own estimation, raised hackles by questioning student enlistments and received the applause of packed houses in Cambridge. The national press registered violent dissent. A Chicago newspaper suggested he should be tarred and feathered. Even

Oliver Wendell Holmes Junior took exception to "the self-righteous and preaching discourse" then in fashion at his alma mater, and confessed to pleasurable feelings at hearing "some rattling jingo talk" in counterpoint to the pacifist bleatings of Norton, James, and others.[44]

When McKinley was assassinated in September 1901, there was outrage in some journals over Harvard's alleged incitement of his anarchist murderer. Eliot himself had dismissed the late chief executive as "a narrow-minded and commonplace man," before McKinley tactfully withdrew his name from honorary degree consideration in the face of alumni protests. Along with an honorary degree, McKinley's successor was showered with advice. Eliot urged Republicans writing their 1904 platform to reject what he called "an American government with Filipino assistance" in favor of "a Filipino government with American assistance." In a period of political awakening, the Yard resounded to student appeals for the Single Tax Club, the Diplomatic Club, and the Harvard Men's League for Women's Suffrage. Nor were the University's president and faculty reluctant to lecture their countrymen about responsibilities or shortcomings.

Like Frederick Jackson Turner, who joined the Cambridge fraternity after pronouncing America's physical frontiers closed, Eliot heard the death rattle of rugged individualism. "The greatest good of the greatest number," was his new definition of democracy's mission. For confirming evidence, he pointed to conservation, business regulation, preventive medicine, and reduced work hours, all interlaced in the seemingly impossible, "collectivism which does not suppress individualism."

By 1907, Eliot was modestly downgrading his own chances for the White House, given "the average American's distrust of the expert." Yet he was not deterred from plans to educate a class of public servants allied to the higher professions, and Science highest of all. "Free from the pressure of public opinion, and from the hot gusts of public feeling," declared Eliot of his cherished professional, "he has no occasion to discover and avail himself of the passing wishes or tastes of the multitude." Seventy years before President Derek Bok dedicated the Kennedy School of Government as a training ground for America's civic managers, Eliot urged a school of public service. Delayed by the 1907 panic on Wall Street, the idea led ultimately to the Harvard School of Business Administration instead.

Meanwhile, Eliot himself rode a wave of public veneration. Whatever he had to say, a national audience seemed eager to listen. From his pen came essays with titles like "The Forgotten Millions" and "Family Stocks in a Democracy." There was the presidency of the Civil Service

Reform League to occupy his time, not to mention the International Health Board, the Rockefeller Foundation, and the Carnegie Endowment for World Peace. He was a trustee of Boston's Museum of Fine Arts, president of the General Conference of Unitarian Churches, and an outspoken advocate of birth control before mildly scandalized Edwardians.

Before he resigned in November 1908, Harvard's president seemed to many a permanent and indestructible fixture—like that stony-faced Puritan on Cambridge Common. At his resignation, Eliot quoted old Dr. Arnold of Rugby, who said that a man was no longer fit to be a headmaster when he could not come up the steps two at a time, and added: "Now I can still do that." He didn't wish his retirement to be spoken of with regret. "It is touching to find that feeling, but I think it is something to be looked forward to with hope. We must all set to work to find some young, able active man for the place. He can be found; we shall find him."[45]

The tributes flooded Cambridge. Theodore Roosevelt praised him for having democratized Harvard. Undergraduates cheered their "Prexy" wherever he appeared. "How absolute is the belief of President Eliot in the truth!" marveled the *Harvard Graduates' Magazine*. "It unites the assurance of the scientist and the convictions of the moralist. . . . He is the Man Doing." The object of all this flattery did not have his head turned. On the contrary, the day after his plans were revealed, he told his wife that two-thirds of the faculty had come up "to view the remains."[46]

There were disappointments to come. Eliot's preferred candidate, David F. Houston of the University of Texas, was passed over in favor of a man neither young nor in sympathy with Eliot's priorities. The outgoing president, confided Lawrence Lowell to friends, looked upon the College "chiefly as a place for learning the subjects that would practically best fit a man for his subsequent career." Not so Lowell, who was hardly enamored of the first decade of the twentieth century. Unable to match Eliot's imperturbable faith in human progress, he was openly contemptuous of practical eduaction. The worst thing Harvard might do, wrote Lowell, was to make young men look upon thinking "as a means of earning bread." Still more offensive to Eliot was his successor's distrust of most graduate training. As Lowell put it, "No one goes into a graduate school in order to acquire a love of learning."[47]

However galling, such remarks were drowned out in the roar of approval for Eliot's performance. A study of America's leading universities early in the new century established Harvard's primacy for all to see. The nation's oldest college was also her richest. She offered more courses than any rival, taught by the largest, most respected faculty in the land. Of a thousand leading scientists, 237 had studied at Harvard, 171 at Johns Hopkins, 93 at Yale. Only the elective system seemed in danger of failing to survive its champion—that, and Eliot's long-held belief that a three-year course should be adopted in order to hasten the start of professional schooling.

At the age of seventy-four, the First Citizen of the Republic embarked on a farewell tour. During its course, he delivered three dozen speeches on such elevated subjects as "A Liberal Education" and "Some Reasons for the Failure of Universal Suffrage in Cities." He stalked away from muckraker Lincoln Steffens when the journalist urged classes in legislative corruption and legal bribery. Would Steffens have Harvard teach the steps necessary to halt such dishonesty, inquired Eliot, literal as ever. "No no," Steffens responded sarcastically, "I don't mean to keep the boys from succeeding in their professions—intelligence is what I'm aiming at, not honesty."[48]

With Lowell's inauguration in October 1909, Harvard embarked on a different course. From his new address on Brattle Street, Eliot might be forgiven for wondering if it were to be a U turn executed by his bustling successor, a pillar of genteel Boston who was as much a behaviorist in thought and preference as Eliot was an advocate of laissez-faire and individual latitude. The old man affected nonconcern. He had his round-the-world travels to occupy him, along with the "Five Foot Bookshelf," his unprecedented effort to condense the world's great literature for those Americans not fortunate enough to attend Harvard.

Fittingly, the editor of the Harvard Classics anticipated a secular millennium, to which Harvard would make a substantial contribution. In Eliot's Eden revisited, machines would replace human sweat. Rational belief would shoulder aside superstition. Warring nations would discard their animosities. Not long before the First World War, Eliot unveiled his highly personalized Religion of the Future. Such a faith would not be based on authority, he claimed, temporal or spiritual. Neither would it tolerate gloom, asceticism, or disharmony with "democracy, individualism, social idealism, the zeal for education, the spirit of research, the modern tendency to welcome the new, the fresh powers of preventive medicine, and the recent advances in business and industrial ethics."[49]

"Nobody's name lives in this world to be blessed," he once revealed, "who has not associated his life with some kind of human emancipation, physical, mental, or moral." So Eliot the Emancipator soldiered on, living out his legend, rejecting ambassadorial posts, musing half-seriously about becoming Postmaster General, writing inscriptions for Washington's

Union Station and a host of other structures throughout the land, riding his bicycle, sailing each summer, and growing old with something close to charm. As his rigidities were converted by a more frivolous generation into quaintnesses, so his exactitudes softened in the solution of time. When a friend suggested that he direct his chauffeur to a grove of "lovely old trees" under which he had played as a boy, Eliot interrupted, "Not lovely trees, noble trees."[50]

His optimism never dimmed. Having heaped praise on Woodrow Wilson's proposed League of Nations, after Lodge and his fellow senators engineered its rejection, Eliot refused to despair. "When a good cause has been defeated," he told a friend, "the only question that its advocates need ask is when do we fight again." He reprimanded Nicholas Murray Butler for titling an article "Is America Worth Saving?" because, as he explained, "I believe that the right way for guides of American opinion is never to question or entertain a doubt about the future of the United States." He confessed to a friend the hope that he might never outlive his personal faith in democracy.

In time, Eliot came to resemble the aging author whose fame increases the less he writes. The popular press began to call him "Last of the Puritans." At eighty-five, he journeyed to Washington to take part in Wilson's postwar Industrial Conference, only to see it break down in acrimony between the representatives of labor and management. Six months later, he gave tacit approval to election of "a rational Catholic" to the Harvard Corporation.

It was hard to get him to reminisce, Eliot's family told the *New York Times*. "With him it is always next month, next year, the future of humanity."[51]

He informed one correspondent, "I have never been able to see that any of the Heavens or Paradises described in sacred or profane literature would be even tolerable for a person who had had fairly happy experience of earthly life. The idea of an eternity of rest is positively repulsive to any man or woman, primitive, barbarous or civilized, who has had joy in work."[52]

When the New York Civic Forum presented him a gold medal and a stand-in assured the audience it would be a cherished memento, Eliot bridled. The last such award given him, he wrote waspishly, had been cherished first in the vault of the Cambridge Trust Company and later in a Museum of Fine Arts safe. Besides, he preferred bronze to gold. He had not bothered to listen to the proceedings carried over a friend's radio. Broadcasting was simply "a means of spreading much ill-considered talk all over the country. Is it going to be like the omnipresent noise which automobiles have introduced into both city and country life," he wondered, "or like the distracting roar of aeroplanes overhead?" A rare whiff of discontent with man-made advance, this outburst was also one of several ways in which the public monument displayed a private whimsy.[53]

Thousands gathered in the Yard to celebrate his ninetieth birthday. When the festivities were over, Eliot leaned across a game of dominoes and told his second wife, Grace, that he'd been able to hear everything said that day, with the single exception of one ministerial prayer. "And that," she replied, "was not addressed to you, my dear." He repeated the story for days.

Within a few months, Grace Eliot died, and the widower asked to see the infant grandson of the same preacher whose prayer had escaped his earlier hearing. "I wanted to hold in my arms a life that was just beginning," he explained. In August 1926, Eliot himself was struggling for breath, an old warrior calmly awaiting an honorable discharge in the salt-scented air of the Maine coast. On Sunday the 16th, he informed his son that his life would end in precisely six days. Dying on a Saturday, he explained, would be convenient for the family, as Sunday trains were more comfortable than their weekday counterparts.

For once, his will failed him. Seven days went by, until he suddenly announced, "I see Father!" A nurse asked if there was anything he wanted. "I see Mother."

Then his eyes closed, and with them the most remarkable career in all of American education. The boy whose scarred face set him apart had grown a hard shell over his sensitive nature, and fashioned a great university to match. Having furrowed the soil and planted the seed, his serenity might have been temporarily disrupted amid Lowell's season of harvest. For the Harvard that filled Appleton Chapel at the old man's funeral seemed in full retreat from electives and graduate training and social atomization. But Lowell's restoration was itself an historical pause in the course laid down by the man Harvard called King Charles.

"The best is yet to come," Eliot informed an admiring nation not long before his death. "Let us hail the coming time." Characteristically, he also inserted amid his prophecies a condemnation of tobacco and an endorsement of tea's sober virtues. His serenity never left him. On the day of his son's funeral, he had told his wife to reflect on all the happy people in the world. When James Russell Lowell pondered democracy's inclination to create a higher average of man in place of the highest possible Men, Eliot lodged a protest. He was sorry to hear such reservations expressed, said Eliot. Personally, he opposed even the contemplation of failure.

Doubt, like grief, waged an unequal struggle with Charles William Eliot. "Straight and solemn as Hamlet's Ghost," he appeared to George Santayana. To us, he is as American as George Washington, Carrie Nation, and Commodore Vanderbilt. Eliot deserved the acclaim he attracted, in those fulsome years when he became one more of the public monuments for which he was always providing inscriptions of oracular common sense.

CHAPTER TWO

The Great Assimilator

Where shall wisdom be found and where is the place of understanding? Surely it should be where the pressure of interests is lowest, where passions should be least inflamed, where men are most free to think and write their own thoughts, where the anxieties of the present do not exclude the contemplation of the past and drawing therefrom a horoscope of the possibilities of the future.

—A. LAWRENCE LOWELL

WHEN NEWS of Eliot's retirement reached the public just one day after the 1908 election which ushered Theodore Roosevelt out of the White House, the entire country seemed anxious to have a hand in the ensuing conclave. Newspapers in Minneapolis and Salt Lake City urged the Corporation to install TR in University Hall. A more populist stance was adopted by Josephus Daniels, editor of the Raleigh, North Carolina, *News and Observer.*

"By all means, [Theodore] Roosevelt should be elected president, John D. Rockefeller bursar and Elihu Root professor of political economy if Harvard is to teach absolutism, greed and usurpation," declared the man who, as Woodrow Wilson's Secretary of the Navy, was also Franklin Roosevelt's supervising officer. One Ohio daily pressed the case for William Jennings Bryan. Then the head of the Harvard Clubs of America weighed in: Roosevelt, he insisted, was too radical to win a single Overseer's vote. Eventually, the President himself doused the scheme with cold water. He knew the Harvard Corporation, said TR. In looking for Eliot's replacement, its members would prefer the Back Bay to Oyster Bay. As usual, his political instincts were sound.[1]

For good measure, Roosevelt offered some discreet encouragement to his friend and contemporary Abbott Lawrence Lowell. In a White House visit soon after Eliot's announcement, Lowell confessed to doubts about his chances of becoming Harvard's president. Nonsense, said TR. For good measure, he volunteered to assist Lowell's campaign publicly—by declaring his own support for another candidate.

Around Cambridge, more than a few of Lowell's admirers thought him a civilized Roosevelt. The two men had much in common, quite apart from their quarterdeck manner, distinguished lineage, and membership in what TR labeled "the governing class." Both men were accustomed to center stage; neither shied away from the personal pronoun or hesitated when presented the opportunity to transform their immediate surroundings. Lowell battled his faculty as Roosevelt baited Congress. Charles William Eliot had proclaimed that a university was the last place in the world for a dictator, that "Learning is always republican. It has its idols, but not masters." When he was elected, Lowell set out to disprove the maxim. In the process, he rejected Eliot's laissez-faire approach to education and exerted his own energies toward shaping a very definite type, a man of parts reminiscent of his own family's most public-spirited members.

In his autobiography, TR asserted that "the evil development of Harvard is the snob, exactly as the evil development of Yale is the cad." Lowell agreed. "I believe that the future of this country is in the hands of its young men," he said at the time of his election, "and that the character of its young men depends largely upon their coming to college. And in college," he went on, "I believe their character depends not merely on being instructed, but mostly on their living together in an atmosphere of good fellowship."[2]

Heavily influenced by William James's behavioral theories, Lowell envisioned an end to Eliot's elective anarchy. In its place would arise a social community patterned on Britain's most ancient universities. In his Harvard, everyone would work, and work hard—even the sons of the rich. He confessed to fear the day when a future constitution might guarantee the right to life, liberty, and the Ph.D. (Not that Lowell paid much heed to advanced degrees. Never having earned one himself, the crusty Brahmin liked to entertain alumni by recalling the diligent if misguided grad student pursuing studies on the left hind leg of the Paleozoic cockroach.)[3]

One trait Lowell shared with both Eliot and Roosevelt. "I have laid awake just two nights," he informed one questioner. The first, said Lowell, followed a heated debate over a plan to merge Harvard's engineering school with that of neighboring MIT, "and I have forgotten what the other was about."

"I shall be told that I am struggling against the spirit of the age, which is . . . plutocratic," he admitted on another occasion. "It is also true that the very object of a university is to keep before men's minds those things that lie beyond the spirit of the age."[4]

Lowell has been cast by some as a kind of Back Bay Lear. Yet he played many characters—the rich man of simple tastes, the gentleman who loathed gentlemanly C's, the passionate theorist of democracy whose personal conduct was suavely autocratic. Upton Sinclair called him a tool of electric light industries. His cousin thought him a snob. To clubmen evicted from their comfortable sloth and forced to pay for the privilege of dining in one of Lowell's Houses, he was a traitor to his class.[5]

Lowell came by his contradictions as the product of a long line of successful merchants and philanthropically minded financiers. The first of the family migrated to America from Bristol, England, in 1639. One Lowell was appointed to high office by George Washington. Another took up the cudgels against Jefferson and his democratic dogmas. In 1836, John Lowell bequeathed a quarter-million dollars of his cotton fortune to found the Lowell Institute, an early attempt to bring free instruction in science, religion, history, and literature to a wider public. The president's father earned the gratitude of abolitionists for his staunch support of the antislavery cause in Bleeding Kansas.

Powerful ties of tradition and blood bonded the Lowells. As an old man, Lawrence could be seen swinging along Boston's Esplanade at his customary four miles per hour, coatless against a blustery wind off the Charles River, his ruddy face dominated by blazing blue eyes and a luxuriant snowy white mustache. There was no deviation from the blue suit, tan shoes, and boiled shirt he wore year-round, nor the two gold studs, large as quarter dollars, which were first worn by his father seventy-five years earlier. Lowell married his first cousin, Anna, opened a Boston law office with her brother, and governed Harvard through a Corporation that included another cousin, Episcopal Bishop William Lawrence. (It was Bishop Lawrence who charmed New York banker George Baker on the golf course into supplying five million dollars to construct a school of business administration early in Lowell's regime.)[6]

The president himself disclaimed any talents for raising money. He left that to others, he said, being unable to bring himself to join the mendicant class. Even with tongue in cheek, Lowell could hardly escape the narrow hierarchy which restricted his sympathies while concentrating his prodigious energies. If Eliot combined Jay Gould and Cambridge Common in roughly equal measures, Lowell was a perfect coupling of State Street and Cecil Rhodes.

His sister, Amy Lowell, was acclaimed for her poetry and lampooned for her cigar smoking and other eccentricities. As a child, Amy had composed her first poem while in Chicago, en route east from California.

> *The folks go*
> *on the lake*
> *in sailboat*
> *and barge.*
> *But for all*
> *of its beauty*
> *I'd rather go home*
> *to Boston,*
> *Charles River,*
> *and the*
> *State House's dome.*

At least emotionally her brother never left Boston. Late in life he would lament that Harvard was the only decent thing the city still possessed. But he entered its presidency in the twilight of America's self-proclaimed Athens. William Dean Howells had long abandoned Chestnut Street for Fifth Avenue, followed by Edwin Arlington Robinson. Longfellow and James Russell Lowell (Lawrence's uncle, who boasted that *his* Cambridge residence, Elmwood, was built Tory and would die Tory) were in their graves at Mt. Auburn. Emerson and Hawthorne were gone, alongside clipper ships and the China trade. Old elites were being displaced in the new century. Darwinian tests supplanted yesterday's deferences.[7]

Change had already begun to transform Boston's insularity by 1856, the year of Lowell's birth. Irishmen and Italians were pouring over gangplanks barely a mile from Beacon Hill, finding refuge in enclaves of their countrymen. But Lowell's boyhood did little to open his eyes to a wider world. As a member of Harvard's Society of Fellows, Arthur Schlesinger Junior once heard the patriarch describe the 1860 presidential campaign: he alone of the Boston establishment's children spoke up for the cause of Abraham Lincoln, prairie railsplitter, against the Whiggish doctrines of John Bell and Edward Everett. The child was merely repeating his father's political doctrines, but in a social circle that was narrow and politi-

cally homogeneous, such liberal views were unacceptable. It was one of
the few times in Lowell's life that he felt the sting of exclusion.[8]

He prepared for Harvard at home, and entered the Class of 1877,
in which he quickly distinguished himself by a tightly coiled energy and
a taste for hard mental labor. The former found release in long-distance
running. As a sophomore, Lowell took both the half-mile and mile races
on the same afternoon and annoyed his competitors by looking over his
shoulder at them. He had just wanted a little extra incentive, he explained
afterward. No such bait was required in the classroom, however, where
Lawrence earned a Phi Beta Kappa key and began a lifelong defense of
the organization. Equating criticism of PBK to requiring the same amount
of milk from every cow, he asserted his preference for one man of talent
to ten ordinary fellows.

Following his graduation in June 1877, Lowell entered into a law
practice with his cousin, John Francis Lowell. He continued to display
his athletic prowess, customarily running up six flights to reach his office,
and trotting back and forth between downtown and the Marlborough
Street residence to which he soon brought a stately bride. The Lowells fit
neatly into a world not seriously challenged until the Great War that began in 1914 shattered class lines. Sublime in its self-confidence, secure on
the summit of responsible wealth, patrician Boston was a custom-tinted,
valedictory world where upstairs and downstairs lived in mutual depen-
dence, and acquisitive greed was dismissed as parvenu. Wintering on Commonwealth Avenue, taking summer flings at Bar Harbor, it had Harvard
as ballast to steady its ship.

Bishop Lawrence said that while proper Bostonians might criticize
the College of Cardinals, they would never find fault with the Harvard
Corporation. As late as 1905, the annual selections of the exclusive
club, Hasty Pudding, were listed in their order of choice in the Hub's
newspapers. When he discovered that the Boston Harvard Club was
stocked exclusively with Fairy Soap, one reporter was called to account
by his managing editor: it was the policy of his paper, he said, not to reveal such things about "nice people."[9]

At home, Lowell surrounded himself with medieval armor and dusty
spears, souvenirs of many journeys abroad. They gave 168 Marlborough
Street a faded congeniality, an effect its owner enhanced with his quaint
Abraham Lincoln collars and frock coats first popularized by Prince Albert. Yet he was discontented. Finding little satisfaction in the law, Lowell
served a term on the Boston School Committee and at the same time began to dabble in the affairs of his alma mater. In a long article written for
the *Harvard Monthly* in 1887, he took issue with Eliot's elective system.

This did not deter him, a decade later, from joining the college's new department of government—America's first—nor from rising to become an influential member of Eliot's star-filled faculty.

By 1900, Lowell was a full professor, speaking to four hundred undergraduates in his Government I course, and confirming a scholarly reputation first noticed in his book *Government and Parties in Continental Europe.* A year later, he had his first encounter with Franklin Roosevelt. It set the pattern for all those to come. Lowell had invited his old friend Theodore Roosevelt to address a course in constitutional government. Hoping to avoid a mob scene, the two men agreed to keep the appearance a secret. They did not reckon with TR's cousin Franklin, then an aspiring *Crimson* reporter, who telephoned Lowell's residence and asked to be put through to the Vice-President of the United States. TR came on the phone, expressed delight at hearing from his youthful cousin, and promptly spilled the beans on the forthcoming lecture. Franklin rushed to the *Crimson* with his scoop, setting the scene for two thousand curious undergraduates to mill around Lowell's lecture hall the next morning. The professor was not amused, even if TR was.[10]

Another reporter's dispatch from the Yard at the time of his election pointed up the similarities between the country's outgoing president, and Harvard's incoming one:

> There is never a lull while he talks. He is dramatic; he acts what he says. He does not stand in one place, but walks up and down the entire platform. He talks with his hands, arms, feet, his whole body. . . . Sometimes his voice breaks into a high pitch . . . but it is never monotonous. His phraseology is colloquial, full of illustrations, analogies, parables, and vivid sketches of the persons involved in the subject. Often he resorts to dialogue to bring out the two sides of a question. His face is never the same for two seconds. He makes grimaces, he laughs, he gets excited in the heat of imaginary controversy. The words tumble out of his mouth, sometimes get mixed, but the meaning is always clear. The speaker's personality dominates the entire room and he himself is always the most interesting thing in it.[11]

•

*It is said that if the temperature on the ocean
was raised, the water would expand until the
floods covered the dry land; and if we can increase the intellectual ambition of college students, the whole face of our country will be
changed.*

                              —A. LAWRENCE LOWELL

EVEN BEFORE his inauguration in October 1909, Lowell had signaled his
dissatisfaction with Eliot's curriculum. There was, claimed Lowell, "too
much teaching and too little studying" in Eliot's university. Personally,
he continued, every man with health on his side ought to pursue classroom honors. It was a subject he would return to often. In 1908, concur-
rent with publication of his magnum opus, *The Government of England—*
a work favorably compared with Lord Bryce's seminal review of the
American polity—Lowell had overseen a committee charged with devising tests for scholarly rank. Its criticism of the untrammeled freedom of
Eliot's elective system was implicit. (Small wonder, then, that the retiring
president should spend the rest of his long life hectoring his successor
from a sinecure on the Board of Overseers.)

While other educators might attack the American college, or question its usefulness, even as a forge of character, Harvard's new chief held
otherwise. "I believe in the college as the core of the academic life, and
as such it will continue at Harvard." In his inaugural address, he quoted
Aristotle on man as a social animal, before asserting the college's unique
role in developing his social powers. Rejecting Eliot's campaign for a
three-year degree, Lowell outlined his own academic notions about undergraduate tutorials and proposed creation of freshman dormitories,
which he felt would foster a much-needed sense of community. He also
hinted at a revised plan of studies he called concentration and distribution, a reform designed to restore a parallel sense of intellectual community without reverting to the deadening recitations of the oldtime academy. His cousin Bishop Lawrence said it all portended a radical break
with the past. "No," Lowell responded, "the same old ship on the same
old course, only on another tack." Given the scope of his dissatisfaction
with the status quo, this was a disingenuous if tangy figure of speech.

One neighbor boy, accustomed to seeing the president of Harvard
emerge from his modest residence at precisely the same hour each morning, first to go horseback riding and later to proceed with stately stride to
Appleton Chapel for morning prayers, confidently fixed his gaze on the
house early in October 1909. He was in for a surprise. The new president

did not ride a horse, and his gait was anything but kingly. Instead, Lawrence Lowell burst through the front door with a green bookbag slung over his shoulder and sprinted like the old runner he was, to reach his pew as the last toll of the bell declared God's scholars in session.[12] Clearly, Harvard was on a new course.

The challenge of remaking Harvard was daunting, even for one of Lowell's energies. Under Eliot, its reach had assumed worldwide proportions. From an astronomical laboratory in Peru to excavating archeologists in Samarra, the University performed ever more functions. Preeminent as ever, its faculty was no less quarrelsome. The divinity school suggested a little of the diversity enshrined by Eliot. Taking their places beside the Unitarian Old Guard were six trinitarian Congregationalists, two Baptists, and one apiece from the Anglican, Roman Catholic, and Jewish faiths.

Lowell reserved most of his early fire for the elective system. "The individual student ought clearly to be developed so far as possible," he announced, "both in his strong and in his weak points, for the college ought to produce, not defective specialists, but men intellectually well rounded, of wide sympathies and unfettered judgment. . . . The best type of liberal education in our complex modern world aims at producing men who know a little of everything and something well."[13]

Eliot's electives produced many things; truly liberal education was not among them. John Reed, the young socialist later entombed in the Kremlin Wall but better known in college as author of *Diana's Debut*, the 1910 Hasty Pudding Show, recalled that Harvard under Eliot was a glorious hodgepodge. Men who came there for a good time could get what they wanted and graduate having learned little of substance. On the other hand, those in serious pursuit of knowledge could find pretty much anything they might desire from the world's storehouse of learning. Free from control, undergraduates could live and do as they pleased, just as long as they attended lectures. "There was no attempt made by the authorities," wrote Reed, "to weld the student body together, or to enforce any kind of uniformity. Some men came with allowances of fifteen thousand dollars a year pocket money, with automobiles and servants, living in gorgeous suites in palatial apartment houses; others in the same class starved in attic bedrooms." The typical Harvard class included every sort of crank, misfit, poet, and philosopher, a great lumpish mass whose very size ruled out intimacy or coherence.[14]

Some among the more politically committed had joined Reed's Socialist Club, and petitioned the faculty for courses in left-wing thought. Catholics had formed their own organization, as had Russian and Polish Jews. Eliot had found all this social and ideological diversity congenial to his nineteenth-century liberalism. His elective system was its academic counterpart. A precocious minority found it to their liking. Others abused it. "Say," exclaimed one undergraduate of the period, "what a glorious farce this so-called college education is!" One of his classmates, more enamored of tackling on the gridiron than of grappling in the library, cobbled together a potpourri of undemanding lectures. "I know it's queer," he told a visiting relative, "but I couldn't help it because I had to take things that wouldn't interfere with football practice."[15]

Administrators had complaints of their own to register. Charles Francis Adams, who completed twenty-four years of service as an Overseer just before Eliot's departure, was disturbed to find that undergraduates had less exposure to instructors in the modern college than they had in his class of 1853. Examination papers substituted for personal contact. The average college man, said Adams, was a face lost in the academic mob. Van Wyck Brooks went further, writing that Eliot's stress on graduate schooling was transforming the college degree into little more than the requisite passkey to a law school or medical lab.

It was one thing to praise Eliot for having loosened the corset binding higher education, quite another to find either symmetry or purpose in the shapeless creature that resulted. The subsequent flood of specialized learning and professional methodology seemed to Lowell to threaten the American college's historic mission to provide a mellowing acquaintance with the humanities. In an era of instant status and vulgar wealth, this was something that humanists believed more than ever worthy of preservation.

In assessing blame for such laxness, Lowell minced no words. The chief failing of the elective system, he said in a 1909 address, lay in its undermining of scholarly competition and its assumption that opportunity for self-development could be realized while weakening the stimulus to exertion. Like the Caucus Race in *Alice in Wonderland*, "every one begins and ends where he pleases, save that he must take at least a certain number of courses; and, as on that famous occasion, little interest is taken in the distribution of prizes." Although no doubt youthful rivalry could be carried too far, as in ancient Athens where only men of exceptional strength took part in field sports, still, Lowell felt, the natural competitive urge could be played upon to provide a healthy incentive for learning.

A century before, English universities had lifted their standing through resort to prizes and honors. Some took exception to this, as Lowell acknowledged, arguing that the muses ought to be wooed for more worthy motives, "but it is our province to make the most of men as they are, not to protest that they ought to have an innate love of learning.

The problem of human nature, the question of whether we could have made it better if we had presided at the creation, is too large to discuss here."

So Lowell set out to convey the majesty of learning, and break the back of popular resistance to hard intellectual labor. He insisted that college must prepare young men for active citizenship, to consecrate part of their time and force to the state. Excellence in studies was a prerequisite for making good citizens. Refinement of taste was also required, yet culture must be broadening. "The intellectual snob," said Lowell, "is as repellent as any other." True culture, which expanded mental horizons, eschewed any sense of superiority. Eager to share its riches with others, it resembled the glow of fire in a cold room. As Lowell phrased it, "It is a form of social service of a higher order."

For proof, Lowell cited Japan's Samurai warriors, a privileged caste who carried a sword in one arm, a stylus for writing poetry in the other, and who earned their status through long and arduous training, self-sacrifice, and renunciation of facile indolence. "Can we expect that of our men?" the new president asked. "We can expect nothing else if we convince them that the demand is serious." Lowell's ideal student—whatever his social rank or national background—would crave the chance to use his power to noble ends, "and if the end fires his imagination, he is not deterred by the discomforts in the path."

You cannot lift a blanket, Lowell liked to say, by taking up but a single corner. The reforms that followed implemented this meritocratic approach, and moved the *New York Herald Tribune* to claim that no man, Eliot included, did more to change the current of educational thought in America. First came the system of concentration and distribution, which replaced freewheeling electives with a common competitive framework in which everyone had to play by the same rules. Henceforth, each student would take six of his sixteen undergraduate courses in a single department or field, while distributing at least four more among literature, science, history, philosophy, or mathematics. Students had to plan their education.

In addition, Lowell instituted general examinations to take place at the end of the senior year (two or three written tests administered by a board of examiners and supplemented by an oral exam for honors candidates) to unify the planning process and provide a specific goal toward which to work. For the first time in half a century, the Harvard racetrack had a single finish line. Lowell himself explained the function of the general examination as preparation for a life in which the ability to think was far more important than mere regurgitation of data. Its object, he wrote, "is not so much to find out what facts the student knows as to find out how far he has grasped their meaning, how fully he can apply them, how far his studies have formed a part of his being and developed the texture of his mind; in short, not whether he has been duly subjected to a process, but what, as a result of it, he has become."

Having established the exams, Lowell took the next step and provided tutors to guide students from their first selection of what other universities called a major to the gauntlet line of general and oral examiners. The use of tutors, intensive individual instructors, was borrowed from Oxford and Cambridge, although Lowell's tutors did not enjoy the exclusive control exercised by their British counterparts. In Lowell's Harvard, young men found themselves advised by senior professors as well as graduate students. Each week they met in groups of two or three for hour-long conferences in which a student might report on recent reading or write a short essay. Between sessions, work assigned by the tutor filled in gaps while encouraging the habit of independent study.

Some departments, notably Chemistry, held back from tutorials. Others embraced them with enthusiasm, if only to correct abuses by the intellectually sluggish which Eliot had been inclined to overlook. At a time when the College's academic standards were far lower than today, and when 85 percent of those who applied were admitted, Lowell wished to extract what latent gifts lurked in his future stockbrokers and bond salesmen. Stimulated by tutorials, one youth interested in little but horses was moved to write an honors thesis on the effects of macadam roads and horse-drawn vehicles in eighteenth-century England; an athlete was led into banking, and a classmate who had chosen literature out of deference to his family transferred to his real love, zoology. The tutorial system became one of Harvard's most distinctive ornaments, and one of Lowell's greatest achievements as well.[16]

Shortly after his election to the presidency, Eliot had encountered a friend who promised him success if only he could display one quality he had not previously exhibited. Did this refer to knowledge of men, the president asked? Good judgment? Appreciation of scholars? To all three, the response was negative. Well then, Eliot demanded, what could it be? "Patience." Eliot at forty could afford to be patient. Lowell entered office at fifty-three, something he never stopped lamenting. It was Eliot's triumph that he outlasted his enemies. It was Lowell's tragedy that he outlived his friends.

One friend asked what he would do if a decision went against him, and Lowell replied that he'd go home and take it out on his wife. He didn't lose often. Deciding to shelter the Yard, the president built a protective circle of dormitories and a palatial residence for himself and future Harvard executives. Lacking any sense of sound—in later years, he became almost totally deaf—he put his new president's house so close to the old one that kitchenware could be passed between their windows. Streetcar noises provided a jarring accompaniment. Typically, Lowell acknowledged hearing them the first night he spent in the house, and never again thereafter.

He was no less deaf to the cries of those outraged by his plans—ultimately thwarted—to merge Harvard's engineering school with MIT's, or to unite the divinity school with nearby Andover Theological Seminary. The president did battle with Felix Frankfurter over his proposal that a member of the Corporation be added to the law school faculty, and riled both undergraduates and alumni with his outspoken disapproval of Louis Brandeis's nomination to the United States Supreme Court.

However, Lowell's willingness to tamper with his predecessor's atomized, freedom-loving University, which reflected a society where wealth and talent were randomly distributed, generated the most widespread resentment. Men were not interchangeable parts, Eliot had said. "No two can have an equal chance in life by any possibility, because their means and powers of meeting the experiences, riches and opportunities of life are different. . . . A just social philosophy will not undertake to fly in the face of these facts of nature." To Eliot, it was simple: democracy's mission was to pursue happiness and security for all, while avoiding what he called "a monotonous, tiresome and unnatural equality."

Lowell disagreed. Long before he was chosen president, he had warned Eliot of the need to construct dormitories within the Yard to combat cliques of privilege thriving along the Gold Coast. He urged vigorous steps be taken against "a snobbish separation of students on lines of wealth" that would ultimately demolish any claims Harvard might make as a nationalizing force. "I fear," he went on, "that with the loss of that democratic feeling which ought to lie at the basis of university life, we are liable to lose our moral hold upon a large part of the students." This was the man who had spurned election as an undergraduate to the final clubs for whom his name alone would open any door, and who preached to the end of his presidency the absolute necessity of avoiding his own error, that of shutting himself up with a small, congenial group of like-minded associates.

"One of the greatest advantages Harvard has over almost all colleges," he remarked to students, "is that we draw the most diverse minds from the most diverse places. . . . Gentlemen, I am at the end of my escalator. I have reached the bottom. You are at the top, on the way down and wondrously wise. A freshman always knows more than he ever will again." To employ some of that knowledge, Lowell proposed to build dormitories just for freshmen. Since one third of any college education he attributed to life beyond the classroom, what mattered most was the atmosphere and traditions in which a youth was immersed upon his arrival there.

All this was in line with Lowell's belief that the pupil and not the courses he took formed the heart of a Harvard education. In place of Eliot's laissez-faire, he would bring good influences to bear. Henceforth, parents and headmasters of incoming students would receive written inquiries seeking information about a boy's needs and capacities. A board of Freshman Advisers was established, and assistant deans were assigned to each year's class. The process of transition was further eased with a special freshman week of introductory activities, headed by Lowell's personal greeting. The freshman dorms first opened in the fall of 1914 were criticized by many as bastions of St. Grotlesex privilege, their spaces allotted by a mysterious yet undeniable system of caste, including a Category X for Jews. Lowell's subsequent attempt to enforce a Jewish quota for the college reinforced public disapproval. Yet both were consistent with his lifelong bias against hyphenated citizenship.

The president surprised none who knew him by welcoming his friend James Byrne as the first Catholic member of the Corporation. Well-placed Bostonians knew of his regard for William Cardinal O'Connell, a prelate of similarly autocratic temperament with whom Lowell could sometimes be seen strolling across Boston Common, arms flailing away in vigorous support of whatever he was espousing at the time. O'Connell, no less than Lowell, spoke for a society whose class lines were clearly demarked, and whose special pride was its own cherished if naive belief in a social scale ascendable to all who were willing to subordinate their own identity to the demands of Brattle Street and Louisburg Square. Lowell's freshman dorms were built to entice such defections from racial or ethnic solidarity. (Fifteen years later, Lowell was finally able to afford this same opportunity to upperclassmen when his house plan was instituted.)

A barely constitutional monarch who diagnosed Harvard administration as "tyranny tempered by assassination," Lowell embodied the Progressive impulse toward government of the elect. Modern Puritans struggling with a society grown enormously complex, impersonal, and corrupt, Progressives like Roosevelt and Lowell hoped to systematize as well as extend democracy. So they campaigned for recalls and referendums, city managers and regulations of product standards. They offered up their own expertise, never more so than when Princeton's erstwhile president Woodrow Wilson, fresh from his battle against college dining clubs, became governor of New Jersey and William Howard Taft's successor in the White House.

College men, it was tacitly understood, were about to assume greater responsibility in national affairs. And Lowell, the former government professor, was determined that Harvard men predominate in TR's governing class. Intent on raising classroom standards, he was equally resolved to banish the weather and sports as the common denominator of American conversation. This accounted for his insistence on what he called self-education, which for Lowell was a lifelong process. Expressed at the college in the tutorial system, measured by oral examinations, it was rooted as well in the camaraderie and conversation of the freshman dorms and later the upperclass houses, and codified in a plan of studies deeply grounded in at least one field of inquiry, while allowing at least fleeting exposure to many more. The alternative, he once warned, would be life in a national village, wherein each citizen had command of a separate vocabulary of one hundred words, and no one knew the auxiliary verbs.

With concentration and distribution, general examinations, tutorials, and the freshman dormitories in place, Lowell continued to embellish his master plan. At his behest, the faculty in 1924 permitted candidates for honors degrees to reduce their course load from sixteen to fourteen, thus enabling them to pursue independent studies, attend lectures of special interest, or simply devote more time and energy to a thesis. Later still came the Reading Period, two and a half weeks near the end of each term during which lectures ceased and upperclassmen could work by themselves on readings and essays assigned by instructors and tutors.

In defending his changes, Lowell the mathematician had plenty of statistics to buttress his claims of success. Contrary to popular expectations, for instance, Harvard students freed from the calendar during the Reading Period did not desert Cambridge for pleasure domes or theater parties. On the contrary, library circulation more than doubled as did book sales at the Harvard Cooperative Society. Best of all, the number of those pursuing academic honors soared—from 9 percent in 1900, to nearly 40 percent three decades later.

Having rescued scholarship from social ostracism, Lowell now moved on to tackle the more vexing issue of class feeling. Along the way, a world war and the strains accompanying America's crusade for global democracy invaded the Yard. They raised as never before dilemmas of academic freedom in a time of patriotic excess. In responding to the outside challenge, Lowell showed he hadn't lost his capacity to surprise.

The elms of Harvard Yard were dying in 1914, their demise a sad, symbolic preview of events half a world away. The next spring, Samuel Eliot Morison, returning from an intellectual sojourn in the midwest, found himself in a virtual armed camp. Harvard's medical and dental schools had dispatched ambulance and hospital units to Europe. Recent graduates eager for a taste of glory had slipped across borders to enlist under the Canadian or British flag, or to don the kepi of the French Foreign Legion. Back in Cambridge, two refugee teachers from the bombed-out Belgian university at Louvain were welcomed. Professor Kuno Francke announced his conversion to U.S. citizenship. A vigilant watch was maintained around a stone lion donated by Kaiser Wilhelm to the Germanic museum.

In the spring of 1915, a chapter of the Collegiate Anti-Militarism League was formed. The *Harvard Illustrated Magazine* urged silence as a prudent response to foreign bombshells. "It behooves every college paper to muzzle war utterances without further delay. . . . Harvard has enough troubles, football and otherwise, of her own to care for, without borrowing any of those three thousand miles away." At least one recent graduate was appalled at this pronouncement. "The summit of solemn priggishness," said Walter Lippmann of the magazine's ostrich-like stance, before recalling "the suffocating discretions, the reservations, and the bland silences of my own undergraduate life . . . when we suffered from a whole herd of sacred cows . . . and transferred our loyalties, our enthusiasms, and our pugnacity to the mighty business of beating Yale."

Two men, each a stranger to blandness, were already exerting themselves to condition America for war. Lowell was one. The other was a bowler-hatted, pocket-watched lawyer straight out of a Louis Auchinloss novel, named Grenville Clark. Born on Fifth Avenue in 1882, Clark was accustomed to private rail cars, Porcellian Club bacchanals, and the company of his fellow law clerk, Franklin Roosevelt. A Bull Moose Republican on good terms with both wings of the argumentative Roosevelt clan, Clark by 1915 was convinced that the United States would one day be dragged into the war. So he persuaded General Leonard Wood, then Army Chief of Staff, to undertake the training of business and professional men, twelve hundred of whom showed up at an old army post in Plattsburgh, New York, that summer. More than a year before Woodrow Wilson asked Congress to declare war on Germany, federal funds were supporting Clark's Plattsburgh movement, which would ultimately supply the armed forces with sixteen thousand officer candidates.

The *Crimson* refuted General Wood's call for similar drilling of college students. But Lowell beamed approval when Wood himself came to Cambridge in the autumn of 1915 to conduct a course in military science, a forerunner of ROTC. The next year, Harvard went a step further, establishing a department of military science and tactics. Lowell invited the French government to dispatch a small platoon of instructors; Fresh Pond was soon encircled by trenches. A sea of canvas tents flooded the ground at nearby Waverly, as a thousand or more young men marched about with rifles and bayonets, hurling imaginary grenades, preparing for a war that Lowell was eager to join. Even were it possible to stay out of the war at the cost of self-respect and sea rights, he wrote, America could not forever hold aloof from the fighting. "There is something better in life than selfish ease and material prosperity, better than life itself, and that is the civilization, the moral principles, that make life to us worth living."

By April 1915, when student publications were calling for isolation and Grenville Clark was dreaming of Plattsburgh, the president of Harvard had joined with William Howard Taft and thirty other notables in formulating a League to Enforce Peace. As usual, Lowell dominated the proceedings. He more than anyone else was credited with persuading Taft that force could be used to compel nations to submit their disputes to judicial review. A few weeks later, a convention assembled in Independence Hall announced the League's program. It called for a judicial tribunal to hear such arguments not already settled through negotiation, a Council of Conciliation to ponder lesser differences, and—Lowell's own contribution—the use of military and economic coercion against any member that went to war without first entrusting its grievances to the League.

Where Eliot had assumed such rational behavior from statesmen, his successor now set a furious pace of toil to achieve it. He wrote articles, made dozens of speeches. He sat on the dais in the spring of 1916 as both Woodrow Wilson and Henry Cabot Lodge pledged to use force in the name of peace. He helped raise money and found hundreds of local chapters. He suffered in silence when Wilson asked delay of any public framework for a postwar organization on the grounds it might tie his own hands. To Colonel Edwin House, the president's closest adviser at the time, Lowell warned that Wilson might be losing control of the situation.

In April 1917, with a dramatic address to the nation, Wilson reasserted his authority, throwing off his country's historic isolation and justifying entry into the war as a heaven-blessed crusade for democracy itself. The next day's *Crimson* carried an obscure if erudite proclamation. "RAGNAROK," it read, "doom of the gods" in Scandinavian mythology.[17]

Lowell was similarly apocalyptic. "Civilization as we know it," he said in Philadelphia a month later, "has reached a point where it must preclude war or perish by war, and war can be precluded only by a conquest of the world by a single power, or by an organization of many nations to prevent its recurrence." Germany, no doubt, would prefer the former course; Lowell demanded the latter.

Before the first doughboys reached European soil, however, Lowell's attention had been drawn away from the global struggle to a homegrown tempest. In stark contrast to the lofty appeals for universal amity in place of small-minded nationalism, America that spring was in a frenzy of contempt for all things German. Congress had already enacted the Espionage Act of 1917, fixing fines up to $10,000 and prison terms of as long as twenty years for anyone behaving disloyally. The mails were declared open for inspection. Foreign-language newspapers were subject to banishment. A minister in Vermont was sentenced to a fifteen-year jail term for praising Jesus as a pacifist. Hundreds of conscientious objectors were put behind bars. So was Socialist leader Eugene V. Debs. German books were yanked from library shelves, sauerkraut renamed liberty cabbage, records of Beethoven or Brahms smashed for their incendiary rhythms. Iowa's governor declared that all telephone conversations in his state must henceforth be in English.

Harvard was not immune to this storm. Long before Washington moved to clamp down on dissent, Cambridge was arguing about Hugo Munsterberg, a feisty, dogmatic philosopher who loudly proclaimed his fidelity to the Fatherland and sorely tried Lowell's patience with his campaign for martyrdom. The pigeons in his backyard were suddenly whispered to be carrying messages to spies. Others insisted they'd seen Munsterberg mailing letters to the kaiser.

When the professor offered to stay away from faculty meetings, Lowell swept the suggestion aside. But when a wealthy alumnus offered the University ten million dollars on condition that it dispense with the German sympathizer, the president could no longer pretend to look the other way. Munsterberg, plainly delighted with the ruckus, volunteered to resign as soon as the donor deposited half his bequest with the Corporation. Lowell's fury was directed at both men. He returned Munsterberg's letter, "feeling sure that hereafter you will regret having written anything which could be supposed to show a lack of respect for the University." He also let it be known that academic freedom was not for sale.

Munsterberg dropped dead in a class two years later, but the issue of professional loyalties would not go away with such finality. At Columbia, Nicholas Murray Butler declared antiwar sentiments to be treasonable.

State-supported schools in California, Illinois, Michigan, and Missouri conducted minor inquisitions against those deemed lackluster in their patriotism. Lowell set to work at making his report for 1916–17 a treatise on the university, its obligations to society, and the academic's liberty to take issue with whatever struck the public fancy. It was unequivocal, it was eloquent, and it became the standard by which Harvard and the rest of American higher education would be judged, then and later.

First of all, Lowell declared for absolute freedom of inquiry and advocacy for the classroom instructor. "He must teach the truth, as he has found it and sees it," he wrote. Students should not be compelled to listen to a professor of Greek harangue against vaccination, or economists declare for Bacon's authorship of Shakespeare. A professor speaks to his class as a professor, said Lowell, not as a citizen. By his appointment, he gains no special privileges. But neither does he forfeit any rights common to others. He might do harm to the institution he was pledged to serve by extreme or injudicious remarks. Yet Lowell was willing to accept such risks. "The objections to whatever restraint upon what professors may say as citizens seem to me far greater than the harm done by leaving them free." After all, members of other professions were not precluded from speaking out. To accept a chair and a muzzle simultaneously would require a man to surrender part of his liberty to a board of trustees. What's more, if a university were to censor what its faculty members might say, then it tacitly accepted responsibility for whatever came out of their mouths. Wartime did not erase this fact.

"There is no middle ground," wrote Lowell. "Either the university assumes full responsibility for permitting its professors to express certain opinions in public, or it assumes no responsibility whatever, and leaves them to be dealt with like other citizens by the public authorities according to the laws of the land."[18]

While the war of words raged, so had the fighting in Europe. Over ten thousand Harvard men enrolled in one army or another. Nearly half became officers. Cambridge itself took on a martial flavor, as boatloads of naval cadets filled dormitories and classrooms. A government-operated radio school took over Memorial Hall and nearby science labs. Cambridge Common disappeared beneath wooden barracks. Appleton Chapel was closed to conserve coal; morning prayers were transferred to the faculty room of University Hall. The chemistry department and its rising young star, James B. Conant, produced poison gas and masks to ward it off. Historians researched the past so that a postwar peace conference might better reorder the future. Marshal Joffre left the trenches of northern France long enough to accept an honorary degree.

In other fields besides Flanders, bright hopes beckoned, only to be crushed beneath personal animosity and politics as usual. Seventy-two thousand persons applied for tickets to a Symphony Hall debate between Lowell and Henry Cabot Lodge over Wilson's League of Nations. "Let us not go through a dark tunnel of umbrageous words," declared the senator, "with nothing to see at the end but the dim red light of internationalism." Lowell took the opposite tack. Although willing to see modifications in Wilson's Covenant, he nonetheless deplored the gunslinger mentality espoused by Lodge. It was the man who saw the world through a gunrange, not the one looking for common interests, who endangered peace and stability, he insisted. The better people agreed with Lodge, said the wags; the best with Lowell.

The president made a serious slip of the tongue before he escaped the platform. Turning aside his rival's reverence for Washington's Farewell Address and its stringent ban on American involvement abroad, Lowell likened it to the Ten Commandments—both among the greatest of documents in their day, both in need of adaptation to current conditions. Idaho's crusty Senator William Borah took him to task. Lowell he charged, was belittling everything truly American. It was a familiar allegation against Harvard.

In the end, there would be no American entry into the League. Instead of protecting the survivors against their own lack of reason, Lowell assumed the somber task of memorializing the dead. He commissioned John Singer Sargent to paint murals in Widener Library, and composed what was, to him, a suitable inscription:

> *Happy those who with a glowing faith*
> *In one embrace clasped Death and Victory.*

Lowell explained his choice of words in a 1919 baccalaureate sermon. Those who had fallen on the field of battle could never be charged with weakness or error. "The fate of those who died was the more heroic, that of the living more continuous and perplexing. . . . It is they, the soldier dead, who died in the light, and we, who live on in the dusk."

The living must grope to find their duty in a twilight and through a labyrinth, said Lowell. His own groping produced his landmark defense of academic freedom. It also stumbled over racial barriers and religious quotas. It was the same aristocratic sense of mission and self-certainty that directed each endeavor, the same thirst to assimilate and mold young men according to Marlborough Street standards. To his admirers, Lowell was consistent with his conscience in both causes. To critics, however, in the second he was sadly at odds with the spirit of the democratic crusade to which he paid tribute in chapel prose and artists' murals.

We live, but a world has passed away with the years that pushed to make us men.
— WILLIAM DEAN HOWELLS

THE WAR to end all wars had an ugly sequel. A nation that had sacrificed a hundred thousand of her sons to rescue Europe from itself turned inward, rejecting the ungrateful continent and imposing new barriers to the politically or economically homeless. Intolerance ushered in the new decade. The Ku Klux Klan boasted four million members by 1924, its emblems of hate lighting up southern and midwestern skies. Neither political party could bring itself to denounce the violence or endorse antilynching laws. When Wilson's red-baiting attorney general, A. Mitchell Palmer, launched an attack on radical elements, he had plenty of help from flag-wavers anxious to apply their own exacting tests of patriotic fervor. A Connecticut clothing salesman spent six months in jail for publicly criticizing capitalism and John D. Rockefeller. An Indiana jury acquitted a naturalized citizen of murdering an alien who had said "To hell with the United States."[19]

Books proclaiming Nordic superiority won praise from naturalists. The *New York Times* expressed fears that the country might be "mongrelized." After Congress passed the Americanization Act, states chimed in with legislation requiring aliens to learn English. The 1921 Immigration Act established quotas that heavily favored northern and western Europe. Later in the decade of normalcy, the walls were raised still higher to prevent millions of eastern Europeans from entering the country and altering its ways. The first federal census to show a majority of the population living in cities was taken in 1920. Yet many Americans reacted savagely when Sinclair Lewis set out that same year to satirize small-town life in *Main Street*. It was as if the country had lost its historical virginity, and could only respond by denying the very changes that were visibly transforming its landscape and culture. Everywhere, it seemed, there was a yearning for cohesion, mingled with contempt for Old World values and vices.

Harvard rejoiced in the internationalism of its generous alumni; the new Harvard Fund reported gifts from every state and fifteen nations. Even so, the backlash overtaking the rest of America, poisoning Wilsonian idealism and hardening social attitudes, did not spare Cambridge. "Don't go around looking like a Bolshevik," urged a local advertisement for O'Leagua hair tonic. More significantly, war-ordained survival of the fittest implied extinction of the unfit. So declared one alumnus writing in the *Harvard Graduates' Magazine* for December 1919. He went on to decry John D. Rockefeller's professed creed that each man was entitled to earn his own way and inhabit a decent home, to play, learn, and love in a society where such opportunities were ensured by industry and government together.[20]

Few undergraduates took issue with this attitude, despite entreaties from the Liberal Club and its publication *The Gadfly* (edited in part by a pacifistic youth named J. Robert Oppenheimer). Foreshadowing their later endorsement of the colorless Newton D. Baker over Franklin D. Roosevelt, Harvard Democrats in mock convention whooped for Virginia's venerable Carter Glass, a conservative Jeffersonian who believed in sound money and states' rights. In November 1924, Calvin Coolidge swept the college vote. Year in, year out, students expended less energy on crusades of any kind than on entering and enjoying the charmed circle of club life. A quarter of all undergraduates belonged to one of the final clubs, submitting to a social code as inflexible as any dictated by fashion. One member was suspended by his fellows for the ungentlemanly act of appearing hatless in Harvard Square.

Throughout the paneled rooms of clubby Harvard—though by no means limited to such quarters—the Dry Decade was anything but. A bathtub hooch in the basement of Kirkland House dispensed a near-lethal imitation of Alexander's liqueur, blending homemade gin with chocolate ice cream. C. Douglas Dillon, later John Kennedy's Treasury Secretary, couldn't recall anyone who attended chapel regularly, but he remembered vividly a taxi stand before the Porcellian Club from which regular deliveries of bootleg Scotch were made to the thirsty young men inside. When President Lowell built his Houses, it was claimed he designed stairwells to avoid the spectacle of drunken students falling over backward and breaking their necks. (Elevators were ruled out, in Lowell's words, "because people do not enter on terms of familiar intercourse on elevators.")[21]

While Lowell sought to insulate Harvard within its walls, even he could not hope to stem the tide of external cynicism and complacency that followed the dislocation of war. Unlike Eliot, he had always cherished a view of the University as a cloistered retreat, a sanctuary earning its privileges through graduates who would somehow raise the overall level of public discourse. In the Twenties, the old man's vision seemed— like Woodrow Wilson's of a rational world order—a mirage.

No two people voiced quite the same opinion about Harvard's president. Had he squandered Eliot's intellectual patrimony, as some alleged, or rescued the American college from hatchet-faced specialists? Was he a taskmaster to the elite, or merely a snob? A foe of Gold Coast privilege, or the architect of Harvard's self-glorification? The questions were not easily answered. For how could a consensus form around one who exasperated his friends as often as he confounded his enemies?

"In aristocratic societies," wrote Alexis de Tocqueville, "the class that gives the tone to opinion and has the guidance of affairs, being permanently and hereditarily placed above the multitude, naturally conceives a lofty idea of itself and man. . . . The effect is to raise greatly the general pitch of society. . . . They facilitate the natural impulse of the mind to the highest regions of thought, and they naturally prepare it to conceive a sublime, almost a divine love of truth."

At his best, no man better incarnated de Tocqueville's idealized aristocracy, with its haughty contempt of what the Frenchman called "material enjoyments and small pleasures," than Lowell. De Tocqueville would rather do anything, he once wrote, in preference to living like "a potato," his dismissive label for small-souled bourgeois life. So would Lowell.

On the other hand, "aristocrat" though he might be, Lowell was not the prisoner of class prejudice he sometimes seemed. For example, there was the case of Harold Laski, a junior faculty member who had outraged Brahmin sensitivities at the time of Boston's police strike in the fall of 1919 by declaring his own sympathies for the strikers. Lowell's personal opposition to the walkout was clear, even before he recruited two hundred Harvard students to fill the depleted ranks of law enforcement. He had no fondness for Laski, still less for the socialistic doctrines espoused by the young visitor from Oxford. Yet when demands circulated for Laski's head, he was immovable. "If the Overseers ask for Laski's resignation," he remarked to a friend while crossing the Yard, "they will get mine!"[22]

In the postwar atmosphere of whispered accusations, Lowell again belied his reputation for blind conservatism in his handling of the Zechariah Chafee affair. In April 1920, Chafee, a law school professor, vigorously questioned the conduct of a case being tried under the Espionage Act. After the convictions were upheld by the Supreme Court, Chafee and others signed a petition for executive clemency. Prominent among the signers was Chafee's colleague, the controversial Felix Frankfurter, who had aroused considerable disapproval by his public demand for U.S. recognition of the new Soviet government. A year went by, and an Overseer named Austen Fox submitted a petition of his own. The work of prominent law school graduates, the petition accused Chafee of inaccurate statements in the *Harvard Law Review,* and called for his dismissal. In fact, the real source of anger was Chafee's support for clemency, and Frankfurter's approving echo. Frankfurter the Zionist, defender of radicals, and all-purpose gadfly, was always a lightning rod for conservative faultfinding. Fundraisers for the school were repeatedly and bluntly informed that so long as the controversial professor remained on the faculty, the financial taps would stay dry.

No one was less approving of Frankfurter than Lowell, who thought him "first rate in intelligence, but defective in character." But Chafee was no radical, except when it came to the principle of free speech. When the law school's visiting committee gathered at the Boston Harvard Club in May 1921 to adjudicate the case, they discovered the president himself conducting Chafee's defense. Given the lurid denunciations carried by local newspapers and the ingratitude displayed by liberals like Upton Sinclair, it was a thankless task. But Lowell carried the day, 6–5 (Benjamin Cardozo supplying the margin of victory), and when it came time for Chafee to dedicate his book *Free Speech in the United States,* he discharged his debt nobly. "Abbott Lawrence Lowell," he wrote, "whose wisdom and courage in the face of uneasy fears and stormy criticism made it unmistakably plain that so long as he was President no one could breathe the air of Harvard and not be free."[23]

Not only was Lowell unpredictable, he was also monumentally self-assured. When a colleague asked how he was able to reach important decisions so quickly, he had a ready answer. "That is perfectly simple," he said. "Everyone has his own pattern of thinking, and can see immediately when a given question comes up what relation it bears to that pattern. Either it fits or it doesn't. The decision can then come at once."

No one doubted Lowell's decisiveness. In the uncertain light of the Twenties, it was his vision that seemed strangely dimmed. At a time when political repression vied for newspaper space with racial persecution, when restless minorities were making demands for long-postponed equality, and co-educational colleges such as Swarthmore and Oberlin were breaking new ground in women's education, Harvard seemed to withdraw into its golden shell. For instance, when a vacancy arose in the philosophy department, Lowell's emphasis on personal character caused him to veto Bertrand Russell's appointment. Arthur Lovejoy was regarded by the department's chairman as the most eminent philosopher in America, yet Lowell rejected him as "a mischiefmaker." Lovejoy's chief mischief, it would seem, lay in his active support for the new American Association of University Professors.[24] The president also turned down John Dewey, because of his age, before finally settling on Alfred North Whitehead.

With faculty matters as elsewhere, Lowell exercised astonishing personal authority. The story is still told of his impromptu encounter with a young instructor to whom he'd taken a fancy. Learning to his dismay that his friend was about to leave Cambridge, his academic progress having been blocked within his department, Lowell granted him tenure on the spot.[25]

Others were less fortunate. When an elderly professor was revealed to the president as a homosexual, Lowell summoned the man to University Hall (where the president's habitual pacing often cowed visitors into the far corners of the room) and demanded his resignation on the spot. He had devoted his life to Harvard, replied the professor. What was he expected to do now? What would President Lowell himself do, if he were in his shoes? "I would get a gun and destroy myself," said Lowell.[26]

Another of Lowell's blind spots was in the area of women's education. A visitor once casually suggested the need to admit women to the Harvard Law School. Not wishing to appear discourteous, Lowell simply changed the subject, only to have the idea presented again. The president was forced to vent his anger by kicking the door to his office. "I should make it plain," he remarked finally, in his even, clergyman's voice, "this isn't going to happen while I am president of this university." Spoken like a man whose Harvard had denied Madame Curie an honorary degree, and who had himself rebuked a correspondent for urging equal pay for male and female schoolteachers. "The men are rendering a service which the women cannot," he informed her. On the other hand, he supported establishment of a state university in Massachusetts in part because of the educational opportunities it would provide females. From his own experience with the Lowell Institute, he judged women "more anxious for general culture" than their male counterparts.[27]

He wished, he said to his wife over breakfast one morning, that their Savior would instruct them in what to do with the Negro in America. Until that time, he would donate to Booker T. Washington's work at Tuskegee, in Alabama. Had he done nothing more, he might have escaped the public outcry that enveloped Harvard in the unsettled Twenties, when his assimilationist policies were put to their most severe test.

Lowell had warned as early as 1887 that the Irishman talking and writing and working for the cause of Ireland could not at the same time claim to be a good American. "What we need is not to dominate the Irish," he went on, "but to absorb them. . . . We want them to become rich, and send their sons to our colleges, to share our prosperity and our sentiments. We do not want to feel that they are among us and yet not really part of us."[28]

At the time of his inaugural in 1909, Lowell had complained, "The College itself falls short of its national mission of throwing together youths of promise of every kind, from every part of the country." However, this mission apparently did not apply to youths who were Negroes. Late in 1921, rumors began circulating of a deliberate policy to exclude blacks from the freshman dorms. A few months later, a dissenting petition bearing 143 alumni names was received at University Hall. In January 1923, the story went public when Roscoe Conkling Bruce wrote Lowell asking him to clarify Harvard's position regarding his own son, a product of Phillips Exeter. Lowell replied that owing to the compulsory nature of dormitory living, the College had not seen fit to include the black man in a freshman dorm.

Bruce was stunned. "To proscribe a youth because of his race is a procedure as novel at Harvard until your administration as it is unscientific. However unpopular the Jew, the Irishman and the Negro may be in certain minds and certain sections and at certain times (wartime not being one), the fact remains that the distribution of human excellence in each of these races, as in the case of every other race, begins at zero and ends at infinity." Then Bruce touched a still more sensitive nerve. "After Charles W. Eliot, Harvard cannot escape the grave responsibilities of leadership in American life. And one leads by ascent to higher levels after the manner of scholar and statesman, of poet and prophet; not by descent."

To friends, Lowell confided there had been trouble just the previous summer on account of blacks in dorms. He remembered a member of the medical school faculty who avoided Cambridge for Johns Hopkins because black students were received at Harvard. "We owe the Negro the opportunity for the best possible education," he wrote Professor Albert B. Hart, "but I do not feel that we owe him compulsory contact with people where it is not mutually congenial; nor do I think it would be right to give up a plan of compulsory residence which is for the benefit of the vast majority of our students because it conflicts with the theoretical principle of treating everyone alike."[29]

When the NAACP attacked Lowell for countenancing Ku Klux Klan tactics, the president responded with the curious argument that to voluntarily segregate Negro men within the dormitories reeked of Jim Crow. Opinion in Cambridge was sharply divided. One club president told the *New York Times* that the University of Virginia was right not to compete with a Harvard team whose roster included a black man, while another athlete asserted that the college must own up to the issue frankly, saying, "The Negro problem is on our hands and we have to face it. Either he must be educated up to our view or a caste system developed." In the 1920s, this passed for racial liberalism.

Before long, the Alumni Bulletin entered the fray, assailing Lowell for disloyalty to principles in effect at Harvard since long before the Civil War. One alumnus told of a southerner in the Class of 1877 who had called upon President Eliot, angry over the presence of two blacks in his classroom. Eliot had declared that while the University would regret the young man's departure, it would manage to go on without him. In his book *Conflict of Principle,* published in 1932, Lowell said publicly what he had long held in private, namely, that racial distinctions were and would remain America's most perplexing dilemma. By then, the Corporation had refined his initial stand, reaffirming the right of every freshman to live in a dorm, while requiring blacks who hoped to do so to find a roommate on their own. Along with raised prices, this had the practical result of enforcing segregation. As late as the 1950s, an indignant resident of Lowell House could ask if the only students permitted the luxury of single rooms were Negroes and homosexuals.[30]

More controversial still was Lowell's simultaneous attempt to restrict the Jewish population of the College, which had climbed from 7 percent in 1900 to over 21 percent by 1922. Under the guise of limiting total enrollment, Lowell published a statement clumsily singling out Jews. Consistent with his view of the University as a melting pot, the president went so far as to lump Jews with blacks, Orientals, and French Canadians "if they did not speak English and kept themselves apart." As the freshman dorm issue simmered just below the surface, Lowell was writing a prominent alumnus, "To a limited number of Jews we can do a vast deal of good in making them American; but if the numbers increase largely, they cling together and are affected comparatively little."

In the days when the top floor of one freshman dorm was referred to as Kike's Peak, and yet another student abode was called Little Jerusalem, Lowell set out to disperse Harvard's Jews as well as limit their numbers. "The summer hotel that is ruined by admitting Jews is not ruined because the Jews are bad in character," he wrote in 1922, "but simply because other people stay away, and the Jews themselves cease to come." From New York, Franklin Roosevelt's law partner wrote the president approvingly. Felix Frankfurter, on the other hand, was incensed. Lowell, he told Walter Lippmann much later, was "a refined Adolf Hitler."[31]

"Meet a scrupulous Jew," Lowell once said, "and you meet the best of men and citizens. He is certain to be an idealist." Although his remark was patronizing, Lowell was not without supporters, even in the Jewish community. Jesse Isidor Straus, Arthur Lehman, and members of New York's New School for Social Research came to his defense. In truth, the struggle was between Jews as much as with Gentiles, between those eager to serve in Lowell's private army of the elite and others less willing to dispense with their cultural and political traditions. Rabbi Isaac Mayer Wise, the great Reform organizer who preferred German literature to works of the Jewish Enlightenment, and who proclaimed his American Way even as he dispensed with prayers for rebuilding the temple at Jerusalem, had for half a century carried the torch of assimilation. Wise derided later immigrants for their "semi-Asiatic Hassidism and Medieval orthodoxy. . . . We are Americans," he declared, "and they are not. . . . We are Israelites of the nineteenth century and a free country, and they gnaw the dead bones of past centuries."[32]

No such benefit of the doubt was granted Lowell in his own milieu. Corporation member Thomas Perkins told his son he wished the old man wouldn't talk about things he knew nothing about. Harvard didn't have a Jewish problem, he continued, just the latest batch of immigrants reluctant to abandon their national identity. Lowell compounded his error by leveling charges against Jewish undergraduates, blaming them for stealing books from Widener Library. Overseer Julian Mack, himself Jewish, discovered that the total theft amounted to a single volume.[33]

After a stormy faculty meeting at which Lowell's longtime friend Arthur Holcombe registered stiff opposition to a quota—he could not face his freshman class, said Holcombe, and expound on American democracy in the face of such a policy—Lowell did not speak to him for two years. Typical of the thirteen-member committee Lowell named to break the impasse was Chester Greenough, who as the first master of Dunster House took pains to locate all five Jews under his charge in the rear of the building, overlooking a destitute neighborhood. When the next year's quota was fixed, said Greenough, he should receive credit for two Jews in place of one, a "particularly obnoxious" fellow named Smuckler.[34]

Ultimately, Greenough's committee came in with a report paving the way for a thousand-man limitation on incoming classes, and a new admissions plan permitting students in the top seventh of their high school classes to be admitted without examinations. Though designed to reduce the number of Jews without a formal quota, the new plan had the more welcome result of speeding Harvard's transformation toward an academic melting pot.

Still not satisfied, in November 1925, Lowell penned a confidential letter to a member of the Corporation complaining that the Jewish presence was more pronounced than ever. He knew of only one method of dealing with the problem, "a selection by a personal estimate of character on the part of the Admission authorities, based upon the probable value to the candidate, to the College and to the community of his admission." The language was deft, the implications blunt: by 1926, candidates were required to submit photos as well as background information regarding any change in paternal name.

Lowell was wont to act impetuously, without considering the implications of his actions, which occasionally caused embarrassment for Harvard. For instance, at track meets, his fervent encouragement of Harvard's athletes grazed the rule against coaching and ran the risk of disqualifying the entire team. A similar rashness propelled him into the center of the national debate over the fate of immigrants Nicola Sacco and Bartolomeo Vanzetti. In 1920, the pair were convicted of the murder of two men in a southeastern Massachusetts bank holdup. Trial judge Walter Thayer made little secret of his antipathies for the men, one a peddler of shoes, the other a peddler of fish. When the trial was over, a series of appeals and a public campaign spearheaded by Felix Frankfurter led Governor Alvah Fuller to appoint a three-man committee to review the transcript and weigh evidence of misconduct against a jurist who publicly boasted of having rebuked "those anarchist bastards."[35]

Lowell was named to chair the committee. He secured that dubious honor by racing up forty-one granite steps to the governor's office, beating out his elevator-riding colleagues. The trio proceeded to retry the case in their own minds, Lowell in particular downplaying Sacco's alibi. In the end, they sustained Judge Thayer's death sentence. Unsympathetic to anarchists and agitators and as ever sure of his own rightness, Lowell had not only rushed to judgment but had dragged Harvard—in the public's eyes, at least—after him. On the morning of August 23, 1927, browsers at that Beacon Hill citadel, the Boston Athenaeum, found in every magazine a white slip declaring, "On this day Nicola Sacco and Bartolomeo Vanzetti, dreamers of the brotherhood of man, who hoped it might be found in America, were done to a cruel death by the children of those who fled long ago to this land for Freedom."

Hardly less embarrassing was the public revelation, soon after a wealthy alumnus bequeathed the University five million dollars, that Harvard was firing a group of its scrubwomen. The Massachusetts Minimum Wage Commission had demanded the College pay each woman 37.5 cents per hour, but Harvard refused to go over 35, claiming that a twenty-minute rest break was worth the difference. Protesting alumni called such attitudes harsh and stingy. On Christmas Day 1930, a group of alumni led by Corliss Lamont presented the women with three thousand dollars in back pay, privately raised. It mattered little that Yale paid their workers even less, that Lowell believed a few male heads of households might be both more efficient and more deserving in a time of spreading economic sickness, or that provision was made for every one of the women deemed to be "a good worker." The president had blundered once again, his tactlessness exposing the nation's leading university to shafts of ridicule.[36]

In December 1924, amidst the wild scrimmage over Harvard's admission policies, the much-loved dean, LeBaron Russell Briggs, submitted his resignation. Seventy years old, a neat, prosaic figure who had given nearly half a century to the place, Briggs's own words of formal parting might provide the most charitable assessment of Lowell's handling of quotas and laborers alike. "I have made lots of mistakes and displayed many kinds of ignorance," wrote Briggs, "but not many persons can care more about the college."[37] Lowell cared about the college as much as any man. His failure to live up to his own demand for social education recalls nothing so much as Wolsey's deathbed lament that if he had cared for his God as much as his king, God would not have left him to die alone.

James Michael Curley, mayor of Boston, once visited the red brick President's House designed by Lowell's cousin to resemble an ancestral mansion on Newburyport's High Street. The two men had a memorable encounter. Over the fruit cup, Lowell asked the mayor to appoint one of his relatives to a supervisory post at City Hospital. Curley ruled this out on grounds of age and experience. The president fixed him with a beady-eyed stare. Then he stalked out. Curley buzzed for the maid, who brought his entree. More buzzing brought subsequent courses, but no sign of Lowell. Finally, Curley directed the maid to bring him a large glass of Old Granddad and a smaller quantity of ice and water. When he had finished, he let himself out of the house without ever again laying eyes on his host.

Such behavior was accepted, more or less, as the price of Lowell's undeniable achievements, not the least of which was an endowment three times what it was in Eliot's day. New buildings were going up everywhere. ("Now we shall have enough scientific equipment to develop fifty Pasteurs," rejoiced the president on a tour of the freshly constructed Mallinckrodt laboratory. "But I don't expect to see them. As soon as professors have all the equipment they require, they are swallowed up in the details of administration.") The curriculum had been given a strong dose of Lowellian purpose, and there was widespread agreement that classroom performance had never been higher.

The president himself had a yeasty charm still attested to by men who as boys had found him alternately picturesque or terrifying. One freshman stumbling around the quadrangle of McKinlock Hall, as yet unfinished in September 1926, saw a portly gentleman emerge from the scaffolding. "May I assist you?" the man inquired. The boy stuttered his room assignment and they were off, dodging ladders and stepping over cans of paint. In the Common Room, the old man paused to admire the Harvard chair he had designed. "Welcome to the college," he announced. "I hope you will be very happy here. My name is Lowell; President Lowell."[38]

It was meant to be funny but it was unfair when the *Lampoon* urged a monument to mark the site where the president spoke to a freshman. In fact, he could often be seen chatting away with undergraduates on the back seat of a transom returning from a Pops concert at Symphony Hall, or bantering at one of the boisterous teas convened each Sunday in the elegant brick President's House. In the spring of 1927, a melee broke out in the Square between local police and a thousand students hurling eggs and waving fists. Following dozens of arrests, Lowell himself showed up in an East Cambridge courtroom to post bond for his surrogate sons and loudly protest police brutality.

When the *Lampoon*'s own editors printed a fictitious issue of the *Crimson* announcing Princeton's victory over Harvard and the subsequent death by shock of the Princeton football coach, the president placed them on a month's probation. However, gentleman to gentleman, Lowell acknowledged the wit of a Poonie cartoon depicting a huddle of grossly fat gridiron stars with the caption, "Come, let us root for dear old Princeton." That, he informed the not so contrite humorists, was in good taste.[39]

Undergraduate humor notwithstanding, Lowell was far more visible and decidedly more vocal than Eliot, who had rarely strayed after students and who, near the end of his presidency, predicted a permanent halt to construction of new student housing. His successor delighted in disproving the assertion, waving his walking stick like a field marshal's baton as he guided distinguished visitors through the freshman halls which preceded his Houses in the area between Mt. Auburn Street and the Charles. Eliot Perkins's brother and a roommate were studying in their entry one day when they heard a knock on their door. "Come in," they shouted, only to be answered with a second round of tapping. Again they told their visitor to enter, and again came a dull rap. Finally, one of the boys called out, "Piss on the floor and swim under."

At that moment, the door opened to reveal A. Lawrence Lowell escorting a set of parents through the well-appointed facilities he regarded as hatcheries of gentlemen. There was no reprimand, no stony silence. The students' own embarrassment gave a whole new dimension to Lowell's phrase "self-education."[40]

Long before it opened its doors in 1932, secular controversy had engulfed Lowell's new Memorial Church. "A stupendous mockery" said the *Crimson,* this totem in brick and wood, this war memorial that wouldn't be filled more than three times a year. The proposed structure was too big for the Yard (an argument used earlier, to no effect, against the frowning bulk of Widener Library). An infirmary or athletic complex would do more to enhance student life. Others shunned utility altogether. What Harvard really needed was a campanile, they said, with a bell-ringing society patterned after those of Oxford and Cambridge.

Raising an $800,000 building fund touched off fresh outbursts. Was the church to be open to all faiths, or would it merely reflect the liturgy of Lowell's Cold Roast Boston? Would honors be paid to a trio of Harvard men sacrificed in the kaiser's beaten army? Lowell brushed the complaints aside. The church would have bells, he decreed, to satisfy the Oxford-Cambridge crowd. He would donate the largest one himself, anonymously, and compose a suitable inscription: "In Memory of Voices That Are Hushed." German names would be excluded from the monumental chamber in which a stone Valkyrie and fallen warrior kept vigil over the names of the Allied dead. In the floor, set in bronze, was the college seal, with its three open books and the motto "Christo et ecclesiae," Christ and the Church.

Planning for his church, the president visited Andover's exquisite chapel. He stalked up and down its aisles, inspecting architectural details like a clerk of the works. "Fuess," he called out to his companion, "look up there. Look at the capital on those columns . . . that's the difference between Harvard and Andover. You have cherubs. We have lions."[41]

Howard Mumford Jones said of the resulting structure, with its graceful spire and stout brick wings, that it was half Emily Dickinson and half Mae West. Lowell paid no heed to such remarks. Memorial Church held the heart of his Harvard.

With equal self-confidence, Lowell also put his mark on Harvard's natural landscape. Old men plant trees, he said, because they recognize they won't live to see results of their life's work. So Lombardy poplars sprouted along the Charles. Hurrying toward the Yard one day, the old man spotted something that angered him. "Who planted that tree?" he demanded, waving his stick at a trunk deviant from his master plan.[42]

Although Lowell was not an early riser—people who got up early, he would say, were conceited all morning and sleepy the rest of the day—he more than made up for it, occupying nearly every waking moment personally overseeing every aspect of Harvard's affairs. Having discarded polo and billiards as time-wasting diversions, the president was heard to finish his morning prayers while running downstairs to breakfast. He denied rumors that he tossed alumni letters into the wastebasket, but nevertheless resented the time they took to answer. With the same reckless disregard for rules which made Lowell think he could avoid Beacon Street traffic by driving across Boston Common, the man whom reporters dubbed the Prophet of the Back Bay was everywhere at once, climbing up and down ladders, dropping in unannounced to sample student cuisine, measuring out paths around Widener Library, challenging his friend Lord Bryce to hurdle campus fences, advising exasperated groundsmen to plant barberry bushes in the Yard—even freshmen would think twice before plunging into barberries, he declared.[43] One day he was even glimpsed emerging from a trench that had been dug in the Yard, clutching fragments of ancient china which later became the inspiration for a famous series of Harvard plates. Like Louis XV, who laid claim to all of subterranean France—and the coal sure to be mined there—Lowell's possessiveness was unbounded.[44]

"All who have meditated on the art of governing mankind," Lowell said, quoting Aristotle, "have been convinced that the fate of empires depends on the education of youth." True to his belief in social as well as intellectual instruction, Harvard's president fretted over students' tendencies to segregate themselves according to wealth, geography, religion, and club allegiance. For instance, all but a handful of the Class of 1923 who entered final clubs were private school men. The wrestling team was virtually unique among athletes in having a public-school-bred manager. Running track and music hall alike took their tone from Groton and Andover. "Private school men come here with a surplus of education," said Charlton MacVeagh, a dissenting *Crimson* editor, "and instead of increasing the surplus they draw on it." Most of their days, he concluded, were dawdled away in idle amusement. Twice as many boys from the public high schools were elected to Phi Beta Kappa; a similar imbalance prevailed among honors recipients.[45]

As usual, Lowell had a plan to combat the problem. Thanks to their size, their resources, and their natural allure for the talented, universities like Harvard were best suited to help form what he called "a national type of manhood." Such advantages were offset, however, if Harvard duplicated big city anonymity. "Character and self-reliance are more developed by being a man of mark in Ravenna than by belonging to the mob in Rome," said Lowell. In building his freshman dormitories, he had thrown in his lot with Ravenna over Rome. For twenty years, he dreamed of similarly housing the entire College. But money was tight. The president himself joked about his "perpetual attempt to assist poor millionaires to make a wise use of their surplus possessions."[46]

Then, in the fall of 1927, he struck pay dirt. A Yale graduate named Edward Harkness, his pockets filled with Standard Oil dollars, paid a visit to University Hall. Harkness envisioned an honors college, a single subdivision consisting of a master, tutors, and the most promising of upperclassmen. He had taken the idea to his own alma mater, only to be put on hold. Miffed, he went to see Lowell, who grabbed the money like manna from heaven. When Harkness's initial offer was later bolstered, the one college became seven Houses. And Lowell's greatest experiment in democratic elitism was launched.

Like so many of his innovations, the House plan was essentially conservative. Waking to its implications, Lowell's faculty demanded open debate. Undergraduates were no more eager to be herded into Houses, watched over by senior professors, taught outside the classroom by junior instructors, encouraged to join intramural teams in preference to the reassuring bonhomie of Pork or Pi Eta. Harvard men required no "broad undergraduate intercourse," vowed the *Crimson,* nor any "artificial cross-sectioning." Warming to the fight, Lowell did not so much persuade the faculty as stampede it. Having courted the Student Council ever since his inauguration, he was delighted to enlist its aid now. When construction finally got underway, he even relaxed his firm rule against press interviews, merrily escorting reporters around the skeletal forms of two structures named for Henry Dunster and his own dynasty. "We have finally smashed the Gold Coast," he exulted.

The Houses were to be seminars in living, where different ideas and outlooks would clash around the dinner table and in the Common Room. Self-appointed arbiters of taste made sport of Lowell's preference for pseudo Georgian; in fact, the buildings were a faithful reproduction of a world doomed to extinction even before the panic of 1929. For example, when architects raised the subject of garages for each House, Lowell asked why. The designers explained that each House master would require a garage for his car. "Oh, that's all right," replied the president, "they can have the man bring it around front." On the other hand, when the garages were finally buillt, Lowell made certain they were consolidated in a central locale. That way, "the men" would be able to enjoy each others' company when not on duty.[47]

Wishing to expose rich students to those of lesser means, and blend lower-class members with the senior supermen, Lowell saw the House system as the crowning point of his design for Harvard. Each building was equipped with dining rooms, common rooms, and ten-thousand-volume libraries. House tutors carried on the work of concentration, while intramural teams and improvised traditions engendered fraternal order, and the wide range of friendships no less than the heady conversation broadened sympathies and strengthened the curriculum. All of this added up to Lowellian self-education at its purest.

By the fall of 1931, nearly all of the seventeen hundred available beds were taken. Not all undergraduates were required to live under an official roof; Jews and blacks were pointedly discouraged from doing so. Yet Lowell and the House masters who assigned individual rooms to the vast majority of Harvard students opting for membership in the president's social and intellectual fraternities looked forward to a time when the proudest clubster—already compelled to pay for meals he preferred to take elsewhere—would end his holdout and join the new order. "In the meantime," Lowell announced, "the loss is theirs." The Houses, he noted in one of his final reports, were mother-of-pearl, shells in which jewels might grow. With a look of self-satisfaction, he pointed to crowded libraries. "Evidently, the habit of reading is growing among our undergraduates."

The new mood of ordered liberty proved contagious. After 1931, no chaperon was required when young ladies were entertained, even after seven in the evening, so long as the visiting party consisted of three or more, and the master or senior tutor furnished written permission. (Harvard did not proceed as far down the path of experimentation as Dartmouth, which briefly permitted students to wear shorts in place of trousers. But then, Yale was still embroiled in protests over compulsory chapel.) Room rates were scaled according to individual means, with third-floor quarters overlooking the handsome quadrangle of Lowell House budgeted at $360 a year, and singles at $120 set aside for scholarship students grateful for attic privacy.

The Houses had gone up as the American economy spiraled downward. Lowell moved swiftly to cut budgets wherever possible. Groundskeepers took a 10 percent pay cut. Waitresses and porters at the Business School accepted three dollars less in their weekly pay envelopes. The president reduced board costs and looked for ways to make House rooms more affordable still. He vetoed as inconsistent with his standards of individual dignity one suggestion that needy students be hired as waiters. But he gloated when the dining halls showed a profit of $40,000, channeling the windfall to a student employment fund and slamming the door on the need for assistance from Franklin Roosevelt's New Deal.

Among sociologist David Riesman's friends in the Class of 1931, life went on much as usual, talk of yachts and summer places muffling the anguish of Depression America. George Homans, with whom Riesman later served on the Harvard faculty, was one year behind him. One of his roommates who liked to play the market made sport of the downturn that had begun in October 1929. "Of course I shall double my money at the end of this year," he predicted. More realistic was the fifth-year progress report compiled by Nathan Pusey's Class of 1928. In their ranks were to be found five chauffeurs, eight bellhops, four golf caddies, ten sailors, eighteen salesmen, three milkmen, six tobacco pickers, 301 Republicans, 59 Democrats.[48]

In the spring of 1932, the Square hosted another student donny-brook. Once again, eggs flew and trolley cars were rocked on their tracks. Cambridge firetrucks charged into the crowd at high speed, and the local district attorney denounced this latest assault on decent society. When freshmen shouted for Harvard Hall's bell clapper and beer, Moscow newspapers called it a food riot, while San Francisco journals diagnosed hunger for a little Radcliffe companionship as a more likely cause of the disturbance. Such pranks aside, the Depression tightened its grip on undergraduate life, especially on those for whom a decline in scholarship funds portended disaster. Lowell scrimped where he could—firing the scrubwomen was one such gesture—and husbanded resources compiled during the days of plenty. Refusing to cut faculty salaries in the depths of the Depression, he stood firm against a proposal to hold charity football games to benefit the unemployed. "This is yielding the principle that our athletes shall not be used for public shows to collect money," he insisted.[49]

Nineteenth-century industrialism was a most unconservative damsel, and Lowell had been no more than its reluctant suitor. He scorned those who held business to be mere moneymaking and therefore outside the dignity of the university. "If this be so," he said, "God help the United States of America." As early as 1924, his school of business had over six hundred students from forty-four states and eleven nations. Its casebooks utilized by a hundred other colleges, its Bureau of Business Research at the back of three thousand firms, the school paved the way for other graduate spinoffs in education, public health, architecture, landscape, and city planning. Ironically, the College's best friend presided over a near-tripling of graduate enrollment. The autocrat to whom one astonished professor was directed to secure a bookcase for his temporary office (Lowell kept a

notepad for such requests in his coat pocket) granted far more independence to the farflung regions of his educational empire than his liberty-
loving predecessor had.[50]

But he would not compromise with the age; this white knight
forever charging into controversy was frequently unhorsed but never
vanquished. In 1933, an airplane dragging a promotion for a local tire
company interfered with Class Day ceremonies along the Charles. "As
this was done with the express purpose of distracting the audience," the
president protested, a claim for damages in the amount of $10,000 seemed
the only way of preventing a recurrence.[51]

Even now, he had plans for further expansion. All along he had
been seeking ways to encourage gifted scholars to pursue post-college
studies without condemning them to the Ph.D. treadmill; now he hit on
the Society of Fellows. The creation of Lowell and Lawrence J. Henderson, a red-bearded Francophile who shared the president's disdain for
most graduate education, the Society was meant to combat mass-produced
mediocrity and advance the cause of "the rare and independent genius."
In 1925, Henderson had been dispatched to study the prize fellows of
Trinity College, Cambridge. He was joined there by Alfred North Whitehead, Charles Curtis of the Harvard Corporation, and English professor
John Livingston Lowes. They returned with plans for a rarefied family, to
consist of seven members from the faculty and governing boards, who in
turn would supervise up to two dozen junior fellows, none older than
twenty-five, who would be subsidized for up to two years of independent
writing or research.[52]

Hoping for just such a plan, Lowell had deliberately instructed his
architects to leave rooms vacant in Eliot House. When no other donor
could be found, he promised two million dollars of his own money, nearly
all he had, to fund the Society. On the evening of September 25, 1933,
the first of Lowell's Fellows sat down to dine. They were the forerunners
of McGeorge Bundy, Arthur Schlesinger Junior, Noam Chomsky, Daniel
Ellsberg, and hundreds of others who would staff future Harvard faculties
and enrich the worlds of science, literature, and politics. Lowell himself
composed the words that are still read aloud as a kind of academic oath
to each incoming band.

> You will practice the virtues, and avoid the snares, of the
> scholar. You will be courteous to your elders who have ex-
> plored to the point from which you may advance; and helpful
> to your juniors who will progress farther by reason of your la-
> bors. Your aim will be knowledge and wisdom, not the re-
> flected glamour of fame. You will not accept credit that is due

to another, or harbor jealousy of an explorer who is more fortunate.

You will seek not a near but a distant objective, and you
will not be satisfied with what you may have done. All that you
may achieve or discover you will regard as a fragment of a
larger pattern of the truth which from his separate approach
every true scholar is striving to descry.

His own favorite description of a university's labors, said Lowell,
was to be found on John Wesley's monument in Westminster Abbey.
"God buries His workmen, but carries on His work."

In November 1932, his own work hobbled by increasing deafness,
his personal life thrown into shadow by the death of his wife of fifty-one
years, his sympathies out of touch with a restless, self-doubting age,
Lowell asked his physician, Roger Lee, whether he should resign. He
didn't want an immediate answer, he told fellow Corporation member
Lee; he wanted his friend to think it over. All too obviously, what he
really wanted was to be asked to stay on. But Lee was no more inclined
than his patient to indulge in drawing-room deception. The next day he
told Lowell that after considering the matter carefully, he believed now
was the time to go with grace.

Grabbing a piece of paper on his desk, Lowell scribbled out a terse
letter of resignation. Flinging his pen down, he shoved the note at Lee.
"There," he muttered, "you've got what you wanted."[53]

When the news was made public, gracious words filled the nation's
press. "It is not too much to say," claimed the *Boston Globe,* "that today
an idler cannot get into Harvard, and if he did get in he could not stay
in." Thomas Perkins summed up the attitude of many, even those occasionally rubbed raw by the old man's prejudices. "You've never shirked
or quibbled. . . . You've won or lost on every point fairly. And you've
never played for your own hand." A retired professor told the president
he must feel like God on the evening of the sixth day.[54]

At a farewell dinner early in 1933, Lowell's classmate Edward Martin read a commemorative ode whose wit could not obscure the brutal
truth of a nation turning its back on former idols. He concluded,

> *The business school is doing fine,*
> *But business—where is that?*
> *A lot of tinsel's lost its shine,*
> *A lot of tires gone flat!*
> *A lot of glory's on the brink,*
> *A lot of fame's grown dim;*
> *But Lowell—lots of people think*
> *There's lustre still on him.*

Not all were so forgiving. In December 1938, the Prophet of the Back Bay appeared at Lowell House for his customary birthday celebration, complete with High Table lampooned by the *Crimson* as an attempt to look smart in pants borrowed from Baliol. As a procession formed up, the University's head of security, Charlie Apted, ventured ahead on a whim. What he discovered when he reached the Senior Common Room convinced him that his impulse was more than a lucky guess. For there, all but hiding a giant birthday cake, was a hand-lettered placard reading "Sacco and Vanzetti Might Have Lived To Be Eighty-Two, Too."[55]

When Lowell left his post in June of 1933, he turned down an offer to become U.S. ambassador to the Court of Saint James and accepted instead the chair of the Motion Picture Research Council. Deriding Franklin Roosevelt's National Recovery Administration for giving sanction to monopolistic practices in the film industry, Lowell engaged in a long-running spat involving not only the NRA's colorful director, General Hugh "Ironpants" Johnson, but Marie Dressler and Eddie Cantor as well.

"To me the times are discouraging," he wrote a friend early in 1936. "My sister had some verses, 'If only the good people were clever, and only the clever were good.' "

Although sympathetic to the new Securities and Exchange Commission, he was an unabashed critic of the New Deal. "Philanthropy out of other people's pockets is not in itself a moral virtue," he asserted. "On the other hand, mutual sacrifice for the good of others or posterity is wholly good." Character meant more to a nation than economic prosperity; self-reliance could not be bought with federal greenbacks.

Then there were the personal consequences of the Depression. Lowell lost nearly $200,000 of his own funds when the Swedish industrialist Ivar Krueger committed suicide, and the gilt-edged firm of Lee, Higginson and Company went into receivership. "I'm getting rather worried about the Lowell family," he revealed not long after. "There's nobody in it making money anymore."[56]

In the last summer of his life, sitting on the porch of his retreat at Cotuit, he protested the ravages of time. "I never thought I should live to be a decrepit old man," he remarked. His companion tried to offer solace. Wasn't it better to be a decrepit old man, he asked, than a decrepit young one? "No," Lowell replied testily, "it isn't. If I had been a decrepit young man, I should be used to it now."[57]

It was no exaggeration, Lowell asserted, to review history by considering the chief priorities of conquering nations over those conquered.

In 1600, they were to change religion, in 1700 to change trade, in 1800 to change laws, in 1900 to change drainage. An eighteenth-century man compelled to play by twentieth-century rules, Lowell insisted his sights were fixed fifty years in the future. Accordingly, he compared his curricular reforms to a well-balanced diet, the educational equivalent of proteins, fats, and carbohydrates. He was quietly boastful of having been arrested for speeding at the age of seventy-seven. But his acceptance of the new social order was grudging. "The inherent defect of democracy," he liked to say, "is that it is no one's business to look after the interests of the public."

At the beginning of 1933, Harvard prepared to alter its arm's-length view of the democratic process in America. For a quarter-century, it had been governed by a man who passionately wanted to remake the country in his own college's image. Now, to its own surprise as much as that of nearly everyone else, it would entrust its fortunes to a man who wished to reverse that order.

CHAPTER THREE

A Dorchester Mr. Chips

Science and Puritanism merged in Jim Conant. His scientific rigor replaced the Puritan vision of an austere God; his human straightness kept the colonists' sense of equality. . . . His was the faith of Jefferson and Franklin, but espoused in a more crowded, more complexly pressing age when the first faith was harder to keep.

—JOHN FINLEY
longtime Harvard classicist

To discharge the responsibilities which have been thrust upon us by the modern world, we shall have to change the outlook of young men. We can no longer allow them to believe that the normal career of a college man is to go out and make a private fortune. . . . It is in the administration of President Conant that the first generation of Harvard men will be trained for these newer responsibilities.

—WALTER LIPPMANN

THE CORPORATION that met behind closed doors throughout the winter of 1932–33 kept hearing complaints about the University's indifference to test tubes. George Kistiakowsky, himself among the nation's leading physicists, complained about a shortage of promising young scientists on the faculty. Harvard, he told Thomas Nelson Perkins, was losing ground in this vital field, precisely when a new generation would most require a thorough grounding in it. There must be new methods of teaching brought to bear, he argued, and a fresh emphasis to match Lowell's on the humanities.

Soon after, Perkins was sent to speak with Kistiakowsky's colleague and intimate friend in Chemistry, James Bryant Conant. He came away impressed. So did George Homans, another member of the Corporation, who dropped by to munch on Grace Conant's toasted muffins, and stayed to solicit her husband's candid assessment of the University and its prospects. Others had a different agenda in mind, and different candidates to carry it out. Conant had one of his own: Kenneth Murdock, a gravely ironic professor of colonial and literary history, with the stiff-backed stride of an ex-ensign, an adroit, precise intelligence, and a taste for Mozart and Keats. As Lowell's dean of the faculty at thirty-six, and master of Leverett House during its relaxed infancy, Murdock had displayed impressive administrative gifts. No one knew the place better, or surpassed the judgment he had displayed in advancing the careers of such talented young men as F. O. Matthiessen, Perry Miller, John K. Fairbank, and B. F. Skinner. Yet Murdock, says one who knew him well, was like the ivy that crawled up a telephone pole. Lowell provided the pole.[1]

One Harvard man who traveled to New York about this time ran into a friend who pressed him for details of the job search. At the moment, he said, Ken Murdock was in the lead, only to have his companion shake his head. What was wrong, asked the first man. "No class," replied the second.[2]

Having played together as boys, Murdock and Conant had forged a fast friendship as undergraduates. The English scholar was best man at the chemist's 1921 wedding. So it came as no surprise when Conant sang Murdock's virtues to Perkins. But while he praised Murdock, Conant's incisive anlysis of what was wrong with Harvard, especially the dangers lurking in the costly tutorial system, moved Corporation members to add his own name to a short list of contenders.

Public speculation involved an array of possibilities, including Eliot's old secretary, Jerome Greene, Clarence Little of the University of Michigan, Navy Secretary Charles Francis Adams, Lewis Perry, principal at Phillips Exeter, Henry Shattuck, the University's treasurer, and much of the Corporation itself. Most eager for promotion was Grenville Clark, a recent addition to the governing board whose candidacy was undeclared but apparent. It is uncertain whether any formal ban on such a promotion was adopted within the Corporation's ranks (George Homans's son maintains there was), but still, Clark posed enough of a threat to propel Lowell into preemptive action. Despite what outsiders believed, his candidate was not Murdock, on whom he had soured, but the even younger head tutor of Kirkland House, Edward Whitney. Lowell said after he left the presidency that he had made few mistakes, but when he did make them, they were apt to be beauties—and Murdock was one of them. His protégé had been seen crossing the Atlantic in the company of a woman not his wife. This, in a community where Episcopalianism was considered an insuperable barrier to presidential ambitions, was a fatal weakness. For this reason alone, Murdock was out. Not realizing this, Murdock never forgave his onetime friend Conant for his failure to persuade the men around Lowell of his fitness to succeed to the presidential office.[3]

As the soft undertone of speculative conversation filled the men's clubs and stag dinners favored by the Corporation, little discoveries were made which enhanced Conant's darkhorse appeal. He liked beer better than cocktails, was moderate in his smoking, had a wry sense of humor, and had gained a well-earned reputation for administrative skill while chairing the chemistry department. Lowell resented the department's disdain for tutors, and there had been an earlier incident in which Conant and Kistiakowsky had approached the Rockefeller Foundation for substantial grants without first obtaining sanction from University Hall. Yet, contrasting the chemist to Murdock the fallen angel, Whitney the neophyte, or Clark the corporate lawyer of dogmatic cast, the aging president was inclined to take a gamble.

Before a decision could be reached, the *Lampoon* staged a roisterous burlesque of the whole solemn process. On Washington's birthday, 1933, a special edition of the *Crimson* hit the streets of Cambridge, announcing a stunning piece of news: the election of a new president, Henry Eliot Clarke, Class of 1904, of Evanston, Illinois. The Associated Press was among the first to disseminate a profile of Lowell's successor, "a business Messiah", and friend of Franklin Roosevelt, whose wired congratulations were also reported. The list of Clarke's achievements was a long one. It included a trusteeship at the University of Chicago and wartime service alongside food czar Herbert Hoover, a directorship of that year's World's Fair, and membership on the Hyde Park, Illinois, school committee. To top it all off, Clarke was revealed to be a member of the Aeropagus Club, "a discussion group which disbanded in 1910." A bookish entrepreneur from the west to replace a scion of the Back Bay: it seemed almost too good to be true.

It was. Henry Eliot Clarke was a figment of the *Lampoon's* imagination. Hardly had the hoax been revealed to red-faced newsmen, however, than the Corporation moved into the final stage of its own deliberations. Thomas Perkins entered the process in earnest. He demanded amplification of Conant's strictures against departmental decline and his support of the German university ideal. Charles Curtis and Grenville Clark followed Perkins. Then Perkins returned with a blunt inquiry as to whether Conant really wanted the job. Lowell was prepared to support him against Clark. Such, at least, were the rumors reaching Conant's ears.

On Monday, April 24, the scientist was in his lab when the telephone rang, carrying news of an impending visit from Mr. Lowell. A few minutes later, the old man swept in, sat down, and coolly informed Conant that the Corporation had elected him president of Harvard. Formal ratification by the Overseers, he went on, would take an additional two weeks, however, and there was no guarantee of their consent. As the conversation continued, it was obvious that Lowell expected little from the new man, an attitude Conant inadvertently strengthened by asking about his salary. The incumbent brusquely informed Conant that he gave to the University; he did not take.

Conant felt anything but elation. Not long after, following his final lecture to Chemistry 5, he returned home, closed his front door, and gave way to tears. One chapter of his life was ending. He never would lose his interest in the field that had engaged him since, as a small boy, he had begged his Dorchester father to add a lean-to onto the family residence which he could convert into a smelly, smokey den of scientific inquiry. He might still return to the lab on weekends, tossing pebbles against their windows until a custodian let him in. But the Nobel Prize his colleagues had so confidently forecast for him was now forever beyond his reach.[4]

There were other causes for apprehension. Conant became president at a moment when Harvard was weary of the carpenter's hammer. Professors and administrators shared a common dream of reestablishing their supremacy. The outside world conspired to thwart this ambition, not just because the Depression imposed financial austerity, but also because of the rise of significant rivals at Michigan and California, Stanford, Wisconsin, and Columbia.

In writing his sister about his election to what he called "the most thankless job in the U.S.A.," Conant had a wistful, almost forlorn tone. Enjoy his success while she could, he advised. "You'll have plenty of years of hearing and reading many nasty things about me if I'm not mistaken." Personally, he planned on making no unnecessary enemies. Yet he harbored few illusions. "It will be interesting and I hope satisfying but on the whole unpleasant and trying—a very very lonely job. From May 8th until I retire, it will be very hard to find anyone who will speak absolutely frankly and fully to me about any Harvard matter.

"Pray for me," he concluded. "I shall need it."[5]

The author of this letter was hardly the cold fish perceived by others. He displayed more than average self-confidence, and for all his reputed hostility to organized religion, he held more than a trace of Calvinistic fervor, at least on the subject of imperfect mankind. Who was this scholar elevated so abruptly to the highest position of its kind? Even before his deliberately frugal inauguration in October 1933, preliminary estimates flew across the Yard. Yet no consensus formed, for little about Harvard's new leader was obvious.

> *Bryant has a formula for everything. He will be*
> *a success.*
>
> —JENNET BRYANT CONANT,
> *on her son, James*

WITHIN twenty-four hours of his surprise selection, Conant did two things his austere predecessor hadn't done in twenty-four years: he rode the subway and talked informally with reporters. Informality was to be a hallmark of the Conant years. On the ballroom floor of Lowell's sumptuous presidential residence the new president and his two sons spread out their toy railroad tracks. That's what all ballrooms should be for, explained Conant. Later, one of the boys appeared in Hearst newspaper photos alongside friends leaving a Young Communist League bookstore. The president offered him a swap: in exchange for Ted Conant's abandoning his ideologically controversial cohorts, his father would subscribe to the *Daily Worker*. (Mrs. Conant's only comment once the paper began arriving at 17 Quincy Street was that the comrades didn't spell very well.)[6]

Harvard information officers had a difficult time finding anything colorful for their new president's biography. Conant suggested that perhaps the press might be interested in his recent investigations of hemoglobin and the blue blood of the horseshoe crab. Hardly, they responded; the last thing the University needed in 1933 was to have people reminded of blue blood. In fact, there was little to connect Conant with the aristocracy of Beacon Hill, part of which questioned the wisdom of going all the way to Dorchester for Lowell's successor.[7]

Conant's father, James, had been a drummer boy in General George McClellan's Peninsula campaign of 1862. Refusing after Appomattox to join the Grand Army of the Republic when others around him wore their GAR membership badges as tokens of political influence, James Senior returned from the Virginia battlefront to become an illustrator. As a talented wood-engraver, his drawings appeared in such publications as *Gleason's Pictorial* and *Ballou's Monthly.*

The girl Conant's father married was Jennet Orr Bryant, daughter of a Bridgewater shoe merchant who in 1933 was still remembered by his neighbors for having left a sickbed to cast a vote for William Jennings Bryan. A familiar figure at local and state Democratic gatherings, Seth Bryant bequeathed to his daughter a Swedenborgian creed that verged on free-thinking. Jennet's son never forgot her disdain for trinitarian doctrines. "Mother basically was a dissenter," he wrote. He proved to be his mother's son.

One way or another, people were always being surprised by the man known as JBC. It had been that way ever since boyhood, when young Bryant, as he was called, had impressed Roxbury Latin classmates at the end of their fifth year by scoring an impressive eighteen points in his preliminary examination for Harvard. As an undergraduate, in the fall of 1910, he had gone to 5 Linden Street, "Mrs. Mooney's Pleasure Palace" to the irreverent. There he had made the acquaintance of John Marquand, with whom he invented the "Two Beer Dash," a diversion which tested who could grab a Boston-bound streetcar, down two large glasses of brew, and retrace his route in the shortest possible time.[8]

Conant's diary shows an unpretentious youth, fond of Pink Ladies ("Wooh! Boom!"), long walks in weather "cold as blue blazes," and the ink-spattered comradeship of the *Crimson* office. "Worked like hell," he noted after chasing the paper and grinding dolomite in a laboratory one day, while at the same time fretting as schoolboys have since time began over how he might stretch his allowance.[9]

Half his class were natives of Massachusetts. A majority had never traveled abroad. Yet in June 1912, Conant, the boy from Dorchester's Ashmont section, found himself attending a fraternity convention in Madison, Wisconsin. What he saw inspired one of his earliest displays of catholicity, precursor to the national university he would shape a generation later. He was much impressed with the midwestern boys' "utilitarian broadness and . . . and their ability to find solutions for problems rather than their exclusive scholastic knowledge of chemistry." They, on the other hand, had mixed feelings toward Harvard and the east generally, he noticed, although they showed "consideration and respect for our age, spirit of learning and our *men*.

"We certainly have much to learn from their openness and general broadness of personality as well as their proper degree of earnestness," he noted, "while they could well imbibe some of our academic and scientific spirit and possibly some of our appreciation of *culture,* i.e., the desire for an enjoying of things which are not in themselves materially fruitful or clearly useful."[10]

After Madison and Cambridge, Conant went on to successive careers in a chemist's lab and the drab mufti of a World War I volunteer manufacturing deadly Lewisite gas for the government's war effort. Finding himself in the midst of a heated debate over the usefulness of scarce rubber pipe versus abundant steel—the latter, it was feared, might all too easily be corroded by acid—Conant turned away from his squabbling colleagues. While they fought, he calmly devised an experiment using steel on hand. Soon he discovered that by diluting the acid with another substance, its corrosive effects could be diminished. "The answer to an issue is an answer," Conant told his associates, "not an argument."[11]

Upon his return to Cambridge, the gifted young scientist joined the Harvard faculty as an assistant professor of chemistry. Before long, he was employing his deductive powers in courting Grace Richards—Patty to friends—the daughter of Harvard's leading chemist. Before their 1921 marriage, the suitor confessed to his prospective bride three overriding ambitions: to become America's leading organic chemist, to serve as president of Harvard, and to hold a Cabinet office, "perhaps Secretary of the Interior." The last objective reflected Conant's love of the strenuous life, which found expression in Alpine climbs and early-morning ascents of New Hampshire's Mount Monadnock, all rationalized according to the puritanical code equating vacations, however exhausting, with the maintenance of health.[12]

Following his wedding, Conant's energies were put to the test in several directions. His family was soon increased by two small boys. In addition, there were a host of flattering offers from institutions outside Cambridge. He was wooed by the University of California for his researching talent rather than his classroom skills, and sought out as a well-paid consultant by the Rockefeller Institute. Instead, he became chairman of his own department at Harvard. None of this did much to alter his homely ways. The Sheldon Emery Professor of Chemistry continued living in a plain, two-and-a-half-story house on Cambridge's Oxford Street. He drove a cheap car, and his personal frugality—reinforced since childhood by a family of women who imagined themselves destined for penury—was the stuff of household legend.

Conant's approach to politics, like so much else, was uniquely his own. "A hard-boiled realist . . . a progressive without being a radical or a freak," in the words of his teacher and later colleague N. Henry Black, Conant "was not noticeably Republican." Indeed, he voted four times for Franklin D. Roosevelt, a fact which in years to come would cause him considerable problems with conservative alumni. Around the Faculty Club, he was remembered as a persistent critic of pre-1929 capitalism, one who accurately bet a colleague that Herbert Hoover would be lucky to carry six states in 1932.[13] Yet his distrust of government's excesses was palpable. "Never let the state camel get its nose under the tent," he warned a friend in urging support for the cause of educational television in the late 1940s.

In truth, Conant's ideology was less important than his instincts, and his rigorous deductive approach to life and politics. He was not sanguine about human perfectability, and yet he shared the scientist's belief in the gradual advance of knowledge, along with an individual conscience which Emerson himself might have handed down. Politically as intellectually, he preferred the yeomanry to nabobs. It was second nature for Conant to yield his subway seat to a black woman passenger; likewise, he preferred discussing chemical reactions to theological dialectics.

In the words of the *New York Herald Tribune,* in choosing Jim Conant, like Charles Eliot a chemist of clinical insights and spartan manner, Harvard had crowned a commoner. Others seconded this view, stressing the obvious differences between Lowell, the retiring legend, and his little-known successor. It was Marlborough Street versus Dorchester Bay, religion against science, the rich possibilities of social instinct giving way to the quantifiable truths of deductive logic. That was just the start of their divergences. Lawrence Lowell was a thoughtful bully who addressed his closest friends as if he were at a public meeting. Conant was a hardheaded prophet preaching the glories of a classless society, who took almost childlike pride in being named one of America's ten best-dressed men. Lowell waved his walking stick, and ivy-covered Houses rose from the riverbanks. Conant built few buildings (although he invited Walter Gropius to design purely functional structures at the law school and elsewhere), but he reconstructed a faculty in decline.

Lowell's academic philosophy was rooted in the traditions of the older, more established British society. Conant's educational views paid lip service to the Britain of his ancestors, but in their concern for boys of lesser means and greater talents than the Boston aristocracy could produce, they were a legacy from Thomas Jefferson and John Dewey. "Each honest calling, each walk of life has its own elite," he declared, "its own aristocracy based on excellence of performance. . . . You will become a member of the aristocracy in the American sense, only if your accomplishments and integrity earn this appellation." A descendent of Oliver Cromwell, Conant never lost the old concept of stewardship by those he chose to label "the academically talented." Early in his presidency, Conant told reporters that he hoped to abolish phrases like "the privilege of higher education" and the very adjective "higher." Such fidelity to his own brand of Jeffersonian democracy neatly dovetailed with Franklin Roosevelt's proclamation of a new estate for the forgotten man. But it did little to win the loyalty of Harvard's Bourbons, who took to calling their new leader Greasy Jim.

"I make no claim to being a proper Bostonian," Conant would write in his memoirs. His name didn't show up in the Social Register for two years after his election, and he astonished Overseer Ellery Sedgwick by explaining that while his family had been seven generations in Massachusetts, he was its first representative to Harvard. "He seemed proud of it," Sedgwick concluded, shaking his head. "I'd have been ashamed of it."[14]

While Lawrence Lowell had taken unabashed delight in the West Indian waiters whose noiseless tread in House dining rooms duplicated the quiet deference of downstairs for upstairs (the kitchen of Lowell House contained a special ice cream mold so that chocolate renditions of the Lowell coat of arms might decorate frozen confections served up at High Table), Conant chafed under the social demands of his office. His discomfort on board Thomas Lamont's yacht, moored in Connecticut's Thames River for the annual Harvard-Yale regatta, was unconcealed. His one perk of office was a separate key to a basement men's room in University Hall, augumented by a faded limousine which he directed his student chauffeur to drive like a mountain buckboard. Don't worry, he told Fred Glimp, then a student, later a Harvard vice-president. "When I'm in this thing, I like to move."[15]

Beginning in the fall of 1933, Harvard itself began to move away from what it had been under Lowell. One of Conant's early decisions as president was to end the seven o'clock bell which since 1760 had faithfully announced morning prayers—prayers he rarely attended. On his first visit to Memorial Church, Conant wasted no time in displaying his personal skepticism, brusquely telling Dean Williard Sperry that should cross or candles ever be placed on a handsome new communion table, he would not again show his face in the church. Whether out of duty or because he enjoyed an intellectual challenge, Conant did become reconciled to Sunday services, especially when his friend Reinhold Niebuhr occupied the pulpit. Still, he permitted his son to read detective stories during the sermon. "He had a very high standard of morality, just short of religious zeal," according to David Bailey, for many years secretary to the Harvard Corporation. But "whether Greek baptism means sprinkling or dunking—about such issues he couldn't care less."[16]

As a boy, Conant had liked to generate static electricity by rubbing a hot water bottle against the family cat. Now the angular, sandy-haired Yankee was about to strike fresh sparks. When Robert Frost visited Cambridge early in the Conant presidency to present the annual Charles Eliot Norton lectures, the poet and the scientist circled each other warily. Conant invited Frost to 17 Quincy Street (which he scornfully labeled "this bulk of a Presidential Mansion"). Their conversation turned to current events, Conant expressing admiration for a recent White House speech in support of the embattled teamsters' union. Frost grunted his disapproval. FDR ought to have entitled that address "Every Man's Home His Own Poorhouse," he remarked, for it presaged a time when every teamster would live off government charity. "You have a bitter tongue," said Conant.[17]

Yet Conant harbored reservations of his own about Roosevelt's methods. He was a frugal New Englander who saved string, shut down Harvard's film distribution service, and justified coeducational classes because it offended his sense of thrift to continue the old practice of having Harvard faculty members cross Cambridge Common to repeat their lectures to Radcliffe students.

Entrusted with an annual budget in the tens of millions, Conant developed his own fail-safe technique for discouraging cash-hungry visitors. In one corner of his office sat a large crystal ball. When the conversation turned to fiscal matters, Conant would rise from his seat, stretching his long legs before striding over to gaze into his prop. Whipping a cloth from the object of his attention, bending low to peer into its depths, within seconds he announced that an answer was at hand. The supplicant rose from his seat, followed in his host's steps—only to find magnified before his eyes an emphatic "No!".[18]

Hereafter, Sunday teas at 17 Quincy lacked the zestful intimacy of Lowell's day, when the president was apt to engage boys whose families he knew personally in animated conversation about the fishing off Cotuit. Now the talk flowed haltingly at best; charm had taken a sabbatical. Yet to those who listened closely, the echo of Eliot's assertive baritone was easy to detect.

Before a New York audience early in his presidency, Conant spun a tale combining equal parts of confidence and modesty. He was reminded, he said, of the experience of Sir William Osler, the great medical man who once went touring Canada in the muddy springtime, only to discover at one remote outpost a sign with the warning, "Choose your rut now; you will be in it for 35 miles." Educational contemporaries would soon learn for themselves what a few intimates had already guessed, namely that Jennet Conant's boy had chosen his particular rut long ago, when praising the muscular democracy of Wisconsin's fraternity men. In his new office in University Hall, Lowell's successor hung a cartoon with a revealing caption: "Behold the turtle. He makes progress only when his neck is out."[19]

That was as close as Conant ever came to a formal inaugural address, having dispensed with elaborate inaugural ceremonies even as the *Havard Graduates' Magazine* deplored such surrender to an age weary of processions and the punctilio of state.

> *The world does not need more followers. It has*
> *too many already. Don't acquire the habit young!*
> —JAMES BRYANT CONANT,
> *to the Class of 1938*

THOMAS NELSON PERKINS set the tone of Conant's first meeting with the Harvard Corporation. "Now fellows," he remarked waggishly, "we have a brand-new president; let's raise hell with him." Reality, reflected in newspaper headlines and stock quotations, annulled the humor in Perkins's joke. Before the session broke up, Conant reiterated his by-now familiar plea for new men in place of new buildings. However, his mention of new money with which to support them touched a raw nerve, for even with the College's upcoming tercentenary celebration to spur alumni generosity, few around Conant wished to contemplate a fund drive in the depths of the Great Depression.

Like the nation from which she had become at least temporarily estranged, Harvard was struggling to throw off the infection of self-doubt. Asked in the wake of Black Tuesday to define the future of America's endowed colleges, one Washington official had replied, "I didn't know they had a future."

When the Class of 1928 issued an appeal for information on post-college activities, complacency ranked near the top of the list of unaffordable luxuries ruled out by a tailspinning economy. Among the responses received was one from Nicholas Biddle. He had spent the summer following commencement in a transatlantic sailing race before settling in posh Milton and finding comfortable employment with Lever Brothers. But for every Biddle, there were twice as many like a classmate of his who, despite having been reduced to occasional teaching and chopping wood, penned a stiff protest to Roosevelt's National Recovery Administration and the country's general drift to the left.

An aspiring investment banker had found himself jobless for over a year, he reported, until a shorthand and typing course paved the way for secretarial work and a reasonably stable position with New York Edison. For him at least, the Depression was over. But others were less fortunate. "I haven't missed a meal yet," confided one product of the business school, "but I have had some close calls." Despite their own brush with impoverishment, many alumni (not just woodchoppers) were vocal in their opposition to Roosevelt and his policies, pinning blame for both on their alma mater. "I think too many Harvard men are or try to be political radicals, 'parlor socialists,' " said one. "Their idea seems to be that it is necessary to criticize what exists, and whatever it is, is all wrong."

Another prescient graduate forecast the intense struggle Conant would be forced to wage. "The stranglehold of Brahmin New England on Harvard should be broken," he wrote, "for New England now has fitting rivals in the United States whom Harvard might well deal with."[20]

Little of this carried beyond the bell jar of alumni magazines. In 1932, fewer undergraduates had sold apples than had joined a torchlight parade for Herbert Hoover's beleaguered reelection campaign. Sharing the cynicism of a generation reared on H. L. Mencken and Charles Beard, young Sam Beer, later a mainstay of Conant's government department, didn't bother to vote that year. More committed was the student columnist who urged a compulsory course in the study of communism. After all, he wrote, Soviet Russia was to be credited with the Gosplan, worker self-respect, and a Red Army "of extraordinary military and cultural force."[21]

Amid the wreckage of fallen idols, the individualistic ethic still thrived. As one writer in the spring of 1933 put it, "Propose to the average student the notion of 'doing something for Harvard' and he will respond as would a passenger to whom the suggestion had been made that he do something for the railroad." Yet even individualism was about to be redefined. Walter Lippmann spoke with a prophet's tongue when he predicted that Conant's presidency would be the first to train college men for careers useful to the public.

Members of Conant's faculty were already providing examples of what Harvard men might do in this regard. A feud brewed between the dean of the business school and rivals over rights to staff Roosevelt's New Deal, a political revolution condemned by many professors. These were the years, John Kenneth Galbraith remembered, "when you could hold a faculty meeting every Friday on the Federal Express bound for Washington." Galbraith exaggerated only slightly the influence and ingenuity represented by Harvard men like Lloyd Garrison, chairman of FDR's National Labor Relations Board; Thomas H. Eliot, Charles Eliot's grandson who served the New Deal as chief counsel to the Social Security Commission; Ben Cohen and Adolf Berle of the "Brains Trust"; economists in the mold of Stuart Chase; diplomat-administrators such as Archibald MacLeish; and assorted regulators, bureaucrats, and brainstormers like Charles Wyzanski, Leon Keyserling, Thurman Arnold, and Telford Taylor.[22]

James Conant's own agenda fit neatly the spirit of Roosevelt's reforming juggernaut. Ushering in a strong west wind of reform that soon had Harvard men talking of a New Deal for America's oldest university, during his first months in office, Conant dropped spring football practice, April and November grades, daily class attendance records, and most of the college's language requirements. Out went the Rank List, nearly as venerable as Harvard itself. A new Faculty Council was instituted, a kind of permanent academic town meeting to replace the unmanageable convocations of Lowell's day.

Conant's concern for the less affluent led to the March 1935 opening of Dudley Hall, the first dining room and study center for student commuters, many of them Jews. Talk of a local Jewish problem faded, even as local wits brought appreciative chuckles with their mock praise of Winthrop House's progressive spirit in switching its bias from anti-Irish to anti-Semitic. Conant discarded any semblance of quotas.

A decade before the G.I. Bill of Rights brought a broad cross-sampling of the American family to Cambridge, Conant proposed to shake up the place in three crucial ways: diversifying the student body, broadening membership in the Corporation and building up the faculty. First, there were his National Scholarships, which prompted one wag to congratulate Harvard for at long last joining the United States of America. "In the future even more than in the past," said Conant in his first annual report, "we should attract to our student body the most promising young men throughout the nation. . . . We should be able to say that any man with remarkable talents may obtain his education at Harvard whether he be rich or penniless, whether he come from Boston or San Francisco." Substituting brilliance for family, generous means, or good form, Conant hoped to convert a college overwhelmingly reliant for its population on the eastern seaboard into the national academy that had been urged by Eliot and endorsed by Lowell. In the process, he would necessarily cut it adrift from its local moorings, installing meritocratic competition in place of New England's stony humanism.

In 1934, the Corporation voted money for ten fellowships, all reserved for boys from the midwest. A year later, the south received its due. Academically, the program was an unquestioned triumph. All ten of Conant's first group of National Scholars graduated with honors. Eight joined Phi Beta Kappa. Even so, the alumni were reluctant to increase their funding for the program, and the president was plainly disappointed that boys from south and west of the Mason-Dixon line able to pay their own way did not materialize. From the outset, applications for fellowships overwhelmed Harvard's thin resources. By 1940, the college was turning down four hundred would-be students a year.

Then there was the Corporation itself. In Conant's mind, it was ripe for expansion beyond the borders of New England and the canyons of lower Manhattan. But not until 1948 did he dip a toe in these treacherous waters; the ensuing uproar shook official Harvard to its core. No such delay slowed his third approach to nationalizing Harvard, however: repairing and adding to its faculty.

In the summer of 1933 when Conant assumed office, Harvard, according to one observer, was still princeps, but no longer facile princeps. The University itself, which under Eliot had grown into America's largest, approached its 300th anniversary surpassed in size by sixteen schools. Widener Library boasted three million volumes in its congested stacks, but the Library of Congress, the New York Public Library, even the upstart Huntington Library at San Marino on the Pacific coast had all pulled even. President Conant insisted on a national reputation for his school, yet nearly 40 percent of all freshmen entering the Yard in September 1933 listed Massachusetts as their residence.

Robert Hutchins, the *enfant terrible* from Chicago, took obvious delight at foretelling the end of Harvard's special status. Discovering how to be clubby was not the highest learning in the groves of academe, Hutchins told an audience at Phillips Exeter in the fall of 1934. To his own way of thinking, New England faced a choice. Either she could do what had to be done in order to resume her leading role in American education, or she could rest on yesterday's laurels.

Conant himself admitted as much. If Harvard failed to attract men of the highest caliber, both as students and faculty, then there were no panaceas which would restore the University to the front rank. Gone were the Kittridges, Wendells, Palmers, Taussigs, Channings, Nortons, Jameses, and Harts who had taught under Charles William Eliot. One recent study had gone so far as to award Hutchins's University of Chicago top honors in the academic world, with eight of the country's leading departments, compared to seven for Harvard.

Not wishing to hurt the feelings of sensitive dons, Conant vowed to search for outstanding men wherever they could be located. He believed that raising the overall quality of the student body and enhancing academic and personal amenities would provide incentive for gifted teachers to settle in Cambridge, and insisted that nothing stand in the way of gathering the most distinguished creative scholars in the world.

The institution Conant was demanding, the *Harvard Graduates' Magazine* warned, had the air of being a Sabbath not made for man, "a body dedicated to the worship of its own activities." Harvard might lure Nobel-winning scientists, but if these men refused contact with undergraduates, of what use were they outside the laboratory? Student grumblings lent credence to such speculation. Conant did nothing to disabuse this with his candid statement that excellent teaching would not, in itself, assure a young man's career promotion.

Holding fast to his own criteria, Conant soon unveiled such new stars for the local firmament as William Langer, Francis T. Spaulding, Walter Gropius, and Marcel Breuer. A thin trickle of foreign refugees escaping Nazi persecution freshened the pool, while scholars still green in the last days of the Lowell era came into their rich inheritance.

Apart from enhancing personnel, Conant found imaginative ways to pursue intellectual excellence without sacrificing utility. When in 1935 a newspaper publisher's wife bequeathed a million dollars to the University, Conant invented the Nieman Fellowships, enabling a dozen promising journalists a year to study whatever they wanted, across however broad a range of interests each man might bring to the task. Even though a million dollars wasn't enough to found a conventional school of journalism, the practical theorist in University Hall designed a fresh approach to the subject. And by doing so, he exposed future scribes to, among others, Walter Lippmann, William Allen White, and Henry Luce.

Another experiment, initially more promising but ultimately less productive, was made possible when Felix Frankfurter persuaded former New York congressman Lucius Littauer to donate two million dollars toward the training of government professionals. As Conant well knew, this would pay for the construction of a building, but little else. Starved for funds, the Graduate School of Public Administration, composed of political scientists, economists, historians, social psychologists, and lawyers, nevertheless pioneered in midcareer schooling. It would not prepare men to get jobs in the public sector, but instead refreshed those already so employed with the latest techniques in their field. Small as their numbers were—the first class numbered fifteen—and feeble as the school's financial base might be, the enterprise set a pattern for other midcareer training programs.

Before Conant was through, Harvard was hosting fellows not only in journalism and public administration, but in labor issues and agriculture as well. In addition, the president launched a series of University Extension lectures that held the Harvard umbrella over all of Greater Boston, encouraged the University Press to branch out into general topics, and began the nation's first summer school (which boasted the nation's first air-conditioned classrooms).

Conant also paved the way for Harvard to involve itself in educational broadcasting. He invited Charles Sitmann of the British Broadcasting Company to join his faculty, and himself served as a consultant to the Carnegie Commission's first study of the subject. Envisioning the future of public broadcasting as a Chautauqua of the airwaves, a permanent electronic town meeting, Conant advised public television advocates against shiny hardware and a programming emphasis on ballet and symphony. Far more important was a source of dedicated funding and substantive on-air discussion of current issues.

In the 1940s he argued for an expanded Lowell Institute, one incorporating all the leading cultural and educational institutions of Greater Boston. Having achieved this, Conant approached the Filene family for funds with which to purchase a television license, and in 1945 WGBH, a UHF station unlike most of its counterparts in other markets, was born.[23] Conant then opened Harvard's lecture halls to the cameras. As a result, local airwaves carried John K. Fairbank and Edwin O. Reischauer. When sister stations on the fledgling National Educational Television network were desperate for programming, kinescopes of the E. L. Godkin and other Harvard lectures were distributed throughout the country. A generation later, WGBH would telecast Vietnam teach-ins from Memorial Hall, and debates over war policy between Henry Kissinger and Hans Morgenthau.

Conant's predecessor, Lowell, liked to compare American universities to a tessellated pavement, fields of learning divided into squares of black and white and red, with professors steeped in a single subject holding forth in each individual square. Out of his desire to avert departmental isolation had come the House plan. Assign men of different fields to different Houses, he believed, and the resulting mix would inspire more than memorable conversation around the dinner table.

While Lowell sought instructional coherence through tutorials, distribution requirements, and general exams, Conant preferred to tackle the problem from the faculty's end of the field. In 1935, as part of a tercentenary fundraising drive, Conant set aside money to endow University Professorships for scholars of the first rank who would be utterly free of departmental restrictions. The chair for such a man would be fitted to his personal specifications, not the other way around. He could roam as he wished across disciplinary bounds, teaching as he saw fit, conducting research, or simply pondering. It was Conant's declaration of war against horizontal development. And it set the tone for later campaigns to salvage the hard-pressed School of Education, promote cooperation between departments, and encourage higher standards for faculty promotion.

Conant's pursuit of coherence went beyond simply loosing departmental bonds. He sought cohesive beliefs which would provide a sense of unity not only in his college but also in his country, in a time when both were plagued with self-doubt. Appointing a committee to review the extracurricular study of American history, he hoped that somehow a knowledge of the ancestry of ideas could bind the liberal arts tradition and tailor it to suit the modern age. "A true appreciation of this country's past," said Conant, "might be the common denominator of any educated man's equipment so that men could face the future united and unafraid." (This marked the beginning of what would become a lifelong quest for Conant, and sowed the seeds for his post-World War II program of General Education.)

1933 was quite a year for Germany, America and me. Hitler rose to power, Franklin Roosevelt took office, and I became president of Harvard.
                                    —JAMES BRYANT CONANT

CONANT HAD A TASTE for making history as well as interpreting it. "If a university is to be alive for generation after generation," he said, "the institution in question must be in all times and all places . . . the connection between the scholar's activities and the burning questions of the day." After barely a year in office, Conant had the opportunity to test this theory in one of the first of many controversies which marked his presidency. If nothing else, he shared with FDR a knack for making the right kind of enemies. In 1934, he was confronted by a Falstaffian figure out of German comic opera, a Harvard man who happened to be Adolf Hitler's favorite pianist.

At six feet, four inches tall, his bearish frame hunched over a piano keyboard or gliding through the elegant salons to which his family pedigree admitted him, Ernst "Putzi" Hanfstaengl was an unlikely acolyte of National Socialism. The grandson of New England Sedgwicks and Civil War generals on his mother's side, Putzi traced his father's line to a Munich art publishing house and the privy council of Saxe-Coburg-Gotha. In the first weeks of 1923, Hanfstaengl made the acquaintance of Adolf Hitler, the unprepossessing agitator behind a Bavarian right-wing movement, the National Socialist German Workers Party (NSDAP). Like others, he was mesmerized by Hitler's platform oratory.

For his part, Hitler was entranced by Hanfstaengl's social connections, his access to Munich's galleries and concert halls, and his vigorous if unorthodox keyboard style. In one memorable scene, Hanfstaengl, Harvard '09, astonished Hitler with a rendition of football marches from his American alma mater. "That is it," Hitler shouted, "that is what we need for the movement." And as the future leader of Nazi Germany marched back and forth in the role of political drum major, imagining the powerful effect of such music upon his mass rallies, Putzi was launched on the strangest sidebar yet to his comfortable brush with bohemia. Before long, the pianist had adapted Harvard's rallying cry, "Fight, Fight, Fight," into "Sieg Heil, Sieg Heil," a blood-rousing anthem for the New Germany.[24]

Following Hitler's disastrous Beer Hall Putsch in November 1923, the ex-corporal took temporary refuge at Hanfstaengl's home outside Munich. Later, Hanfstaengl became a sort of unofficial court jester to the Nazi inner circle and self-appointed ambassador of goodwill from the Third Reich to America.

In the spring of 1934, Hanfstaengl went to Cambridge for his twenty-fifth class reunion. "Beware of Nazis Bearing Gifts," warned the *Baltimore Sun* at the unwelcomed visitor's arrival. Striding down the gangplank in New York harbor, Hanfstaengl clutched busts of German heroes from Von Gluck to Hindenburg intended as presents for his alma mater. He also wished to donate a thousand dollars for a scholarship fund, earmarked so that some deserving Harvard man could see for himself Hitler's New Germany.

Inappropriate as the gift of the busts might be, the scholarship offer struck the Corporation, and Conant in particular, as being in even worse taste. Equally offensive was the German's designation by his classmates as aide to the class marshal, ordinarily a purely honorary title but one which assured the publicity-loving Hanfstaengl a place in the sun for days to come.

Nor did the *Crimson* help things by urging an honorary degree for the German emissary. The Student League suggested that perhaps Harvard might devise the degree Master of Concentration Camps, or Bachelor of Book Burning. Putzi himself basked in the attention. Accompanied by four state troopers dressed in identical blazers and white flannel trousers, he didn't blink an eye when undergraduates filling Harvard Stadium greeted him with parodies of the Nazi salute and a raucous performance of "Ach du Lieber Auchenstein."

Such showmanship was embarrassing enough to Conant and the Corporation. Worse was Hanfstaengl's use of a nonpolitical event to serve his own ends. The president's remarks on Class Day were interrupted by shouts from a group of anti-Nazis who chained themselves to a nearby fence, protesting Hanfstaengl's tainted money. Shortly afterward, with unconcealed satisfaction, Conant announced the Corporation's formal rejection of the Berlin scholarship.

The *Crimson* raised its voice in protest. "That politics should prevent a Harvard student from enjoying an opportunity for research in one of the world's greatest cultural cities is most unfortunate and scarcely in line with the liberal tradition of which Harvard is pardonably proud," it asserted. However, dozens of other journals came to Conant's defense. The *New York Post* attacked what it called "budding young Fascists" on the *Crimson*. "Bully for Harvard," declared the Boulder, Colorado, *Camera*. A Richmond newspaper recalled the recent purge of 198 academics, while the *Boston Herald* took pleasure in seeing the "Veritas" on the University seal become something more than a meaningless Latin verb.

Conant dropped charges against the Class Day demonstrators, leading Hanfstaengl to accuse the president of fostering bolshevist subversion. The Yankee from Dorchester, he predicted, "will be proved antiquated in the future." Then he returned to his homeland, soon to fall from official favor, his key-banging renditions of Wagner relegated to private salons.

In 1935, Harvard conferred honorary degrees on Albert Einstein, Thomas Mann, and former Chancellor Heinrich Brüning, all victims of Nazi persecution. Having assumed Harvard's presidency on the same day that Nazi hooligans kindled a bonfire of books outside the gates of the University of Berlin and Joseph Goebbels pronounced the death of "Jewish intellectualism" from a swastika-draped podium nearby, Conant kept a wary eye on the country he knew intimately from extensive travels.

In this, he set the tone for others. For even as Conant's emphasis on modern vocation and relevant studies took the place of Lowell's humanist belief in character building, Harvard classrooms devoted to sociology and economics encouraged political expression. The September 1935 issue of the *Harvard Advocate* featured "So You're a Parlor Pink," billed as an attack on "nice, humane, middle-class intellectuals who toy with communistic theories." Young Arthur Schlesinger Junior contributed a review of proletarian theater to the same journal. A month later, Hitler was convicted in a student mock trial, and many faculty members joined Samuel Eliot Morison in opposing a teachers' loyalty oath approved by the Massachusetts legislature. Conant's opposition to red-baiting legislators was easily drowned out by Hearst editorials and American Legion resolutions. Pressed by liberals on his faculty to disobey the new law, the president refused. Work to elect a new legislature, he advised Morison and others. In the meantime, little consolation was to be had from a supplemental ruling exempting riding academies and beauticians' schools from the hated oath.

At Harvard as elsewhere, tempers were hardening, the lines of division growing more apparent. Six hundred undergraduates gathered to vent their anger at militarism and to proclaim their allegiance to the pacifist spirit of the Oxford Oath (under which students at that ancient seat of learning publicly proclaimed their refusal to fight for their country or king). Pranksters, assembled under the banner of Michael Mullins and his Chowder and Marching Society, ridiculed such notions. Some traversed the campus chanting Hitler's name in a car mounted by a machine gun.

In the fall of 1935 a conservative alumnus gained access to Hearst columns with an assault on a government textbook used at Harvard whose attitude toward the Constitution he found flippant. A few months later, a congressman from Texas raced to the House rostrum to warn of impending revolution after a Soviet flag was discovered flapping from a pole in front of the new Supreme Court building. At the base of the pole, police had found an article entitled "Down With Capitalism," prophesying that Americans would one day soon find a red banner flying over their highest tribunal of law. The editors of the *Lampoon* had been so taken with the idea that they had promptly executed it, much to the consternation of Representative Thomas L. Blanton and the PWA worker forced to give up his blowtorch so that firemen could reduce the Poonies' red flag to cinders.

All of this was harmless enough, a comic counterpoint to the moderate views which still dominated Cambridge. Alfred Landon would prevail, but only barely, in the 1936 voting on campus. But beneath the surface flowed quickening currents of disenchantment. Restive over the state teachers' oath, faculty liberals were unhappy at Conant's willingness to live with such restrictions. Campus traditionalists, on the other hand, took exception to the changes at Harvard since Lowell's departure. Dropping Latin was only one of the outrages Conant was forced to justify, often with dry bemusement. After suffering through a long, urbane critique by a Latin-loving professor at the Signet Society, the president rose to reply, in a style which Ovid himself would have recognized. He had come to praise the Signet, said Conant, not bury Caesar.[25]

Ideologies aside, some among his faculty faulted Conant for a decision-making style they thought needlessly brusque. When Felix Frankfurter dropped by to discuss a replacement for Roscoe Pound as dean of the law school, he suggested that it might be a good idea first to review the school's overall needs, along with the general qualities to be sought in the new man. Conant cut him off. He wanted a list of names. "That's the difference between us," he explained to Frankfurter. "You are a lawyer, accustomed to move from the general to the particular. I am a scientist, trained to move from the particular to the general."[26]

Conant's playful sense of humor occasionally got him into trouble with his flock. When he filled Pound's old chair at the law school with James Landis only to have Landis generate heated controversy by publicly endorsing FDR's maneuver to pack the Supreme Court with justices favorably inclined to New Deal legislation, Conant was inundated with letters protesting his choice. Roger Ernst, a prominent lawyer and principal Unitarian, claimed that it was as if the governing bodies of Harvard, having selected a dean for the divinity school, were to learn subsequently that he was an agnostic. Didn't he exaggerate the situation, Conant wrote back. "Isn't it as though, after having selected a dean of the divinity school, we were to discover that he was a Unitarian?"[27]

Urged by the faithful to undertake a large fund drive for the divinity school, Conant agreed on one condition: that no prospective donor be guaranteed a place in heaven. Wounded by such remarks, Old Guard alumni applauded a regular at New York's Harvard Club who boasted of having thrown a pie at Greasy Jim. An older colleague tottered up to the president and leaned over across a dinner table they were sharing to bark, "I want you to know that I hate the Harvard Law School."

But however much he might share Franklin Roosevelt's disregard for the old Brahmin gods, Conant could not afford to discard their commandments entirely, mainly because the collection plate had to be passed. The level of giving by alumni had plummeted by over half since Lawrence Lowell's last year in University Hall, and continuing hard times and the specter of confiscatory taxation blunted the appeal launched in advance of Harvard's tercentenary in 1936. The amount ultimately raised, around five million dollars, fell far short of expectations, and inspired fresh complaints that Conant disdained the unpleasant but vital chore of endowment-building.

> *He who enters a university walks on hallowed ground.*
>
> —JAMES BRYANT CONANT,
> *September 1936*

TO BOTH friends and foes, the tercentenary celebration gave Conant a second chance to seize authority and to escape the looming shadow of Lowell, whose retirement had done little to lower his profile. Two Harvard presidents in the same room, Conant quickly discovered, meant one too many. Now he faced six months of public festivities, to which the whole academic world was invited, and which he was expected to share with the Roosevelt-hating Prophet of the Back Bay.

Like virtually anything associated with Harvard, her 300th birthday aroused the argumentative. One was Summerfield Baldwin, Class of 1917, self-proclaimed gadfly whose hobbies included "scandalmongering, purchase of worthless manuscripts, the formation of gigantic and Utopian enterprises, and memorizing all the titles of all the books in Widener Library." Baldwin had proposed "The Society for the Prevention If Necessary By Force of Any Pageant in Connection with Harvard's Tercentenary in 1936." By all means, said Baldwin, let there be books written, orations delivered, even a cake with three hundred candles. Only no pageant. He needn't have worried. Conant was unlikely to look with favor upon pageantry in any form. Instead, he promoted the celebration for its wider implications, especially "the aspiration of mankind toward a universal fellowship, based on reason."

Unity was an ironic leitmotif for an academic festival in the third week of September 1936. Throughout the world, chauvinism and dogma absorbed national energies. In Africa, Italian forces consolidated their hold on Haile Selassie's Ethiopia. In Spain, Francisco Franco's followers fought communists in a bloody civil war, with Pope Pius XI denouncing the "Satanic persecution" carried out by Bolshevik sympathizers. There were Russian pilots on the streets of Madrid, while overhead the German air force conducted a dress rehearsal for World War II.

As Europe tottered, Nuremberg's Adolf Hitler Platz echoed to the troops of one hundred thousand brownshirts. Thousands more took part in what were billed as "defense demonstrations," with bomber squadrons, motorized infantry, fast-firing anti-aircraft batteries, and light tanks crashing through barbed-wire barricades. There was even a new goosestep for crowds to admire. Not quite as high as its predecessor, it was easier to maintain in the closed ranks of parade formation. "A chickenstep," said one foreign observer.

Earlier in the year, Germany had broken with the Versailles Treaty and Locarno Pact, reoccupied the left bank of the Rhine, and successfully tested the military and diplomatic will of the Western democracies. "We are not missionaries of our political creed," Hitler insisted to the cheering throngs at Nuremberg. "If anyone is in a position to complain of intolerance, surely we are." Yet a few breaths later, he declared democracy a passing stage, and accused Soviet Jews of promoting a doctrine "as bestial as it is mad."

A Moscow newspaper returned the challenge. Hitler, it claimed, had as much chance of ever seeing the Ukraine as his own ears. In an England riveted by the romance of King Edward VIII and an American divorcée, Fascist leader Oswald Mosley marched at the head of a line of anti-Semites bound for Whitechapel. The *London Times* retracted its declaration that Nazism, unlike communism, was not meant for export.

In the United States that autumn, a bitter election campaign matched Franklin Roosevelt against Alfred Landon, FDR ravaging malefactors of wealth, Landon warning that the profit motive was about to disappear. "If the present Administration is not beaten in 1936," shouted the Republican National Committee, "the American plan of government may be lost forever."

After seven years of depression, Americans accustomed to thin resources demanded good generalship. They listened approvingly to their president. In their leisure, they devoured the newly published *Gone With the Wind*, hummed Richard Rodgers's score from *On Your Toes*, rooted for Joe Louis against Max Schmeling, and stayed glued to the radio for late-breaking bulletins from the New Jersey town where Bruno Richard Hauptmann was on trial for the kidnapping and murder of Charles Lindbergh's baby. Only a handful of Americans that year had the time or inclination to read Freud's autobiography or John Maynard Keynes's *The General Theory of Employment, Interest, and Money*. Few outside intellectual circles paid much attention to Carl David Anderson's Nobel Prize in Physics (awarded for his work on the positron), the death of Ivan Pavlov, or the birth of the Ford Foundation.

That fall the shrill disorder of a splintered globe was temporarily put aside. As scholars from every state and from forty countries, in brilliantly colored cloaks, in white tunics and brown kimonos, in drab mortarboards and velvet fezes, crowded the streets of Cambridge, Massachusetts, to congratulate America's oldest university on her 300th anniversary. Those who put together Conant's academic coming-out recognized pride as the natural property of museum custodians rather than subversives of the status quo. Harvard had its glass cases. Much was put on display for the nearly 70,000 visitors who dropped by in the weeks before September's observances. Conant himself slipped unobserved into one tour group setting off from Wadsworth House, where nine earlier Harvard presidents had lived.

But the true theme of the celebration lay elsewhere. In assessing her mission, Harvard would look to the future. She would attempt the imposing feat of unifying the world of knowledge. Invitations poured out, ten thousand in all, to the most eminent scholars in the world to participate in an unprecedented symposium lasting three weeks and structured to break through the artificial membrane dividing scientist from humanist, theorist from practitioner.

Not everyone said yes. Albert Einstein declined the invitation as a protest over inclusion of scientists from Germany's Reich. George Bernard Shaw reacted as if asked to stroll naked down the Strand. "If Harvard would celebrate its 300th anniversary by burning itself to the ground and sowing its site with salt, the ceremony would give me the liveliest satisfaction," he had written back, "as an example to all the other famous corrupters of youth, including Yale, Oxford, Cambridge, the Sorbonne, etc. etc. etc." A German Nobel Prize-winner was ordered to stay home and serve eight weeks in Hitler's army. Then there was the celebrated biochemist who said he wouldn't adorn the conference if it meant giving up his daily pleasures of boxing and horseback riding. The Harvard faculty scoured Boston and found an elderly Irish boxer, but Otto Warburg stayed away anyway.[28]

Such absences were hardly noted late in August 1936, when 2,500 scholars from five continents, including eleven Nobel Prize-winners, gathered to take the temperature of the physical, biological, and social sciences in the pre-tercentenary conference. Hearst columnist Westbrook Pegler labeled it "Highbrows' Old Home Week." Reporters flocked to hear more than seventy papers read, and struggled to translate into popular prose the erudite, often baffling formulae spun by astronomers and mathematicians.

Professor Elie Joseph Cartan suggested a new approach to the uni-

fied field theory, which had eluded Einstein. A Columbia delegate announced that the sum of two halves, properly calculated, could be greater
than the whole. Sir Arthur Eddington of Cambridge spoke of the constitution of stars, before gauging the number of subatomic particles in the
universe: 3,145, he estimated, followed by seventy-six zeroes. One evening, the conference looked at films of fiery eruptions on the face of the
sun, solar storms shooting out into space a hundred miles or more. En-
zymes within the human bodies, "living and yet not living," were described
as bridges between two worlds. A German scientist revealed a process to
turn sawdust into sugar. Carl Jung and Jean Piaget discussed human behavior with an English specialist on nerve impulses and a Canadian pioneer in endocrine research. A British economist quoted Lewis Carroll in
explaining the laws of interest rates. Cosmic rays were analyzed alongside
male sex hormones, the decline of the Greek city-state, and eighteenth-
century humanism.[29]

While the great men expounded their theories, thousands of alumni
descended on Cambridge. They were as diverse in their ways as the theories of the brilliant company whose abstruse counsel was splashed across
the front pages of newspapers everywhere. The Harvard Club of Annapo-
lis delivered its greetings in Latin. Its Houston counterpart proclaimed,
"Howdy folks! Hitch your hosses to that Granjero back over yonder and
come get some jerky, beans and yeller bread, whilst I tell you-all Down
East Yankees what a soft time you've had since our paws helped Ole Sam
Houston whip Santa Ana back in 1836."

In compliance with popular wishes, few Old Girls found their way
into the festivities. Harvard in 1936 was still a male bastion, with Radcliffe freshmen each fall handed little red handbooks forbidding them
from appearing hatless in Harvard Square. It wasn't surprising that the
tercentenary's academic family was diverse in all but sex. Harvard's first
tenured female wouldn't join the faculty until 1956, twenty years after
the celebration.

Other alumni, unable to make the long journey, marked the occa-
sion in their own fashion. Fifty members of the Harvard Club of Tokyo
drank a toast to his Imperial Majesty and the President of the United
States. A banker from the house of Mitsui sent a stone lantern, itself three
centuries old, to be placed on permanent exhibit outside Widener Library.
From Oxford's Bodleian Library came Columbus's original 1493 letter to
Arragon's treasurer, describing "the newly discovered islands" of America.
Not to be outdone, the Harvard Club of Shanghai unveiled a marble
dragon for the Tercentenary Theatre, a roofless arena between Widener
Library and Memorial Church. Once the site of pigpens and breweries, it

now was filled with sixteen thousand chairs, each providing the thirty-three-inch seat Harvard's experts judged necessary.[30]

On Wednesday, September 16, in Sanders Theater, James Conant greeted a sea of 554 scholars variously garbed in *bonnets de coeur* from the time of Henry VIII, the green embroidered uniform of the French Academy, tufted caps, and plumed chapeaux. His own faculty looked on from the galleries as the gaunt, solemn-faced president bowed low in receiving homage from his peers. First in line came Professor Saleh Hashem Attia, representing Cairo's Al-Ashar, the oldest university in the world. Second in the procession marched the representative from Bologna. Then, past marble statues of Josiah Quincy and James Otis, came scholars representing Paris, Oxford, and Harvard's parent, Cambridge. For nearly an hour the dons filed by, until the last, Professor Hu Shih of the University of Nanking, reached out to shake Conant's hand. A national radio audience listened in via NBC.

Conant's mind was elsewhere, on the reception for Franklin Roosevelt when he would attend the final convocation a few days later. He had reason to fear public demonstrations, quite apart from the breakfast table snorts of disapproval inspired by Walter Lippmann's pivot away from FDR in the direction of Alfred Landon. Prompted by the activities of Felix Frankfurter in staffing and counseling the New Deal (was Frankfurter *really* a Communist, Mrs. Charles Francis Adams asked Conant at a 1935 dinner party!), Lippmann was quick to warn of those who would turn universities into bureaus in the ministry of propaganda. Hardly more tolerable were those eager to contribute their advice in the formation of national policies. One view struck Lippmann as crudely destructive of academic freedom, the other subtly erosive.[31]

A choice must be made. If private universities wished to remain free of government control, they must renounce any ambition in the field of partisan politics. This did not rule out consultation with professors in their areas of special competence. It did exclude the possibility of academics either running for office or serving as political advisers to those so inclined. "For once they engage themselves that way," concluded Lippmann, "they cease to be disinterested men . . . and having lost their own independence, they impair the independence of the university to which they belong.[32]

Less elevated arguments of statecraft prompted traditional Harvard's antipathy to the new order. Many alumni added to their suspicion of FDR's character flaws a resentment of his treachery to his class. "Perhaps those who have repeatedly told us that educated men should go into politics were on the wrong track," echoed the *Crimson*. "Mr. Roosevelt came of a good family; he had wealth; he passed through the best and most expensive education in the country." The aftermath of such preparation included such grievous boondoggles as the Agricultural Adjustment Administration. The editors wanted it repealed instantly, and a similar fate for Senator Robert Wagner's labor bill, Social Security, and the Neutrality Law. Most of all, however, they thought Roosevelt himself should go. "In the midst of our great Three Hundredth Anniversary Celebration," the *Crimson* concluded, "let the presence of this man serve as a useful antidote to the natural overemphasis on Harvard's successes."[33]

Suspecting political motivations behind FDR's tercentenary visit, Lawrence Lowell, then president of the alumni association, refused to preside over any meeting addressed by his former pupil. After much cajoling, the president emeritus drafted a patronizing letter to the Oval Office. Lowell felt certain that Roosevelt would welcome this opportunity "to divorce yourself from the arduous demands of politics and political speechmaking." What's more, "Do you not think it would be well to limit all speeches that afternoon to about ten minutes?" FDR replied correctly.

But Lowell would not let the matter drop, and soon the President of the United States was blowing off steam to Felix Frankfurter. FDR considered staying in Washington to attend the International Power Conference rather than his alma mater's anniversary. "What is your slant on this one?" he asked Frankfurter, before concluding with an eloquent expression of his own discontent: "Damn."[34]

On the morning of September 18, as Roosevelt's special train drew near and silk-hatted marshals assembled the thousands of alumni in the Tercentenary Theatre, Conant fretted about possible heckling. As the presidential limousine appeared on Massachusetts Avenue, there were scattered cries of "We Want Landon!" Roosevelt, in cutaway and top hat, managed a look of amusement.

Shortly before ten o'clock, loudspeakers sputtered to life with a live broadcast of the bells of Southwark Cathedral, hard by the London neighborhood of the college's first benefactor. The sheriff of Middlesex County stood to call the gathering to order. Governor James Michael Curley brought greetings from the Commonwealth of Massachusetts, and stayed long enough to grate Republican sensibilities. Half a century before, said Curley, Harvard had been honored to host Grover Cleveland. Today, its special guest was Franklin Roosevelt. "Both of them are Democrats, strangely enough." FDR looked stricken.

Next came a Latin oration, Professor Samuel Eliot Morison's historical address, tributes from Paris, Oxford, and Cambridge, and a long, eye-glazing ode performed by John Masefield. A steady drizzle tapered off and then Conant was on his feet, clutching a keynote address which would take the place of his long-postponed inaugural. His words and the manner in which he spoke them would set his seal on the proceedings. More important, they would confound humanists doubtful of the scientific lab's civilizing impulse.

In the elms facing the speaker's stand, cameramen filmed Conant nervously peering at the sky. "Such a gathering as this," he began, "could come together only to commemorate an act of faith." He touched on the college's Puritan roots, and the long winter that nearly killed them in the ground. For despite propitious beginnings, enthusiasm for education had waned as Harvard's founding fathers went to their graves. Her sitting president cited the harsh assessment of a visiting Oxford scholar in 1867: "America has no universities as we understand the term, the institutions so called being merely places for granting titular degrees." In truth, said Conant, the tercentenary commemorated "a hope the fulfillment of which was long delayed—delayed, indeed, until within the lifetime of many now present here this morning. . . . The real past which we salute is but yesterday."

Conant's words did not glitter, but his vision soared, and his audience was at his side as he wondered whether America could evolve a civilization equal to her opportunities. A hundred years earlier, powerful doubts had been expressed over the prospect of democratic cultivation. Those fears had been disproved. But it was only a down payment on success. The towering aspirations of Harvard's founders were even less reflected in other lands, where learning had possessed but a transient splendor.

"A wave of anti-intellectualism is passing round the world," said Conant. "But the anti-intellectualism of the present is in part a protest—a most ungrateful protest, to be sure—against the benefactions of the learned world. It expresses a rebellion against the very triumphs of applied science, against the machines from which we would not be separated and yet towards which we feel a deep resentment."

To bring order out of the chaos of progress—this too, was part of the academic tradition and of Harvard's own mission of service. "Those of us who have faith in human reason believe that in the next hundred years we can build an educational basis for a unified, coherent culture suited to a democratic country in a scientific age, no chauvinistic dogma, but a true national culture fully cognizant of the international character of learning."

To accomplish this, Conant prescribed the study of history, "for he who is ignorant of what occurred before he was born is always a child." Topical controversies must be traced back, far beyond the front pages of daily journals. The essential precondition for such probing was exactly what was missing in many classrooms abroad:

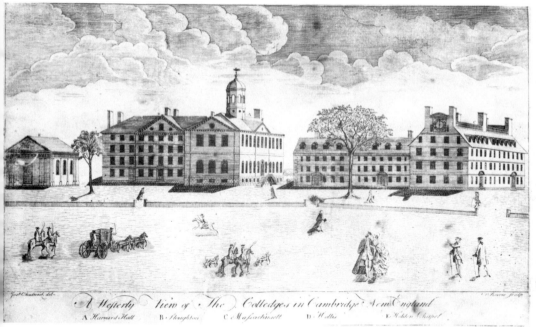

A Westerly View of The Colledges in Cambridge New England
A. Harvard Hall   B. Stoughton   C. Massachusett   D. Hollis   E. Holden Chapel

"Boston town meetings and our Harvard College have set the universe in motion." So John Adams claimed of the provincial academy dependent for its survival on assistance from the state. By 1770, the first college in the colonies was already the object of attack from religious and political traditionalists. Four of the buildings in this engraving by Paul Revere of 18th-century Harvard still stand today.

"We seek to train doers." For forty years, Charles William Eliot presided over Harvard, during which he transformed the old "College of Divines" into an instrument of national purpose. To millions of admirers he was "First Citizen of the Republic," his views solicited on issues from U.S. imperialism to birth control.

THIS PAGE:
"The same old ship on the same old course—only on another tack." Few men differed more radically in style or outlook than Eliot and A. Lawrence Lowell. For most of his presidency, Lowell chafed under the presence and criticism of the legendary figure he called "old man Eliot." Most paradoxical of Harvard's presidents, Lowell broke the stranglehold of exclusive clubs and replaced Eliot's electives with a common competitive framework. But he also drew angry comments for his clumsy efforts to restrict Harvard's Jewish population and maintain a whites-only policy in freshman dorms.

OPPOSITE PAGE:
Top left: "I make no claim to being a proper Bostonian." Forgoing a career in chemistry (and perhaps a Nobel Prize) was just the first of many trials to beset James Bryant Conant. In the years before Pearl Harbor, he urged American participation in the war, debating members of Harvard's Corporation who were convinced of Hitler's ultimate defeat.
Top right: After the war, Conant and Harvard both reached new heights of prestige. At the June 1947 commencement, Secretary of State George Marshall unveiled the rescue plan for Europe that would bear his name.
Bottom: J. Robert Oppenheimer, Conant and Vannevar Bush—architects of the atomic age—who helped usher in a permanent and mutual reliance between higher education and a federal government eager to tap its expertise.

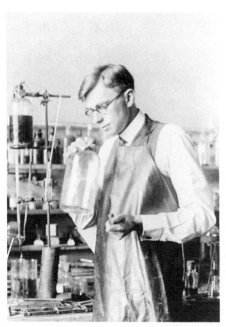

For the most part, the non-political Pusey was content to leave the national spotlight to such Harvard graduates as Felix Frankfurter and John F. Kennedy, shown here at the 1956 commencement.

In the late 1960s, however, neither Harvard nor her president could avoid political involvement. This time the challenge came from the left and from within the university community. By the end of his presidency, an embattled Pusey, shown here with deans Fred Glimp and Franklin Ford, was keeping dossiers on those he called "brickthrowers."

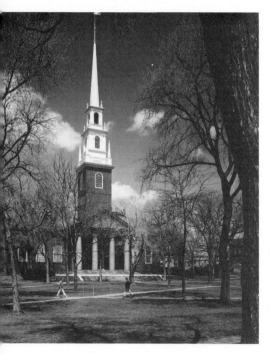

However traditional Pusey might be in his theology—in a 1958 fracas over Jewish weddings in Memorial Church, he declared the University's church a Christian institution—his avant garde taste in architecture changed the face of Harvard. "Incinerator Gothic" asserted critics, while Pusey's pathbreaking department of visual studies was housed in Le Corbusier's Carpenter Center—likened by the irreverent to two copulating pianos.

"The Bust" followed a student occupation of University Hall in April 1969. It led to a student strike and the overhaul of Harvard's governing structure. It also hastened the end of Nathan Pusey's term of office.

I

2

The deans of Arts and Sciences have had an enormous impact on Harvard and her presidents in the twentieth century. (1) Paul Buck, dean of faculty under Conant, and Harvard's only provost. (2) McGeorge Bundy, brilliant, decisive, and often a thorn in the side of his nominal superior, Nathan Pusey. (3) Franklin Ford, installed by Pusey after Bundy left for Washington. Ford was engulfed in the era of student protest and was violently evicted in the University Hall takeover. (4) John Dunlop, Harvard's "Lion Chancellor," who combined political savvy with disarming candor to rebuild a shattered university. (5) Henry Rosovsky fathered Harvard's Core Curriculum and restored a sense of institutional purpose all but lost in the turbulent sixties. (6) A. Michael Spence, young enough to be considered a possible successor to Derek Bok in the president's office.

3

4

5

6

Derek Bok, Harvard's twenty-fifth president, arrives for a deliberately informal inauguration in October 1971. In the years to come, he would dramatically restructure Harvard administration, challenge his own graduate schools to modernize their methods of instruction, and revamp undergraduate education.

Bok, the necessary man, "a wonderfully fine human being" in the words of one associate, "with a totally contemporary mind." While such qualities may be required for managing modern-day Harvard, they add little to the university's legend.

. . . absolute freedom of discussion, absolutely unmolested inquiry. . . . The origin of the Constitution, for example, the
functioning of the three branches of the Federal Government,
the forces of modern capitalism, must be dissected as fearlessly
as the geologist examines the origin of the rocks. On this point
there can be no compromise; we are either afraid of heresy or
we are not. . . . Harvard was founded by dissenters. Before
two generations had passed there was a general dissent from
the first dissent. Heresy has long been in the air. We are proud
of the freedom which has made this possible even when we
most dislike some particular form of heresy we may encounter.

The rebuff to Berlin's ideological masters was clear, as was the president's disapproval of the Massachusetts teachers' oath. More explicit still
was the challenge contained in words once spoken by Charles William
Eliot, now woven into Conant's own peroration. A university, according
to Eliot, was a "society of learned men" gathered around a common objective: "the incessant, quiet, single-minded search after new truth, the
condition for both the material and intellectual progress of the nation and
the race." How, asked Conant, would the American people further that
progress? A hundred years hence, the record would be read. Harvard
would have a prominent place at the bar. "With humility but with hope
we look forward to that moment," he concluded. "May it then be manifest
to all that the universities of this country have led the way to new light,
and may the nation give thanks that Harvard was founded."[35]
     For a moment, there was thoughtful silence, but then a wave of
applause began rolling through the Tercentenary Theatre, swallowing up
New Dealers and the Great White Father's most bitter foes, crashing at
last upon the stage where the stoical orator, in his plain black gown and
undisciplined mortarboard, laid claim to the mantle of earlier Harvard
presidents, giants named Dunster, Leverett, and Eliot. Lawrence Lowell
and Franklin Roosevelt were equally pleased. After three years' apprenticeship, JBC was Harvard's president in more than title.
     When Roosevelt's turn came to speak that afternoon at the alumni
exercises in Sanders Theater, he recalled Harvard's bicentennial in 1836,
Andrew Jackson's tumultuous presidency, and the worries then besetting
many alumni about the nation's future. Then on her 250th anniversary,
Grover Cleveland was in the White House and Harvard graduates were
no less sorely troubled. "Now, on the 300th anniversary," he revealed, "I
am president. . . ." There was no need to complete the sentence amid
the laughter it provoked.
     Those who feared a political harangue were in for a pleasant sur-
prise, as FDR quoted Euripides on the "many shapes of mystery." He

spoke of changed formations and modernized strategies, all assembled under "the old banner of freedom." Many students had left Harvard, he went on, with more inquiring minds and a healthy appetite for national service. It was of the University's essence that her sons had participated in the great dramas of American development. Now more than ever America needed the Eliots, the William Jameses, the Oliver Wendell Holmeses, men "who made their minds swords in the service of American freedom." The College could not be content with a spectator's seat. In FDR's description, it took on an added dimension, an expanded role in public life and, by implication at least, in political controversy.

> Here are to be trained not lawyers and doctors merely, not teachers and businessmen—here are to be trained in the fullest sense—Men [Roosevelt insisted]. Harvard should train men to be citizens in that Athenian sense which compels a man to live his life unceasingly aware that its civic significance is its most abiding, and that the rich individual diversity of the truly civilized life is born only of the wisdom to choose ways to achieve which do not hurt one's neighbors. . . . It is only when we have attained this philosophy that we can "above all find a friend in truth."

Like Conant's, Roosevelt's words said more by implication than by outright assertion. Both men assumed a mandate for change. In their wake, Yale's president delivered a puckish tribute of his own, noting that the downpour outside seemed to be President Conant's way of soaking the rich. Roosevelt beamed his approval. Then Lowell returned to the podium. Conant wished to adjourn the celebration in the manner of Josiah Quincy, he said, who had predicted in 1836 another gathering of Harvard's sons "from every quarter of the land" after a century rolled away. Only Conant proposed to amend Quincy's predictions by replacing the word *land* with *globe.*

Lowell offered an impromptu second.

> If I read history aright, universities have rarely been killed while they were alive. They commit suicide, or die from lack of vigor, and then the adversary comes and buries them. So long as an institution conduces to human welfare, so long as a university gives to youth a strong, active intellectual life, so long as its scholarship does not degenerate into pedantry, nothing can prevent its going on to greater prosperity.

Flanked by Conant and Roosevelt, the aging lion could not doubt that his world—especially his Harvard—was bathed in the light of a setting sun. But he was too ebullient to bemoan what was past. His nature did not cast him for a tragic role. "In spite of the condition of many things in the world," Lowell concluded, "I have confidence in the future. Those of you, therefore, who believe that the world will exist one hundred years hence, and that universities will then be faithful to their great purpose, will say 'Aye.'" A roar of acquiescence shook Sanders. "Contrary-minded, 'No.' It is a unanimous vote."

The University anthem provided a valedictory:

> Let not moss-covered Error moor thee at its side,
> As the world on Truth's current glides by;
> Be the herald of Light, and the bearer of Love,
> Till the stock of the Puritans die.

The crowd dispersed, the President of the United States returning to his battle with Landon, Lowell to his old man's reverie on Marlborough Street, his successor to a newly enhanced position in University Hall. Barely did the strains of self-congratulation die down before Conant found himself embroiled in fresh disputes. Some of these were purely local. Others, however, opened the way to the international arena which would become a second home for Harvard as well as for her combative president.

CHAPTER FOUR

Mr. Conant Goes to War

*The surest way to ruin a university faculty is
to fill it with good men.*

—A. LAWRENCE LOWELL

THE FIRST YEAR of Conant's presidency was also the first in over a century in which Harvard served beer to its undergraduates. It was a small, but telling, example of how old conceits were breaking down. Instead of shaping the rest of the country, in the Thirties Harvard began to acknowledge how much it was shaped by outside forces and changing mores. At sister campuses such as Columbia, the socialism of Norman Thomas was taken up by disillusioned young men. Even in rock-ribbed New England, there were boys who wouldn't dream of attending class without a coat and tie, who nevertheless flocked to discussions of world revolution and the Popular Front. At Harvard's Dunster House, economists Joseph Schumpeter, Seymour Harris, and Paul Samuelson, among others, debated the course of Keynesian pump-priming. F. O. Matthiessen, a Christian Socialist, drew enthusiastic audiences to his lectures on Emerson, Whitman, and others in the pantheon of nineteenth-century liberalism. Members of the Young Communist League preferred to keep their identities private, but *someone* had to deposit their communiqués at the *Crimson*. The paper's editorial staff was increasingly divided, with isolationists on the right, Bob Taft Republicans in the middle, and liberals mildly enthusiastic about the father of the New Deal on the left, fretful over the glacial pace of social reform.

By 1938, the campus Student Union had five hundred members.

Leonard Bernstein staged Marc Blitzstein's opera *The Cradle Will Rock*
for the Union's theater group. The Union subsequently split open, but
even before the Communists withdrew from it, their presence on campus
was hard to miss. With influence disproportionate to their numbers, they
promoted Dos Passos's *U.S.A.* and John Strachey's *The Coming Struggle
for Power.* Granville Hicks's *I Like America* was a must for many undergraduates, its explanation of radical politics as a desire to see Americans
freer, happier, and more comfortable accepted at face value.

Hicks's appointment in 1935 as adviser in Conant's new program in
American Civilization set off a furor, but Conant rejected calls to withdraw it. He was not an appeaser. But his stubborn streak, so appealing in
defense of unpopular causes and their champions, got him into hot water
in the spring of 1937 in his handling of what came to be known as the
Walsh-Sweezy affair. The controversy was heavy with irony as the democratic Conant fell back on Lowell's strictures against faculty control, the
nonpolitical Conant was forced to play politics and also to apologize for
errors of judgment, and the Conant who criticized capitalism in the Faculty Club was labeled by radicals a closet conservative and a tool of Wall
Street.

However complicated it became, the origin of the Walsh-Sweezy affair was not hard to trace. In the early Thirties, in the wake of their battle
against the state teachers' oath, a nucleus of instructors, young members
of the economics department prominent among them, had banded together to form the Cambridge Union of University Teachers. Although
it was an offshoot of the American Federation of Teachers, the CUUT
was no ordinary union. Going on record against any strike action or other
tactics commonly associated with industrial warfare, it vowed to attack
social, racial, or religious discrimination.

Dedicating itself primarily to political agitation rather than economic, the new organization did not, at first, seem to pose any threat to
Harvard's president. Conant enjoyed public debate. Indeed, when in later
years Paul Freund of the law school questioned how a self-respecting
chemist could put aside primary evidence and sign a petition on behalf
of accused spies Julius and Ethel Rosenberg, Conant replied that precisely
because his scientific colleagues labored under such restraints around their
test tubes, they welcomed the freedom to indulge their feelings in the
realm of politics.[1]

The situation of peaceful coexistence with the CUUT changed, however, when Conant attempted to initiate a new system for faculty promotions. In the 1920s, any instructor who performed well might expect to
spend the rest of his academic life in Cambridge. "Publish or perish"

would come later. As long as the national economy remained buoyant and Harvard's income outpaced expenses, the University could continue to employ teachers whose social graces exceeded their scholarly firepower.

With the Depression, however, such luxury vanished. Conant first raised the sensitive subject of promotion within the ranks when Kenneth Murdock was still dean of the faculty. The two men agreed that a crisis was impending. Between 1924 and 1933, income (from tuition and endowment) for the faculty of Arts and Sciences had soared nearly 85 percent, but from 1933 to 1939, the figure would rise by just 3 percent.[2]

In 1933, when Conant was sworn in, it was conceivable for a man to spend his entire Harvard career as an assistant professor, or to retire with the title of instructor emeritus. The junior faculty was clogged with candidates who had overstayed the limit of four one-year appointments. With the tercentenary fund drive encountering resistance, there was an added fiscal imperative to devise some method for pruning back the payroll. Unwilling to permit a permanent, unhappy clot of men to hold temporary appointments while their employment potential elsewhere was fast fading, Conant was also opposed to retaining promising candidates on annual appointments. That would establish two academic castes, of equal age and unequal status.

Conant would count men, not dollars, in drawing up future budgets. Calculating the age and distribution of present tenured professors, he would direct each department to weigh the chances of its most promising faculty members accordingly. As a result, in the spring of 1937 the economics department, which had seven potential candidates for tenure, was instructed to rank the candidates in preferred order. Two would be advanced, while the others would receive their last appointment, which would be for three years, putting them on notice that their career prospects would best be served elsewhere. Among those receiving the five final appointments the department recommended that April were Raymond Walsh and Alan Sweezy, two popular instructors who were virtually alone at Harvard in using Marxist criticism on the existing economic and labor structure in America.

Although three others in the department also received final appointments, the press seized upon Walsh and Sweezy because of their pro-union activities and their criticism of the profit motive. The legislator responsible for the state teachers' oath had previously demanded Walsh's expulsion for what he called "communistic activities." Now both men were indeed on their way out—and journalists were presented with a golden opportunity to gore the Harvard ox and castigate her liberal-sounding, autocratic president.

Conant made things worse by approving a press release describing the decisions as having been made "solely on grounds of teaching and scholarly ability." These words were not only potentially libelous, but they also seemed to confirm the worst allegations of critics on the left, who regarded Walsh and Sweezy as political martyrs. Conant stepped back from his position in a subsequent report to the Overseers, but the damage was done. Overnight, student committees sprang up to register their anger. The president, the *Crimson* fumed, was notorious for preferring star researchers to good classroom instructors. According to this theory, Walsh and Sweezy were less victims of a political witch hunt than of Conant's alleged disregard for undergraduate education.[3]

Next there entered into the case a new and potentially lethal element. For in the president's discomfiture, former dean of the faculty Kenneth Murdock and his followers, a group known as "the Leverett House gang," perceived their chance at revenge. Preserved in Conant's private papers is a letter from the secretary-treasurer of the teachers' union, Lewis Finer, recounting meetings held in the rooms of a law school professor and attended by, among others, David Prall, a left-wing economist, F. O. Matthiessen, and Walsh himself. From these sessions there emerged a plan to create a committee of inquiry which would serve as what Finer called a packed jury. "Dr. Walsh said the results of the inquiry might be such as to lead to your dismissal," the letter reads. "He stated that Kenneth Murdock was enthusiastically for it, and suggested that the upshot might be your replacement by Professor Murdock."[4]

Soon a band of dissidents, including Murdock, Felix Frankfurter, and Arthur Schlesinger Senior, were calling on the president to investigate the circumstances surrounding Walsh's and Sweezy's dismissals and to set in motion a new system of personnel promotion. Conant seized the opportunity to forestall his critics by accepting their demands and appointing them to the subsequent investigation. The Committee of Eight, as the investigating group became known, issued two reports, one on the dismissals and one on employment procedures. The first, which came out early in 1938, exonerated Conant and the economics department of political or personal favoritism in the dismissals, but faulted the president for having imposed his own rules without adequate consultation. The committee concluded that Walsh and Sweezy had been treated badly, and that they ought to receive new appointments without restrictions on their long-range prospects.

Conant rejected the peace offering. The committee overemphasized the degree to which misunderstanding played a part in the department's original decision, he told the press. To accept its recommendation on

Walsh and Sweezy now, he said, would be "both unwise and impractical."
It was not a popular response. When naming the original committee, he
had promised ample time to reopen the dispute should facts warrant it.
Now he seemed to be reneging on that promise.

A Boston paper reprinted a scorching cartoon from the *Lampoon*,
depicting Conant as a bespectacled witch rubbing his crystal ball and
cackling, "Mirror, mirror on the wall, On whom next shall the axe fall?"
As moderate a journal as the *New York Herald Tribune* found grounds
for concern over the loss of two "brilliant classroom teachers." Others
murmured about presidential dictatorship.

But Conant was no Lowell. Times had changed, and no president
was likely to impose his will or deflect opposition by pretending not to
notice it. Just as the seemingly invincible FDR had failed in his plan to
pack the Supreme Court—a scheme Conant publicly criticized—Conant
was vulnerable on both political and administrative grounds when it appeared that left-wing leanings were grounds for dismissal.

In March 1939, the Committee of Eight issued its second report,
nearly two hundred pages of closely reasoned arguments in favor of
standardizing employment procedures, tenure decisions, and salary levels.
At this point, Conant turned to an unlikely source of help. He recalled the
warning imparted by Lawrence Lowell during his final months in office
that no president could, under any circumstances, allow members of his
faculty a say in the appointment process. Conant dug in his heels, refusing
to allow the entire faculty to consider the report as a body. Instead, he
showed it to groups and individuals. Under such circumstances, discussion
was bound to be inhibited. Few, if any, claimed to know with certainty
how Conant would actually implement the report's findings, among which
was a call for abolition of the assistant professor's rank. Early in April,
the president reported almost unanimous support for the committee's
findings. He also expressed agreement with those who urged flexibility in
administering any new rules.

Harvard, it appeared, had devised its own Magna Charta, with a
strong leader vowing ultimate allegiance to the nobles of his faculty.
However, Conant didn't see it that way. Moving swiftly, indeed, precipi-
tately, to carry out his mandate, within days he had fired ten junior faculty
members, including the president of the teachers' union and the widely
admired literary critic Theodore Spencer. This touched off fresh criticism
from both *The Progressive* and Phi Beta Kappa. Undergraduates formed
a "Student Committee to Save Harvard Education." Faculty members met
in resentful knots, with some proposing a broad inquiry into University
governance. Others, planning for the day of Conant's ouster, were busy
laying the groundwork for Murdock's triumphant reentry to University

Hall. It was common knowledge, gossiped bystanders, that Murdock was meeting with fellow plotters in F. O. Matthiessen's rooms.[5]

Amid all the speculation, core issues tended to get lost, above all, Conant's implacable demand that the faculty contain only the world's finest scholars. (Much later, the president would admit that he had erred in firing all ten men at once. In his naive way, he explained to friends, he thought he was behaving gallantly, cutting through uncertainty and ensuring each man a secure base from which to seek employment somewhere else.) Meanwhile, opposition simmered until a white-hot meeting was held in University Hall in October. An even larger crowd turned out for the next session, at which the chairmen of English, Government, and Biology all demanded a reversal of the springtime terminations. This time, debate was cut off only after a Conant ally proposed the writing of a dean's report, a classic dodge which allowed time for behind-the-scenes maneuvering.[6]

Although temporarily safe, Conant was hardly secure. Dean Wallace Dunham, his friend from the business school, was blunt. The president, he said, had lost the confidence of the faculty. The only thing he might do to salvage his job and keep the historic governing structure of Harvard intact would be to swallow his pride, admit having made mistakes in judgment, and appeal to reasonable colleagues to refrain from any action that might harm the University. Conant disliked the advice. Resenting the attacks which had been going on now for two years, he no doubt rued his own part in displaying Harvard's dirty linen before prying eyes. But he agreed to think it over.

When the faculty next met, on November 7, 1939, it had the scent of blood in its nostrils. Hardly had the meeting been called to order than it voted 140 to 6 to do away with Conant's fledgling Faculty Council. Next came a motion to examine the faculty's role in administering the University itself. Tom Perkins was in the audience that stormy afternoon, not far from Ken Murdock, who remained silent in his seat as his allies did their best to destroy Conant's mandate. Finally, Conant rose to his feet. He wished to point out the grave consequences of the motion before the house, he said. He admitted contributing to the current tension through his own errors, and he all but begged the faculty not to punish Harvard for his personal mistakes.

"You could have dropped a pin," Perkins remembered long afterward, "and everyone would have jumped a foot." When the president finished, a member of the government department moved to table the motion. The ground cut out from under them by Conant's unexpected contrition, Murdock's supporters were overwhelmed.[7]

The fight had reached its climax and the presidency had retained its appointive powers. It had been a very close thing, however, and only with the passage of time would Conant's essential wisdom in the affair become apparent. In the end, neither Walsh nor Sweezy lived up to the academic promise glimpsed by their adherents. More important, the crisis over promotions led Conant four years later to the invention of a striking new system for determining tenure, the ad hoc committee.

In autumn 1939, Conant was pledged to adjust his predepression payroll to a postdepression budget. Even as the controversy over internal promotions raged, Harvard was reminded of her precarious place in the national affections. A few weeks earlier, the United States Senate had passed a bill endorsed by labor chieftains such as John L. Lewis and William Green that would restrict the number of government jobs held by Harvard Law School graduates.

But by now, other fights absorbed Conant's energies. In Cambridge, the debate over America's obligation to Europe was growing warmer. Harvard's president reflected the puzzled frustration of his countrymen.

"The western world is in a quandary," Conant told the first chapel service of the school year. "The forces of violence must be beaten by superior violence and yet without engendering bitterness or hate. Reason must triumph over unreason without being converted in its hour of victory to the very thing it would destroy." America, he warned, might well be the final citadel guarding against such horrors.[8]

Most of the youths he addressed were determined to keep it that way. Too much that was pleasant vied for their attention with the European fracas in those last years before America entered the war. Swing had intruded its syncopated rhythms into Cambridge. The music department undertook a scholarly comparison of Tommy Dorsey and Guy Lombardo. Men wandering the halls of Widener caught the exuberant strains of "You Must Have Been a Beautiful Baby" and "Indian Boogie-Woogie." Outside, political activists carried placards denouncing the Corporation's denial of Harvard Hall to Earl Browder, general secretary of the American Communist party, on the grounds that Browder was under indictment for passport fraud.[9]

Spencer Klaw, the *Crimson*'s new editor, was typical of the undergraduate whose adventurous social life coexisted with a pained social conscience. In an after-hours Boston bar when hookers discovered Klaw's Harvard connection, the young women invariably would ask, "Do you know Jack Kennedy and Torby MacDonald?"[10]

In Eliot House, Franklin Roosevelt's godson would entertain the sons of Robert Taft and Joseph P. Kennedy for bull sessions on isolationism.

For the most part, however, student interest in the war was light-hearted. In the fall of 1938, after the local city council had proposed making Harvard a separate municipality, a loudspeaker emerged from Lowell House's noble façade with the rebellious call: "United we stand, divided we become Czechoslovakia!" The *Lampoon* solemnly demanded a plebiscite for all minorities in Cambridge, along with a buffer state between the University and the surrounding working class community.

A letterwriter in the *Alumni Bulletin* complained about an exhibit of war posters at Widener that it was both "vulgar and emotional" to mount such a display while most of the civilized world held its breath. Student disengagement reached its zenith when, on March 3, 1939, a freshman named Lothrop Withington Junior accepted a classmate's dare and made the nation's oldest university the site of the first public display of goldfish swallowing, which earned the undying enmity of the Animal Rescue League, and provoked angry legislation in the Massachusetts state senate.

When Conant and his Corporation that same month endorsed twenty scholarships for German refugee students, and the ensuing fund drive ran up against a buzzsaw of criticism, an open book protesting Nazi persecution and soliciting undergraduate gifts "to enable German students to live in a free country and to study at a friendly university" was soon filled with more than 150 signatures from Leverett House, led by that of Kenneth Murdock. Such gestures were few amid the youthful resistance to the idea of war.

"We are frankly determined to have peace at any price. We refuse to fight another balance of power war," the *Crimson* thundered. Also expressing antiwar sentiment were the American Independent League, the Harvard Anti-War Committee, the Harvard Foreign Relations Club, and the Pacifist League.

In September 1939, returning students found all sorts of applecarts upset. The first black man to reside in Lawrence Lowell's inner sanctum unwrapped his furniture in Adams House. A student was arrested in October for being the ringlaeder of a group distributing five thousand pamphlets justifying the Hitler-Stalin Pact to the men of Lowell and Dunster. There were five separate meetings in the Yard on November 11, Armistice Day, one of which listened to an impassioned denunciation of the country's "two-faced stand" on Europe's impulse for suicide, while other undergraduates distributed antiwar leaflets at a veterans' march on Boston Common.

In the nation's capital, tempers flared over Roosevelt's call for an amended Neutrality Act, with legislators inundated by mail and editors sharply divided over any relaxation of the arms embargo then in effect.

"There's not going to be any war this year," Idaho's William Borah informed the president. "All this hysteria is manufactured and artificial." J. P. Morgan, in Switzerland grouse hunting, complained that a second European war might interrupt the hunt. Persuaded that the Allies would defeat Hitler, Herbert Hoover judged the dictator's air superiority insignificant to the war's outcome.

From Cambridge, an agitated Conant wrote Alfred Landon, FDR's 1936 opponent and a thoughtful critic of the country's subsequent drift toward battle, that the survival of free institutions was in danger. After twenty years of indoctrination, Americans had accepted their isolation from Europe as permanent, Conant said. "Should we not examine without fear the advantages and disadvantages from our own selfish point of view of every aspect of our foreign policy? Must we not assume that a democracy can make a rational choice on matters of war and peace? If not, war has already defeated democracy on this continent."

In the June 1939 issue of *Foreign Affairs*, Lawrence Lowell urged his countrymen to declare, publicly and without delay, which islands in the Atlantic and Pacific were so essential to the national welfare as to warrant their armed defense. Lowell said he personally would extend the Monroe Doctrine from Guadaloupe to the Azores. But Conant was not prepared for such diplomatic belligerence; it took the Nazi offensive against France and the Low Countries to wrench him from his position of watchful waiting. On the night of May 9, 1940, Conant attended a dinner at which all agreed that when French and German armies finally collided, France's superiority of arms would be made manifest. The next morning there was news of a massive Nazi assault. Just the previous Sunday at his regular tea, Conant had listened to denunciations of British stupidity in Norway's unsuccessful defense. Now, with German invaders advancing on all fronts, the Allied cause was threatened.[11]

Conant encountered disunity in his own ranks over the issue of U.S. intervention in the European conflict, most notably from William Claflin, a Boston broker recently installed as Harvard's treasurer. Claflin reveled in stories of his armed defense of the Hub during the 1919 police strike, and the laziness of the peons on his Cuban sugar plantation. Fearful that Conant might soon call for outright U.S. intervention, Claflin advised him to be realistic. "Hitler's going to win, let's be friends with him," was the way Conant recorded the counsel in his diary. It was counsel that was repeated often in the weeks ahead by isolationist students and hesitant alumni. Claflin's pessimism was a minority view, however, and one which Conant in any event was inclined to dismiss.[12]

At an alumni meeting in New York, Conant was pressured in the other direction by another Corporation member, the old Plattsburgher Grenville Clark. Supported by Clark Eichelberger of the League of Nations Association, another Harvard graduate, "Grenny" urged Conant to join a new pressure group, The Committee to Defend America by Aiding the Allies, whose guiding light was William Allen White, crusading editor of the *Emporia Gazette*. Conant accepted.

Going further, Conant also agreed to address a national radio audience. "I shall mince no words," he began. "I believe the United States should take every action possible to ensure the defeat of Hitler." He called for an immediate shipment of U.S. planes and other war materiel to the beleaguered Allies, stricter controls over imports that might leak to Germany's benefit, and a repeal of all laws preventing U.S. citizens from volunteering to serve in foreign armies. Near the close of his talk, Conant declared war of his own, against all those content to wallow in ignorant apathy. The fight was veering toward America's own shores, he said.

"Can we live as a free, peaceful, relatively unarmed people in a world dominated by the totalitarian states? Specifically, can we look with indifference as a nation (as a nation, mind you, not as individuals) on the possible subjugation of England by a Nazi state? If your answer is yes, then my words are in vain. If your answer is no, I urge you as a citizen to act." A wave of response washed over Massachusetts Hall. "Much abuse from illiterates," Conant noted in his diary.[13]

At a subsequent Corporation meeting, Charlie Coolidge asked if the president planned to endorse Roosevelt for a third term. No, Conant told him; why even make such an inquiry? "Well," answered Coolidge, "you do so many unexpected things!"[14]

Impelling him forward in his unpredictability were student discussions filled with anti-British feeling. At one tea, as attacks on the Empire rained, he invited a young English guest to express his opinion. To his astonishment, the visitor announced that he would rather live under Adolf Hitler than Neville Chamberlain. Swallowing a gasp, Conant wondered how he came by such views. At the London School of Economics, the youth replied. For Conant, this was the closest thing imaginable to rank heresy. Yet he kept his temper, and his equilibrium. Before a Jewish audience of war veterans, he defended the younger generation for its refusal to rubber-stamp war fever while making plain his own distaste for their views.[15]

When the *Christian Science Monitor* polled the Harvard student body, it discovered that 91 percent were unwilling to go to war for the Allied cause; 62 percent opposed extending aid because it might bring the fighting closer to home. The American Independent League claimed over 650 adherents, the Anti-War Committee a hundred more. Forty undergraduates acknowledged belonging to the Young Communist League.[16]

On May 7, 1940, the *Crimson* published an impassioned critique of those who had so readily answered the war call a quarter-century before. A rejoinder was signed by thirty-four members of the Class of 1917. Having experienced war first hand, the alumni wrote, they yet believed that should it come, "it is a man's part to help finish it. . . . Knowing it as Harvard men, we believe it is particularly the honor and privilege of Harvard to be foremost in that leadership."

On June 20, 1940, Secretary of State Cordell Hull appeared in Harvard Yard to accept an honorary degree and to warn against what he called "the massed forces of lust for tyrannical power." "Our American history has not been achieved in isolation from the rest of mankind," said Hull. "There is no more dangerous folly than to think its achievements can be preserved in isolation."

By now, Harvard's president had himself become a convert to Hull's uncompromising position, and was ready to act. Earlier that same week, he had wired Roosevelt his personal support, and urged William Allen White's Committee to Defend America by Aiding the Allies to follow up on the president's controversial declaration in a Charlottesville, Virginia, speech that the United States would materially aid "the opponents of force." He joined White's policy committee, and agreed to sit informally with more militant interventionists convening top-secret strategy sessions in New York City, sometimes at the local Harvard Club, who dubbed themselves the Century Club.

More significantly, on June 14, Conant had accepted an invitation from his friend Vannevar Bush, president of the Carnegie Institution, to help him establish a scientific research committee that would work with the White House to prepare America's defense, and lay the tactical groundwork for massive assistance to the British, now fighting alone after the fall of Paris. In doing so, Conant took a momentous step, with implications for Harvard and all other American universities. Personally, his action guaranteed that he would be an integral player in the dramas leading to the first atomic bomb, the creation of synthetic rubber, and a host of other scientific developments. From the standpoint of the University, Conant's acceptance ignited a storm of criticism, usually whispered, occasionally shouted, about frequent furloughs from Cambridge, and the president's seeming indifference to his academic duties. It moved Conant to decentralize his own administration more than ever, to rely on what he called his heavy deans and especially the man he would make Harvard's first and only provost a year later, historian Paul Buck.

The impact of Conant's decision ranged far beyond the Yard. The National Defense Research Committee (NDRC), which Bush's committee became, was to operate in unprecedented fashion. Unlike the scientific community's efforts in World War I, when chemists and physicists had come together in government labs, this time the government would contract out its orders to the universities themselves, as well as to research institutes and industrial laboratories. Almost no one suspected it at the time, Conant included, but the NDRC would license the marriage of bureaucrat and professor that would so color postwar education.

There was no time to ruminate on such possibilities. With Nazi armies pressing, Conant hurried to the capital to contact other chemists, consider questions of legality (it was technically against the law to assist any other nation's war effort), devise security arrangements, and develop liaison with the British. Funds were diverted from the Carnegie Corporation and his own Committee on Scientific Aids to Learning. Midwestern scientists, true to the region's isolationist sentiments, rebuffed his overtures. Conant chafed under the necessity of describing his work as defensive, knowing it was preparation for armed conflict.

Late in June 1940, he had a pessimistic conversation with Princeton's Harold Dodds. Dodds predicted that the next five years would be a prelude to a dismal future. Conant responded more hopefully that he'd be glad to check back with his colleague in 1950. In his diary he began the first of many references to his Pax Americana, even as he conducted a telephone negotiation with Grenville Clark over a new and potentially explosive bill to create the first peacetime draft in American history. A pro-war speaker was booed at Harvard's Class Day exercises, and loud protests greeted the lecture appointment of a former BBC director. Despite this, Conant stepped up the pace of his involvement. He devised a plan to dispatch to the British a special unit of personnel and supplies from his faculties of medicine and public health. Turning down columnist Joe Alsop's appeal to go on radio for the committee to aid British refugee children, Conant told Alsop to have his cousin Eleanor Roosevelt raise the subject with her husband instead. "Have talked enough!" he declared to his diary.[17]

More and more now, Conant was drawn into the political arena, devising plans to persuade the public to back Clark's draft, pretending to be away from Cambridge while actually conferring with medical experts on how to fight the spread of disease in bombed-out Britain. In Washington, he discussed a "fundamental physico-chemical study of high explosives" (the atom bomb in miniature), saw Undersecretary of State Sumner Welles, and picked up rumors of an impending deal to swap fifty overage U.S. destroyers for military bases in British possessions. In New York, he raised $10,000 from Harvard Club members to establish a British field hospital, and spoke to friends about a new plan to have the business school train reserve officers. "Great news," Conant proclaimed on September 4 when the destroyer deal became official, and attached his name to a public round robin in its support.

Still convinced of Germany's impending triumph, Bill Claflin was as eager as ever to get on with the Nazis. It was a viewpoint Conant dismissed with a snort as typical of "the business appeasement group."[18] On September 24, 1940, addressing the first college chapel of the new school year, the president went further than ever before in refuting such beliefs.

> What is the worst possibility which confronts us—war? [he asked.] So many people think, but I venture to disagree. War is not the worst possibility we face; the worst is the complete triumph of totalitarianism. Such a triumph might conceivably include this republic among the victims as a result of military reversals. Or we might become in essence a dependent state through a policy of appeasement under the coercion of a Nazi system which controlled the seas.[19]

At a meeting of New England college presidents a few days later, most expected the country to be at war in ninety days. (Conant gauged the odds on American involvement at four to one.) Back home, he asked for and was denied Corporation permission to move from Lowell's mansion to a smaller residence; Bill Chaflin led the opposition. The sting of defeat was eased soon enough: October 16 marked the first day of registration for the new draft. In Widener Library and at the medical school, faculty volunteers signed up undergraduates. Ralph Barton Perry of the philosophy department drew six hundred supporters to his pro-Ally American Defense League. Faculty and alumni wives met on three mornings to prepare 37,000 surgical dressings for Conant's British hospital. Samuel Eliot Morison, Crane Brinton, John Fairbank, and Sidney Fay were among the Harvard professors who argued the Allied cause in the newspaper columns of America.[20]

"To all intents and purposes we are already in the war," wrote William L. Langer that fall. "It therefore behooves us to prepare to the limit." Members of Government, Philosophy, and the Harvard Observatory matched Langer's outspokenness, but on the other side of the issue. They insisted that however the American people might lament Britain's defeat, they could not easily be frightened into joining what was, to them, a cynical conflict over the balance of European power.

In November, Roosevelt was reelected (true to the forecast of the *Crimson's* intrepid elections analyst, who awarded FDR all but Maine, Vermont, and the business school). Conant had made up his mind to support the president in the voting booth, though he had told no one, including his wife, so that he might honestly preserve his stance of public neutrality.[21] But later that month, he said on the radio that Americans "would be rightly condemned by posterity if we needlessly become involved in war and squander life and treasure. But we shall be yet more guilty in the eyes of our descendants if we fail to preserve our heritage of freedom—if we fail because of timidity or lack of farsighted resolution."

With this, the dam burst on student opposition. Conant's office was picketed, its occupant lampooned as a warmonger in a halftime skit at the Harvard-Yale game. The *Crimson* excoriated him ("the best we can hope for is a stalemate victory"), and the object of its assault noted tersely, "No fan mail," in the wake of his latest broadside.[22]

Many honestly differed with Conant, or held him up to censure for involving the University in his private crusading. Even White's Committee to Defend America by Aiding the Allies found Conant too militant. Yet he was not deserted. The president of the Alumni Association called a special meeting on December 7, 1940, where a battery of speakers described the dangers to the country and implored participants to join in combating what Conant called "an emergency of unprecedented scope."

Gradually, he began to make converts. Even the *Crimson,* late in October 1940, had shifted to a less unbending line. The Student Union fragmented, with liberal elements walking out and left-wing militants at least temporarily isolated. And when ROTC applications were opened, 250 men in one class sought the fewer than 200 positions.

In early December, Conant entreated Roosevelt to step up his warnings about Britain's peril; that same day FDR presented the idea of Lend-Lease in a press conference. Along with Wendell Willkie and Fiorello LaGuardia, Conant visited Capitol Hill to persuade Congress to endorse Roosevelt's idea of shipping vast amounts of war materiel to the impoverished Churchill government. But FDR had more ambitious plans in mind for the head of his alma mater. At the White House, he proposed to Conant a highly sensitive mission to Britain. His new ambassador, John Winant, would get on well with the opposition Labor Party, said Roosevelt, which he expected to succeed Churchill after the war. Averell Harriman would handle Lend-Lease negotiations with the London government. But he needed Conant to coordinate the scientific communities on both sides of the Atlantic. Conant agreed on the spot.

On February 3, 1941, he broke the news of his impending departure to the Corporation. "Silence!" he jotted in his diary afterward. "Slight approval."[23]

Conant's involvement set a pattern for the rest of his presidency. From now on, he would be caught up in bigger issues than university governance. He might well take as a compliment what *Scribner's Magazine* intended to be an insult, when it inducted him into its Internationalist Hall of Fame. Nor did he blink when isolationist Senator Burton Wheeler attacked him as one of those "too old to go into the front line trenches," yet anxious to provoke a war that younger men would have to fight. From 1941 on, Conant occupied a prominent place near the center of great events, scientific, diplomatic, and political. And his University, fittingly, was transformed into an arsenal of strategic ideas and deadly weapons.

Whenever I feel depressed about the quality of human beings, I recall with emotion the picture of England under fire.
        —JAMES BRYANT CONANT

IN THE SPRING of 1941, Harvard undergraduates were waging a gentlemanly but intense campaign of their own. At one alumni meeting, anti-war students agreed to remove their buttons proclaiming "No Wilson Promises" rather than disturb the social equilibrium. A delegation presented the legendary anglophile Roger Merriman of Eliot House with a toy tank; the professor displayed it with pride on his mantel. Eliot Perkins encountered four seniors in cap and gown, picketing an entrance to the Yard. Recognizing them as students from Lowell House, the master doffed his hat, and the protesters responded with a stiff little gesture—presenting arms as it were, with their placards. At the Faculty Club, Conant was greeted with an inflammatory poster announcing the latest meeting of isolationist forces. "Now that's the kind of thing I like to see," he declared with a fixed smile.[24]

In fact, he had encountered much stronger opposition during his visit to Britain, where fiercely patriotic Cockneys drowned out pacifist cliques in academia. The trip had been wrapped in more than the usual quota of official secrecy. Even the amateur sleuths at the *Crimson* had been unable to uncover the mystery surrounding Conant's February 15 departure. After arriving in Lisbon, Roosevelt's emissary was forced to wait for one of the irregularly scheduled direct flights that were the only way into besieged London. There, he was met by Brenden Bracken, Churchill's parliamentary secretary and his most devoted admirer throughout the wilderness years leading up to the Nazi attack in the fall of 1939.

Within a few days, Conant was sitting in the basement of Number 10 Downing Street, where Churchill was grumpily fretting over the fate of Lend-Lease. "This bill has to pass," he told his guests, before wondering aloud if President Roosevelt might be forced to resign his office were it to fail. "We don't want your men," he told Conant, repeating words spoken in public. "Give us the tools and we shall finish the job."

Temporarily infected by the gloom, Conant wired home his own doubts about the bill's chances (misplaced, as events would demonstrate). Then he launched a personal blitzkreig, lunching with Bill Donovan of the OSS and taking tea with King George VI, conferring with fellow chemists and dining at Claridge's while German bombs fell a few blocks away. The Blitz, he wrote his wife, reminded him of a cross "between fireworks at the Braves' field heard from Quincy Street and a thunderstorm in the 'Massif Central.' . . . I need more practice to be able to tell a bomb from a gun."[25]

Conant was soon able to report progress on the NDRC front ("It's a comfort to be able to do something besides talk to Senators!"). He was escorted through an underground radar center, and greeted with enthusiastic applause at the country's most ancient seats of learning. "Seeing you again," one old friend informed Conant, "is almost as good as peace!" At Cambridge, a fellow scientist handed him a slip of paper with a passage from the 127th Psalm written on it:

> As arrows are in the hand of a mighty man,
> So are the children of his youth.
> Happy is the man that hath his quiver full of them:
> He shall not be ashamed
> When he speaks with the enemies in the gate.

Deeply moved, Conant added a personal postscript: "Cambridge is now speaking surely with the enemy at the gates if not in the gate, and her children are speaking in the clouds with bursts of deadly fire, assisted by many keen minds on the ground directing them as if by magic."[26] The magic was radar, a powerful instrument of defense known to almost no one outside scientific circles, Franklin Roosevelt included—an ignorance Conant was quick to correct on his return to America.

Invited for a second visit with Churchill, this time at his country home, Chequers, Conant listened attentively as the prime minister discoursed on the American Civil War. Turning to Reconstruction, the PM remembered that men equipped to win wars can never make a suitable peace. He also announced that only wars made history, a cue for everyone to join in general denunciation of those who claimed to the contrary that war never settled anything. Afterward, in his car en route to London, Conant heard a British general predict a possible German invasion, while dismissing its chances of success. "These people won't surrender," he said. "They may all be killed, but they won't surrender." It was the same conclusion Conant had reached.

Before leaving for home on April 12, he managed a quick visit to his Harvard field hospital near Salisbury, and a final call at Downing Street. British forces had just been overwhelmed in Greece, and the prime minister was closeted with top military advisors. However, Churchill insisted on seeing Conant in the cabinet room. His words matched the twilight mood of those filing out. "Here we are, standing alone," he told Conant. "What is going to happen?"[27]

At such a time, despair and uncertainty were natural allies. Conant rejected both. At a special Overseers meeting two weeks later in colonial Williamsburg, there was a luncheon in Raleigh Tavern, complete with talk of the Pilgrims and Thomas Jefferson. In the restored House of Burgesses, Conant presented the College of William and Mary with a 1726 copy of its original charter, for over two centuries locked away in a Cambridge archive. Yet for him, like the rest in attendance, embattled present-day England took precedence over George III's distant oppression. To those asking how Britain would win the war the president replied that no one knew exactly. When a friend of Herbert Hoover's suggested that America might best aid the battered nation by confining her assistance to sending supplies, Conant delivered a sharp rebuke. Hitler, he said, would undoubtedly declare war on the United States if he believed she had embarked on such a course. What's more, these supplies must somehow be convoyed to the island kingdom, an undertaking he felt would be impossible without the full support of the American navy. At a meeting with Roosevelt a few days later, the two men swapped stories about prominent figures, Overseers included, whose sympathy for Britain was outweighed by their neutralist sentiments.[28]

Racking his brain for new ways to prop up the faltering British, Conant hit on a fresh expedient. In his earlier visit to radar facilities not far from London, he had learned there was a shortage of both repairmen and more sophisticated engineers with which to supervise radar operations. Why not recruit the latter back home? The idea was promptly reported to FDR, who just as promptly commissioned a corps of reserve officers grounded in physics for overseas assignment as official observers. Secretary of War Henry Stimson asked Conant to expand his scheme to include help for the British Air Force—and more than two thousand men had crossed the Atlantic by the time the Japanese bombed Pearl Harbor, exploding any need for circumspection.

Living with her husband, Patty Conant liked to say, was like living with a jet-propelled missile. After Hitler's invasion of Poland in September 1939, the pace became more frenetic than ever. Somehow, he found time for the NDRC, Harvard affairs, and, commencing in the spring, a new organization, the Office of Scientific Research and Development (OSRD). Chaired by Vannevar Bush, buried deep within the executive office of the president, and intended to augment the continuing NDRC, the OSRD was the offshoot of a top-secret approach to Roosevelt in the fall of 1939, made by Albert Einstein and other physicists who alerted the president to the vast untapped potential of uranium fission. Research had been going on as Conant toured the war zone. Out of an atom smasher at the University of California in 1940, Berkeley scientists had manufactured element no. 94, plutonium.

Conant's initial reaction to all this was skeptical. At lunch with a British counterpart, he openly questioned the value of devoting so many man-hours to a project whose short-range consequences were at best hazy. But he had overlooked the possibility of a bomb, a bomb of tremendous destructive force. Conant asked how such an instrument could be constructed. "By first separating uranium 235," he was told, "and then arranging for two portions of this element to be brought together suddenly so that the resulting mass would spontaneously undergo a self-sustaining reaction."[29]

Conant was persuaded. More important, he was eager to persuade others. Arguing for a crash military program against those who spoke of uranium's revolutionary industrial possibilities, his New England hardheadedness was again displayed in a *New York Times* interview published late in July 1941. A journalist found Conant curled up in his Massachusetts Hall office, long legs knotted, jawbone hidden by his hand as he spoke of the present conflict and America's pending choice. When questioned about the devastation already caused by opposing armies and air forces, Conant raised his eyebrows and responded that civilian casualties were, on the contrary, less frightful than anyone might have forecast at the war's outset. As for ruined property, he merely shrugged his shoulders.

Science had yet to be fully utilized, he went on; Napoleon had made greater use of it than Hitler had to date. He credited Britain's triumph over the Nazi Luftwaffe to technical superiority, puncturing the myth of German supremacy in numbers. He dismissed the fears of those who agreed with Hoover and Lindbergh that the coming of war might permanently restrict America's freedom. "To assume that under the stress of war we shall destroy our form of government or plunge our land into social chaos is to deny the virility of our birthright," he declared.[30]

Outside Conant's window, student attitudes were evolving. The *Crimson* was about to enter the interventionist camp. There were fewer jokes about the paper's "blitzkrieg" up the Charles River "to find a Southwest passage to Wellesley." Two-thirds of those answering an *Alumni Bulletin* poll agreed that professors should take sides on controversial issues of the day. The Nazi invasion of Russia that June crystallized interventionist sentiment, while demoralizing those who had called this merely the latest in an unending series of European border-crossings.

In the Yard, it was not unusual to encounter opposing picket lines for and against U.S. involvement in the war, or rival meetings called to denounce Old World imperialism or to assist Bundles for Britain. In a small office tucked away beneath a Widener Library staircase, George Sarton, a Belgian refugee, was reconstructing from memory a manuscript it had taken him five years to write, that was lost when the advance of Nazi forces led him to bury it in his garden. His hope of returning to retrieve the pages dashed, Sarton toiled away on its replacement.

Conant was spending much of his time in Washington now, warning Stimson's staff of the potential for disaster should the Nazis be the first to unravel the atomic secret. Late in November 1941, after Vannevar Bush had formally urged Roosevelt to proceed with the bomb's construction, Conant became intermediary between Bush and a group of physicists headed by Arthur Compton of the University of Chicago. On a subsequent visit to the White House, Bush and Conant came away with a presidential IOU in the amount of $100,000,000, and signed "O.K., FDR." Leslie Groves, the Manhattan Project's supervising general, would use the document later to convince top-level skeptics that the bomb was indeed a presidential priority.

Conant was in the capital on the eve of Pearl Harbor but hurried back to Cambridge to preside over a mass meeting in Sanders Theater on the evening of December 8.

> Now the days of uncertainty and ambiguity are past [he told his audience]. We can call things by their proper names. Defense work is war work and takes precedence over every other consideration. . . . At the moment the path of duty for many

of you is still uncertain. On the one hand, it is clearly senseless to rush around the Yard engaging in hysterical manifestations of war excitement. On the other hand, no one of you will be unconscious of the fact that he may soon be called upon to serve. For the immediate present the task before us is to carry on as usual. The call from Washington will be coming soon, undoubtedly. In the meantime, you gentlemen of the student body may well stand by for further orders—stand by, but on the alert.[31]

Having been on the alert for over two years, Conant himself was well prepared for whatever might befall his country and college. Out of the war into which both were now plunged would come a new self-image for each, and a set of priorities close to the president's heart.

> *The best thing that ever happened to Harvard*
> *was World War II.*
> —PROFESSOR GEORGE GOETHALS

WITH AMERICA'S formal entry into the war, even Harvard managed to put an end to factions. Twelve months earlier, when Roosevelt's plan to swap aging destroyers for rights to British bases in the Western Hemisphere had been announced, antiwar undergraduates had demonstrated outside the classroom of William Yandell Elliott, an outspoken advocate of aid to the Allies. "Send 50 overage Professors to England," their placards read. Now students flocked to war courses, while Latin, Greek, and philosophy were neglected. Three thousand officer candidates took possession of the law school, along with others training to serve as quartermasters, chaplains, engineers, Navy supply men, and Air Force statisticians. Sleeping in double-decker bunks in overcrowded dormitories, Harvard's newest classes dined in shifts at the Union and awaited the day when a vast new mess hall might rise over the tennis courts on Soldier's Field.[32]

War interrupted many careers but smiled on others. B. F. Skinner's theory of operant conditioning, descended from Pavlov's work with dogs, took on geopolitical significance. Having taught his flock of pigeons to pick out tunes on a player piano, Skinner now instructed them in missile guidance. Norman Mailer left the *Harvard Advocate* for the South Pacific and found the great American novel. Vladimir Nabokov became a research fellow in entomology, while an unknown playwright named Tennessee Williams worked feverishly to complete the draft of his "memory play" in the room of a legal student he'd met while on a Provincetown holiday. *The Glass Menagerie* opened in New York before the end of 1944, making Williams famous and winning for Harvard a footnote in theater history.

Seven weeks after Pearl Harbor, a new course catalog announced year-round instruction. Fresh recruits were taught in accelerated programs to build airports and to speak the language of the country's sudden ally, the Soviet Union. Whatever hardships the conflict might impose, for Conant it brought realization of at least one long-deferred hope: release from Lowell's presidential mansion, which he cheerfully presented to the Navy.

Equally pleased to be free of crystal chandeliers and formal dinner parties, Patty Conant became head of a Women's Auxiliary and hostess to such visiting luminaries as Winston Churchill. On a September 1943 visit, Churchill discussed the atomic research effort with Conant, and denigrated his own biography of Marlborough ("There is too much detail in it," he remarked. "It is static. . . . I should like to do it over in one volume—take three months off to do it"). Following a triumphant address in which the unabashed imperialist predicted that all future empires would be empires of the mind, Churchill reviewed Harvard's cadets in training, and accepted an honorary degree. Then the great man returned to Dana-Palmer House for an assessment. "How did I do, mother?" he asked his wife.[33]

While Patty Conant made careful notes of such historical footnotes, her husband made history of his own. Taking a cut in his $23,000 salary, Conant was soon spending several days a week in a four-room apartment at Washington's Dumbarton Oaks. The gift to Harvard of a onetime U.S. ambassador to Argentina, Dumbarton was headquarters for an intense scientific effort to beat the Nazis to the atomic secret and to cut East Asia's stranglehold of the vital rubber supply.

Before the war, Conant had been escorted around the campus of a nearby university by a dean whose superior was known for his exacting attention to detail. Spotting a bare patch of earth where grass ought to have been growing, the dean grew apprehensive. If his president saw that, he told Conant, there would be hell to pay. Conant sympathized with his plight. "I couldn't even afford to get into housekeeping details if I wanted," he explained. "I just have time to look after dollars and the professors."[34]

After Pearl Harbor, the central functions of running the University were largely entrusted to Treasurer Bill Claflin, Senior Corporation Fellow Charles Coolidge, and above all to a promising historian of American Reconstruction named Paul Buck. Buck's title of provost only hinted at the alter ego relationship he enjoyed with Conant, whom he would serve as a loyal second-in-command for a full decade. Short and balding, he reminded Cambridge observers of Sancho Panza to Conant's Don Quixote. His memory is cherished by many, including the colleague who forty years later recalled "that little man, shifting foot to foot, misusing the English language, yet holding the faculty in the hollow of his hand." It was Buck who would deliver a brisk greeting to the incoming Class of 1946: "You must be trained to win the victory. You must be prepared to live in the postwar period, and both of these tremendous tasks must be achieved in a relatively short time. There can be no wastage, no misspent effort, and no luxuries. We have work to do and we must do it well and quickly. More than our own individual destinies are involved."[35]

Conant had said as much at the June 1942 commencement, whose national importance was highlighted by the appearance of Secretary of War Henry Stimson and Navy Secretary Frank Knox. The flags of the United Nations, as the Allies were now called, clustered around Sever Quadrangle on the resplendent spring afternoon, and all talk of "Mr. Conant's war" gave way to demonstrations of pride. "To speed the day when the Axis Powers surrender without conditions," vowed the president, "we now dedicate the resources of this ancient society of scholars; to speed the day when we can walk once more in the sunlight of human liberty, we stand ready to make whatever sacrifice may be required."[36]

For Conant, sacrifice included a quarter-million miles spent on swaying railroad cars between Cambridge and Washington. "I could be perfectly happy with a permanent Pullman ticket," he joked. But there was nothing funny about his mounting responsibilities as chairman of the NDRC, whose two-billion-dollar budget had to be stretched to permit the development of radar, chemical warfare, and nuclear fission. He was now convinced that fission would work, but first, the theory must be tested. Should the project, soon to bear the name Manhattan, be carried out according to usual industrial practice—that is, in a small pilot plant or series of plants? Or should the scientists go for broke, building enormous facilities based on little more than the laboratory research at hand? Conant decided on the second course and, along with others, he took Roosevelt with him.

Other Harvard scientists—and some precocious undergraduates—followed their president into the war effort. Chief among them were Conant's old friend George Kistiakowsky, physicist Norman Ramsay, who directed the top-secret Delivery Group, Kenneth Bainbridge, who pressed the button setting off the world's first atomic explosion, Donald Hornig, who designed detonating devices, and most crucially, a student of Hindu philosophy and left-wing politics named J. Robert Oppenheimer. Oppenheimer and Conant shared a common impatience to complete the bomb by May 1, 1945. Both men knew they were in a race with scientists in Germany and Japan. But Conant couldn't devote himself exclusively to that task. He had also signed on with Bernard Baruch's crash campaign to speed production of synthetic rubber, to replace the million tons a year lost because of the Japanese occupation of the East Indies.[37]

The American economy was struggling to put itself on a war footing overnight. Top priority was awarded indiscriminately to destroyers and anti-aircraft guns, $100 billion worth of military orders in all. It was soon obvious to a handful of scientists assembled to test and perfect a new weapons system on the scale of an atomic bomb, that only the military could provide an adequate shield and supply line. In September 1942, General Leslie R. Groves, a forty-six-year-old engineer, was assigned to take George Marshall's place atop what was code-named the Manhattan Engineering District. Groves answered to a newly established Military Policy Committee, headed by Vannevar Bush with Conant as his alternate.

From the start, soldier Groves got on well with scholar Conant. Harvard's president, Groves wrote afterward, "had the gambling spirit of New England pioneers." It proved to be contagious. That December, when Enrico Fermi and forty associates produced the world's first nuclear chain reaction in a reactor built over a University of Chicago squash court, the principle was established that atomic power on a practical scale could be manufactured. The long-theorized but still untested superweapon came a giant step closer to reality. Operating under stringent security precautions, Arthur Compton, University of Chicago dean of physics, telephoned his Harvard colleague with a message of historic opacity.

"Jim," he began, "this is Arthur. I thought you would want to know that the Italian navigator has just landed in the New World."

"What," asked Conant, "already?"

"Yes, the earth was smaller than established, and he arrived several days earlier than he had expected."

"Were the natives friendly?" Conant inquired.

"They were indeed," Compton told him. "Everyone landed safe and happy."

"Fine news," said Conant. "I'll be eager to learn what you found on the new continent."[38]

Others at Harvard shared Conant's eagerness. By the fall of 1943, the physics department retained just eight of its prewar roster of forty-four lecturers and instructors. To help fill the gap, chairman Edward Kemble was forced to call up reserves of his own, including European refugees, retired professors still in the Cambridge area, and teachers of English, history, economics, and fine arts, all given quick refresher courses over the preceding summer. "Even three undergraduates and a woman teacher are instructing," marveled the *Alumni Bulletin.*

Amid the demands of war and scientific exploration, Conant found time for other plans for Harvard. According to Paul Nitze, then in charge of purchasing graphite, beryllium, zirconium, mercury, and other metals needed for the Manhattan Project, Conant endorsed his idea of establishing a permanent, postgraduate institution, to be located in the nation's capital, supported by business and government, and directed by a Harvard-led consortium of universities. The new institute would take advantage of expertise gained during the war and direct it toward U.S. foreign policy once peace returned. After agreeing to head up the project's academic side, Conant was unable to convince his own Corporation or Overseers to join in. But Nitze went ahead anyway, aided by Christian Herter, and a few months before Alamogordo the School of Advanced International Studies, now part of Johns Hopkins University, was launched.[39]

At the same time, despite internal fissures and the suspicion of traditionalists, Conant plowed ahead with local University matters. In 1943, he unveiled his single most important reform for Harvard, the ad hoc committee system of choosing tenured faculty. Since the Walsh-Sweezy affair, the president had looked about for ways to institutionalize the principles contained in the Committee of Eight's landmark report. Assisted by mathematician Walter Graustein, who calculated a kind of professorial actuarial chart, gauging the average professorial career at thirty-four years and providing for the first time insight into the University's prospective hiring needs, Conant devised a new system for determining tenure.

The Conant-Graustein formula reduced the president's arbitrary power of appointment, transforming what had been essentially an adversarial system into a cooperative one that enhanced the executive's ability to pass judgment on both faculty and deans. The process was not complex: henceforth, members of the Faculty of Arts and Sciences could remain up to eight years before a formal decision was made about their permanent status. Whether tenure was likely or not, they would have to be informed no later than the seventh year. When vacancies occurred, a special panel, or "ad hoc committee," would be created within the department, composed of Harvard specialists plus men from other disciplines and universities, and the private sector. If there were an opening in Economics, for instance, a minority of jurors might come from the existing ranks of Harvard economists. To this nucleus could be added a government or history professor, an economist from Yale, a government statistician, and a prominent businessman to supply private-sector input. The assembled members were free to propose elevating someone already in Cambridge, or to go elsewhere for the best candidate they could find.

The ad hoc committee would suggest a candidate, but only the president could ratify. Then the Corporation and Overseers must agree before the candidate could be formally invited to answer Harvard's call.

The tenure reform's implications were historic. The addition of outside experts, it was hoped, would dilute departmental logrolling. Theoretically the candidate search would boil down to a simple, painstaking hunt for the most brilliant mind, though not necessarily the most creative classroom instructor. In practice, however, Conant's system inevitably neglected teaching, especially of undergraduates, in favor of original research.

"Conant laid an egg that others hatched," declared W. Jackson Bate, making no effort to conceal his dissatisfaction with what later emerged. Bate is not alone in believing that the new process was weighted against the humanist, whose academic credentials tend to be cumulative, unlike the hard scientist, whose reputation can be earned with a single and early breakthrough. Such criticism notwithstanding, the ad hoc system has done much to maintain the University's standards, not to mention the prestige and authority of its presidents.[40]

Even as Conant pressed ahead with his reform and Harvard scientists worked to perfect poison gas and homing torpedoes, a short, stabbing event reminded the University of what it had been before America's global responsibilities linked it so closely to the government in Washington. Lawrence Lowell's winter had been a bleak one. Deafness had all but ruled out conversation, which he had loved, and his memory had failed. He rarely ventured out and his reading gradually dwindled away, until only the Bible held his attention. Then, one evening in December 1942, the old man was found unconscious in his Marlborough Street library. He died two weeks later, and was buried from the Memorial Church, in a simple ceremony befitting his creed and the reticences of New England. Only one other member of the Class of 1877 survived, and he was too weak to reach Cambridge for the service. In more than one sense, Lowell went to his grave alone.

On the day after Lowell's funeral, Conant returned to his church to mark the passing of generations and anticipate a world as yet but dimly visible through the smoke and noise of battle. It was a different kind of education awaiting the young men bound for the war zone to whom he said farewell that morning, yet one equally vital to reshaping a democracy in the peace for which they all prayed. "Once it is clear in a man's mind that the demands of war are one thing and those of a free society another," he said, "the virtues which are developed on the battlefield reinforce the natural talents. And this education may prove as valuable in the postwar world as years of study in academic halls."

He needn't remind them, Conant went on, that the silencing of guns would not eliminate men's problems. All in common would require courage, endurance, and patience—above all, patience—if the coming peace were to be more than an empty husk, a mere pause in the shooting and slaughter. For the youths seated before him, sacrifice would impart its special brand of knowledge. Freedom won through risk would assume an almost holy significance. On some future commencement day, they would return with an understanding born of great events. For now, he could only quote James Russell Lowell's greeting addressed to Harvard's warriors in 1865:

> *Today, our Reverend Mother welcomes back*
> *Her wisest scholars, those who understood . . .*
> *Many loved Truth, and lavished life's best oil*
> *Amid the dust of books to find her . . .*
> *But these, our brothers, fought for her.*

Conant looked up from his text and out over a field of upturned faces. "Gentlemen," he concluded "with anxious pride, Harvard awaits the day of your return."[41]

> *The prophet himself stands under the judgment*
> *which he preaches. If he does not know that,*
> *he is a false prophet.*
> —REINHOLD NIEBUHR

IN MAY 1943, Conant ignited local flames with a bold article in the *Atlantic Monthly*. Entitled, "Wanted: American Radicals," it lived up to its saucy premise. The author claimed to describe an imaginary type, but those who knew him best discerned autobiography in his appeal for an unsentimental yet high-minded challenge to tradition. Who, he wondered, would succeed the men who had abolished primogeniture at the birth of the republic, or those who had zestfully destroyed the Bank of the United States in Andrew Jackson's time?

In the society around him, the author professed to see at least some of the makings of latter-day insurgency.

> He springs from the American soil [avowed Conant of his heroic rebel], firm in the belief that every man is as good as his neighbor, if not better, and is entitled to a real chance for a decent living. . . . He will be respectful but not enthusiastic about Marx, Engels, and Lenin. . . . No one need to be told that the American radical will be a fanatic believer in equality. Yet it will be a peculiar North American brand of doctrine. For example, he will be quite willing in times of peace to let net salaries and earnings sail way above the $25,000 mark. He believes in equality of opportunity, not equality of rewards; but, on the other hand, he will be lusty in wielding the axe against the root of inherited privilege. To prevent the growth of a caste system, which he abhors, he will be resolute in his demand to confiscate (by constitutional methods) all property once a generation.

Conant's radical would concern himself more with public than private education, and harp on the dangers of federal involvement with either. He would search for ways to decentralize and localize responsibility, while coming to terms with the industrial growth that dwarfed individuals and glorified Washington. Believing in universal employment, "he will rack his brains to find the equivalent of those magic lands of the old frontier." Finally, wrote Conant, the American radical would embrace contrariness. He would stay "as independent as a hog on ice."

To illustrate his point, Conant told a story about an ancestor stopped en route to a town meeting.

> "Don't you know, Ed, there ain't no use in going to that there meeting? Old Doc Barnes and his crowd control enough votes to carry everything they want and more too. You can't make any headway agin 'em."
> "That's all right," replied Ed, "but I can worry 'em some."

Conant provided plenty of worry to his Corporation colleagues. Bill Claflin and other conservatives might entrench themselves in Harvard's wartime administration, but Conant preferred change, and he got it. He permitted junior-college students to transfer into Harvard's sophomore year and eased Business School admissions to reflect the spread of economic instruction to other institutions; he fostered coeducational education, "in practice if not in theory," beginning in the fall of 1944, by shattering the ancient prohibition on women in Harvard classrooms and lecture halls; he ordered that that year's commencement program be printed in English rather than Latin. The editor of the *Alumni Bulletin* took sharp exception to this last step, expressing the hope that it was but a wartime expedient. Along with others, he was in for surprises ahead.

CHAPTER FIVE

Redbook, Red Scare

> *The question has become more and more insis-*
> *tent: what is the right relationship between spe-*
> *cialistic training on the one hand, aiming at any*
> *one of a thousand different destinies, and edu-*
> *cation in a common heritage and toward a com-*
> *mon citizenship on the other? It is not too*
> *much to say that the very character of our so-*
> *ciety will be affected by the answer to that*
> *question.*
>
> —*General Education in a Free Society*
> *"The Redbook," 1945*

WHILE DINING at the Cosmos Club in Washington one evening in November 1942, Conant was approached by William H. Cowley, president of Colgate University, a self-appointed spokesman for an emerging generation of educational theorists. Cowley mentioned an instance when ambitious plans had been put aside by colleagues relying on the familiar refrain, "Look at what Harvard does." In Cowley's view, Harvard wasn't doing enough to justify such claim to leadership, or to counter the conservative thrust of the University of Chicago and its irascible president, Robert M. Hutchins. Hutchins's gloomy view of the long-range survival of the liberal arts had led him to the "Great Books curriculum" (filled, as one critic put it, with pure knowledge, undefiled by time). Hutchins plumped for the faith of the fathers in defiance of the Emersonian notion that each age must write its own story.

Assuming that Cowley was right, said Conant, what would he propose as a remedy? Even granting the substantial numbers engaged in war work, Cowley replied, much of Conant's faculty was inactive. Why not appoint a committee of outstanding men to study the future of liberal education—not only in the local context, but throughout the country? When the war ended, America's leading university would have a program that might inspire and point the way for other schools.

In a few weeks, a second meeting was held, attended by Conant, Cowley, Calvert Smith, secretary to the Harvard Corporation, and Williams president James Phinney Baxter. Smith in particular was seized with enthusiasm. He maintained that if Cowley's survey was done right the report would end up on the front page of every newspaper in America. The problem of how to pay for the inquiry was resolved when Mrs. Bonwit Teller donated $60,000 to the cause.[1]

In early 1943, Conant instructed Provost Paul Buck and a dozen faculty colleagues to undertake a broad examination of general education in a free society. The group's composition was criticized because, although it contained three historians, an equal number of educational thinkers, and one each from the departments of Greek, philosophy, English language, zoology, biology, and government, there was no professor of business and no sociologist. Why such an emphasis on the humanities, especially history? The panel reflected Conant's bias.

For the next two years, Buck and his associates interviewed college presidents and social workers, labor leaders and kindergarten teachers. At first the committee devoted itself almost exclusively to the study of secondary education. The disturbing conclusion was that relatively few high school students enjoyed a rounded schooling. Youths with little use for them were given prolonged instruction in shorthand, typing, bookkeeping, and other vocations, while in the meantime, ten million Americans remained illiterate, and twenty million of voting age had never gone beyond the sixth grade. Even among those who had, for millions the essentials of democracy remained so many abstract ideals, civics book recitations of this battle or that treaty.

But these problems formed only the tip of a much larger iceberg. The Buck committee was grappling with educational theories as old as the republic, Jeffersonian versus Jacksonian, "the one valuing opportunity as the nurse of excellence, the other as the guard of equity." By broadening the basis of government to include all the people, democracy demanded for everyone the intellectual training once reserved for the elite. The education of governors was now the preparation of citizens.[2]

Buck and his colleagues concluded that it was the task of educators "to nurture ability while raising the average." To accomplish this the committee set about to revise the high school curriculum. They were equally anxious to reform Harvard's curriculum, to find replacements for Eliot's electives and Lowell's costly tutors, to define a common core of democratic values and propose ways to acquaint a generation with them, all the while avoiding the slightest hint of indoctrination. It was a formidable undertaking, and the strains were apparent when the committee's 267-page report, which a generation would call "the Redbook," was published in the fall of 1945. Written by several men, including John Finley, I. A. Richards, Benjamin Wright, and Raphael Demos, the report did not even mention Harvard until two-thirds of the way through. Three-quarters of the work dealt with changes in secondary education.

According to Finley, Conant's influence was felt most pervasively in the section on high schools, recalling the president's lifelong devotion to Roxbury Latin.

> Democracy is not only opportunity for the able [declared the committee]. It is equally betterment of the average, both the immediate betterment which can be gained in a single generation and the slower groundswell of betterment working through generations. Hence the task of the high school is not to speed the bright boy to the top. It is at least as much (so far as numbers are concerned, far more) so to widen the horizons of ordinary students that they and, still more, their children will encounter "fewer of the obstacles that cramp achievement."[3]

In an attempt to deemphasize vocational study in high school classrooms, committee members proposed a core curriculum, built around English, the humanities, science, mathematics, and social studies. The object of such instruction was to foster an ability "to think effectively, communicate thought, make relevant judgments, and discriminate among values." Such "general education" courses would be spread evenly across the four years of secondary schooling, rather than concentrated in the first two.

The report returned often to the question of how to reconcile the specialized training required to earn a living with cultural preparation to make life enjoyable and socially useful.

> [The search must continue] for some overall logic, some strong, not easily broken frame within which both college and school may fulfill their at once diversifying and uniting task. This logic must be wide enough to embrace the actual richness and variegation of modern life—a richness partly, if not wholly, reflected in the complexity of our present educational system. It

must also be strong enough to give goal and direction to the system—something much less clear at present.

Then came the heart of the Redbook—and of Conant's search for a "coherent national culture."

> It [the overall logic] is evidently to be looked for in the character of American society, a society not wholly of the new world since it came from the old, not wholly given to innovation since it acknowledges certain fixed beliefs, not even wholly a law unto itself since there are principles above the state. This logic must further embody certain intangibles of the American spirit, in particular, perhaps, the ideal of co-operation on the level of action irrespective of agreement on ultimates—which is to say, belief in the worth and meaning of the human spirit, however one may understand it.

The curriculum proposed for Harvard was a conservative response to radical demands. Six of the required sixteen undergraduate courses came under the "General Education" heading, including one apiece in the humanities, sciences, and social sciences. "Great Texts of Literature" was suggested as a concession to work already advanced by Columbia and carried to an extreme at Chicago and St. John's. Harvard's list of "great books" included Homer, Plato, the Bible, Virgil, Dante, Shakespeare, Milton, and Tolstoy.[4]

In designing social science courses, the committee aimed to ground students in broad issues of social responsibility. Mixing historical perspective with topical immediacy, a course in American Democracy might require students to read standard works such as de Tocqueville and Lord Bryce, and Gunnar Myrdal's *An American Dilemma,* which cast a critical look at race relations in the postwar society. Conant himself agreed to conduct a course in the history of science. Designed for nonscientists in keeping with the report's overall emphasis on cultural breadth and intermingled disciplines, the course reflected Conant's wartime experiences and his conviction that scientists and humanists were woefully ignorant of each other's fields.[5]

The Redbook dispensed with religion, science, and empirical reason alike as adhesives for modern America. To many, this was akin to building a bridge with no middle. If neither revelation nor reason led to the values enshrined in the General Education theory, then who could determine or define which cultural patterns were worthy of preservation? Buck's committee responded that there were self-evident values, "moral principles which command the assent of civilized men." (A dubious reviewer referred to Harvard's special line of communication with the absolute.)

Most of all, the authority of tradition hung over the document, enough to remind a reviewer of the late George Apley's complaint to a friend: "Dear John: I wish there weren't quite so many new ideas. Where do they come from? . . . I try to think what is in back of them and speculation often disturbs my sleep."

Much of yesterday's wisdom, said some critics, is today's banality and tomorrow's baloney. Some attacked the Redbook for containing too much Plato, not enough Freud. Foreign languages were neglected as were radio, television, and other emerging media which might serve as instruments of communal thought. The social activists said the report was too divorced from social disparity and community afflictions. The National Education Association took exception to the committee's prescription for high school excellence. In its report *Education for All American Youth,* the NEA proposed more, not less, functionalism—teaching students how to live in the modern world as consumers and voters, tracing history backward from current events, and rooting such esoterica as economic theory in family life. Instead of Thermopylae or Hastings, the headlines would be searched for current social problems; young women might be drawn to science by first making their own cosmetics. Grammar would be enlivened and literature made more contemporary.[6]

The Harvard committee's response was that it sought to minimize the differences between high school students bound for college and those destined for an assembly line or a tractor. "To the belief in men's dignity," the report noted, "must be added the recognition of his duty to his fellow men. Dignity does not rest on any man as being separate from all other beings, which he in any case cannot be, but springs from his common humanity and exists positively as he makes the common good his own."

Sociologist Jacques Barzun detected the influence of Lawrence Lowell in what seemed to him the first truly American undergraduate curriculum, one "equidistant from Oxford and Heidelberg, and maintaining the perpendicular between them." Nothing published about American higher education in the twentieth century, William Cowley wrote, approached the Redbook in importance or potential. A Columbia scholar retorted that "banal good sense" was not the stuff of historic reform. *The Christian Century* pronounced the document an overdue tribute to Hutchins's University of Chicago.[7]

Other, smaller schools, followed Harvard's example, and much was made of a return to the wisdom of the ages. But Harvard's experiment, and particularly the charter of its birth, should be seen in political as well as educational terms. Firmly rooted in the western tradition (and, for all its talk of American democracy, the product of a European sensitivity), Conant's Redbook was a rallying cry on behalf of an endangered way of life.

Harvard's embrace of the Redbook's national values was as close as modern Harvard dared to come to espousing an official doctrine. As long as eminent professors maintained their enthusiasm for the courses it spawned, and their agreement about the threat it opposed, the Redbook was a success. But by the mid-1950s events had overwhelmed its urgency. A president more interested in bricks and mortar had succeeded to the corner office, and Harvard had begun looking in other directions. General Education lasted for a generation, but sapped of its vitality and mocked for its irrelevance. The University, touchstone of a liberal society, would lose faith in promoting doctrines, even liberal ones, and a new Core Curriculum would arise. Methodology—bloodless, safe, no doubt useful— would succeed to the throne. The American Century would defer to a global perspective, and Harvard, which under Conant had become a national university in fact as well as theory, would reach out further still to the status of international service center, managing consultant to the world.

> *The primary concern of American education today is not the development of the appreciation of the "good life" in young gentlemen born to the purple. Our purpose is to cultivate in the largest number of our future citizens an appreciation both of the responsibilities and the benefits which come to them because they are American and free.*
>
> —JAMES BRYANT CONANT, *1945*

IN MAY 1945, thousands filled the Tercentenary Theatre for a simple, fifteen-minute service of prayer and thanksgiving celebrating the end of the war. On flagstaffs outside University Hall, the hammer and sickle of the Soviet Union flew next to the Union Jack and Old Glory, all three lowered in memory of Franklin Roosevelt. A few weeks later, Conant presided over an abridged Commencement, whose honorary degrees re-

flected the University's preoccupation with the war. The men upon whom
Harvard pressed laurels were all architects of military triumph: Admiral
Ernest J. King, "determined organizer of final victory," Frederick Terman,
a Stanford professor on loan to Harvard for the war's duration and "a
master of the mysterious science of radio communication," and Bradley
Dewey, "whose Herculean labors in a federal office gave us the rubber on
which we now roll to victory." The Phi Beta Kappa poet that June was
Wallace Stevens, Class of 1901. Among alumni elected to honorary membership in the Harvard chapter was the new president of tiny Lawrence
College in Appleton, Wisconsin, a handsome, hearty-looking humanist
just thirty-eight years old named Nathan Pusey.

Conant used the occasion to announce the Redbook's publication
and to glance ahead to the time "when we shall be instructing in the arts
of peace a generation whose valor in war will long be a proud boast of
the American people." His own role in building the atomic bomb, then a
month shy of its violent birth in the New Mexico deserts, was still a
secret, successfully withheld from his faculty, the Corporation, and his
own family.

Late that July, beneath gray skies, Conant stretched himself out on a
New Mexico tarpaulin, raincoat pulled tight, face down and feet toward
a steel tower from which was suspended the most destructive weapon yet
devised. "I never imagined seconds could be so long," he said in recounting the first atomic blast. Kenneth Bainbridge had a different reaction.
"Now we are all sons of bitches," he muttered to Oppenheimer. At the
same time, Conant harbored growing reservations about unleashing a
form of power he'd once thought was restricted to melting polar ice
caps. (In 1964, only his wife's advice would restrain him from depressing
the festive mood of his fiftieth class reunion with the declaration that he
had long since expected Cambridge itself to crumble into radioactive
dust.)[8] Yet he had little patience with historical revisionists who almost
from the birth of the atomic age doubted the motives of those initially
responsible for the bomb's development. At first, he had believed that no
bomb should be dropped without an explicit demonstration of its devas-
tating potential. But later, in the face of criticism that just such a warning
ought to have been given Japan, he took a more pragmatic position.
There were only two such devices in existence at the time, he said. If
notice had been given through some public test and the Japanese had not
surrendered, a single bomb would have remained. If that were to fail, the
entire Manhattan Project would have been for naught. Only a surprise
attack, he insisted, could possibly achieve its objective of cutting the war
short and saving millions of lives.[9]

He bridled at accusations that the nuclear attack was unleashed on Asians rather than Europeans. The bomb had been intended as a weapon against Germany, Conant argued, but the Germans had surrendered that May.

Before returning to Cambridge in the fall of 1945, Conant was asked by the new president, Harry Truman, to assist in formulating U.S. policies with regard to the atomic secret. At the invitation of Secretary of State Jimmy Byrnes, he drafted a long memorandum calling for international control and joint oversight by the victorious Allies, including the Soviet Union. In common with many Americans, Conant later disowned his optimistic opinion that the wartime fraternity of superpowers might survive V-J Day. Yet he stuck to his forecast that even without U.S. cooperation, Russian physicists were likely to have developed their own nuclear device in five to fifteen years.

A few months later, Truman discussed with Conant the possibility of his becoming chairman of the new Atomic Energy Commission. Intrigued by the prospect of spearheading a United Nations campaign for the peaceful use of this newest energy source (his own faith rested on solar generation), Conant entertained the offer for a week before turning it down. Although tempted to escape Cambridge and move permanently into the channels of international diplomacy, he was discouraged by the chairman's subsidiary role in choosing his colleagues. Conant also disliked the presence on the AEC of Admiral Lewis Straus, who would subsequently play a leading role in the loyalty probe of J. Robert Oppenheimer. He was disturbed as well by Truman's abrupt about-face on the May-Johnson Bill, a congressional attempt to structure U.S. oversight of atomic energy which had initially enjoyed backing from the White House, but was later rejected on the grounds that it awarded too much influence to the military. (Such questions of policy combined with personal feuds to point up sharp divisions among the bomb's architects. Just as Conant's Harvard faculty took umbrage at a style of administration variously labeled decisive or dictatorial, so some of his wartime associates joined cold warriors such as Edward Teller to deny Conant the presidency of the National Academy of Sciences in 1950.)[10]

At the end of 1945, Conant resumed his educational responsibilities and dedicated the University's newest tribute to its fallen sons. On the south wall of Lowell's red brick sanctuary were inscribed hundreds of names, including those of Franklin Roosevelt and young Joe Kennedy. The occasion was even more solemn than one might expect, especially for the scientist-scholar who presided over it, his sense of triumph at victory muted by the deadly advances in science he had participated in. Conant gazed through the tall windows of Memorial Church, built as a tribute to the dead of the First World War and now filled with survivors and mourners from a Second, and pointed at Memorial Hall, another reliquary commemorating another fearful slaughter. The president doubted whether Harvard would ever again lay the cornerstone for such a monument. "If the peace is broken once more by a major war, our cultural pattern will be warped and seared and twisted," he said. "If the wave of destruction comes and passes, it is doubtful if the continuity of our three-century-old tradition could be maintained with vigor."

"How shall we behave ourselves after such mercies?" he asked, quoting Oliver Cromwell. Characteristically, Conant was ahead of most Americans in asking that question, and scrutinizing its broader implications.

The war had changed the University as much as it had the country. Women were beginning to demand a fuller share in national life. Having supplied a third of the workforce responsible for the B-29 bomber, they were unlikely to resume their secondary status once the planes returned to earth. Blacks also wanted as much out of peace as they had given to the war, and flocked to join the NAACP and pressure Washington for long-delayed rights. A surge in wartime employment, coupled with higher taxation of the better off, had done more to redistribute national income than any of the New Deal nostrums adopted before Pearl Harbor. Net corporate income was lower in 1945 than in 1941.

Meanwhile, a restless people cut themselves adrift from their roots. Over a million resettled permanently in the west, where plane builders and rubber makers offered employment. The migration altered forever the old patterns of eastern dominance and social noblesse oblige.

Changes outside the Yard were reflected within. Quonset huts sprawled in temporary shabbiness near the law school. Some undergraduates were housed in an old Boston hotel, or as far away as Fort Devens, some thirty miles distant. House dining rooms had gone cafeteria-style in 1943. And that same year, Radcliffe women—"Cliffe-dwellers," in local parlance—were admitted to the inner sanctum of male Harvard. It was said that Conant once returned to the Yard demanding to know what females were doing in his classrooms, only to be reminded that it was he who had signed the historic compact, presented to him by Paul Buck on board one of the countless railway cars in which he had spent so much of the war. However advanced his thinking in other realms, Conant never got over his discomfort at sharing a liberal education with females.[11]

At his first lecture following the war's end, Samuel Eliot Morison swept into the classroom, dashing and authoritative in his navy cape, and promptly ordered the room cleared of females. He had spent several years in the company of sailors, explained the admiral-historian, and he planned on telling stories of his experiences, some of them using nautical language of the kind not found in *Bowditch's Navigation.* For good measure, Morison also evicted a young man, later Harvard's treasurer, for wearing a pink shirt to class.[12]

In Harvard's classrooms, new educational theories were advancing. Before the war, traditionalists like Roger Merriman had taught history in personal terms, with a syllabus ranging from Charles I's pre-execution farewell to the bitter regrets of Anne Boleyn in her cell beside the Thames. Now came a different brand of scholarship, pioneered by Arthur Schlesinger Senior, Merriman's colleague in History, who stressed economics and sociology over biography, and held that Lincoln was less important to American development than the invention of barbed wire.[13]

The judgment of those acquainted with postwar Harvard is virtually unanimous: returning veterans brought to the classroom a seriousness and maturity that were the joy of their instructors. David Aloian, later master of Quincy House, recalls the difference in mood between September of 1945, when he arrived on campus as a sixteen-year-old freshman, and the following January, when Harvard was inundated by vets. At the start of the academic year, according to Aloian, his freshman English writing course was little more than a continuation of what he had known at Exeter. When the older men appeared a few months later, the teachers were challenged, skepticism was heightened, texts were read more rigorously.[14]

Above all else, the G.I. Bill of Rights opened Harvard to a diversity of enrollment and outlook unimaginable when Conant had first proposed his National Scholarships. Nationwide, 2.3 million veterans studied in universities and colleges, at least a third of whom could never have taken advantage of such schooling without the financial incentives the bill contained. During the decade following 1939, the number of people receiving college degrees more than doubled. Converting what had been the privilege of the few into the right of all, the new wave of students forced educators to revamp their standard curricula, to emphasize science and technology, to dispense with old entrance requirements, and to experiment with fresh approaches to those whom Robert Hutchins publicly disdained as "educational hoboes."[15]

Some of the G.I. Bill students enrolled in rumba lessons from Arthur Murray's or studied archery, but most took the program at face value. In doing so, they permanently changed the value systems of the institutions into which they crowded. In the three and a half years following Japan's surrender, Harvard received 60,000 applications from veterans alone. Winthrops and Cabots and Lees were replaced on the Crimson football squad by Dvarics, Gorzynskis, and Flynns. Hundreds of foreigners arrived, transforming a New England college into a polyglot university.

A few years later, a Cornell survey of twelve major universities reported that the school with the largest proportion of Jewish students registered, some 25 percent of its total enrollment, was Harvard. Harvard also reported the most economically diverse student body: a fourth or more from households with annual incomes of less than $5000, a majority from public schools, a large contingent from blue-collar families. Credit for this demographic overhaul was shared by Conant, Provost Paul Buck, and Dean Wilbur J. Bender, whom the president had persuaded to move from University Hall to Admissions in order to protect Harvard's egalitarian thrust.[16]

Like its president, Harvard basked in a postwar glow, its contributions to victory equaled by the new Redbook and a troop of promising recent graduates. Carl Frederick of the government department flew off to help organize a democratic Germany. His colleague Arthur Holcombe had the distinction in 1946 of voting for three former students, including John F. Kennedy and Henry Cabot Lodge, whose divergent party labels mattered less than their mutual allegiance to Harvard and her confident assertion that the United States should be responsible for shaping a newly imperiled world.

By the fall of 1947, General Education featured eight new courses, including Perry Miller's "Classics of the Christian Tradition," Kirtly Mather's "The Impact of Science on Modern Life," and Walt Rostow's "The Institutions and Thought of Western Society." A survey by the Student Council reported enthusiastic support for the program. Up to 80 percent of those enrolled won honors grades.

As General Education took hold, thoughtful observers recognized it as a new form of Harvard assimilation. In place of Lowell's emphasis on manners and breeding, the hallmarks of a gentleman, Conant and Buck had designed a program in harmony with the president's belief in a casteless national family, led by its most academically gifted, yet purified of financial excess and hereditary pride.

Meanwhile, Conant and his staff were busy expanding the University. In 1903, Harvard had received a substantial bequest which in its original form had stipulated aid to the field of mechanical engineering. Since neither the gift nor the field of mechanical engineering retained their 1903 dimensions half a century later, Conant needed to find some way to put the money to work without repeating Lowell's mistake of urging formal alliance with neighboring MIT. He asked his wartime colleague Vannevar Bush to chair a committee to oversee the project. Bush came to his rescue, and the result was the entirely new department of Applied Sciences.

Another innovation, the Russian Research Center, sprang from the fertile mind of Paul Buck. With the war concluded, veterans of Bill Donovan's Office of Strategic Services were at a loss for gainful employment. The OSS had acquired a magnificent library of Slavic literature as well as a large corps of experts, whose talents were being squandered even as U.S.–Soviet relations deteriorated. Harvard historian William Langer had directed the OSS's Research and Analysis Branch, in the process discovering the drawbacks of compartmentalized scholarship. Langer's colleagues were reaching the same conclusion.

At a six-hour meeting convened under the auspices of the Carnegie Corporation, a Harvard professor whose wartime psychological profile of the Japanese had attracted favorable attention was cited for uncovering a new and potentially critical field of topical scholarship. Impressed by the study, as well as by remarks from U.S. diplomats frustrated over dealings with Soviet Foreign Minister Andrei Gromyko on the subject of atomic energy, Carnegie's John Gardner sought a new approach to the baffling, increasingly strident regime in the Kremlin. The best hope lay through the social sciences, he concluded.

In the fall of 1947, Carnegie donated a hundred thousand dollars to Harvard scholars to undertake an exhaustive review of Soviet behavior. From this grew the University's first independent research facility. Conant was not convinced that the idea warranted permanency and was, as ever, worried about the fiscal implications of anything new. He agreed to provide funding only if Buck devised a name suggestive of temporary status. But the Russian Research Center that resulted not only outlived the cold war, it paved the way for other centers, similarly divorced from existing departments, also committed to strategic scholarship.[17]

In the atmosphere of mutual suspicion unfolding in the late Forties, Center directors informed FBI agents before they purchased texts from Cambridge's communist bookshops. But Conant broke with prevailing custom and deliberately sacrificed handsome government contracts by declaring that the University's policy would be to conduct only federally funded research projects whose results could be aired in public. He shut down the sonar assembly line in the basement of Memorial Hall. He cast out room after room of sophisticated gadgetry, much to the displeasure of scientific engineers. From its lofty position in wartime funding, third behind Berkeley and MIT, Harvard soon fell back into the pack.

Conant's definition of a good administrator was "a man who has a worried look on his assistant's face." Backed by Paul Buck and others, he replaced the frowns of academic colleagues with the satisfied expression of the scholar who knows he is appreciated for his individual worth. Conant reorganized Harvard's cumbersome libraries and dispersed academic oversight through a network of senior tutors in Lowell's Houses. He was praised for the deans he chose, men like George Berry (Medicine), Donald David (Business), and Erwin Griswold, who succeeded the controversial James Landis at the law school and went on to carve out his own distinguished niche by opposing the challenge of Joseph McCarthy and others pursuing both Communists and headlines.

Preeminently, Conant focused on recruiting good faculty and keeping them. His Cambridge was filled with such luminaries as Edwin Cohn and Fuller Albright at the medical school, Edmund Morgan and Austin Scott at the law school, Sumner Slichter in Economics, and Percy Bridgman in science. Archibald MacLeish filled the Boylston Chair of Rhetoric. Theodore Morrison took over freshman writing courses, spawning an impressive school of prizewinners, including A. B. Guthrie and John Ciardi.

Postwar students rubbed shoulders with an eminent company of intellectual barons, but they saw little of the president himself. Each morning, before lecturing in his course on the history of science, Conant set aside time for writing. *Education in a Divided World,* published in 1948, was one of several books he wrote during this time which laid out his favorite theme, the need to educate a democratic society in a world polarized by ideology and militarism. He also dealt with an enormous volume of paperwork. Presented with a three-page, single-spaced memo describing the pension plan of a retiring professor, Conant said reproachfully, "Ike doesn't allow this," referring to his wartime acquaintance, now the president of Columbia University. "He won't accept any memo with more than 300 words on one side of the page."[18]

The president pressed forward outside the Yard as well. He lectured on atomic energy at the National War College. He convinced fellow educators to endorse his plan for creating an Educational Testing Service. The achievement tests subsequently drawn up by ETS supplemented the standard college entrance examinations inspired half a century earlier by Charles W. Eliot. Early in 1947, Conant called for establishment of a nationwide system of two-year junior colleges, the logical extension of his General Education scheme. He proposed a national scientific foundation to support university research.[19]

In addition to all this, Conant managed to dine alone with his wife twice a week. Two vacations a year gave him rare time with his sons, neither of whom chose to attend Harvard; they scrambled up the White Mountains, fished for trout at Yosemite. He also found time to dabble in oil painting. Resentful undergraduates thought him remote and perhaps a little bored with their workaday occupations. Yet Conant met regularly with editors of the *Crimson,* faculty members, and a steady stream of other educators for whom he naturally assumed the role of oracle.[20]

His schedule did not include Harvard football games. Although credited with establishing the modern Ivy League by rallying other schools to a common athletic schedule, contests of muscular skill ranked low on his list of priorities. Francis Keppel, who headed his School of Education and enjoyed the relationship of a favored son, remembered Conant's visit with William Bingham, the Harvard athletic director, whom he hadn't seen for years and whose expected call for money for a new stadium scoreboard held all the allure of a dentist's drill. Aware that even the most lavish praise for his distant associate would consume but five minutes of the scheduled half-hour visit, the president hit on a highly personal expedient to frustrate any financial pitch. By calculating on a notepad the cost to Harvard of a championship football team, complete with All-American fullback and tight end, Conant disposed of Bingham's supplication before it ever left his mouth. Such a team would be entirely too expensive, declared Conant, as Bingham's allotted time ran out. His point was not lost on the outmaneuvered coach.[21]

Long before the war, Conant had raised hackles with his vow to infuse new blood into both the student body and the Corporation. His activities during the war had prevented him from carrying out his wishes. Now, with the GI Bill accomplishing his long-cherished goal of democratizing the student body, the president did not delay in promoting a similarly broadened governing board. Until 1947, Harvard's inner sanctum had admitted only three non-Bostonians: Henry James, a New Yorker accepted because of his unique personal bonds of family; Grenville Clark, who could boast similar ties to the Hub; and international banker Thomas Lamont, product of a threadbare youth who concluded his days at New York's exclusive Tuxedo Park, and who enjoyed a warm friendship with FDR. In 1947, James revealed he was suffering from cancer, prompting Conant to look for a successor.

It didn't take him long to settle on a most unorthodox choice. A Baltimore lawyer and descendant of the man who figured so prominently in *Marbury* vs. *Madison,* William Marbury was familiar to Conant through his work in drafting the May-Johnson Act. However, although he had assisted in reconstructing the post-Landis law school, he was virtually unknown to most of the members of the Corporation and was quick to admit that he hadn't the foggiest idea what the Corporation was or whom it included at the time of his selection. Conant wanted him, and he was strongly supported by Grenville Clark. Bill Claflin, however, pressed for an up-and-coming Boston banker more to his liking, one whose election, Conant believed, would tip the scales permanently against his own leadership.[22]

After spirited debate, the Corporation approved Marbury, five to two. Refusing to yield, Claflin pleaded his case against Marbury to the more pliable Overseers, confident they shared his distrust of the outsider. At Leverett Saltonstall's behest, Overseer Charles Wyzanski, a New Deal alumnus graduated to the federal bench, went to ask Conant to withdraw Marbury's nomination. He found the president in a bitter mood. Conant said he wanted carved on his gravestone, "I worked for ten years with Bill Claflin," adding that he had no intention of yanking Marbury on the verge of confirmation.[23]

Confronted with such determination, Saltonstall gaveled Marbury through without the formality of a vote at the next Overseers' meeting. But from that moment, Wyzanski believes, Conant's hold over the governing boards began to weaken.[24] Even with Claflin's subsequent departure, fresh bickering lay ahead. At the center of a major storm was the imposing if sometimes maddening figure of John Kenneth Galbraith, a gifted young economist whose Keynesian views and general adherence to the New Deal was terrifying to conservative pocketbooks. When Galbraith's candidacy for tenure came up in 1948, Clarence Randall, chairman of Inland Steel and head of the Overseers' visiting committee on economics, was violently opposed to granting it. Besides their political differences, Randall had encountered Galbraith's authoritative manner in a wartime dispute with the Office of Price Administration, making his objections personal as well as ideological.[25]

Charles Cabot was equally upset with Galbraith because of his conduct on a European mission to survey results of U.S. wartime bombing of Germany. According to Charles Wyzanski, Cabot's dissatisfaction, which stalled the appointment for a full year, stemmed only partially from Galbraith's official behavior. What really riled Cabot was the economist's manner and deportment.[26]

At a dramatic meeting of the Overseers on Commencement morning, 1948, Galbraith's rejection was staved off only after Wyzanski, taking advantage of the diversion caused by the Harvard band playing outside the windows of University Hall, moved a delay in consideration until fall. He was not acting on a whim. All morning long, the judge had been back and forth between the faculty room and a nearby lavatory, where what he overheard convinced him that Galbraith would never be confirmed in the present atmosphere.

When the board reconvened a few months later, Conant shepherded the nomination past a battery of objections. In the process, he also lectured the Overseers on their responsibilities. The function of the board, he explained, was not to examine the merits of a nomination, "as to which you are not qualified," but only to review the process by which it had been reached. If a nominee had emerged from an ad hoc committee, won approval from the department and relevant dean, and been duly considered by the Corporation and emerged unscathed, the Overseer approval should be all but automatic. No one on the board would consider himself equipped, said Conant, to pass on a professor of Sanskrit, and economics shouldn't be different. "For what you would be doing is applying knowledge acquired thirty years ago. You would be out of touch with the issues, not to mention that most of you would be biased."

Not an uncritical observer of the Conant presidency, Wyzanski credits this last-minute appeal with reversing almost certain defeat. Galbraith received tenure, and went on to delight undergraduates and infuriate colleagues for three decades. But the struggle did nothing to enhance Conant's authority. Together with the brutal campaign to confirm Marbury, this latest uproar only deepened the unhappiness the president was beginning to feel in a job easily eclipsed by the world stage on which he now moved with ease.[27]

Perhaps never before had the nation's destiny been so entwined with that of her leading university. Just twelve months before the debate over Galbraith reached its climax, Secretary of State George Marshall had launched his celebrated European Recovery Program at the 1947 Commencement. In truth, the ERP was more the product of Marshall's deputy, Will Clayton, and others, than Marshall himself, and it had first been mentioned by Dean Acheson in a speech at Delta State Teachers College in Cleveland, Mississippi. Following the positive reception accorded this trial balloon, Marshall advanced his official announcement, originally planned for Amherst's commencement on June 16, to the Harvard ceremony eleven days earlier.

In an address of barely fifteen minutes, delivered in a soft monotone (the secretary wasn't the main speaker of the day), Marshall prescribed a $17 billion transfusion into the Old World's anemic economy. Only then could hungry people regain their feet and, he implied, western forces reclaim the initiative against a rapacious Soviet Union. Across the Atlantic, approval was instantaneous. At home, isolationists whittled away at the package, tightening congressional oversight and delaying final passage for ten months.[28]

In the aftermath of Marshall's address, Harvard undergraduates were ensnared by accelerating tensions between the United States and the Soviet Union. Posters around campus announced meetings devoted to European recovery and the new Britain, UNESCO and the Zionist advance in the Middle East. The John Reed Society marked the centenary of Marxism, while the Law School Forum listened to Joseph Alsop and I. F. Stone debate the question, "Must We Stop Russia?" At the Society for Industrial Democracy, Professor Gaetano Salvemini asked, "Which Way for Italy?" and William Yandell Elliott tackled "The Politics of One World" before the United Nations Council.

The Cold War came as a rude awakening to a generation of liberals whose hopes it dashed. Perhaps no one felt more the disillusionment of those years than F. O. Matthiessen, a Christian Socialist for whom World War II was justified only after Hitler's attack on Soviet Russia. A man of daunting complexity, the brilliant Matthiessen had been a loyal member of Yale's Skull and Bones. As a junior instructor in Cambridge, his homosexuality had turned him against conventional Harvard, with what seemed to him its suffocating climate of genteel snobbery and rigid mores. It was only natural for Matty, as friends called him, to attach himself to the work of Theodore Dreiser, another outsider. Such an artist could transform the short, nearly bald lecturer, with his metallic voice and disdain for platform histrionics, into a powerful speaker, of original insight and contagious enthusiasm.[29]

Matthiessen's public life had been a litany of lost causes. In the spring of 1941, he had addressed the Harvard Peace Strike. Not long after, he rebuked young Arthur Schlesinger for pointing to Winston Churchill as a symbol of hope against the crumbling backdrop of European defeatism, pointing out that Churchill the empire lover represented everything he, Matthiessen, detested. When war touched American shores, Matthiessen embarked on a different kind of combat, taking the side of the American Civil Liberties Union against Boston censors, and working to sustain the teachers' union in its declining years.

Critics competed to praise his masterwork, *American Renaissance: Art and Expression in the Age of Emerson and Whitman*. But Matthiessen found only bitter dregs in the book he wrote from his experience as a visiting professor at the University of Prague, *From the Heart of Europe,* an optimistic forecast of postwar reconciliation between East and West.

When his verdict was rendered obsolete by a Soviet-ordered coup which installed a Communist regime in Czechoslovakia early in 1948 while the book was still in proof, typically, Matthiessen made no changes in the book's text but merely added a lengthy footnote explaining his error in judgment. He once told an associate in private that he guessed he was more a socialist than a democrat.[30]

As the Cold War heated up, he became involved in Henry Wallace's quixotic third-party campaign against Truman. This time, political setbacks foreshadowed personal tragedy. His lover, Russell Chaney, died. The grieving professor was bogged down on a new book that deprived him of student companionship. His most cherished causes were crushed beneath the weight of superpower hostility and a rising wave of domestic intolerance. On Friday afternoon, March 31, 1949, he checked into Boston's Manger Hotel, in the shadow of North Station, asking for "a nice airy room" on the twelfth floor. That evening, he trudged up Beacon Hill to the Chestnut Street home of Ken Murdock, where he sat glumly depressed through a funereal dinner. "Remember that I loved you," he told Murdock and his wife. When they pressed him to stay over, he shook his head. Back at the Manger, he took a call from Eleanor Murdock imploring him to return to their apartment for the night.

Then he sat down to compose a farewell, later discovered alongside his Skull and Bones key. "I have taken this room in order to do what I have to do," it began. "As a Christian and a socialist believing in international peace, I find myself terribly oppressed by the present tensions." On the back of his suicide note, Matthiessen asked that whoever found his body inform Harvard University, "where I have been a professor." The next morning, Ken Murdock was summoned to the Nashua Street morgue to identify his friend's remains, hours after Matthiessen leapt from his hotel window.[31]

Matthiessen was called the first academic victim of the Cold War. This overlooked the professors at Prague's ancient university, whose acquaintance Matthiessen had made shortly before their intellectual lives were brutally destroyed by Soviet-backed "thought" police. But there was a romantic appeal to the statement, and his story has become the stuff of Harvard legend, a preview of the torment about to be unleashed on academia by Whittaker Chambers and Senator Joseph McCarthy.

To this day, the sad, fiery, ultimately vanquished Matthiessen inspires passionate admirers and vehement critics. Three decades after his death, the University belatedly acknowledged his genius, naming tutorial rooms in Eliot House in his honor. History has proved less generous. Within a year of Matthiessen's death, the United States was at war with a Soviet client state on the Korean peninsula. General Education was riding a crest of renewed ideological urgency, and James Bryant Conant, although embroiled in perpetual controversy, was the undisputed leader of American higher education.

The cycles of historical judgment fade in and out as perspectives evolve. Today, F. O. Matthiessen is remembered as a wishful thinker. The president he despised is recalled as a thoughtful patriot whose global perspective did nothing to dull his judgment or weaken his nationalism.

Studying a philosophy does not mean endorsing it, much less proclaiming it. We study cancer in order to learn how to defeat it. We must study the Soviet philosophy in our universities for exactly the same reason. No one must be afraid to tackle that explosive subject before a class. If an avowed supporter of the Marx-Lenin-Stalin line can be found, force him into the open and tear his arguments to pieces with counter-arguments.

—JAMES BRYANT CONANT
Education in a Divided World

No feature of the Hiss case is more obvious, or more troubling as history than the jagged fissure, which it did not so much open as reveal, between the plain men and women of the nation, and those who affected to act, think and speak for them. It was not invariably, but in general, the "best people" who were for Alger Hiss and who were prepared to go to almost any length to protect and defend him.

—WHITTAKER CHAMBERS

THE LATE Forties were discordant years in Cambridge. Fears once addressed on foreign battlegrounds were suddenly turned inward; justifiable pride surrendered to irrational suspicion. 1948 was the year of Truman and Dewey. Williams president James Baxter Phinney spent election night at 17 Quincy Street. The next day he was scheduled to go to New

York to launch a fundraising campaign for his college. He canceled the trip, telling Conant that no one on Wall Street would be in a mood to give money to anyone after Harry Truman's upset victory over Thomas Dewey.[32]

1948 was also the year of the Hiss-Chambers affair. Alger Hiss was a former state department official now president of the Carnegie Endowment for International Peace. Slender, discriminating, well-spoken and well-connected, the prototypical Harvard man, Hiss was being defended by his oldest friend, the Harvard Corporation's William Marbury, against accusations of treason and perjury; his accuser was Whittaker Chambers, a disheveled, slightly disreputable editor at *Time,* an acknowledged former Communist, an alleged homosexual, whose rumpled suits and florid prose were complemented by a messianic personality and a vision of traitors in the nation's attic. The contest between the two seemed uneven when it began before the House Un-American Activities Committee in August 1948. Angrily, convincingly, Hiss denied that he had ever been a Communist, or that he had even known Chambers. Nearly everyone on the committee believed his testimony. The single exception was an intense, bettle-browed Californian named Richard Nixon. In Cambridge, Conant joined in the applause, although he had the discretion to pay his compliments in private.

Following a second round of questioning and Chambers's positive identification of Hiss, however, Conant pressed Marbury, just back from a European jaunt on state department business, to visit him and Grenville Clark at 17 Quincy Street. Clark was especially agitated over the developing situation, which prompted both men to urge Hiss to sue Chambers for libel. Marbury telephoned Hiss (his child's godfather) and requested an update on events since his overseas departure. Others had mentioned the possibility of suing Chambers, their advice set aside in hopes the whole thing might go away. The statute of limitations had long since expired and Communist allegiance was not a crime, in 1935 or in 1948. And congressional immunity had provided Hiss with an impervious shield of legal protection. However, Hiss's public credibility in the face of Chambers's allegations was now beginning to lose its strength. According to Marbury, both Conant and Clark were adamant that the situation had gone too far to ignore; failure to refute Chambers's lurid accusations might be taken by some as an admission of guilt. What's more, argued Conant, the case had taken on a new and worrisome dimension. With election-year rhetoric reflecting growing alarm at Soviet spies and domestic treachery, he feared there would be fresh assaults on academic freedom.[33]

Marbury presented this to Hiss, who in turn urged him to see John W. Davis, who had succeeded Hiss as president of the Carnegie Endowment for Peace, Arthur Ballantine, once Herbert Hoover's Assistant Secretary of the Treasury, and Edward Stettinius, briefly Secretary of State under FDR and Truman. They assessed Chambers to be an erratic bohemian whose checkered career and emotional instability would undermine his veracity in a court of law. Marbury accepted their counsel.

Late in September 1948, Hiss filed suit for perjury. With that, he sealed his fate, catapulted Chambers into a permanent place in history, and unwittingly inaugurated six long years of televised melodrama and national soul-searching. Harvard would play an outsized role in the morality play that followed, her president receiving alumni brickbats, editorial plaudits, and eventually, a place on the international diplomatic scene from his friend Dwight Eisenhower.

In his book *Education in a Divided World,* published almost simultaneously with the first notes of Chambers's overture, Conant warned his countrymen that external threats must be met with internal rigor. To strengthen their position, moral as well as political, he demanded a shift in the forms of public education. Tax-supported schools provided the sinews of democracy, wrote Conant; by dispersing economic and social inequities, they would emphatically dispel any latent appeal held by Marxist doctrine.

Conant's advice was not confined to the classroom. He endorsed the Marshall Plan, Universal Military Training, and NATO, along with federal aid to equalize teachers' salaries and a vigorous pursuit of gifted pupils. He also begged his readers permanently to throw off their distrust of foreign involvements. They must prepare themselves for years to come, he wrote, to traverse "that narrow knife-edge which divides supineness from belligerency. Patience and yet more patience, strength and wisdom to handle strength, a belief in the importance of the historic goals of our unique society, intelligence and courage to cope with problems of terrifying complexity—all these we shall need in abundant measure."

Events in his own backyard testified to the stresses attending such half-mobilization. Fresh from defeat in his campaign against Galbraith, Clarence Randall rose before a Commencement audience, in his capacity as president of the Alumni Association, with a provocative appeal to his fellow businessmen. Wade into academic controversies and political thickets alike, he urged, offering a thinly veiled attack on those who would embrace freedom for the professor while shunning it for the man of commercial enterprise. He sat down to find Conant's expressive features mingled somewhere between a smile and a frown.

"You didn't like it," Randall told his chief.

"Well," replied Conant, "I guess it is all right, so long as it doesn't happen too often."[34]

Dean Acheson, at the Commencement to receive an honorary degree, mounted the podium with a wry rejoinder. Down in New Haven, he told the president, there had been many bold Robin Hoods in past days, but not, as yet, one who was so bold as to raise his standard in the Royal Pavilion itself.

Less fanciful criticism was on the way. In 1949 the Soviets entered the nuclear fraternity and Chiang Kai-shek's government fell. Yet Harvard students were denouncing a Navy ROTC oath—even Young Republicans joined the protesters' ranks—and a *Newsweek* survey reported that Conant's University was one of a half-dozen in the nation with an organized unit of campus Communists. The National Council for American Education issued a stinging indictment of what it labeled "Reducators" at Harvard, singling out by name seventy-six faculty members with affiliations to over a hundred reportedly subversive or front groups, ranging from Educators for Wallace to veterans of the old Abraham Lincoln Brigade of Spanish Civil War fame. Among those condemned for allegedly disloyal activities were Crane Brinton, Randall Thompson, Howard Mumford Jones, and Conant.

With his usual disdain for tactical wisdom, astronomer Harlow Shapley incurred alumni wrath by chairing a New York assembly reputedly devoted to fostering U.S.-Soviet friendship among scientists and litterateurs. English instructor John Ciardi spoke to a gathering of the Maryland Progressive Party, which prompted a Baltimore lawyer named Frank Ober to compose a letter of protest. In Ober's view, the University was condoning the extracurricular activities of at least some faculty members who were giving aid and comfort to foreign enemies of the United States. Such men ought not be employed as teachers, he declared, adding his own refusal to supply financial support for the law school of which he was a graduate unless corrective action were taken.

Conant turned to Grenville Clark for assistance in drafting a reply. Clark's letter quoted Eliot as saying that an American university must be free before it was rich, and reminded Ober of Lowell's condemnation of those who would restrict the public pronouncements of faculty members, however unpopular they might appear. If five million dollars were the price placed on Shapley or Ciardi, wrote Clark, the University would reject it with contempt. Conant added his own postscript. Harvard needed money, he said, but not at the expense of compromising its tradition of freedom.[35]

However forthright the president's statement, it soon conflicted with a public report he had signed, which flatly ruled out employment of any known Communist in a teaching position. Conant tried to reconcile the two positions. As long as he was president of Harvard, he wrote in the spring of 1949, there would be no inquiries into professional politics, no watch made of their activities as private citizens. Distinguishing between government's need to investigate the loyalty of its employees and the university's timeless obligation to avoid witch hunting, Conant stuck to his view that the issue was not heresy but conspiracy, "which can only be likened to that of a group of spies and saboteurs in an enemy country in time of war." From documentary evidence as well as his own experiences in the atomic lab, Conant was convinced that card-carrying Communists were not free agents, but sworn enemies of American freedom.

Undoubtedly, the president felt much better about another response he made on the same issue. Presented with a *Crimson* poll showing that his faculty was against employing known Communists two to one while students took the opposite position by an identical margin, Conant adopted a Solomon-like stance. Asked what he would do if a professor were to stride into his office and announce his homage to Moscow, the hard-headed idealist broke into a grin. "I would send for a psychiatrist," said Conant.

Paul Buck's response was more practical when an internal dispute involving a promising young history instructor named H. Stuart Hughes threatened the new Russian Research Center. An active partisan of Henry Wallace in 1948, Hughes had been named assistant director of the Center, which was, at the time, attempting to define its mandate from the Carnegie Corporation. Under pressure from Carnegie, center director Clyde Kluckholm moved to sever Hughes. The grandson of Chief Justice Charles Evans Hughes promised to scale back his politicking, but it was not enough for Carnegie.

Subtly but effectively, Buck turned up the pressure. As he later recounted in a Columbia University interview, "I told him that I thought in his best interest he'd better just stick to his knitting as an historian for a while and then develop into some position, and then when he's in his forties and fifties he could make his real impact." His offense, in Buck's candid words: he'd been "a little too active a little too soon" on the political front. In fact, Hughes went on to a distinguished career.[36]

The Hughes case pointed up Harvard's dilemma. Defending academic freedom absolutely would cause public scandal. Yielding, even by inches, could infuriate faculty members who were already estranged from their president and who were increasingly alienated from the American political mainstream. Conant and Buck did their best to find a middle way. For the most part they succeeded, holding the place together in the face of the gathering storm while other institutions took shelter by tossing overboard those instructors who were out of step with majority thinking. When UCLA rejected Harold Laski's appeal to speak on campus, Harvard opened the doors of Sanders Theater. A year later, in 1952, after the California Board of Regents dismissed a squadron of Berkeley instructors for publicly opposing a state loyalty oath, four of them became permanent members of Harvard's faculty.[37]

The storm rising in the wake of the Hiss case, which Conant had predicted back in 1948, reached hurricane force in the mid-Fifties in what became one of the most furious domestic conflicts of the century. Harvard was at its eye, though by then Conant was no longer at the helm. The furor was accidentally touched off by a curiously charming, laughingly unprincipled junior senator from Wisconsin. On his way to a Lincoln Day speech in February 1950, Joseph McCarthy was startled to hear an airline hostess greet him by name. "I'm glad somebody recognizes me," he replied. Recognition was not a problem for McCarthy after he told the Ohio County Women's Club that he had uncovered the names of 205 onetime Communists known to the secretary of state, who even then were "working and shaping the policy of the State Department." When the press sought details, McCarthy backtracked. He had actually been referring to "bad security risks," he claimed, not Communists. But the senator had tasted fame and found it to his liking.

Buried within his Wheeling, West Virginia, jeremiad was a populist assault on those he accused of selling America out. The objects of his attack were "not the less fortunate, or members of minority groups . . . ," he claimed, "but rather those who have had all the benefits the wealthiest nation on earth has to offer—the finest homes, the finest college educations, and the finest jobs in the government that we can give . . . the bright young men who are born with silver spoons in their mouth [*sic*]." In his lexicon of resentment, striped pants became a code word for Eastern Establishment diplomatic disloyalty, and the governing elite that had been schooled at Harvard and other eastern universities became an irresistible target. McCarthy did not invent this sport. He was descended from a long line of breastbeaters who had railed at Charles Eliot as a Red and had denounced as pacifists professors unhappy with the Spanish-American War. Unlike them, however, he had television to disseminate his message, at least until his overheated image burned out in that cool medium.[38]

In a baccalaureate sermon delivered that June following McCarthy's first salvo, Conant took for his text the passage from St. John, "In my Father's house are many mansions." The house of many mansions had a single foundation, said Conant, laid in a society's transcendent values. Harvard had, by now, become almost a sidebar to his public campaigning against whoever threatened the American house and all it contained.

With the outbreak of hostilities in Korea that same month, Harvard's president, who considered himself the coldest of cold warriors, returned to the national headlines. He was in the vanguard of the Committee for the Present Danger formed to steer public opinion away from the America First isolationist doctrines of Herbert Hoover and Robert Taft. In a December 1950 article in *Look* magazine, Conant demanded the immediate conscription of up to three and half million men to be sent to Europe for as long as a decade. In assembling this titanic force, a breastwork against Soviet expansion, he would permit no deferments for college students or for anyone else.

A month later, Conant submitted a plan to Secretary of Defense George Marshall. He proposed to take a year off the standard college calendar for returning soldiers, to shorten graduate studies and to rotate essential faculty members in government service, rather than surrender them to Washington for the entire length of battle. Congress rejected Universal Military Training, however, in favor of a modified draft. This kept the colleges filled but at a cost of mounting resentment among the less academically favored. "It is obvious," wrote Conant with Yankee understatement, "that such a policy does not make for national unity."*

At the end of January 1951, students began reporting to the third floor of Phillips Brooks House to receive free subway passes and directions to the Boston Army Base. The old double-decker bunks stamped USN were still in the Houses, and the dining halls had only just gotten rid of the metal mess trays left behind by earlier classes bound for the Western Front instead of the 38th Parallel. The *Crimson,* now firmly anchored in the internationalist camp, berated left-wing students for a onesided Peace Poll and the Liberal Union for its part in a strike at the Revelation Bra Company. Harvard Progressives tried to stoke the fires of militancy by inviting singer Paul Robeson to appear on campus. Their efforts were no more successful than those of a hastily formed Peace Council, which fractured as soon as the ink on its mimeographed petitions dried.

In the Square, gray flannel suits were on sale for $39.95. Each year the editors of the *Crimson* elected a Miss Radcliffe. But changes were

---

* Fifteen years later, when the same policy was applied to Vietnam it turned Harvard and other universities into moral pressure cookers, stuffed with unhappy men who couldn't shake a sense of guilt for being spared from a war they didn't want to fight anyway.

taking place at Harvard. There were only four blacks in the Class of '52, but before the end of the year, Harvard had both a chapter of the NAACP and a cross burned outside a Yard suite inhabited by black students. Although patrons of the Club 47 on Mt. Auburn Street opted for sweet jazz and bitter coffee over political agitation, and the dime brew at Cronin's was preferred by many to membership in the Harvard Society for Minority Rights, yet four hundred members of the Silent Generation crowded into a 1955 concert by Pete Seeger.[39]

In 1951 the University bid farewell to its crew of House bedmakers, "the one last remnant of gracious living," in the words of the football team's head cheerleader. Bill Bingham, Harvard's athletic director for twenty-five years, also left. Conant's revamped Harvard had little space for Lowell's "biddies" or the affable but defeat-prone Bingham. The alumni were restive, and a new Overseers Committee on Athletics tolled the bell for gentlemanly mediocrity.

The president continued to kick over beehives, even within the closely guarded councils held every other Monday with the six men who aided him in governing the University. There was a protracted, bitter dispute with Grenville Clark over the Arnold Arboretum, which ultimately was resolved by the Massachusetts Supreme Judicial Court, plus a private contest of wills between Conant and Clark over the latter's adherence to what Conant labeled "World Government or Bust." In addition, there was a dispute over the status of the Divinity School, which Conant had first hoped to drown like a kitten, and then to convert into a kind of ecclesiastical Nieman Foundation for visiting divines. But the president yielded, however reluctantly, when Clark and Buffalo attorney John Lord O'Brien volunteered in 1950 to raise a two-million-dollar endowment for the school for which God had not taken it upon Himself to provide.[40]

Conant would contain his doubts about the school and its mission, but not his basic skepticism or outright hostility to organized religion in the public classroom. The latter pitched Conant against the Catholic hierarchy of Boston, and its redoubtable archbishop, Richard J. Cushing. In a strongly worded address to the American Association of School Administrators in April 1952, the dogma-hating Conant criticized the role played by private and parochial schools in American life. Such candor was more or less taken for granted by now, along with his habit of giving large chunks of advice, solicited or not. What really landed the president in hot water was his declaration that social equality and the fluidity of condition celebrated by de Tocqueville might be eroded if Americans were to follow the example of Australia, where belief that religious instruction ought not be divorced from secondary education had inspired a dual system of schools, with local control overrun in the name of a state-ordered program of studies.

Many Protestants, Catholics, and Jews, he acknowledged, were united in concern that secularism in the classroom was undermining popular values. But, committed as he was to public education, hopeful as he was about its unifying drive and democratizing power, Conant thought that demands for taxpayer support of private institutions suggested "that American society use its own hands to destroy itself."

Archbishop Cushing wasted no time in responding. Conant's statements were sure to aid and comfort the enemies of parochial schooling, he wrote, and were altogether astonishing coming from a Harvard president "in this late year of grace." Skillfully, Cushing shifted the battle away from religious indoctrination, toward the issue of nuns teaching black children who, until recently, had been deprived of such instruction because of community attitudes—presumably authentic, if warped, expressions of the popular consensus Conant championed. The argument wasn't exactly fair, but it was effective. For once the old scientist seemed bested on his own turf.[41]

Imbued with Eliot's suspicion of the Catholic clergy, Conant went so far as to urge those accepting the gift of Dumbarton Oaks in Washington, D.C., to word the deed in such a way as to permit Harvard, should the need arise in the distant future, to pull up stakes and walk away from a Massachusetts in thrall to the Roman hierarchy.[42]

In the fall of 1952, Conant was nearing his sixtieth birthday, a weary man out of patience with academic life. "You get tired of exercising the same muscles," was the way he put it to Bill Marbury. When a newly elected Dwight Eisenhower invited his friend to serve as High Commissioner to the Federal Republic of Germany, it took him only twenty-four hours to telephone his acceptance to John Foster Dulles. In his diary Conant confessed that he hadn't the slightest idea where he might find himself four years later. But at least he would not be chained to what he exasperatedly called *"this* job."[43]

"Thunderous silence" greeted his revelation to the Corporation on January 1, 1953. "I've got a piece of news for you that may come as a bit of a surprise," he laconically informed University publicists twelve days later. "You've seen the rumors in the papers? Well, they're true."

"Holy smoke!" sputtered one of the visitors. The rest of the University rubbed its eyes in disbelief. "It seemed ten steps down," said Mc-George Bundy, "for the president of Harvard to merely run Germany."[44]

Conant's surprising decision set off much speculation and jockeying for position. Bundy's own name figured prominently on a list that included Paul Buck and a hefty number of deans, professors, and House masters. One undergraduate climbed a tree and announced he would not come down until the Corporation anointed John Finley, the much-loved humanist and philosopher-king of Eliot House. Bundy, professing a lack of interest in the job, linked his Yale pedigree and the continuing preoccupations of congressional investigating committees. Talk of his candidacy, proclaimed Bundy in a sly twist on Harry Truman's memorable phrase, was nothing more than a blue herring.[45]

Like the Roman curia, the Harvard community had its own "fat pope, thin pope" theory of succession. Eliot, the scientist, followed by Lowell, the humanist, followed by Conant, the scientist, followed—by whom? There were plenty of candidates to speculate about, but one thing was already decided. This time, the Corporation wanted a man who would give himself unreservedly to the University and, above all, to the College. Twenty years earlier, Lawrence Lowell had advised his successor that to be successful in the job, he ought to think of it as a marriage. Lowell had justified his suffocating style of leadership by simply loving Harvard more than anything else. But Conant was cut from different cloth, and however much prestige his globetrotting enterprises bestowed upon the school, those who shared Lowell's outlook had grown restive in the loveless marriage that began in 1933.

In the public mind and media spotlight, Conant had succeeded in nationalizing Harvard. His successor would have to deal with the limitations this imposed, as well as the opportunities it presented. For instance, tuition hadn't been raised between 1928 and 1948. With the rest of the Ivy League and hundreds of smaller colleges looking to Cambridge as an example, any president willing to state forthrightly the case for increased tuition—and increased salaries, endowment, and scholarships as well—would in effect be performing a valuable national service, legitimizing a similar appeal by others.

But the very size of the modern university restricted the freedom of its chief executive, as did its increasing reliance on outside sources of funding, subject to political whims or economic fevers. Conant's successors could no longer command support by divine right. America was no longer the intellectually timid, hierarchical society it had been in the late nineteenth century, when scholarly frontiers were defined by a handful of corporate potentates and academic inventors. Now in the company of many first-rate institutions, Harvard was hardpressed to retain Conant's meritocratic brass ring.

In Eliot's time the school was cast as a natural training ground for a ruling elite of dispassionate experts. That image never disappeared, even if succeeding generations draped it with garlands of public service. In their own ways, both Lowell and Conant had embroidered the pattern. But here too, the University bartered away part of its sovereignty for more of its status.

After World War II, the university that had created National Scholarships and been intellectually enriched through the G.I. Bill, the university whose leading personalities had campaigned openly for U.S. involvement in the fighting and then gone on to assist in building the bomb that ended it and in negotiating the postwar alliances that formed its uneasy aftermath, had become de facto national property, to be argued over and scolded and shouted at when it failed to please everyone—which was nearly always. In making Harvard a national possession, Conant had made it more than ever the target of both the right and the left. Government funding was only the most obvious lever available to political overseers. No less important, if harder to calculate, were the exaggerated feelings of alumni enamored of the school's special role, and the constant scrutiny of a press corps pleased to discover an institution whose name was a catchword for controversy—Harvard's authorities were rarely shy about tossing off a quotable opinion or an instant explanation for things alien to most reporters.

For Conant's successors, the new facts of life were further complicated by internal shifts requiring more of a president's attention for the greasing of departmental machinery, carrying out architectural blueprints, wining and dining potential donors, protecting against faculty poachers. There was both less time and less inclination for involvement beyond the Yard.

Finally, the choice confronting the Corporation in the spring of 1953 reverberated with the echoes of 1908, when the undergraduate College faced starvation at the hands of Eliot's rapacious graduate schools. Insofar as this was a recurring issue, the Corporation was on familiar ground. However, the Harvard fashioned by James Conant was a faithful reflection, not alone of one man's liberalism, but of a society comfortable enough with its own values to undertake a missionary avocation. General Education was a Cambridge platform for modern man, hammered out by Conant, Buck, and a self-assured community of dons. After 1953, Harvard, in league with much of the American Establishment, began to lose that sense of coherence. More than ever aware of its power, it seemed uncertain of its purpose. In search of unifying themes, it turned inward.

Conant had been able to preach his gospel to America and to the world in no small part because the University had permitted him the luxury of a provost who shared his beliefs and was equipped to administer Harvard in his absence. In eliminating the job of provost, the Corporation guaranteed that subsequent presidents would pay more attention to their own backyard. They would proselytize less, administer more.

After 1953, the University performed more functions than ever before. It advanced knowledge in ways its founders could not have imagined possible. But the question arose: was Harvard doing the other thing for which it was established, perpetuating a learned ministry (in the modern, secular sense, a cultured set of rulers)? If Harvard could no longer settle on a common set of values prerequisite to citizenship, what did that say of the country's fragmentation, the will of its leaders, the drift of its opinion makers, and the balkanization brought on by pluralism run amok?

The Corporation didn't intend such a result, but the reality is inescapable. When Conant left Harvard, value-oriented education lost its best friend. His vision of a university both national in scope and peerless in its acceptance of moral burdens was destined to be superseded, ironically enough, under a successor whose personal commitment to that dream was more verbally explicit than Conant's own.

As Cambridge settled in for a long, delicious feast of speculation, Conant prepared to confront McCarthy face to face during the confirmation hearings on his nomination as ambassador to Germany. Eisenhower had appointed a cadre of Harvard men to his diplomatic corps, establishment figures like Winthrop Aldrich, C. Douglas Dillon, John Davis Lodge, and Charles E. Bohlen. This was more than enough to displease elements of the Taft wing of the GOP, for whom such men were all too enamored of tweed and bowler hats. In presenting his Harvard classmate to the Senate Foreign Relations Committee, Leverett Saltonstall explained that Harvard presidents were expected to be controversial figures. Michigan's Homer Ferguson remarked that Conant had certainly maintained the tradition.[46]

After Drew Pearson revived Conant's old problems with the Catholic hierarchy in print, the nominee managed to defuse senatorial objections in a private session. On the second day of February, he went before the committee in an open hearing to which opponents came well-armed. One of them zeroed in on the old "American Radical" article, reminding his audience of Conant's desire to confiscate and redistribute private property. Robert Taft hurried to Conant's aid on that one, asking whether the final paragraph of the piece didn't dull the edge of the president's advocacy. "You are in," a State Department functionary whispered to the nominee, and anyone familiar with Taft's prestige among conservatives could understand the almost audible sigh of relief that swept the committee room.

Only later did Conant discover how close his nomination had come to being scuttled. McCarthy had invited a youthful William F. Buckley to prepare a speech summarizing his case, including Conant's opposition to congressional probes of alleged Communist activity at Harvard, his attacks on private and parochial schools, and his wartime endorsement of Henry Morgenthau's drastic plan to economically dismember a fallen Germany. Behind closed doors, Taft argued with his headstrong colleague. McCarthy eventually settled for sending a letter to Eisenhower which contained what Ike called "wild charges."[47]

Freshman Senator John F. Kennedy lent only grudging support to the nomination of his fellow Bay Stater, going out of his way to reassure Catholic constituents that had the job in question been U.S. Commissioner of Education instead of High Commissioner to the government in Bonn, he would have cast a negative vote.

With more haste than decorum, Conant was confirmed and sworn into office. "This really is the end of a chapter," he wrote following his final Harvard Commencement. "Sense of great relief. My successor promises to be excellent but with different ideas." When he left Cambridge to Nathan Pusey, he would put it behind him once and for all, with a single exception. "I'll be damned if I'll give up my dentist."[48]

Conant returned home from Germany in 1957 to spirited bidding for his services. The *Boston Herald* enthusiastically suggested him as a possible running mate for Richard Nixon in 1960. Instead, he chose, at John Gardner's bidding, to undertake an exhaustive study of the comprehensive high school in America. Aided by a staff of high school principals and instructors, Conant plunged into the subject with zest. After visiting fifty-five institutions, he published a book with the surprising admission that too little was being done for the gifted pupil, especially those top 15 percent who were the country's secret weapon in the national game of catch-up being played because of Russia's unexpected coup in launching the first satellite to orbit the earth.

Having warned of the dangers in neglecting America's most promising youngsters, Conant next embarked on an entirely different campaign. His book *Slums and Suburbs* was based upon a disturbing round of visits to all-black high schools in Chicago, St. Louis, and Detroit. This led him to coin the oft-quoted phrase, "social dynamite" to describe the festering inequalities of ill-financed academies, half of whose students never completed the course. Consigning more and more black youth to urban joblessness, he wrote, against a landscape without hope, was like stockpiling flammable material in an empty building in a city block. Yet Conant displayed insensitivity of his own in claiming that token integration would achieve less for disadvantaged youth than an infusion of federal money into their classrooms. His opposition to busing upset many black leaders. It also ensured heated controversy and immense book sales.[49]

In the early 1960s, Conant turned his attention to the preparation of American teachers. He was harshly rebuked by the NEA and others who thought he was a turncoat for questioning current methods of training. Conant found it easy to brush aside such complaints, just as he was able to concentrate on the work at hand while associates rushed to watch a Columbus Day parade pass under their Manhattan window. One of the men, carried away by the music, remarked gingerly, "Dr. Conant, I like marching bands."

"Oh?" responded the chairman, who felt such frills as marching bands had no place in the modern high school, "you do? . . . Hm." A five-second pause. "Let's see now, we were discussing this point in chapter three."[50]

Conant's appearances in Cambridge were well spaced. He returned to inspect the latest experiments in organic chemistry. He gave substantially toward a new library for the school of education. Nathan Pusey's Harvard, he said, was like another world from that much smaller institution he had guided. Conant liked his successor personally and was moved to wire approval following Pusey's forced eviction of University Hall occupants in the spring of 1969. He was also grateful for the kindnesses of Pusey and his wife, who later lived in the same building on New York's East Side when Pusey left Cambridge for the Mellon Foundation.[51]

The old man's thoughts often strayed back to Massachusetts Hall. Not long before his death, Conant looked out the window of his apartment at the nearby East River and asked Pusey if he weren't seeing Harvard Square. To his daughter-in-law, he confessed what must have been, for a scientist of rigorous deductive powers, the ultimate indignity. "You know," he said of his occasional memory lapses, "the worst thing about this is that you cannot believe a word I say."[52]

Spoken with the lifelong passion for empiricism implanted early in the Dorchester photoengraver's son, Conant's lament ushered in a sad time of physical and mental decline. Before encroaching deafness and a wave of small strokes forced him to curtail his writing, Conant matched wits with William F. Buckley on Buckley's television program, and faulted Richard Nixon's administration for its neglect of education and science. He turned against a Vietnam War he had once supported and cast a ballot for George McGovern over Nixon in 1972. David Riesman encountered him on the porch of the handsome inn at Hanover, New Hampshire, the college town where Conant now spent half the year, and found that old fires still leapt at criticism of the comprehensive high school.[53]

To the end fastidious, he kept up his handsome dress, at least until the summer of 1977, when he went to die in a Hanover nursing home. The ranks of his Cambridge contemporaries were much diminished by the following April. But there were more than enough admirers to fill Memorial Church (for a thoroughly secular ceremony Grace Conant agreed to only after considerable persuasion by official Harvard). They heard John Finley pay graceful tribute to the father of General Education, and George Kistiakowsky recall his old companion the cultural preserver and social innovator, "a cool Yankee who could be a warm friend." The presence of such a man, said Kistiakowsky, had left an indelible imprint on this century's America. For that, they were all enriched.[54]

President Derek Bok, who had succeeded Conant's successor by then, had not known Conant during *his* presidency but acknowledged being influenced daily by his decisions. No president, Bok said, could be adequately assessed while in office. Only after a generation had come and gone could his memory be interpreted with perspective. A president could make brilliant speeches, captivate alumni, raise huge sums, and build great buildings, "but if he neglects the quality of appointments, the institution will inevitably erode under his leadership. Conversely, however dull and uninspired a president may seem, if he can manage somehow to guard and enhance the quality of the Faculty, the University cannot fail to prosper under his guidance."[55]

Bok's criteria seemed overly defensive and far too narrow to admirers of Conant's boldness in asserting the national preeminence of Harvard. In fact, they reflected a changed culture, wherein the University could ill afford the kind of presidential outspokenness which might touch off student protests and rile alumni whose financial support enabled it to survive and prosper. They stamped Conant as the last of his breed, something the *New York Times* judged a national calamity. "There is not now at any major university a leader concerned with the whole of American education," the *Times* concluded.

In his eulogy, Bok seemed to accept such developments with dry eyes.

A meritocracy, after all, had little room for sentiment, hardly more than the deliberately restrained commemoration held to mark Conant's passing. As a student of physics, no one better than Conant would have understood that for every action must come a corresponding reaction. Derek Bok's definition of presidential leadership said volumes about a Harvard obedient to that law.

CHAPTER SIX

The Bishop from Appleton

*Our search is successful. Harvard will have a
president who believes in God!*
—THOMAS W. LAMONT
Member of the Corporation

*We thought we were getting St. Thomas
Aquinas; We wound up with Tom Sawyer.*
—JOHN FINLEY
Master of Eliot House

CONANT COULD NOT have chosen a worse time to announce his resignation. Even as he prepared to clean out his office, Joseph McCarthy was
sharpening his attacks on higher education in general, and preparing to
do battle with Harvard in particular. This was just one of the headaches
plaguing the Corporation, which would have to choose a successor before
Conant's departure for Germany, an event that could not be put off later
than midsummer 1953. At the same time as they were deciding what
Harvard needed and who might best meet those needs, the men of the
Corporation were compelled to take a stand on the growing issue of
Communist subversion of the classroom. Pressure to come forward on
this issue was already intense but it was further exacerbated because the
whole educational world was looking at them, curious and more than a
little fearful about what Harvard might do.

When two *Crimson* editors stole the *Lampoon's* mascot, a large

metal stork named Ibis, and presented it to Stalin as a gift from American students, and then the Poonies retaliated by reporting this flagrant
example of Communist sympathizing to the McCarthy committee, it was
funny. The laughter died quickly, however, when McCarthy attacked
Harvard for its decision to retain three instructors who had supported the
Communist cause in the Thirties.

The nation's intelligentsia were understandably jittery. The University of Washington fired three tenured academics in 1953. University of
California regents approved a loyalty oath, and discharged two dozen professors who held back from signing it. In Chicago, Robert Hutchins flatly
rejected a state board of inquiry's efforts to force his university's hand.
Hutchins admitted that students protesting the probe might have been
guilty of objectionable conduct. But "Redness and Rudeness are not the
same," said Hutchins, who made it clear that he was on the students' side.
It was a minority position.

In subsequent months, additional attacks were launched against the
New York City public school system. Rutgers and the University of Kansas City reacted to a Senate investigation by evicting faculty members
who took the Fifth Amendment rather than discuss their past or present
involvement with Communism.[1]

For Harvard, the issue had been raised with dramatic urgency early
in 1953, when McCarthy's Senate colleague, William Jenner of Indiana,
had charged Assistant Professor Wendell Furry and instructors Leon
Kamin and Helen Deane Markham, with Communist involvement. It was
apparent that Harvard was vulnerable to such attacks even before Jenner's
committee summoned Furry to Washington in February. For one thing,
there was the Alger Hiss connection. Not only had Corporation member
William Marbury defended Hiss, but three nationally known graduates—
Felix Frankfurter, Francis B. Sayre, and Charles Wyzanski—had served as
friendly witnesses during the Hiss perjury trial. The University already
had a reputation as a breeding ground for radicalism, and Conant's repeated joustings against the established order had done nothing to alter
that. It was no surprise that the Corporation almost panicked when Furry
refused to comply with the committee's request for information about
his past and the names of others who might have been compatriots in
subversion.[2]

The strict fifty-year rule enforced by University archivists makes it
impossible to reconstruct the chain of events with absolute accuracy. But
the agonized reappraisal of the instructors' backgrounds and Harvard's
obligation to due process survives in the memories of participants. "We
didn't pay any attention to the bastard," claims Paul Cabot, then Univer-

sity treasurer. However, both Joseph Alsop and William Marbury remember a February 27th call Overseer Alsop made to Corporation member Marbury loudly protesting the Jenner probe and urging the Corporation to declare support for the beleaguered Furry. The faculty's response was more equivocal. "A real Communist is a traitor under discipline," said Professor William Yandell Elliott. "He is a Charlie, not a Joe, McCarthy." Attacking "pseudo-liberals . . . who were burned playing footsies with the Communists," Elliott spoke for many who were offended when Furry declined to cooperate with his questioners.[3]

With Conant about to depart for Germany, the burden of formulating official policy fell squarely on Provost Paul Buck, aided by Alsop, Senior Corporation Fellow Charles Coolidge, and others. The issue at hand was simple: Should Furry's resort to the Fifth Amendment disqualify him from membership in the Harvard family? If the University's answer had been yes, "Harvard would have been the Judas goat for everyone else," says Alsop. "If we gave way, it would have been the first battle of Bull Run all over." Agreeing with Alsop, several of Furry's science colleagues threatened to resign en masse were his services dispensed with.[4]

Three weeks after Alsop's first telephone call to Marbury, Edward Mason, dean of the graduate school of public administration, proposed a basis for handling the issue. On March 17, Mason wrote to Buck suggesting that Furry be reprimanded for having given false information to federal investigators who in 1944 had queried him about possible ties to the Communist party, and for later withholding his action from the governing boards. This was significant misconduct, argued Mason, but warranted nothing more than a probationary slap on the wrist.[5]

McGeorge Bundy, then a rising young member of the government department (and considered a possible Conant successor), strongly supported the Mason view in a letter dated April 21. With this evidence of faculty sentiment in hand, Buck advised the Corporation to take the Fifth Amendment into account, but only as one factor—and by no means the determining one—in weighing a faculty member's assurance that he was no longer under Communist influence.[6]

On May 1, anxious to settle the matter in time for the arrival of a new president, the University had crafted its final position. No one presently in thrall to Communist doctrine would be retained on the faculty; but no one would be fired for past association with it. Nor would anyone taking refuge in the constitutional protections afforded by the Fifth Amendment be punished for it. Furry's attempt at concealing the past made him a special case, and he would be formally reprimanded for it (but even he would go on to receive full tenure in the early 1960s). In the crucial test, then, Harvard had not buckled.

The Boston Catholic Archdiocese praised the judicious manner in which the Furry case had been handled. The *Baltimore Sun* added, "As has so often happened in the past, this venerable institution follows no preconceived formula but tackles a difficult problem in its own way—with results that will be helpful far beyond the confines of Harvard itself."

As events would demonstrate, McCarthy had only begun to fight. But Harvard was too preoccupied with its search for Conant's replacement to give the Wisconsin senator more than a fraction of its time. Although the University in 1953 was more than ever aware of its special position at the head of the educational community, it had no intention of adhering to Conant's national agenda, or of selecting a replica of Conant. As a token of just how far the Corporation was inclined to go in seeking an alternative—especially one capable of tapping the financial wellsprings neglected by the retiring president—Charles Coolidge, first among equals on the governing board, suggested to dean Erwin Griswold of the law school that Harvard consider David Rockefeller.[7]

Preposterous, snorted Griswold; coming so soon after Dwight Eisenhower's troubled Columbia presidency, Harvard's selection of Rockefeller would hit the academic community like a water balloon dropped from the tower of Memorial Hall. (Still, the idea didn't die there. As late as the Monday morning on which the press was given Nathan Pusey's name as Conant's successor, Corporation member Thomas Lamont, at a Ritz Hotel breakfast meeting with Charles Wyzanski, returned to Coolidge's vision—with no better luck.)[8]

Pusey's name had entered the contest late, almost by accident, at a time when Corporation members were increasingly frustrated by perceived flaws in the local contenders. Government department prodigy McGeorge Bundy at thirty-four was too young, and perhaps too arrogant, though Walter Lippmann had urged his candidacy. Long-time Eliot House master John Finley was too much the gentlemanly humanist. Scientist Paul Doty seemed genuinely reluctant when he was approached; in any event, the Corporation was unlikely to anoint another man of science to fill Conant's shoes. Provost Paul Buck was scratched from the list because of a reputation for being a natural second-in-command. As a result, the Corporation was only too glad to hear from Sheridan Logan, secretary to a New York educational trust fund, of the impending visit to New York of a Wisconsin educator named Nathan Marsh Pusey. It wasn't the first time Pusey's name had come up. It had already been put forward by Henry Wriston, president of Brown, and Victor Butterfield, another distinguished academic, who had both known Pusey since 1935.[9]

At that time Wriston had been president of tiny Lawrence College in Appleton, Wisconsin, and Butterfield was a member of his faculty. Together, Wriston and Butterfield had devised a new venture in general education. Long before Chicago's Robert Hutchins and others popularized what would become known as the Great Books scheme, the two men had been determined to conduct a broad survey of Western cultural traditions. They only needed the right young instructor to breathe life into the concept. They found him in Nathan Pusey, whom Wriston recalled as the son of an Iowa schoolteacher and a disciple of Harvard's irascible Irving Babbitt. Like his mentor, Pusey could be relied upon to shun fashionable causes for moral education of the timeless variety.

"Too many modern teachers commit the error of teaching students to see the evils and shortcomings of society without at the same time pointing out the evils that exist in themselves," Pusey lamented. Young minds should have liberating experiences, he thought. This seemed far more important to him than the ability to identify the President of the United States, "though I recognize there may be considerable irresponsibility in the attitude."[10]

Pusey could trace such beliefs to some powerful influences. As a boy in Council Bluffs, Iowa, he had listened to his widowed mother read aloud from *Pilgrim's Progress,* and the experience foreshadowed events in his own life. Even before he arrived in Cambridge as a scholarship student in the fall of 1924, there was about the young Iowan something of Christian confronting Mr. Worldly Wiseman. Irving Babbitt and other instructors only reinforced Pusey's moral certitudes, above all his belief in the civilizing mission of education. It was these qualities that Wriston and Butterfield saw in 1935 when they were scanning the horizon for a teacher who shared their own faith in the humanistic agenda. Their judgment was soon confirmed. "That man's crazy," exclaimed one disbelieving colleague of Pusey in those days. "He's got sophomores reading Aristotle's Aesthetics. Sophomores can't read Aristotle's Aesthetics!"[11]

Pusey proved otherwise. He went on confounding cynics in other schools until in 1944 the trustees of Lawrence summoned him again, this time to take over Wriston's job as president. Pusey plunged afresh into the classics, creating a new course for every entering student. In a kind of intellectual waterbath drawn from all fields, he assigned physicists to read *Hamlet,* taught English majors Darwin, required that art historians discover John Stuart Mill. Pusey became something of an infant prodigy, shaking up faculty traditions and shaking loose corporate cash for art centers and science labs.

Pusey did not pretend to be in the mainstream of practical instruction. "Not the scientific exploration of things," he warned, "not the scientific examination of the behavior of groups of people, but the living, vivid acquaintance with the adventures of the human spirit—this it is which especially can stretch the humanity that lies in a man . . . and needle it into its fullest growth."[12]

He had yet to publish a book, and he never entirely escaped the frowning disapproval of those Harvardians who would later dismiss him as a president on the theory that he would not have been qualified to earn tenure. But in Appleton, Pusey won respect as a teacher who cared about other teachers, who raised their salaries, who modernized their surroundings, and who played havoc with their comfortable habits. Above all, he lifted their morale at a time when the scholarly life in America was fast losing its special allure.

Under Pusey's guidance, Lawrence College undertook the greatest building campaign in its history. He doubled the meager endowment. He reached out into the private sector for support. He recruited outstanding teachers (so much so that Lawrence candidates for Ford Foundation research fellowships regularly won national competitions against better-known colleagues).

Along the way, he displayed the dogged certainties reared into him at his mother's kitchen table. Beginning in 1947, disillusioned by what he saw as the postwar world's wickedness, Pusey called for a greater role for religion at Lawrence. Political ills were far less important than psychological and spiritual ones, he contended. "College people," he wrote in 1949, "believe that something can be done about the state of the world, not blatantly, crudely, or self-righteously, but quietly, intelligently and persuasively, and especially in and through individual lives." In a world made noxious by demagoguery and insecure by spiritual malaise, in a time whose temper was illiberal, vindictive, and repressive, it was the responsibility of the liberal arts college to foster in the individual the courage and faith to seek out truth. "Especially the faith," he concluded, "for . . . the whole world now looks to us for a creed to believe and a song to sing."

Perhaps not the whole world, but certainly that portion inhabited by the Harvard Corporation looked to Appleton, Wisconsin, in the spring of 1953. Urged on by Wriston, Butterfield, and Sheridan Logan, Corporation members Tom Lamont, Paul Cabot, and Keith Kane, a New York lawyer and Episcopal vestryman who had replaced Grenville Clark, met for lunch with the unsuspecting Iowan at the Wall Street offices of J. P. Morgan and Company. Also at the meeting was George Whitney, who in addition to being chairman of the board at Morgan Trust was also president of the Harvard Board of Overseers.[13]

Unaware of the real reason for this impromptu gathering, Pusey hoped for nothing more than scholarship money for Lawrence. The luncheon dragged on, however (four hours instead of the allotted two). When it was followed by another invitation to come to Boston, Pusey realized that these men, who kept talking of their interest in the College, who implied that Conant had been guilty of negligence and who were now anxious to hear Pusey's remedies for that neglect, were assessing him as a possible successor.[14]

Pusey's examiners gleaned little from his undergraduate record. In the Class of 1928's album, his was one of the shortest biographies. It didn't even list his captaincy of Harvard's successful contest against Yale in a *Time*-sponsored "brain quiz." Nor could classmates provide much insight. Indeed, at the class's twenty-fifth reunion dinner, where the white smoke first puffed, there were mutterings of confusion and surprise. "Pusey," said one representative Old Boy, "who the hell is he?"[15]

Reporters asking the same question discovered a family man who went to church twice on Sundays, didn't own a television set, and disdained golf. Digging deeper, they unearthed a warm trail of controversy at Lawrence, where, depending on one's perspective, Pusey's religious convictions made him alternately steadfast or obstinate. His certitude did not end with Sunday's benediction. At least one college trustee had quit in protest over the modernistic design of a new campus building, which reflected Pusey's surprising penchant for the avant-garde in architecture. A few traces of youthful rebellion cropped up, including an undergraduate protest over Boston's ban of H. L. Mencken's *Mercury*. But mostly there was obedience to Babbitt's strictures against topical morality and political shrieking, an echo of the professor's harsh judgment on those who assumed that the only significant struggle between good and evil was social rather than individual.

Among the rumors circulating about the potential president was one alleging him to be a teetotaler. This Tom Lamont dashed on a scouting expedition to Appleton that spring. Relax, he telephoned Harvard treasurer Paul Cabot, he had just downed a couple of martinis with Pusey himself. Other stories were less easily dispelled. In some quarters it was whispered that Babbitt's disciple was not the professor's intellectual equal and that he had abandoned the basketball court after his freshman year so that he would not have to forfeit his scholarship. It was said that he had been unhappy as a graduate student in Cambridge, plowing through Widener's stacks in preparing a Ph.D. thesis on fourth-century Athenian law. "If you ever catch me around here again," he was quoted as telling classmates, "you can shoot me."[16]

With such information to promote misgivings, not all Harvard's governors were eager to embrace the new man—even as an alternative to David Rockefeller. Overseers Joseph Alsop and J. Robert Oppenheimer questioned Pusey's intellectual candlepower, and suspected that in its haste to be rid of Conant's disputatious ways, the Corporation was condemning Harvard to a period of quiet self-satisfaction, duplicating the national slumber induced by Eisenhower. Theirs, however, were the only dissenting votes cast.[17]

In the last days of June 1953, the graduate student who, with typical modesty, had once doubted his own credentials to be part of the Cambridge community was back for good. A handsome six-footer of 180 pounds and forty-six years, Pusey was voted the best-looking Harvard president ever by a secretarial poll. He pronounced himself "stunned" by his sudden elevation to the most coveted throne in all of American education. Characteristically, he had barely occupied it before stepping into the more familiar confines of the pulpit.

> *Harvard is not a college limited in the reach of its influence, and entering here you become citizens of no mean city. This University is now organically related to all parts and sections of our country—indeed to the whole world—and it touches almost every aspect of its life. Having chosen to come here, and in turn been chosen, it follows that your interests must grow patiently but steadily into commensuration with a vastly enlarged perspective. And it follows, too, that they must deepen.*
>
> —NATHAN PUSEY
> *September 1953*

HOWEVER ELSE he might differ from Conant, Pusey shared his predecessor's disdain for ceremonial excess. This was unfortunate, because in choosing a deliberately frugal inaugural in the fall of 1953, the new president missed an opportunity to lay out his own objectives, and to gain loyalties of a Harvard faculty suspicious of anyone who was so public in attending Sunday services and Saturday football games. But Pusey preferred to let deeds speak louder than words. Cynics suspected that most of his conversation was reserved for God.

Armored in his faith, Pusey never lost the monklike appearance of one who lived apart from the world. To admirers, he seemed a vestigial figure from the past, a lineal descendant of Increase Mather who felt perfectly at home sitting on the seventeenth-century throne reserved for presidential use on Commencement Day. When Giles Constable received tenure in the government department, Pusey called on him, as was his habit, to express congratulations. Constable leaped to his feet and addressed the president as Sir, a title he had previously reserved only for his father.[18]

To detractors, who cringed when he told them that "the queen of theology" would again receive her proper due, or when he sat mute at gatherings of faculties over whom he presided in the most nominal fashion, Pusey was at first a riddle, later an embarrassment, "an academic ballbearing," as one senior professor put it. He did not spellbind, like Lowell, or lose himself in vast causes, like Conant. To a community of sparkling wit and omnivorous intellect, he offered personal rectitude and discriminating judgment.[19]

He could astonish his closest collaborators with a literalness devoid of humor. When Charles Whitlock, who functioned in effect as Pusey's vice-president for community relations, revealed a job offer from the Rhode Island School of Design, he expected to be met with sympathy and a touch of fatherly counsel. Instead, he was greeted by a look of puzzlement, followed by a resolute declaration. "Charles," Pusey intoned, "resist temptation." "You know," Whitlock told a colleague, "if it had been said in humor, I would have thought it funny. But it wasn't."[20]

Such stories, repeated and embellished, set Pusey apart from the rest of Cambridge, but the president himself didn't seem to mind. He understood from previous experience what it was like for an outlander to arrive in Cambridge, to be plunged into its vortex of ideas and egos, to grope for a pattern and discover interior purpose. The campus he had known as an undergraduate in the 1920s had been in love with excess. Boys enamored of gin and flappers found little time and less tolerance for those they labeled "Christers." Pusey looked back at the era, and was grateful for the personal awakening that Harvard had inspired in him, despite its social climate.

Now in a time divided by politics and ravaged by messiahs of far right and left, Pusey turned to traditional faith as an antidote to cynicism. Combining his personal piety with very modern instincts, one of his proudest directives as president brought women into the choir that sang at Memorial Church. It was done quietly in the spring, so that no one noticed the change until the following September. In the meantime, however, Corporation members were apprehensive. "Well, Nate," said one, "that'll be the end of you."[21]

A much more publicized campaign to restore religion at Harvard gave Pusey a platform from which to display his liberal, pluralistic approach to the subject, and more than a little personal courage as well. "He's an Episcopalian," said one close friend of the president, "but he lacks the buffed-down political sense of Episcopalians and Catholics. He's really a rock-hard Calvinist."

Within days of his election, Pusey had launched a major fund drive for the moribund divinity school. Once a flourishing academy, the school now had only three professors, a handful of part-time instructors, and a dreary, outdated preoccupation with the sort of methodological scholarship popular in nineteenth-century Germany. It had virtually no constituency outside the old Unitarian precincts of Back Bay and Beacon Hill. Impressed after spending a weekend with Pusey in New York, John D. Rockefeller Jr. donated a million dollars toward revitalizing the place. With this plus millions more from only slightly less well-heeled laymen, Pusey brightened the faculty with Paul Tillich, the University of Chicago's Amos Wilder, Lutheran Krister Stendahl (an avid spokesman for his native Sweden's Christian youth movement), plus Catholics, Jews, and holy men from the East. Arthur Darby Nock, who in the new order was assigned classes in comparative religion, astonished a Christmas week gathering of the American Philosophical Association in Philadelphia. "Fancy seeing you in this den of iniquity," exclaimed the president of Vanderbilt. "Oh, that's quite all right," Nock replied. "I'm professor of all the religions that aren't so."[22]

Pusey hired George Buttrick of Manhattan's Madison Avenue Presbyterian to preach in Memorial Church. Buttrick was a powerful speaker who made a significant contribution to the campus-wide revival of religious interest. Signs of that revival were visible everywhere. In the first freshman class at the College after Pusey became president, twelve men opted for the Episcopal ministry. Membership in the Harvard Catholic Club more than doubled. And Sunday night lectures on such abstruse topics as "The Dead and Absent God in Modern Theology" drew standing-room-only audiences to the Hillel Foundation.

"There don't seem to be any other answers outside of religion," one student told *Newsweek* in April 1957, when that magazine became the latest journal to report on Harvard's sudden interest in Christian humanism. "We are a generation looking for a creed. Students have to find some meaning for their existence beyond a bad grade. I guess you just have to have a God."

As a man who already had a God, Pusey could not have been happier with this turn of events. He believed there was a direct connection between current intellectualism and events of the twentieth century. Two world wars, the rise of fascism, the brutalization of humanity, all combined to promote "a growing sense of tragedy and an awareness of mystery." The theme, an old one with Pusey, was now shared with a body of scholars more accustomed to splitting atoms than calculating the number of angels on a pin.

Dispensing with Conant's anti-Catholic bias, the president did the unthinkable: he called upon Boston Cardinal Richard Cushing, who administered a lesson in political logrolling of the hoariest kind. Harvard scientists were worried about a bill in the state legislature outlawing experiments on laboratory animals. Only Cushing had the personal clout to sidetrack the bill before passage, so Pusey arranged for this audience with His Eminence, and brought with him an expert from the medical school, who outlined for the cardinal the many social benefits that would be lost if animal experiments were prohibited. This went on until an impatient Cushing interrupted. "That's all very well," he said. "But how many votes have you got?"[23] The question amazed Pusey, whose grasp of the cynical core of politics was tentative. It also laid the groundwork for a whole new relationship with the cardinal and the church he represented. In future years, Cushing became a frequent visitor to the Cambridge campus, even preaching in Memorial Church, and his successor, Humberto Madeiros, continued the courtship.

Pusey's willingness, in his first major address as president, to tackle head-on his predecessor Charles William Eliot's bromidic Religion of the Future was even more unconventional. Before a packed house at the divinity school, he did not question Eliot's credentials as a moralist, only as a prophet. Eliot's enemies had been churches, creeds, priests, anything supernatural or insufficiently scientific. Pusey suspected that Eliot would have dismissed the central doctrine of the faith, Christ's mission to save sinners in a sinful world, as "so much twaddle."

> President Eliot had a creed, whether he admitted to it or
> not. It is there implicit in every line of his address. But in our
> time most of us will find this an inadequate one. What this
> proves, I think, is that our need was not then and is not now to

get rid of creeds, but rather to examine into them, and now again, more especially, to find an adequate one for our time. We need to know, but we need also to believe, and what we want especially to do is to believe knowingly and to know with conviction.[24]

Then, using words as certain to enrage Faculty Club agnostics as they would please church-going alumni, Pusey boldly suggested that Harvard was failing in her ancient mission of educating a Christian ministry—especially if one took an expansive view of a ministry unlimited in membership by formal training or ecclesiastical garb. To the president, every thoughtful individual was a member of the Church's army, and woe to those who yielded to "the all but universal adoration of the State, and . . . almost idolatrous preoccupation with the secular order, the accumulation of knowledge, and with good works."

As the immediate heat generated by Pusey's divinity school address cooled, its long-range implications struck the Harvard community full force. He had meant what he said, and he intended to continue saying it. Those who had bargained for a safe, quiet successor to Conant had mistaken Pusey's equanimity for weakness. The new president was turning out to be surprisingly strong, with definite ideas of his own. As an example of his assertiveness, the president tried (unsuccessfully, as it turned out) to convince the faculty of Arts and Sciences to make Paul Tillich a tenured professor. He was unafraid of incurring the wrath of Boston's possessive elite, who were resentful of his penchant for nominating deans from west of the Mississippi. Comfortable in the presence of a kitchen cabinet which came to include David Rockefeller and Douglas Dillon, he was quoted as saying that one of the joys of his new position was the exposure it afforded him to the very wealthy. To money-starved professors, it didn't always matter that the results of such hobnobbing could be seen in new buildings and better equipment.[25]

It was from the mouths of just such faculty members that Pusey received his most stinging appraisals. "We couldn't be choosey, so we took Pusey," ran one popular assessment during the president's early years. Much of the resentment was academic snobbery, pure and simple. Much could be traced to his sacerdotal manner and muscular Christianity. In effect, the divinity school speech was Pusey's inaugural address. As such, it not only set the tone for his presidency, but also alienated a large part of Harvard's vigorously secular family.

What saved him from more public censure was Joe McCarthy's continuing threat, and his own response to it. Here, Pusey rose to the occasion, and in the process redefined his university's status in American life.

For by the 1950s, Harvard could hardly expect to bestride American education as in days of old. In times of trouble, however, it might still occupy a unique position, if only as shield and defender of less fortunate or famous institutions. Pusey grasped this, and acted accordingly. It remains his finest hour.

"It is hard to establish good principles when there is almost no belief in principles," Pusey had contended while still at Lawrence, "and we are, collectively, a sadly unprincipled lot." Pusey's remark was aimed at the malaise and insecurity which struck deep roots in the postwar era. He might have made this complaint about his fellow Appletonian, Senator Joseph McCarthy, whom he knew as an occasional companion on train trips through the Wisconsin countryside. Thinking Joe McCarthy a slaphappy character of bawdy stories and boozy vulgarity, Pusey did not regard him as a national villain per se. "What scared me," he recalled long after, "was why the public was so scared about Communists."[26]

McCarthy was more pointed. He hadn't forgotten that Harvard's new president had signed a booklet critical of his record in office during his 1952 reelection campaign. Out of anger, McCarthy secretly tape-recorded Pusey reacting to negative remarks planted by a McCarthy staff aide, and displayed a genuine, if baffling, outrage at what he heard. "I do not think that Pusey is or has been a member of the Communist Party," McCarthy told a Boston columnist in June 1953. "However, while he professes a sincere dislike for communism, his hatred and contempt appear to be infinitely greater for those who effectively expose Communists and injure the Communist cause."[27]

McCarthy earned public censure for this from his hometown newspaper. Pusey, the upstanding teacher and the moderate liberal, was protected from the senator's animus. His university was not so fortunate. Out in Appleton, conceded Harvard's new president, a lot of people confused crimson with red; McCarthy was only the most prominent.

If the Corporation had reckoned on ending the communism-in-the-classroom controversy first stirred up at Harvard by Wendell Furry with its cautious defense of professors whose only crime was to invoke the Fifth Amendment, it only betrayed its ignorance of the hard-charging Senator McCarthy. Within six months of its decision to retain Furry and two months of Pusey's inauguration, the professor was called before McCarthy's own investigating committee and loudly criticized for his uncooperative attitude. Warming to the attack, McCarthy warned parents that should their children be sent to Harvard, they would risk Communist indoctrination.

Harvard's new president took the unprecedented step of convening a mass press conference to deny the allegation. He also restated Harvard's opposition to keeping any known Communist on its faculty, and publicly dared McCarthy or anyone else to name a single member of the party among his teaching staff. Of a hundred thousand Americans who had attended the University over the years, said Pusey, only a few dozen had involved themselves with such causes. This only proved that "there is almost nothing that at least some Harvard men do not get into!" Acknowledging the earlier presence of a cell of fourteen graduate students and instructors, Pusey drew attention to the University's half-dozen Nobel Prize-winners and to others whose contributions in medicine, atomic energy, radar, sonor, business management, and the arts were deemed historic.[28]

McCarthy pressed ahead with a bill to end gift-tax exemptions for any educational institution employing those he called "Fifth Amendment Communists." He dubbed Harvard "a real privileged sanctuary" for academics refusing to divulge possible affiliation with the party. "We hope to do something about that in the not too distant future," he vowed, a few days before Furry and instructor Leon Kamin were indicted on charges of contempt of the United States Senate. Governor Christian Herter of Massachusetts advised the Corporation to fire any professor invoking the Fifth Amendment as a shield against McCarthy's questioning, a view seconded by Overseer Ralph Lowell. But Pusey made an artful dodge: he agreed that there was no place at Harvard for subversives, but refused to dismiss anyone as long as the Corporation adhered to its own firmly stated policy.

In January 1954, McCarthy was in Boston ridiculing both Furry and Kamin. Of Furry, he said he found it inconceivable that a great university "should keep this kind of creature teaching young Americans." Furry responded that he did not wish to protect the guilty from prosecution, but "merely to secure the innocent from persecution." Kamin added that his duties as an American did not require him to become a political informer.

Throughout his interrogation, McCarthy stressed the word *Harvard* with sarcastic emphasis and reserved his sharpest fire for her mild-mannered president. Even before the contempt charges collapsed under their own weight, journalists generally were more impressed by Pusey's quiet defense than by McCarthy's melodramatic accusations. The *St. Louis Post-Dispatch,* noting that both Furry and Kamin had waived their own immunity from self-incrimination, pronounced that Americans everywhere were in Pusey's debt. "Our first university judges by the old standards rather than by the new hysterics," it claimed. "For this, due honor to Harvard."

At the end of the month, Pusey told alumni that the danger of Communists on college faculties had passed, that subversive influence had been "fantastically exaggerated." The real challenge confronting Harvard and other institutions of higher learning, he said, was how to motivate young people to think for themselves, to buttress democracy in an age when individuality sold at considerable discount. After that, he made a personal hit at the National Press Club, defending the nation's universities against "the other gentleman from Appleton, Wisconsin." In the same speech, he expressed his opposition to the whites-only policy of the local Harvard Club, and good-naturedly entertained queries as to whether Harvard might award McCarthy an honorary degree. Pusey's faculty passed a resolution praising the president for his "serene and quiet courage." The American Civil Liberties Union gave him an award.

All this should be kept in mind when pondering a related controversy which would not erupt until a quarter-century after the fact, in a heated exchange of letters published in the New York Review of Books. The debate revolved around the exact code pursued in 1954 by McGeorge Bundy, the new dean of the faculty of arts and sciences, Pusey, and the governing boards in the cases of historian Sigmund Diamond and sociologist Robert Bellah. As prospective appointees who had belonged to the Communist Party in the 1940s, both men were closely questioned by Bundy about their earlier sympathies and their colleagues who might have shared them.

In the summer of 1977, Diamond, who had gotten access to files on the case through the Freedom of Information Act, charged that he had been pressured by Bundy to "name names" of onetime party members or forfeit a job counseling foreign students and lecturing part-time in history. He had willingly talked to Bundy and the FBI of his own past conduct, he said, but he had refused to inform on others, and so he had lost the appointment.

While faulting Diamond for insufficient candor at the time the job was offered, Bundy responded that a distinction had been made between academic and administrative positions. Precisely because Harvard was so embattled in its defense of higher education, Bundy wrote, it could not afford "to behave foolishly in its administrative appointments."

Robert Bellah then leaped into the debate with similar charges. He had been an undergraduate when he joined the party in 1947, and was a graduate fellow at the University of California at Berkeley seven years later when Bundy discovered his background and called him to account.

He, too, had refused to point a finger elsewhere, passing up a one-year instructorship rather than yield to conditions set down by Bundy. Responding to Bellah's charges, Bundy said he had disagreed with Corporation policies in Bellah's case, although at the same time he admitted that until 1956, the senior governing board had attached "negative weight to incomplete candor on the part of ex-Communists, even for teaching appointments." (Ironically, in a climate far removed from the tense Fifties, both Diamond and Bellah would later receive Harvard appointments.)[29]

As the controversy waxed, it spread from the pages of the *New York Review of Books* to those of *Time, Newsweek,* and other mass journals, reminding Harvard anew of its stature and vulnerability alike. Once again, it was a target, only this time from liberals, angered that it had insufficiently resisted McCarthy's assaults in an attempt to protect its own from the eddying currents of the period. Much was made of the apparent contradiction between the University's public stance as self-appointed defender of academic freedom, and in-house probes, complete with surreptitious taping, implied threats, sexual innuendo, and collusion with public authorities.[30]

Pressing his case, Diamond sifted historical evidence for details of how University officials had obtained details of his past behavior. From the FBI? Had Conant, he demanded, lent personal assistance to surveillance activities? Had the Bureau passed derogatory information on to other institutions? Turning such inquiries aside, Harvard refused to bend the fifty-year archival rule or permit outside scholars to weigh the documentary evidence for themselves. ("When my journals are published," said Wellington, "many statues must come down.") As a result, the University still remains under suspicion.[31]

In the furious exchange of letters involving Bundy, Diamond, and Bellah, some essential facts were overlooked. First, whatever its initial doubts, the Corporation had defended Furry and his colleagues. Second, considering the political atmosphere of the time, it's not surprising that there was behind-the-scenes questioning of would-be instructors and administrative personnel. Third, and most important, in the end, McCarthy was tested by Pusey, and Pusey prevailed.

What happened in Cambridge in 1953–1954 held far-reaching consequences. According to John Dunlop, then an economics professor, later a dean in two Harvard administrations as well as Gerald Ford's Secretary of Labor, "McCarthy certainly raised Pusey's Hooper rating." As such, his victory cast a false light over the man for whom political activity was a distasteful prerequisite of his job. At the height of his duel with McCarthy, Pusey expressed his feelings in words that would assume ironic overtones fifteen years later. "The number of undergraduates who get excited about political problems is not large," he declared in May 1954. "Most of them are above that sort of thing."[32]

Even as he said it, Pusey was mistaken. Anyone who walked through a Harvard dorm that spring, observing the television sets tuned to the Army-McCarthy hearings that finally led to the senator's downfall, could see it for himself. Pusey preferred to look elsewhere.

In the spring of 1958, his view was fixed on Memorial Church, Lowell's monument to Harvard's World War I dead. When a squabble erupted over the use of the church for Jewish weddings, Pusey's critics were given the opportunity they had been looking for. The dispute was touched off by a local rabbi's objection to the required presence of a Christian minister at such services. On the other side, it seemed that glasses were being broken as part of the ceremony and tearing the crimson carpet of the church, something the Reverend Buttrick was unwilling to allow to continue. Too hastily intervening on Buttrick's side, Pusey appeared intolerant of the very pluralism to which he was naturally inclined. The church, he claimed, was Christian, although nondenominational.[33]

With that, the lid was off an already overheated kettle, and foes of the president rose up to denounce him, Buttrick, and the shade of Lawrence Lowell. Eliot's aged secretary, Jerome Greene, called Pusey's stance shocking. Some angry descendants of Harvard's war dead demanded the removal of their family name from memorial tablets. A delegation of senior professors petitioned Pusey to open the church to all faiths.[34]

John Finley declaimed eloquently on the University and its traditions, only to have Pusey reply, "It's all right, John, as long as you don't confuse Harvard with God." Historian Perry Miller, whose lifelong study of New England's Puritans had done nothing to draw him to their church, or any other, asked angrily if he would be allowed a funeral service there. Pusey replied that Miller would—if he could find a preacher to perform it.[35]

At the height of the wrangling, Miller lashed out at Pusey, whom he charged with making the faculty victims of "pietistic fallout." Law professor Archibald Cox was more generous, even though initially he was astonished to hear the president say that there had never been a great man who rejected the doctrine of original sin. Only later did Cox perceive Pusey to mean that anyone who aspired to greatness must first appreciate the underside of humanity. Few of Cox's associates were so willing to look beyond the literal.[36]

Two weeks after it began, the fracas over Memorial Church died down, but only after the Corporation publicly distanced itself from the president's reflexive position. Henceforth, the Christian character of the church was reaffirmed. But its doors were also thrown open to non-Christian services. Pusey returned to more pressing matters. Even those inclined to criticize his judgment were willing to hold their tongues early in 1958, when the president launched "A Program for Harvard College," an eighty-five-million-dollar fund drive, five times the size of any college fund drive previously attempted.

"He came along at a time when the College needed someone to love her," recalls one close adviser. Not only the College, but its faculty—for whom Pusey felt near reverence—stood to benefit. At Appleton, he had been appalled to discover that workers in the local wire factory earned four times as much as his teachers. With "A Program for Harvard College," he could redress such imbalances. At a time when inflation was low, Pusey could engineer a salary increase that was genuine. University resources could multiply, and the multiplication would be real.[37]

The immediate and practical benefits of such a drive—more buildings, laboratories, scholarships, endowed chairs, and research centers—might be strictly local. But Pusey did not confine his ambitions to Cambridge alone. Realizing that Harvard's example carried weight throughout the academic community, he granted three across-the-board salary increases in the first four years of his presidency. Meanwhile, the sound of construction crews filled the air. Though in many ways he might be judged a traditionalist, when it came to Harvard's public face, Pusey was contemporary. (When the monumentally ugly Memorial Hall caught fire in 1956, the president hardly bothered to conceal his disappointment that the flames had not been more thorough.) More than thirty structures rose in commemoration of the new era. Many were stark, even bristling in their uncompromising modernity. Incinerator Gothic, they were labeled. Some won worldwide renown, like Le Corbusier's visual arts center, likened by the irreverent to a pair of copulating pianos. Several would be virtually falling down within fifteen years of their completion, an ironic postscript to the Pusey years.[38]

More important than the buildings themselves were the things that went on inside them. Conant had been many things—but he was no savant. His eye for men was better than his ear for music. At annual concerts of the Boston Symphony Orchestra held in Sanders Theater, he could be glimpsed casting glassy eyes at Latin inscriptions high above the stage, translating from a language that he was inclined to bury. Pusey, however, was a man of far-reaching interests. His personal enjoyment of the arts helped lead Harvard to build an undergraduate theater and to launch a pioneering discipline in visual studies. Instead of the traditional emphasis on art appreciation (something to be endured in dutiful little tours of local galleries), Pusey stressed participation and individual expression.[39]

National interest in Harvard throughout this period was undiminished. When CBS's *Omnibus* visited the Yard in the mid-Fifties, twenty-two million viewers watched as Tenley Albright skated, the Hasty Pudding theatrical troupe rehearsed, deans conferred, the Peabody Museum exhibited, and Pusey explained Harvard's colonial origins and its subsequent transformation.

Then, as later, Pusey seemed ill-at-ease before the footlights, but he would always try. Professor Raymond Vernon recalls standing at his side in a Memorial Hall blood-giving line as attendants repeatedly jabbed the president's arm. Pusey's face showed the pain caused by their efforts to locate a large enough vein and Vernon suggested that perhaps he should abandon the attempt. He couldn't do that, Pusey replied. "They tell me it's good for the University's image."[40]

His own image mattered less to him, even if his leadership role eroded and authority shifted from the president's office. The real leaders of modern Harvard were in the research labs and lecture halls; they were the men challenging frontiers in science and medicine, behavorial studies and social theory. Following in line with Paul Buck's Russian Research Center, the University developed separate institutes devoted to cognitive studies, computers, population control, the Middle East, East Asia, Latin America, Hellenic studies, and urban policy. Cutting across institutional and departmental boundaries, the centers recast Harvard's relationship to the outside world. As they began to provide society with needed expertise, influence naturally gravitated away from Massachusetts Hall in the direction of the experts.

Pusey's quiet unassuming style contributed to this erosion of authority. His lack of glamour contrasted sharply with the assertive manner of his new dean of Arts and Sciences, the brilliant, acerbic McGeorge Bundy. Bundy's role in recruiting faculty stars was pivotal, but his habit of jumping up at faculty meetings to announce "The president feels . . ." could rile even his imperturbable superior. Later on, the dean's relationship with Pusey would be described as a trial run for his equally prickly service alongside Kennedy's self-effacing Secretary of State, Dean Rusk.

Bundy had been a classroom legend at Groton, the first Yale student in history with three perfect scores on his college entrance exams (dubbed "Mahatma Bundy" in the 1940 yearbook), and a distinguished addition to the Society of Fellows founded by his great-uncle, Lawrence Lowell.

He had participated in D-Day planning, been a speechwriter for John Foster Dulles, written a biography of Henry Stimson, and been a much admired, highly visible government instructor at Harvard. (*The Lampoon* honored Dean Bundy as Worst Supporting Performer of the Year, in recognition of his part in a University promotional film.)[41]

Extraordinary as Bundy's resume was, it was not enough at first to earn him tenure for he had never taken any government courses, graduate or undergraduate. "All I can say," concluded Conant in 1951 when he finally gave his assent, "is that it couldn't have happened in Chemistry."[42]

Bundy and Pusey might be seen as opposite ends of Lawrence Lowell's Harvard: Pusey, the grind from Iowa, scratching his way toward success and struggling in his self-proclaimed role as *paterfamilias;* Bundy, the gold-medal debater accustomed to command, the scholar of fluent versatility, who could talk with equal assurance to scientists or playwrights. Bundy's credentials for carrying on in Conant's scholastically rarefied tradition were beyond doubt. All that was uncertain was his humility. As a Yale associate put it following news of the Pusey-Bundy teaming:

> *A proper young prig, McGeorge Bundy,*
> *Graduated from Yale on a Monday*
> *But he shortly was seen*
> *As Establishment Dean*
> *Up at Harvard the following Sunday.*[43]

In fact, Bundy, the anti-bureaucrat, managed the trick of wooing the Establishment even as he kicked sand in its face. "I'm so sick of these rich businessmen," he sighed near the end of the College's big fund drive. He was just as cavalier concerning academic sensitivities. When some departments threatened to oppose outsiders like Lillian Hellman, David Riesman, and Erik Erikson ("Freud wouldn't get through an ad hoc committee," declared one veteran of the process), Bundy went over their heads and created independent chairs.[44]

At the same time, he stroked faculty egos. As one Corporation member of the time said, "He let himself be pushed around. No wonder he was popular." When John Kenneth Galbraith needed a leave of absence to write *The New Industrial State,* he went to Bundy. Pusey, by contrast, once replied to James Watson, one of the discoverers of DNA, who had informed him that a West Coast trip would keep him away from Cambridge for a couple of days longer than expected, that he must "return or resign." Around Massachusetts Hall, the malady suffered by those who'd gone to the president hat in hand only to be turned down with magisterial phlegm, was named "Post-Pusey Depression," PPD for short.[45]

Bundy later would comment that the Harvard faculty liked to believe that each of its members was a potential candidate for the National Academy of Arts and Sciences or the American Philosophical Society. Yet even the faculty was awed when Bundy delivered his first address. The speech was a masterful tour of the academic landscape, detouring long enough to break down Harvard's budget in flawless style, without a note in hand. A friend explained afterward that Bundy had been fascinated by his discovery in the pages of Macaulay of a similar presentation by the younger Pitt, who at twenty-four astonished the House of Commons and created his own instant legend.[46]

Conant had said that Paul Buck was superb at handling the faculty, "but you have to tell him what you want him to do." No one ever said that about Bundy. When he received a memo he acted on it promptly, often by the time he had reached the signature at the bottom of the page. Pusey was a strict constructionist who left most decisions to his cabinet of deans. In this way, Bundy and Pusey complemented each other. At their first group meeting, Erwin Griswold addressed the president airily as "our representative to the governing boards."[47]

At gatherings of the Society of Fellows, Pusey would sit virtually ignored. Yet when a guest bothered to seek him out, as did William Bossert, later master of Lowell House, he was in for a surprise. Bossert recalls the single most perceptive conversation of his Harvard career during one such visit, as Pusey analyzed his Appleton bête noire Joe McCarthy from all angles—psychological as well as political, the heavy-drinking jokester as well as the heavy-handed destroyer of careers.[48]

The student body at the Harvard Pusey inherited from Conant was vastly different from what it had been when Pusey himself was a student. Ironically, probably neither Pusey nor such other illustrious alumni as John F. Kennedy and Franklin Roosevelt would have been admitted to the new Harvard, where more stringent tests of selectivity replaced the prewar standards of social and economic standing. Since the late Forties, inspired by the liberal spirit of James Conant and the G.I. Bill, admissions director Wilbur Bender had developed a sprawling alumni network to help recruit promising applicants from all over the country. By 1960, it had over four thousand members and was entrusted with a $150,000 budget to attract black youths from the South and farm boys from the great plains. Meanwhile, Boston Latin alumni were pressed for the first time by sharp youngsters from Jamaica Plain and Roslindale. All this was in keeping with Conant's National Scholarships and Lowell's academic melting pot, designed to break down social distinctions and to develop character *in loco parentis*.[49]

Although Harvard was pleased with the growing pool of bright applicants for the freshman class in the late Fifties, fresh debate erupted over Bender's admissions policies and the concept of the University's mission they projected. This controversy provoked another of Harvard's periodic attempts at self-definition. Opposed to Bender were the merito-crats, captained by Conant's old friend, chemist George Kistiakowsky. Before becoming Dwight Eisenhower's White House adviser on science, he had been a veteran of the Russian White Army, and a torpedo maker for its American counterpart. Kistiakowsky had won a ten-dollar bet from J. Robert Oppenheimer that the first atomic device would in fact detonate. Kistiakowsky's temper could be equally explosive, as he proved in a flareup over promotional material being mailed to prospective Har-vard applicants. What generations of admissions officers called "the Rollo Book" stressed pictures of happy undergrads lolling by the banks of the Charles, shooting baskets in Lowell's cavernous Indoor Athletic Building, or raising their voices heavenward in the University choir. For a research scientist like Kistiakowsky, all this frolicking, however vener-able, gave the University an image of superficiality, dilettantism, or worse.[50]

At one contentious faculty meeting, he claimed that too much money was being spent for too many library books, many of which should be banned. More seriously, he demanded a clarification of the University's mission. Who had a right to a Harvard education? How could the school best fulfill its national obligations? Should Harvard continue to adhere to the Lowellian vision of an educated gentry at a time when secondary schools, public and private alike, were assuming those same responsibili-ties, when television broadened perspectives, and when paperback editions of Freud and Marx were introducing young Americans to a semblance of culture? Or should Harvard take the next logical step in its evolution by narrowing its focus to the top one percent of graduating high school seniors, as determined by Scholastic Achievement Tests, and refining its instructional methods to satisfy the urgent need for scientists, engineers, statisticians, and others who could answer a complex society's growing appetite for expertise?[51]

Kistiakowsky's one-percent solution would discard *amor patriae* for electron accelerators and proton racetracks. It might even produce, in Bundy's phrase, "a freshman class composed entirely of promising or-ganic chemists." Yet in stating a preference for hard sciences over soft humanities, Kistiakowsky was not unaware of the reforms Bundy himself had introduced in that direction. In 1955, for example, an advanced-standing program was begun, permitting students who had already com-pleted some college level work to move ahead at a faster pace. Eventu-

ally, a fifth of all incoming freshmen would skip their first year altogether. Not long after, Independent Study was initiated in the College
as well as the Graduate School of Arts and Sciences. Starting in 1959,
there were Freshman Seminars to speed the way toward graduate work
(and incidentally hasten the decline of Conant's General Education).[52]

In response to Kistiakowsky, Bender pleaded openly for a class
whose diversity of experience and outlook matched its intellectual promise,
a college "with some snobs and some Scandinavian farm boys who can
skate beautifully and some bright Bronx pre-meds, with some students
who care passionately about editing the *Crimson* or beating Yale. . . .
Won't even our top one percent be better men and better scholars for
being part of such a college?"[53]

Bender won his argument for admissions criteria that considered
other qualifications in addition to standardized tests. He thereby prodded
the College into recruiting those who were not, in the faculty's con-
descending words, "destined to win Nobel prizes and who will not
accomplish 'break-throughs' in any field of scholarship, but who nevertheless exhibit strengths which can make them important contributors
to the life of their country and their time." Henceforth, a candidate's potential for extracurricular achievement would be mingled with his demonstrated classroom performance. If he could write a symphony, design
an apartment building, build a memory bank, juggle the student body
presidency with hospital volunteer work—if he could, in short, demonstrate *leadership*—his chances for admission were raised several notches
above those of the one-dimensional grind.

To make it possible for such aspirants to realize their goal, Pusey
supported a new system of need-blind financial aid, a costly reform
which fulfilled the final chapter in Conant's nationalizing process. The
result was not exactly what Pusey had in mind, especially when "leadership" in the late Sixties consisted of berating the administration and lock-
ing deans in their offices. In the meantime, however, campus mixers
teemed with Merit Scholars, most of whom had been reminded from an
early age that they were special. Their view of Harvard's significance
roughly matched their own self-estimate, and neither was notably modest.

Bender's bright young students felt they assumed a responsibility to
make an imperfect world perfect. At their best, they were remorseless in
their precocity, stimulating in their company, and challenging in their
conversation. At worst, they were neurotic, opinionated grade hounds.
Onlookers noted a syndrome called "Valedictorian's Ego," wherein over-
achievers were thrown together, forced into mortal combat to justify their
well-worn halos.

The dean of admissions addressed incoming students in September 1961 as the greatest freshman class in the history of civilization. There was laughter, one who was there remembered, but it was of the nervous variety. "We could die now, child martyrs," Andrew Holleran said, "and it would be all right—we would go straight to Heaven. We were Harvard undergraduates, members of a long and illustrious army. Harvard itself was almost beside the point: getting in, having gone, were the prodigious things."[54] As an example of what they faced, one class opened its blue exam books and found that they were asked to write a three-thousand-word essay "comparing the concepts of wisdom and justice held by the authors of the Book of Job, the Book of Ecclesiastes, and *Prometheus Bound.*" Robert Frost scanned the list of books assigned in a General Education course and said it was more reading than he managed in a year. Those who passed such a gauntlet were entitled to a sense of accomplishment. Unfortunately, when John F. Kennedy entered the White House and surrounded himself with a covey of Harvard professor-politicians, self-congratulation became all too easy.

Such boasting wasn't Nate Pusey's style. Nevertheless, he was engulfed, first in the exaggerated pride engendered by Kennedy's triumph, and then in the cruel disillusionment ignited by his assassination. Harvard would climb to dizzying heights of institutional hubris before plunging into virtual civil war, as the bright promise of January 1961 gave way to Vietnam, the civil rights revolution, the recognition of mass poverty and social exclusion, and a generation of disenchanted youngsters eager to pin the blame for society's ills on an institution that was no less guilty in thinking that it was capable of curing those ills.

> *We should not only use all the brains we have,*
> *but all that we can borrow.*
> —WOODROW WILSON

IF THERE WAS to be a dominant theme to the Pusey era, it was its internationalism, expressed in the colorful dress of Africa and Asia in the Square, and in the tongues of a hundred nations mingled with the drawl of the American South and the New Englander's broad A. From the mid-Fifties on, undergraduate calendars fairly bulged with events dramatizing newfound access to Buddhist philosophy or to Germanic art. On any given day an ambassador from Ghana might be competing for student interest with a New York urban planner, a lecturer from Tokyo on the Japanese economic miracle, a display of Baroque painting, and a concert by the Juilliard String Quartet.[55]

The president reflected the University's newfound appreciation for the wider world. At a Mexico City gathering of the International Association of Universities, Pusey discerned a host of issues relevant to emerging lands as to ancient citadels of learning. What was the proper relationship of the university to the state? What of the preoccupation with science and material needs which together posed a threat to humane values? What of the explosion in student enrollments, unmatched by an equal rise in creative scholars or brilliant instructors?

While Pusey enlarged Harvard's vision, much of the rest of the world returned his favor. Early in his presidency, United Nations Secretary-General Dag Hammerskjöld, while waiting to receive an honorary degree, thumbed through a list of Ph.D. theses. Hammerskjöld's favorite was "Sex Differentiation in the Embryology of the Reptilian Nose." A few months later, Fidel Castro stood before a crowd at Soldier's Field and disavowed any intention of turning Cuba's recent revolution into a Communist triumph.

Pusey was able to realize many of his international ambitions through assistance from the American Establishment, especially from private foundations willing and able to finance scientific research, educational television, and new methods of classroom instruction. If Harvard didn't exist, ran the Cambridge joke, the Ford Foundation would have had to invent her. Encouraged by the Foundation's generosity, the University flung itself into global enterprises. The law school set up an International Legal Center to train scholars from the developed world and fiscal officers from the developing one. In 1955 the business school had established an Office of Overseas Relations, planting seeds of administrative instruction in France, Turkey, and Italy. The school of public administration diagnosed Pakistan's economic health, and journalists from the British Commonwealth and Asia were invited to become Nieman Fellows.

Harvard sent experts to staff management schools in Switzerland and Guatemala, to provide health services in poverty-stricken areas of the Third World, to raise awareness everywhere of environmental and nutritional urgencies. The divinity school had its Center for World Religion. Engineering and Applied Physics, in tandem with other specialists, advised India on how to control its rivers. The Development Advisory Service did what its name implies in Columbia and Korea, and the school of education signed a contract to supervise Nigeria's first comprehensive high school. Harvard even devised an ambitious international Tax Plan, guiding multinational businesses through the intricacies of taxation in fifteen countries.

Foundations weren't the only outside forces to call the shots in what historian Daniel Boorstin termed the Hotel of the Mind. America had traveled far since the first federal Office of Education assembled its numbers, and Justin Morrell's land-grant colleges echoed to the tramp of raw-boned scholars. Now, government was in the classroom with both feet. First World War II, then the Cold War, and the challenge posed by a Russian satellite the size of a grapefruit caused Washington's investment in higher education to spurt a hundredfold. By 1960, three-quarters of all university research was funded by the government, much of it at the behest of the Defense Department.

With Pusey's consent and Washington's cold cash, Harvard now became a research university par excellence. The medical school typified the new affluence. In the twenty-five years from 1935 to 1960, its annual research budget had soared from $200,000 to more than $5 million. Of the ninety endowed chairs added to the Harvard faculty during Pusey's first decade, medicine claimed twenty-six. A similar pattern cropped up at other universities. Overwhelmingly, the bureaucratic Medici skewed their patronage in favor of the physical and biomedical sciences. Only 3 percent of federal aid in 1960 was earmarked for the social sciences and less than that went to students of Virgil or Platonic discourse.[56]

Between 1953 and 1963, Harvard's share of the federal bounty rose from $8 million to over $30 million. Washington sponsored 95 percent of Division of Engineering research, 90 percent of the physics department's research, and two-thirds of Chemistry's. However, with the outside funding came outside restrictions. For instance, the National Science Foundation imposed a limit on extra income for its Fellows, which, as a practical matter, deprived the University of the teaching capacities of its most talented graduate students. Campus administrators were regulated by the Department of Health, Education and Welfare, the Atomic Energy Commission, the National Institutes of Health, and NASA. As Clark Kerr, president of the University of California, noted, the danger was less one of federal control than of federal influence. "One of the quickest ways to lose a faculty member," he said, "is by refusing to accept the grant he has just negotiated with his counterpart in Washington."[57]

Earlier than most, Pusey grasped the threat such government influence posed to an already splintered educational community. So he cast himself as counterweight to what he called "a frenetic, concentrated effort to produce . . . hundreds of thousands of scientists and engineers." Faithful to Conant's ban on classified research, Pusey cautioned against preoccupation with scientific projects of immediate use for the military. Such work, he claimed, was for other hands.

In 1959, federal dollars exceeded Harvard's tuition revenue for the first time and a concerned Pusey proposed and then chaired an unprecedented review of the government's relationship to academia. "The role of the university cannot be one of withdrawal from the world," his report concluded. "But it will serve society well only as it remains true to its essential nature—a university, not an agency of government." However, having broken the path, the prudent, institutionally constricted president would not travel very far down it. On balance, he decided with his fellow educators that the federal giant was useful, as long as it didn't roll over and crush the object of his ardor.

Meanwhile, there appeared in the immediate aftermath of World War II a whole new breed of professor, the educator-entrepreneur. One of the most distinguished was I. A. Richards, who had been lured by Conant to the American Cambridge from his native England. "Technology to the rescue," proclaimed Richards, who with Charles Kay Ogden had conceived and developed a simplified language known as Basic English in the 1920s, and had reorganized China's educational structure a decade later. Along with a colleague, Richards founded Language Research, Inc., which sold two million copies of "English Through Pictures" and used closed-circuit television to teach Puerto Rican children English.

With professors like Richards venturing boldly into the marketplace, it was only a question of time before Harvard's force-field overlapped that of its wartime collaborator, MIT, whose research activities had led to involvement with industry as well as government. Indeed, by the early Sixties, people were talking of a new University of Cambridge, encompassing both the immediate academic community and the sprawling region of private scientific and other research establishments carved out within the high-tech corridor of nearby Route 128.[58]

Such had not been the case with Harvard. As Vannevar Bush described it, "Here you have the spectrum between pure and applied. MIT is at this end, in touch with business. And Harvard is at this end, in touch with the clouds." When an electron accelerator was proposed in 1961, the distance between the two seemed to shrink abruptly. The schools agreed to share the new facility, which relied heavily on government contracts for its livelihood. Inevitably they became entangled in Greater Boston's web of private research and development firms, which had names like Itek and Avco, and with MIT's own spin-off, Mitre. Because of its close ties to the Air Force, for which it manufactured missile warning systems, and with which it exchanged lab staff, Mitre further blurred the distinctions between government, business, the military, and academia.

> Verbally, at least, Pusey took exception to such developments. However high our opinion of ourselves, [he told a Brown University audience early in his presidency] universities are not the creatures of modern industrial society. Nor should they be enslaved to that society. . . . The present chief danger for a college or university is then that, from preoccupation with business life, or from fatigue, or from a lack of grasp on what the spirit means for life, it will yield to the pressures that are always working to make it conform itself to the world—not at the world's novel, creative best, but at its less thoughtful, almost meaningless ordinary.[59]

In any case, Harvard was hardly as independent as it liked to think. If the University had sufficient wealth of its own, enough to do without military contracts, that was largely because of such corporate angels as IBM. In 1964, IBM donated five million dollars for a ten-year review of technology's world-wide impact. For its money, IBM bought more than prestige. It also obtained some of the best academic minds in the market, including executive director Emmanuel G. Mesthene, former Harvard director of students and RAND Corporation economist and later White House special assistant for science and technology. The economics department was famous—or infamous—for its outside connections. Some, like the ubiquitous Galbraith, restricted their off-campus activities to public service. Others, including Wassily Leontief, Otto Eckstein, and Carl Kaysen, alternated officeholding with business consulting. Ed Mason, of the Center for International Development, was a troubleshooter for the State Department, the World Bank, and the Agency for International Development.[60]

The potential for conflict of interest among Harvard's star players was dramatized when prominent economist John Dunlop, wearing one hat as consultant to the President's Committee on Urban Housing, simultaneously wore another as spokesman for unions seeking to restrict minority hiring in LBJ's Model Cities program. George Baker was dean of the business school when President Johnson named him one of the public's representatives on a commission studying ways to improve postal operations. Simultaneously, Baker chaired the Transportation Association of America, a trade group of common carriers whose interest in a privatized post office was presumably more than theoretical.[61] Other Harvard officers joined Baker in lending their presence to corporate boards at Ford, Socony Oil, Raytheon, Litton Industries, Lockheed, and John Hancock Insurance. Pusey, unlike his counterparts at Princeton and Columbia, turned down such invitations, but this did not prevent Harvard from suffering acute embarrassment when it was revealed to be the largest single shareholder in Mississippi Power and Light, whose board of directors also included members of the local White Citizens' Councils.

With faculty energies so diffused, Harvard in the Sixties justified as never before its tongue-in-cheek description as an assemblage of different departments held together by allegiance to one central heating plant. While nine Nobel Prizes added luster to its outside reputation, Pusey's beloved College began to drift. Marooned amid growing specialization, General Education suffered from the demise of generalists. Few professors were inclined to stand in front of undergraduates and survey history from the Roman Empire to World War I. Rather, factional scholarship paved the way for special-interest disciplines such as women's studies, Third World perspectives, and ecological ethics. In 1963, Pusey commissioned a faculty review of the undergraduate curriculum, but the panel, chaired by Professor Paul Doty, was divided in its findings, and the president himself declined to press for reform. Even the prospect of change was enough to stir up vigorous opposition among the faculty to the idea of *any* mandatory course requirements.

That same year the president's educational preferences were made clear in a compilation of his speeches entitled *The Age of the Scholar*. For the most part, the volume was excoriated by reviewers as a desert of clichés only occasionally relieved by an oasis of provincialism. Daniel Boorstin claimed that Pusey's remarks were full of fear of the outside world, fear of practicality, and fear of applied science, and dismissed his talk of God and intellectual purity as "sanctimonious mishmash." Far more attractive to Boorstin was Clark Kerr's "multiversity," which, in its revolutionary potential, Kerr buoyantly compared to nineteenth-century railroads and twentieth-century automobiles.[62]

Some reviewers sympathized with Pusey's obvious concern for individuals over institutions. However, accepting his view that learning was a force for moral good as well as a means for technical advance, these critics also wondered how the modern university could be both an instrument of national purpose and a dispassionate critic of government policies. Organizers of the first round of Vietnam teach-ins might not have realized that in their preference for independent evaluation they stood closer to Pusey's vision of Harvard than to Kerr's California octopus. (Of course, in *his* later, unyielding support for ROTC, Pusey did violence to his own arguments.)

By then, however, nearly anything Pusey might say would be so many words to the wind. For however much Pusey declaimed about the glories of Plato and the isolated grandeur of the academic village, as the Sixties proceeded past Hue and Woodstock, Watts and Morningside Heights, his distance from the reality on campus grew in proportion to his distaste for politics. The combination of defense and national security contracts, the charms of private industry, and the refracted glory of public office had made Pusey more than ever the brakeman on a runaway train.

It would require exceptional leadership to make sense of this intellectual witches' brew. It would take a virtual miracleworker to achieve institutional unity against the additional onslaught of a society undergoing its own disintegration. Already suspect among much of his faculty, a man more emotionally attuned to the Age of Eisenhower than to the New Frontier, Pusey coupled the touch of Croesus with the starchy manner of a Deerfield headmaster, a combination which, while ideal for the Fifties, was ill-suited to the decade now opening before him.

> *I intend to be an ivory-tower President.*
> —JOHN F. KENNEDY
> *January 1961*

ALONG WITH a majority of Americans, Nathan Pusey had liked Ike. America had wanted a rest. Harvard similarly had needed time to soothe nerves worn raw during the Conant years. Most of the University community, however, had been inclined toward Adlai Stevenson, Illinois' elegant, ironic governor, who was much more to its taste than the war hero from Abilene, who scrambled his syntax and disdained open warfare with Joe McCarthy.

In 1961, Eisenhower stepped down to make way for Jack Kennedy. Pusey, however, clung to office, as uncomfortable with celebrity as Schlesinger, Galbraith, and Bundy were eager for it. In a time when charisma outweighed character on the scale of popular values, Harvard sophisticates found it easier than ever to laugh at a man who likened youthful minds to ripening blossoms, and who roused considerable grumbling by banning lunchtime cocktails at the Faculty Club.

Kennedy's election raised Harvard's national profile anew. Pusey, having replenished the University's finances, rebuilt her shabby plant, inaugurated a host of new programs, and taken a prominent part in the

national religious renewal, could hardly foresee how the election of a
Harvard alumnus as President of the United States would impact on his
own career. He imagined no calamity worse than the loss of a few
faculty stars to the new administration. In the weeks that followed the
election, students at the graduate school of public administration discovered that Economics 169 was missing its professor; Kennedy had
asked David Bell to come to Washington to wrestle with the federal
budget. Ed Mason was busy surveying the economy of Uganda. Government instructor Arthur Maass was examining Spain's water laws, his
colleagues Arthur Schlesinger and Carl Friedrich were engaged in West
Coast lecturing and a Texas seminar on Hegel, respectively.

At a post-election party, McGeorge Bundy and other Harvardians
speculated on the precise job each might land once Kennedy took office.
Eventually, more than fifty realized their ambition, a platoon of techno-
crats who spearheaded a nuclear test ban with the Russians, developed
new analytical tools with which to gauge the success of Keynesian economics, advised the angry president in his showdown with Big Steel.[63]

Four members of the incoming Cabinet were Harvard men: Robert
McNamara of Defense, Treasury's Douglas Dillon, Labor Secretary
Willard Wirtz, and the president's own brother, Attorney General Robert Kennedy. They were backstopped by middle-level Harvard appointees
like Solicitor General Archibald Cox, special assistants Richard Goodwin
and Kenny O'Donnell, ambassador to Japan Edwin O. Reischauer, and
Richard Neustadt, who was assigned the herculean task of government
reorganization. As head of the National Security Council ("You can't
beat brains," said Kennedy of his new NSC adviser), McGeorge Bundy
had his own, privileged entree to the Oval Office. John Kenneth Galbraith, in his capacity as U.S. envoy to India, was a special favorite of
Mrs. Kennedy's—so much so, and to such prominence, that Pusey objected when the *New York Times* ran a photo of the two at a Swiss ski
lodge, identifying Galbraith as a Harvard professor.

Not everyone thought Kennedy's fondness for Harvard alumni well
placed. Arizona's Barry Goldwater complained that, having exhausted
the supply of PT-boat men, touch-football players, and ushers at Kennedy family weddings, the president-elect was now robbing the Harvard
faculty. James Reston predicted that soon Cambridge might have nothing
left but Radcliffe. And when Minnesota's Orville Freeman, about to be
sworn in as Kennedy's Secretary of Agriculture, was asked by newsmen
how he got his job, Freeman replied that he wasn't entirely certain, but
he thought it had something to do with the fact that Harvard didn't have
a school of agriculture.[64]

Skeptics professed to see a brain cartel in the making, a dangerous if well-intentioned alliance between Harvard, her sister universities, the foundations bankrolling creative thought, the RAND Corporation, the Council on Foreign Relations, and others who together forged what sociologist C. Wright Mills in 1956 had dubbed the power elite.

Robert Frost advised the new president to be more Irish than Harvard. The advice wasn't necessary. Grasping the limitations of expertise in popular government, JFK was therefore able to perform the educational and inspirational functions assumed by his Harvard-educated predecessors, Theodore and Franklin Roosevelt. To Nate Pusey, he explained his decision to put an American on the moon in terms reminiscent of William James's search for a social bonding agent short of war.[65]

On a visit to Harvard Yard in December 1960, the president-elect was mobbed by five thousand exuberant undergrads. ("Weld Is a Depressed Area," read one banner hung from Kennedy's old freshman dorm.) The successful candidate delighted students by promising to go over their grades with President Pusey, and by granting the campus radio station an exclusive interview about his proposed Peace Corps.

Pusey ribbed his most famous Overseer about depopulating his university for the New Frontier. At the same time, he was anxious not to offend the man whose post-presidential career was already expected to revolve around a Harvard-sited library. Kennedy once speculated to Newsweek's Ben Bradlee that he might succeed Pusey in Massachusetts Hall. (Or, on the other hand, he mused, he could always become his brother Bobby's Secretary of State.) In more serious conversations, he anticipated a professor's chair at his old alma mater—but not before January 1969. When a member of the Corporation expressed regret over having supported Nixon in the election, the new president jauntily assured him there were no hard feelings and that he would have a chance to rectify the error in 1964.[66]

Pusey wasn't so sure. His own doubts, rooted in Kennedy's failure to stand up to Joe McCarthy or lend personal backing to his 1957 effort to strike a loyalty oath from federal scholarship grants, were reinforced at a 1962 White House meeting where every attempt to discuss the future Kennedy library was put aside by Kennedy's shaken recollections of how Nikita Khrushchev had tried to bully him at their recent Vienna summit. But Pusey was able to forget such incidents, and Harvard's Republican president grew to admire America's Democratic one. At the same time, Kennedy's ties to the College grew stronger, especially as the Harvard connection came to be seen as a political asset.[67]

In the last spring of his life, JFK invited his fellow Overseers to meet at the White House. John L. Loeb cherishes the memory of sitting up one night with the President of the United States, who lay on the floor of Abraham Lincoln's bedroom, reliving his past and treating guests to a Cook's Tour of a troubled present. Around 10:30 p.m., Kennedy got to his feet and excused himself. He was sorry he couldn't stay longer, he said, but Alabama's governor, George Wallace, was giving him grief. Then he was off to grapple with a very different kind of antagonist from those discussed in the lecture halls of Cambridge. The next morning, Kennedy was in the State Dining Room fussing over seating arrangements like the mother of the bride, checking and rechecking that afternoon's menu.[68]

Kennedy had a ready response to a crusty visitor who took exception to patronage of "that son of a bitch Galbraith." Why did his visitor think he'd sent Galbraith to India, he asked. How much further from the nerve center of policy could the professor go?[69] Kennedy didn't mean a word of his witty rejoinder. His regard for Galbraith was warm and genuine. But it showed just how far he'd progressed in the politician's art since his first, unsuccessful race for freshman class president. And it reminded thoughtful observers (at least those who belonged to the Bender School of Admissions) of Harvard's continuing opportunity to provide the nation with more than just the makings of a presidential brain trust. The University must educate potential presidents as well, equipping them to harness intellectual talents without becoming their prisoner.

In an early class of 1940 report, after noting carefully his wartime exploits, journalistic forays, and community services, Kennedy wrote, "I am pessimistic about the future of the country." His pessimism moved him to do something about that future. However tragically his presidency ended, he—and Harvard—would have had far less impact had Joe Kennedy's boy opted for molecular theory, jet propulsion, or the metered genius of Homer.[70]

Early in his presidency, Pusey had a recurring dream in which he was faced with an onrushing locomotive. In his restless hours the president anticipated the turmoil of a decade that would run over him. It became fashionable to say that the 1960s really began on the afternoon of Jack Kennedy's violent death in Dallas. Of course, history observes no such neat parameters. Conventional accounts of those unconventional days treat the traumatic student occupation of University Hall in April 1969 as a climax, more or less logical, to a period of crushed hopes and blasted opportunities. But the forces that tore Harvard apart and led to University Hall had been festering for years.

The fabric of the Harvard community had begun to unravel long before its vulnerability became apparent to the outside world. For a century, Harvard had chosen contemporary men for its leaders, only to suffer when the times passed them by. Eliot had constructed a great institution, to bequeath after forty years in office both curricular chaos and social fragmentation. Lowell had put the pieces back together and forged a distinct identity for the place, but what had been a solution in the early part of the century, by 1933 was a problem. Conant had thrown open Harvard's windows, aired out its fusty, insular pride, and replaced social tests of personal merit with cerebral ones. Before he was through, Harvard was less than ever New England's plaything. But it paid a price for the divorce, an alimony measured less in dollars than in ambience, cohesion and sense of purpose.

With distance inevitably came dilution of an older, gentler culture. In 1939, a majority of all Harvard instructors had degrees from the college. In the Sixties, less than a third did. Over the same period, new faculty members were recruited not for their knowledge of Harvard nor for their commitment to undergraduate education, but because an ad hoc committee had judged them preeminent in their field. Because of the admissions policies of Conant, Bender, and Buck, there was now less segregation between high achievers and clubby good fellows. Along with higher standards came stiffened competition, a loss of civility, a weakening of institutional bonds. McGeorge Bundy recalled a preponderance of fine scholars over large men. "There were not enough whole men among us at any rank," he wrote in retrospect, "and there was not enough modesty. . . . We may well have been the best in the country—but we foolishly supposed that made us good enough."[71]

That was just the beginning of Harvard's problems. Swamped by returning veterans, flush with federal dollars, the postwar University (despite Conant's privately expressed desires) had been reluctant to curb admission. One House master remembers an early meeting with Pusey at which the president placed a chart upon an easel, mapping Harvard's growth ever since Eliot first decreed she should be biggest as well as best. With the sole exception of wartime, noted Pusey, the line of enrollment rose as if foreordained. Certainly he wasn't going to stand in the way of progress.[72]

Few stopped to ponder how much of her shape Harvard might lose as the money from Washington flowed in, new labs and Houses shot up, the lines of freshman registration lengthened, and the University's sense of mission became global.

When Columbia and other universities caught fire in the late Sixties, Harvard refused to think itself vulnerable. After all, it wasn't a slumlord or perched in a racial tinderbox. It didn't carry on classified research for the Pentagon. Most of all, it had Lawrence Lowell's Houses to foster communication between faculty and students. This, like other mantras of the period, proved an exercise in self-hypnosis. Eating three meals a day with the same people, sharing their concerns, tolerating their foibles; all this was supposed to foster a sense of community. At one time it had. Eliot Perkins, for a quarter-century master of Lowell House, could recall when Lowell's residents numbered 290 rather than 450, and it was possible for him and his wife to know every sophomore "in civilized fashion." Those were the years when each House's population was culled personally by its master (appointed for life) from among a few prep schools, leavened with public school graduates, a sprinkling of Jews, and an occasional black.[73]

John Finley was another of the old school of masters. His Eliot House had an unmistakable patois. Each year, Finley pored over freshman files, probing friends and interests, interviewing each applicant, writing in his own hand letters of recommendation for every senior who sought one. Along with a well-earned reputation as home to preps and jocks, Eliot House also boasted twenty-eight Rhodes scholars in Finley's twenty-six-year tenure.

It did not—at least until the advent of co-residency and the age of computer-driven selections in the late 1960s—feature any women. "I'm not quite sure people want to have crystalline laughter falling like a waterfall down each entry of the House at all hours," said Finley. "I should think it would be a little disturbing if you were taking advanced organic chemistry."

Originally, House masters were to serve as a kind of presidential cabinet, with responsibilities of advice and peace-keeping far beyond their individual establishments. Thus, when a Harvard lab was occupied during a 1967 protest in which a Dow recruiter was held hostage, Finley was on the scene. He had as much right as anyone to be there, he told demonstrators. Besides, some of his boys were inside. Likewise, Kirkland House's Arthur Smithies would hasten to University Hall in the first hours of the student occupation two years later, to argue in vain with members of the Progressive Labor Party and other ideologues for whom argument was as distasteful as popular balloting.[74]

Lowell had envisioned academic as well as cultural preparation on the House menu. But the postwar rise of science, with its elaborate laboratory equipment, rendered this an old man's delusion. General Education's emphasis on large lecture courses further sped the decline of Lowell's vision. So did the gradual ossification of tutorials, as senior faculty members showed less inclination to add tutoring to their list of duties. Resentful of Sixties students who wanted to make history rather than study it, many professors were driven away from the Houses and they became bricks without straw.

The erosion of the House system mirrored what was happening in all areas of the University as it expanded to a scale unthinkable in Lowell's day. It was fitting that in 1963 Clark Kerr should choose Harvard for the unveiling of his "multiversity," neither cloister nor research organism, but a vast inhuman grid of services and specialties, consultancies, and experiments. ("Every time he said university," recalls sociologist Richard Herrnstein, "I said shoe industry. And you know what? It worked just as well. Yet there really ought to be some difference.") [75]

CHAPTER SEVEN

Children of the Storm

*The great American frustration is a numb, un-
formed persistent sense . . . that we, as Americans, . . . have somehow lost control of the
management of our human affairs, of the direction of our lives, of what our ancestors would
have called our destiny. A curious automatism,
human in origin but not human in action, seems
to be taking over.*

—Archibald MacLeish

In the Fifties, Harvard had seemed an academic Eden. McCarthy had
riled its equilibrium, the Battle Over Memorial Church had ruffled its
calm, but in spite of all that, the consensus was that scholarship had taken
precedence. It was the closest thing then in existence to Lowell's Boston
phalanx or Conant's coherent national culture; it was *something* into
which students might be assimilated.

However, as the Sixties wore on, Harvard discarded academic gowns.
Like coats and ties, they were replaced by sackcloth and jeans. A new orthodoxy emerged, composed of equal parts liberal guilt, the alienation of
black youngsters annexed by the white Establishment, remorse over the
country's Vietnam adventure and Harvard's alleged complicity in it, and
anger at the University's physical encroachment into local neighborhoods.

However unintentionally, Nathan Pusey seemed to embody the era's
guns-and-butter mentality. At one moment, he sounded an alarm about a
new serfdom for scholars in government, business, and the military.

Though universities have a concern and responsibility toward the everyday world, their primary, their fundamental responsibility lies totally elsewhere. This is for basic investigation, for the pursuit of learning almost for learning's own sake. . . . It is possible for a university without being aware of it to slip into a servile relationship with the culture in which it finds itself and so betray its real reason for being.[1]

Yet, at the same time Pusey also cheered a utilitarian ministry. "Wherever the affairs of men call for intellectual analysis, discrimination, criticism, formulation, concern, here must the university follow." Before an audience in New Delhi in 1962, he called Harvard part of "the supranational network of universities," and a powerful contender for world peace.

In the Sixties, in Cambridge and in Washington, the belief took hold that nearly anything was doable, given enough money and expertise. America could fight a war in Vietnam as well as the brushfires of urban unrest at home. Harvard could serve the regime in power and look its conscience straight in the face. It could become Washington's anteroom while still clinging to its traditional status as privileged sanctuary. Having ignored a 1956 warning from prospective Overseer John Kennedy about the dangers accompanying too close a relationship between temporal and academic power, the University wound up crunched between the two, and its claim to special status in the ruling order crumbled. So did the internal adhesive Theodore Roosevelt called fellow-feeling.

In a golden age, in those days of bright color,
we dreamed of a world better for everyone.
—FAYE LEVINE
Radcliffe, Class of 1965

IRONICALLY, the era that would be preoccupied with revolutionary change opened with a half-serious stand for tradition. In April 1961, two thousand students assembled before Widener Library to register their anger at Harvard's decision to abandon the Latin diploma. The Corporation had been forced to this unhappy reform in abrupt recognition of the mortality of one elderly man who, for as long as anyone could remember, had painstakingly hand-lettered each year's batch of graduating certificates. Now he was showing unmistakable signs of age. And so Pusey, priding himself on his modern outlook, concluded that the time had come to issue new diplomas, machine-printed in English. A year later, Vatican II would win acclaim for casting out the Latin Mass. But this was Cambridge, not Rome. Besides, the president might have anticipated trouble when the Harvard Coop sold five hundred Latin copies of a famous children's book, *Winnie Ille Pu.*[2]

It was later rumored that at the very hour the crowd was gathering, Pusey was in his living room relaxing with a copy of Virgil. For he, unlike the vast majority of Cicero's partisans, could read the language, which he proved by addressing the crowd in its preferred tongue. The irony seemed lost on the demonstrators, who soon were filling Massachusetts Avenue with chants of "Latin Si, Pusey No."

Since protests on behalf of anything classical were deemed preferable to tipping over street trolleys, the administration's initial response was one of indulgence. Then the *Crimson* found its voice. It was bad enough, the editors noted, for the president to have denigrated a Harvard diploma as "merely a gesture from the Corporation." Infinitely worse was his failure to keep one ear sufficiently close to the ground to detect rumblings of student dissatisfaction. The paper charged that Pusey was insensitive, not only to undergraduate wants, but also to the values and beliefs of contemporary Harvard. Further, it said he ought to refrain from taking public positions—or sticking to them with his customary rigidity—until he had a better sense of both.

"The lesson that the President must learn," the *Crimson* declared, "is that the governing of Harvard, like the governing of any institution, is a matter of politics. And in politics good intentions are not enough."[3]

All this was a mildly humorous preview of a decade in love with slogans and enamored of mass political action. Politics was on many minds that spring of 1961. In May, Laos shared the headlines with the disastrous CIA-backed invasion of Cuba's Bay of Pigs. In the Yard, demonstrators angered by the right-wing John Birch Society inspired The Committee Against Misguided Picketing and its equally frivolous rival, The Committee to Repress Anti-Pickets. Members of the Student Council upbraided their conservative president, Howard Phillips, because of his public criticism of the Peace Corps. Barry Goldwater addressed campus Republicans. And the Club 47 welcomed the first of a string of what the *Alumni Bulletin* called "thoughtful, long-tressed girl folk singers," in the mold of its most famous performer, Joan Baez.

By the time Baez took her leave, local student priorities, like the times, they was a-changing. Carrying the banner of global disarmament and social justice was a new protest group named Tocsin. A spin-off from the Committee for a Sane Nuclear Policy, Tocsin lived up to its name by demonstrating outside a local Woolworth's on behalf of southern blacks who were being denied access to department-store lunch counters. In 1962, Tocsin's faculty adviser, H. Stuart Hughes, ran for the U.S. Senate against Kennedy's brother Edward, a member of the Class of 1954. Demanding a nuclear test ban treaty, an end to CIA-sponsored coups, and a thirty-five-hour workweek, Hughes was endorsed by Bertrand Russell, made a strong showing in the *Crimson's* poll, and received fifty thousand votes statewide.

But Tocsin and its members were soon absorbed into two new nationwide organizations, Students for a Democratic Society (SDS) and the Student Non-Violent Coordinating Committee (SNCC). Conceived to battle injustices more burning than English-language diplomas, SDS and SNCC were by-products of conventional liberalism. Initial funding for SNCC came from the AFL-CIO; SDS was formed when Young Democrats and Young Socialists joined with veterans from Americans for Democratic Action and the NAACP in Port Huron, Michigan, for an organizing conference in June 1962.

It was a tiny band with which to remake a society. In the wake of Port Huron, barely eight hundred members belonged to SDS. But they had passion on their side, plus Tom Hayden, a twenty-two-year-old sometime journalist who served as leader of the group from the University of California. Hayden had found a dissenter's paradise at Berkeley, where J. Edgar Hoover and the House Committee on Un-American Activities competed in unpopularity, and where John Kennedy was faulted for his gradualism in civil rights and nuclear disarmament. (Though he had first been beguiled by Kennedy, asked later whether he had been inspired by the president, Hayden replied, no—just politicized.)[4]

Back in the fall of 1961, when sit-ins were escalating throughout the South and James Farmer's Freedom Riders were pricking millions of consciences on the plight of blacks victimized by legally sanctioned discrimination, Hayden had been deep in Mississippi. He wasn't witnessing a movement, he told colleagues, but a revolution, and, "We had better be there." Less than a year later, his anger and resolution crystalized in the Port Huron Statement, SDS's birth certificate. Assailing the sterility of American life, its lack of community, and its inequities of social weight and economic power, Hayden's polemic reads in places like one of Pusey's chapel exhortations.

"We oppose the depersonalization that reduces human beings to the

status of things," it declared. "We would replace power rooted in possession, privilege, or circumstances by power and uniqueness rooted in love,
reflectiveness, reason and creativity." To achieve its goals, SDS proposed
a radically broadened "participatory democracy," with special emphasis on
the nation's campuses. For nowhere, the group said, was modern life devouring humane values more rapaciously than in the university—once a
shrine to the liberal arts, now a market stall dispensing the latest hardware to business, government, and the military. The Old Left was to be
conscripted into Hayden's battalions, but on his terms. (As someone said
afterward, Communists were valued mainly for their mimeographing
skills.)[5]

To assert such doctrines with any degree of confidence might have
seemed faintly absurd. America in 1962 was not Paris in 1848, nor was
John Kennedy to be confused with the Orleanist Louis Philippe. But even
at Harvard, home to the power elite, where until now the politically alert
were satisfied to teach low-income children to make gifts for local or-
phans; even here, SDS could tap wellsprings of discontent. Ten percent of
students responding to a 1958 campus poll called themselves radical,
twice as many were for socialized medicine, and a third believed in government ownership of all basic industries as well as immediate, unilateral
suspension of nuclear testing by the United States. A majority wanted the
government to recognize the People's Republic of China.[6]

Student impatience with the status quo had its faculty counterpart.
Prominent instructors like sociologist David Riesman spoke out against
the University's ties to the military. Others attended peace conferences
aimed at relaxing Cold War tensions. But, however impassioned these
feelings might be, they were expressed in civil fashion. In the fall of
1962, when a senior fellow at the Russian Research Center proposed "destructive criticism of a destructive system," he was booed. A few months
later, Franklin Ford, Bundy's successor as dean of the faculty of Arts and
Sciences, won appreciative chuckles for his tongue-in-cheek comparison of
the University to pre-1789 France. Both, said Ford, were "irrational, frequently unjust, tradition-bound, and culturally distinctive." If anyone tried
to explain Harvard rationally, Ford cracked, "it would come down in a
shower of blood."[7]

Around Cambridge, the genial, pipe-smoking Ford, a specialist in
German history, was widely viewed as Pusey's revenge for having endured nearly a decade in Bundy's penumbra. When Bundy left to join the
Kennedy Administration at the start of 1961, Pusey had muttered that
he'd like the experience of running the place himself for a change. Then,
for the next eighteen months, he wore two hats, straining relations with

his faculty with an impolitic promise to return Bundy's old chair "some-time this side of the immediate future."

Such actions displayed both sides of Pusey's love affair with Harvard. For years, he had felt shut out of faculty councils. Now he wished to get to know the members of Arts and Sciences, their strengths and weaknesses, as he had known his colleagues in Appleton. At the same time, shoulder-ing such additional burdens inevitably reduced the president's contact with undergraduates. With the benefit of hindsight, Corporation member Al-bert Nickerson diagnosed a condition which, untreated, contributed much to the institutional unraveling of the Sixties. "Harvard was still being run like a small private school. But it wasn't one. Because of tradition, every-one resisted the idea of structure." Pusey most of all. "We tried to get him to establish a more complete administrative set-up. But he couldn't bring himself to do it. We were pushing him so hard, and he was resisting so steadily—we had to pull back or see him explode."[8]

Even after Ford moved into Bundy's old office in University Hall, Pusey was absorbed by administrative demands inevitable for any execu-tive of so large and growing a concern. The University's worldwide repu-tation exacted a price, in presidential travel overseas, in heightened de-mands from the press, in an ever-expanding array of academic functions on campus. Before long, the teacher who had hoped to recreate in Cam-bridge the personal rapport he'd known at Lawrence, who early in his administration had been a familiar sight at Glee Club concerts and fenc-ing matches, gradually withdrew from public sight. The man who took to calling himself "the last old-fashioned college president" failed to grasp the irony of his self-applied label.

In truth, Pusey was a transitional figure, in many ways a victim of his own decency. He disliked surrounding himself with subordinates in Massachusetts Hall, preferring to husband financial resources for research and instruction. Even Harvard's historically decentralized administration, which on the surface might be expected to relieve the president of certain responsibilities, did not in practice work out that way. For Pusey was a conscientious delegator, at his meticulous best in recruiting deans to ride herd on the University's nine schools and twenty-eight departments. With a sublime confidence in his own judgment, and with the outside world pressing him as never before, it became easy for Pusey to avert his eyes from student unrest or faculty room discontent.

His own priorities were spelled out in a report marking ten years in the president's office. Fueled by the economic good times of the early Sixties, Harvard's universe continued to expand. The University received forty million dollars a year in private gifts and still more from Uncle

Sam. By 1963, there were new chairs in Oriental Art, Iranian and Korean Culture, and the General Theory of Value. Ninety-seven buildings were constructed or rehabilitated, and the University's budget tripled. Thanks to Pusey and his fundraisers, the endowment was fast approaching a billion dollars. Aided by an expansive administration in Washington, and a Congress so compliant that Barry Goldwater likened it to a Xerox machine, Harvard launched its own version of Lyndon Johnson's Great Society. During Pusey's reign in Massachussets Hall, the University's permanent population swelled from three thousand to eighty-five hundred, her tenured faculty rose from 122 to 277. The course catalog ballooned to seven hundred pages. For his professors, Pusey turned the spigot, and out flowed noncontributory pension plans, disability benefits, life insurance, hospital care, loans for those inclined to invest in real estate or add still another degree to enhance the holder's luster.[9]

There was too much intellectual wizardry to include in any president's report. Backed by the Arabian-American Oil Company, experts from the School of Public Health developed a vaccine against trachoma. At the University's cyclotron, proton beams were used to treat brain tumors. The effects of human weightlessness were investigated in the new Guggenheim Center for Aerospace Health and Safety, while astronomer Fred Whipple unveiled a system to track satellites, and Norman Ramsay's maser device led to the most accurate clock on earth. Computers were just coming into their own, their advocates predicting that they would do for modern scholars what the printing press had done for monks who once passed their days illuminating manuscripts—drive them from the monasteries, force them to look technology squarely in the eye. One professor at the law school fed three decades of statistics on juvenile crime into a computer. Someone else had resort to the marvelous machine in tracing the authorship of the Federalist Papers.[10]

Another, less welcome innovation disturbed the local peace. In December 1962, Dean of the College John Monro assailed Harvard researchers who were promoting the use of hallucinatory drugs, particularly psilocybin, LSD, and mescaline. Assistant professor Richard Alpert and lecturer Timothy Leary lodged indignant protests against what they called Monro's hysteria. The pair insisted that no evidence existed to prove such mind-altering drugs "uniquely dangerous." In fact, they said, there was no reason to think them any more harmful than psychoanalysis or four years in Harvard College.[11]

On Good Friday 1963, Leary presided over a gathering in the Boston University Chapel, after which divinity students reported having experienced religious insights foreign to most reading lists. Within days, Harvard dismissed him, the first such firing ever. A month later the University terminated Alpert's contract as well. Getting evicted from the Harvard faculty brought both men instant notoriety. (It also sharply curtailed their access to drugs permitted in the lab.)

Harvard's official reasons for the dismissals—frequent absences from Cambridge—were overshadowed by Alpert's revelation at a well-attended press conference: two hundred Harvard undergraduates, he claimed, had sought him out hoping to sample his potions for themselves. The gurus might be gone; not so the drug culture, now exposed for the first time. More than a few of those undergraduates who had been unsuccessful with Alpert had better luck in Harvard Square, where sugar cubes soaked in acid could be had at five dollars apiece. Even after the University placed four students on probation in the fall of 1965 for smoking marijuana, cheap Mexican dope remained a staple of campus party-going.[12]

Like nudity and obscenity, drug-taking became classified as a political act. Others called it hedonism, simple if not pure. Irving Howe, a stalwart of the Old Left, spoke for many who were disturbed by what appeared to be young people's undue preoccupation with political style over strategy. In his opinion, they were more concerned with "how to live individually within this society, rather than how to change it collectively." Such strictures were lost on Berkeley protesters who in 1963 carried signs instructing readers not to fold, spindle, or mutilate the bearers. For them, as for others of their generation, modern life itself was the culprit, and they wished to register their unhappiness with a society whose pursuit of profit threatened individuality and the very landscape around them. Rachel Carson's *Silent Spring* helped foster environmental awareness; and Cambridge police were called out to disperse fifteen hundred demonstrators trying to rescue sycamore trees from a highway overpass.[13]

Another topic of heated debate was the changing role of women, an issue sparked by the publication in 1963 of Betty Friedan's *The Feminine Mystique*. Until now, women's rights at Harvard had been relegated to the shadows. To be sure, the University had awarded an honorary degree to Helen Keller in 1956 (following a heated debate between Overseers loyal to Miss Keller and others supporting Eleanor Roosevelt), but no woman would take a place on the larger governing board before 1970. In between, Radcliffe opened a center for women's studies, but when a female editor of the *Crimson* made a runoff election for class marshal, the Undergraduate Council refused to count her votes. The same body protested that opening Lamont Library in Harvard Yard to women would inevitably damage what it called the male emotional stability factor.[14]

Pusey risked it anyway, taking the next step in his largely unpubli-
cized campaign for educational equality. In fact, Pusey was never given
credit for his personal commitment to coeducation. As his Radcliffe counterpart, Mary Bunting, made clear in a later Columbia Oral History Project interview, he was genuinely eager to consider a merger of the two
schools as early as 1965. The first Harvard president ever to address Radcliffe's governing board of trustees, he also pioneered in establishing a single, coeducational graduate school, and hoped to cap his presidency with
a final merger between the main University and the offshoot originally
dubbed "the Radcliffe Annex." The latter would fall victim to opposing
forces in the spring and summer of 1969, when tumult in the wake of the
University Hall uprising combined with a conservative backlash from
Radcliffe alumnae to stymie Pusey's ambitious plans.[15]

While debates over honorary degrees and library privileges engulfed
the governing bodies, outside forces began to demolish traditional sex
roles. In November 1963, a three-judge panel in Manhattan ruled *Fanny
Hill* obscene, and Boston newspapers headlined spurious sex orgies at
Harvard. Neither surprised Cambridge. There had always been a certain
Chaucerian strain in the local fraternity. Deans who sought to regulate
undergraduate social lives had merely encouraged generations of young
men to discover the joys of sex before dinner. As John Kenneth Galbraith
summed it up, "When Harvard College was in part a privileged academy
for the socially visible, it needed to assure parents that their more retarded
offspring would have the supervision of men of the scoutmaster type who,
however ineffectually, would try to protect them from the natural penalties of indolence, alcohol or lust."[16]

What really offended Galbraith was evidence that the administration's maternal drives were intact. Prompted by postgame shenanigans during the 1963 football season, Dean Monro wrote a cautionary letter to the
future leaders in his charge. Munro was shocked that half of all college
women were losing their virginity by the time they gained a diploma, and
he vowed to fortify Harvard's parietal rules. In a subsequent address in Memorial Church, Pusey took a different tack. He had hoped to have "a quiet
intramural talk" about parietals, he informed a student audience, but before he could do so, exaggerated press accounts had produced a backwash
of alumni letters, most demanding a forthright denunciation of immorality in all its forms. No such disclaimer was required, said the president.
Nor was Harvard to blame for a popular culture preoccupied with sex:
the pornography on local newsstands was, according to Pusey, the work
of adult America.

Thus, a double paradox was born: young people who rejected the

University's authority over their lives and yet were quick to accuse that same institution of a callous disregard of values, and a president who blamed the press for distorting youthful behavior, even as the undergraduate stream drifted away from him. Pusey, like a lot of American fathers, wanted to keep a little peace in the family, so he washed his hands of the affair. And so the parietals remained on the books but were ignored in practice. They mocked the very authority they were supposed to uphold. The net effect was to dramatize the well-meaning but ineffectual leadership of a man sincerely trying to please differing constituencies, but whose efforts satisfied almost no one.

"In such a state of society," Plato wrote, "the master fears and flatters his scholars, and the scholars despise their masters and tutors. . . . Old men condescend to the young and are full of pleasantry and gaiety; they are loath to be thought morose and authoritative, and therefore they adopt the manners of the young."

In paying tribute to Robert Frost in a speech at Amherst in October 1963, President Kennedy's eloquence matched the beauty of the season. Men of power, he said, made an indispensable contribution to national greatness. But so did those who questioned its uses, "especially when that questioning is disinterested. For they determine whether we use power or power uses us. When power leads man toward arrogance, poetry reminds him of his limitations. When power narrows the area of man's concern, poetry reminds him of the richness and diversity of his existence. When power corrupts, poetry cleanses."[17]

Three weeks later, the speaker himself was being eulogized. Nowhere did Kennedy's assassination have such resonance as at Harvard, an academy already torn between poetry and power. The first bulletin from Dallas sent people racing toward the *Crimson* newsroom, to huddle around a clacking wire service machine. Others lurched in the direction of darkened, silent Houses. Young men wept on the grass of the Tercentenary Theatre, or sat numb with grief beside a glassy Charles River. Mingled with the tears was a sense of guilt. "We felt as if one of the very best of us had been shot," the *Crimson*'s Faye Levine recalled, "that we had committed some grave oversight in letting it happen."*[18]

Before his Amherst audience, JFK had chosen to quote one of

* The unwarranted sense of self-importance that led to the students' feeling of guilt over John Kennedy's death also colored their anger at his successor's course in Vietnam. From the middle through the later Sixties, no dining hall conversation was complete without declarations that if only enough *Harvard* students refused to fight Lyndon Johnson's war, the leader of the free world might reconsider.

Frost's uncharacteristically sanguine appraisals of the human family. Had he been a seer, the president might instead have selected the poet's bitter reproach to New Deal equalizers, penned in 1936 in the aftermath of Lawrence Lowell's disputed decision to fire a dozen scrubwomen:

> *No memory of having starred*
> *Atones for later disregard,*
> *Or keeps the end from being hard.*
> *Better to go down dignified*
> *With boughten friendship at your side*
> *Than none at all. Provide! provide!*

In Washington and Cambridge alike, those in power provided much in the 1960s. In the end, however, unable to purchase gratitude, they went down to a chorus of angry shouts.

The years between 1964 and 1966 were good ones; as one chronicler put it, post-Leary and pre-draft. The Faculty Club menu still offered horsemeat, a last vestige of World War II rationing. President Pusey had two entries in the local phonebook, one for his family and another for their servants. After someone calculated that the American Friends Service Committee spent 13 percent of its time propagandizing for world peace, the organization was deemed political and dropped from the Harvard-Radcliffe Combined Charities. Four times as many Harvard students signed petitions supporting Lyndon Johnson's Vietnam policy as opposed the escalating war. The Spee Club welcomed its first black member. And the turnout was disappointingly small when Mario Savio, eager to export his west coast brand of student rebellion, came to Harvard to denounce what he called "a knowledge factory . . . plugged into the military and industry, but not to truth."

At Berkeley, Savio and his cohorts had dubbed themselves the Free Speech Movement. Free Speech was an early example of Sixties protesters' Orwellian doublespeak, destined for a place alongside the "liberation" of occupied buildings and the "real learning" enshrined in such late Sixties Harvard courses as "The History of the Self" and "The Political Relevance of Encounter Groups." Like so many protest movements of the period, the Free Speech movement encouraged the view that society's shortcomings might be changed as quickly as a TV channel. It was no accident when, in the course of the violent student rebellion at Berkeley in 1964, Savio declared "an end to history." The emphasis was now on the contemporary, Pusey complained, "as if learning itself is not relevant!"

Yet, in the wake of the Berkeley disruptions, touched off by the administration's refusal to permit student dissidents to wage their campaign on official property, Harvard's president commended the conscience of the restless young who echoed his own critique of "the stifling, all-pervasive cheapness of the life around us." In his baccalaureate address in June 1965, Pusey looked over his shoulder at Savio's protest of the previous autumn. Granted, Berkeley had witnessed crude displays of force and manifestations of a revolutionary power struggle. But most of those who were disturbing the peace of America's campuses cared less for Marxist polemics than for democratic promises. They were moved to action over civil rights, poverty, and their nation's conduct in Vietnam. Just as important, he said, was their resentment of "an alleged growing indifference on the part of the faculty toward students, especially undergraduate students, the rights of students to be heard and to participate in the formulation of policy, especially education policy, and . . . excessive concern on the part of the administration officers for problems outside the institution at the expense of more important ones."

Typically, Pusey qualified his commendation. Protest, of itself, he contended, signified neither virtue nor achievement, but rather awareness of shortcomings in themselves and in others, of abuses and chicanery; above all, of human need—these things were timeless. He cited Henry Adams, both Roosevelts, Walter Lippmann, and John F. Kennedy as "patient people who could bide their time, not people who would spend their power to protest in a single youthful effort, justified or misguided, but individuals who throughout their lives would keep on working constructively to strike what blows they could for advance. And it is to this latter tribe we hope students have elected to belong." Fight the good fight, Pusey seemed to be saying, but don't get carried away.[19]

It was all perfectly reasonable. Unfortunately, reason authorized little of what happened in the Sixties. The student attitude Yale president Kingman Brewster dubbed "Nowism" was no exception. Nowism placed sensory experience ahead of conceptual knowledge. It dismissed objectivity, mocked detachment, and praised participation and spontaneity in place of academic specialization and cloistered research. Sociologist Jacques Barzun characterized Sixties students as a campus proletariat impatient with restraints and governed by impulse, the inevitable product of progressive education and what his colleagues liked to call the permissive-expressive home; this army of the young had been constantly reminded by college presidents and American presidents that theirs was the best educated generation in history.

In fact, it was the most easily bored. Barzun might have been describing students in Mexico City or Indianapolis when he wrote of those who from infancy had been told "that ideas and books are meant to be provocative, that speakers must be stimulating, that the best teachers are exciting; they have come to believe all this and are restless when not in the presence or pursuit of some detonating mixture." Yet this excitement as defined by the mass media was a dangerous fallacy. In Barzun's view it was the opposite of interest and the enemy of academic calm. In one, time raced and thoughts blurred. In the other, every minute was savored, its passage regretted.[20]

At Harvard, young Americans found themselves inside an institution whose impersonality and confusion of purpose encouraged a belief in untutored emotions and disenchantment with anything beyond their immediate control—which seemed to be nearly everything. So Harvard students went to the barricades to confront the symbols of their impotence: the government that drafted them into its armies, and the University's much more vulnerable semi-government, which they punished for its claims to neutrality.

A majority of those involved in the ensuing disruptions were private school graduates, many from wealthy families, most embarrassed if not ashamed of their advantages. After a 1967 visit to Cambridge, New York Times columnist Russell Baker accused Harvard of perverting modern education. "We have debased the college degree," he wrote, "by turning it into a shabby visa which admits the holder to the exclusive privileges of employment and promotion in the ruling industrial-governmental-social establishment. . . . And so, in the midst of so much safety, one broods upon the doomed who have to pay for it."[21]

There was no shortage of brooding at Harvard in the late Sixties. Undergraduates, dissatisfied with the pallid distribution requirement General Education had turned into, became allied with graduate students who were caught up in their own fierce competition, aware that for each one from their ranks who would win tenure, five more would fall short. Pusey could build new housing for aspiring professors, he could raise their wages and enhance their titles, but he couldn't shield them from the draft, nor generate loyalty to an institution rather than a career.

He was even less able to contain the combustible feelings of Harvard's newest minority. By the end of the decade, the University's black population would quintuple. Even before that, blacks at Harvard formed a critical mass no longer manageable by dispersal. "Before a group can enter the open society," declared black power advocate Stokely Carmichael, "it must first close ranks." Most of the newcomers rejected traditional pluralism for racial solidarity. The fact that such students preferred to live in Pusey's glass and concrete boxes was easily explained, according to a Leverett House tutor: men from Watts and Roxbury associated Lawrence Lowell's Georgian enclaves with plantation life, not Kuumba gospel concerts or classes in Swahili.[22]

Typical of the new black student was Sylvester Monroe, who later became a *Newsweek* reporter. Monroe entered Harvard in 1969, after attending an all-black high school in Chicago's South Side. He chose to live with white students his first year but soon regretted his decision. Questions about soul food and hairstyles made him feel like a sociological guinea pig. He narrowed his range of contacts, restricting future roommates to members of his own race. Failing to connect *Beowulf* to the black experience in America, he walked out of class. Dissatisfied with Harvard's traditions, he and other blacks timed their departure from Leverett House's sophomore dinner to coincide with the master's opening remarks. He joined the Association of African and Afro-American Students—Afro for short—and endorsed the group's call for a separate Third World Center and full department of Afro-American studies.[23]

"This demand for black studies grows out of guilt of the past when we let ourselves be pushed around," explained a black Nieman Fellow and Harvard recruiter, "guilt by middle class black youngsters who are conscience-stricken because their fathers did nothing for ghetto blacks. This striving for identity is a natural first step."[24]

In their search for community, Monroe and his friends turned to confrontational tactics. Artificial unity seemed better than none, and black nationalism was a bonding agent more satisfying than the exam blue book. But it added a new and destabilizing element to the campus. It also baffled orthodox liberals.

Harvard's first black administrator was Archie Epps III, a pioneer with a flower in his lapel, a scholar's interest in Malcolm X, and a devotion to Pusey's belief in the University as an island of calm reasoning. "Sometimes I think we might do well to return to wearing academic gowns," says Epps, "if only to spell the difference between a university and a political institution." A one-time theology student who as a boy had preferred Beethoven to basketball, Epps was among Afro's first faculty advisers. Along with black professor Martin Kilson of the government department, he founded the *Journal for Negro Affairs,* and he had organized New England's participation in the historic March on Washington in August 1963. As a music tutor in Leverett House, Epps listened spellbound the night two thousand people assembled in the streets outside to hear Malcolm X give his seminar on "Martin Luther King and the Negro Revolution."[25]

As assistant dean of students, Epps tried to befriend black youths plucked from the streets and dropped into an alien culture. He drew the line, however, at black separatism, and his devotion to Harvard as an institution undermined his credibility with many of those he was most anxious to help.

At that, he was more attuned to student sensitivities than most of his administrative colleagues, such as F. Skiddy von Stade, the freshman dean, who was enshrined in local legend as having been the last Harvard undergraduate to appear in Cambridge with his own polo ponies. Von Stade's deputy, Burris Young, was a man of no less impressive cultivation. An amateur archeologist, Young pursued his hobby each summer in Turkey. In between digs, he fretted over young people of the Vietnam era whom he considered too obsessed with politics to savor "leisurely growth and the enjoyment of tradition."[26]

In contrast to the mannerly deans of University Hall were the moralists of SDS. Each camp regarded itself as a lonely outpost of realism and disdained the other as a band of hopeless romantics. Each clung to its own view of the country for which it presumed to speak. To Pusey's generation, America was a nation of pure motives and unblemished generosity; to antiwar activists, it was a land of imperial appetites and official mendacity. One thought it bad form to imprison a Dow Chemical recruiter ("that man could *sue* us!" sputtered Dean of Students Robert Watson). The other found bitter humor in University Hall's denial of a permit to demonstrate against Robert McNamara; a new stand of rosebushes, it was ruled, was unlikely to withstand even an orderly mob.[27]

Etiquette mattered little to SDS militants. Jesse Kornbluth, for instance, after learning of an impending visit by Robert McNamara in November 1966, pondered how to sneak human limbs from a medical lab to hurl at the Secretary of Defense. "No symbols," he told those who proposed settling for butcher shop bones and chicken blood. When McNamara arrived, hundreds of demonstrators forced him from his car outside Quincy House. Unshaken, he told the crowd that he'd spent four years at Berkeley doing many of the things those now confronting him were doing—with one difference. "I was tougher and more courteous." Amid cries of "murderer" and "fascist," McNamara raised his voice. "I was tougher then and I'm tougher now." University officials apologized for the incident. So did nearly three thousand students, and SDS members who appeared in the Quincy House dining room that evening were hooted.*[28]

---

* Although McNamara might be placated, infuriated by television accounts of the incident, Johnson soon ordered an escalation of bombing over North Viet-

In quieter moments, Kornbluth acknowledged that the world might be more complicated than it appeared from Harvard Yard. At such times, he entertained thoughts of accommodation, or at least of listening to other opinions. "But with each passing day," he wrote, "thousands were dying and we were brought closer to our own deaths, so there was not time for caution or experimentation or give and take."[29]

During his college days, Burris Young remembered, anyone sufficiently miserable to want to leave the place for a year could do so. After 1966, and the end of most draft deferments, that option vanished. What remained was a community of brainy, supersensitive people, by their own estimation America's brightest and best, locked inside the Yard like flies in a bottle.

"Whatever was wrong about American society—war, racism, poverty, it could be seen or felt here," says Young. "You could go to class and argue about Keats. But deep down inside you worried about Selma and Vietnam."[30]

In his undergraduate journals, later published as *Push Comes to Shove,* Steven Kelman, a disciple of the Old Left and member of the class of 1970, traced the evolution of radical thinking as draft calls closed off the last remaining safety valves. Kelman followed Tom Hayden's evolution from 1965, when he refrained from taking an official position on socialism (people would decide that for themselves, he said), to 1968, when he embraced Ho Chi Minh's National Liberation Front. At this same time, SDS was proclaiming its own Week of Solidarity with the Cuban Revolution and opposing factions of the group were waving copies of Mao's Little Red Book at one another like combatants invoking God's blessing or curse. To such true believers, revolution seemed imminent, with Vietnam the fulcrum that might tip America in radical directions.

Populism and the New Deal, Kelman said, were movements spawned in anger. George Wallace and Adolf Hitler, on the other hand, were off-springs of popular frustration. For those who wrote letters and knocked on doors for Eugene McCarthy's dump-Johnson campaign in 1968, who marched in the streets and flocked to campus teach-ins against the war only to see Richard Nixon swept into the White House on a conservative tide, frustration was building. A poll of students in the spring of 1969 showed that 40 percent had entered America's colleges with the hope of bringing about change. Some were populists for whom the globe simply spun too fast; others were nihilists whose rant and preference for street the-

---

nam (such, at least, was the story told by historian James C. Thompson upon his return from LBJ's State Department).

ater followed in savage footsteps.[31] (Mark Rudd, the Robespierre of Morningside Heights, told Columbia's president Grayson Kirk that his was a sick society. "Up against the wall, motherfucker, this is a stick-up." Jared Israel, a leader of Harvard SDS's Progressive Labor contingent, spoke contemptuously of "bourgeois civil liberties" and claimed that Martin Luther King's assassination was a step forward in the struggle for black liberation.[32])

Conventional liberalism was SDS's mortal enemy. At Harvard, law professor Archibald Cox was its nemesis before he was Richard Nixon's. A bow-tied Brahmin, Cox detested the Vietnam War yet he agreed to introduce South Vietnam's ambassador to the United States to a hostile audience in Sanders Theater. For his pains, Cox was shouted off the stage and, along with the emissary from Saigon, forced to escape by Harvard's version of the underground railroad ("The steam tunnels are a great thing," says Cox. "You'd be surprised how important they were in those days").[33]

Throughout the late Sixties, as student opposition to the Vietnam War mounted, traditional liberals in Harvard's governing circles clung to their own idea of the University's obligation to serve. In the spring of 1967, it was revealed that more than $400,000 had been funneled to Harvard through CIA conduits, a large chunk of which went to support the summer school's international seminar program run by professor of political science Henry Kissinger. Franklin Ford remarked casually that Harvard was involved in Vietnam "like any other agency or organization of the American people." And Corporation member William Marbury, steeped in the traditions of World War II and the liberal nationalism embodied in his good friend James Conant, roused hostile comment with his defense of the Reserve Officers Training Corps. Criticizing ROTC, declared Marbury, was like slapping a lion in the face, "especially at a time when every university is dependent on federal funds."[34]

On October 25, 1967, protesters trapped a campus recruiter from Dow Chemical in Mallinckrodt Hall. "God, what a mess!" exclaimed Dean Watson afterward. "I'd never seen Harvard students behave this way." Demonstration leader Michael Ansara countered: "It was one of the most exciting days I ever spent at Harvard." Two days later, a follow-up rally heard one student speaker after another denounce such recruitment. As one put it, "It is not the purpose of a university to provide space for murderers to recruit other people to participate in their murders."[35]

Fearing a repeat of the Dow fracas, the CIA canceled its annual round of interviews. Professor Jerome Cohen, a noted China expert, wondered if the Maoist slogan "Politics Takes Command" might not apply to undergraduate Harvard in the spring of 1968, when over a hundred of that year's graduating seniors pledged resistance to the draft, and when one of Cohen's faculty colleagues was forced to spend an entire week negotiating ground rules before U.N. Ambassador Arthur Goldberg could appear on campus.[36]

In April, SDS staged a violent series of disturbances at Columbia University, occupying Low Library. When it was over, Pusey entrusted to Archibald Cox an investigation of the protest and of the Columbia administration response. Although Cox insisted his findings were later misinterpreted, Pusey found them clear enough at the time. By permitting the protesters to stay inside the library for several days while negotiations dragged on inconclusively, President Grayson Kirk had surrendered the initiative. It was a mistake Pusey had no intention of repeating. Not long after, following prolonged discussion with his deans, Pusey reached consensus on what should be done were any Harvard building to fall into radical hands. Police would be called in, not at night, when their presence might touch off mob violence, but soon, before any occupation could gain a foothold.[37]

Almost as important as avoiding such trouble, the deans agreed, was shielding the president from personal responsibility for what was certain to be an unpopular move. Thus, it was decided that Pusey would stay in the background, his natural milieu, while others assumed disciplinary functions. The decision corresponded neatly to the preferences of a man who resembled increasingly a visitor in his own house. Indeed, only a handful were aware of it, but Pusey himself was anticipating retirement. As far back as 1963, at the end of his first decade in office, the president had asked the Corporation to conduct a full-scale review of his stewardship before he would agree to stay on at the helm for another five years. After 1968, he made plain his reluctance to continue in office on more than a year-to-year basis.[38]

And so, at a time when Harvard most required strong leadership, when its curriculum needed overhaul, its administrative shortcomings cried out for reform, its relations with Radcliffe invited redefinition; at this critical juncture in its history, its president acknowledged his own lack of energy to tackle such contentious issues. As events would demonstrate, Pusey had more than enough stamina to defy his radical critics. Tragically, however, he had too little imagination to defuse their unlikely appeal to the vast majority of student moderates.

*It is the disease of not listening, the malady of
not marking, that I am troubled withal.*
                                    —Henry the Fourth, Part II

*I don't have any time to see students. I have a
whole university to run.*
                                    —NATHAN PUSEY
                                    Spring 1969

IN HIS annual report for 1967–68, composed against a backdrop of antiwar marches, draft-card burnings, ghetto violence, and the politicization
of his student body, Pusey congratulated "the vast majority of Harvard
undergraduates [who] went about their essential business seriously and
gaily, as students have from the beginning." He boasted that thirty plays
had been produced, and that Harvard had achieved the best athletic record in the Ivy League. Within a year, however, shaken and mystified by
student violence, Harvard's president would turn to a local clergyman for
solace. "Wouldn't you say the devil is in these people?" he asked.[39]

Despite his lack of sympathy for student rebellion, in his resistance
to prevailing trends and his disdain for those of his countrymen who lived
"shallowly and limitedly in unawareness, self-deception, irresponsibility,
selfishness and unconcern," there was much to link Pusey with youthful
protesters who were contemptuous of an impersonal educational system
which chewed them up and spat them out without ever realizing their
potential. Because Pusey the Moralist was overshadowed by Pusey the
Manager, a distant figure consumed by administrative and bureaucratic
detail, the connection was never made. At a time when personal visibility
could have been a crucial element of leadership, the Janitor Theory of
Nathan Pusey emerged: there was no such thing as a president in Massachusetts Hall, it was claimed, only a distinguished-looking Building and
Groundsman who dressed up in a blue suit for ceremonial occasions.

By the late Sixties, when love-ins were being held in Cambridge
Common at the same hour as the president's weekly tea, more than schedules were in conflict. Pusey inadvertently fed student charges of his hy-
pocrisy when, in 1968, he refused to permit televised coverage of a
campus teach-in against the Vietnam War. "To use technology to assert
a point of view is contrary to the principles of the University," he asserted—not long after Harvard scientists, at Robert McNamara's behest,
had contemplated an electronic barrier that would ward off North Viet-

namese infiltration into the South. Even as the University was displacing Cambridge renters as it expanded into nearby low-income neighborhoods, and the president was pressed to account for Harvard's investment in a southern company accused of racial discrimination in its hiring practices, he responded, "Our purpose is to invest in places that are selfishly good for Harvard. We do not use our money for social purposes." Such positions, while consistent with his view that the University should not take political stands, suggested an immense lack of understanding of what was really happening on his campus and in the surrounding community.[40]

More than ever, Pusey seemed to rely on himself and to believe that God whispered into his ear. His range of consultation shrank to a few intimates in Massachusetts Hall. On the rare occasions when the palace walls were breached, the monarch appeared deaf to popular sentiment. After Tom Crooks, then master of Dudley House, arranged for Pusey to talk with an antiwar student, the president said he couldn't understand the reason for such an appointment; it had been a complete waste of his time.[41]

In a biting characterization of militant students as "Walter Mittys of the Left," Pusey revealed a sweeping view that all student dissidents were harbingers of a new McCarthyism. When he made the assertion, in the spring of 1968, Pusey genuinely believed his University endangered by a fresh wave of anti-intellectualism, made worse because this time the assault originated from within. Yet by lumping general dissatisfaction over Vietnam with the anarchic hard-core militancy of SDS's Maoist fringe, he unintentionally conceded to his harshest critics the tactical advantage.

Pusey was not inclined to argue his case in the press. That task was reserved for Hugh Calkins, a moderately liberal Cleveland lawyer who joined the Corporation in 1968 and who rapidly became Harvard's pipeline to the media. As the president's contacts with the press dwindled, so did his meetings with community leaders. In what few he had, he seemed detached and insensitive. There was the time Boston mayor Kevin White asked Pusey to consider allowing the New England Patriots to use Harvard Stadium until a permanent facility could be constructed for them elsewhere. To Pusey, professional football as a character-builder exercise ranked somewhere between pool and smoking behind the barroom door. Uncomfortable as he was about the game, he was still more dubious about the drinking sure to go on in the stands. "Besides," he continued, "I don't think it really would be good for Boston."

"Mr. Pusey," White interrupted, "on the way over here, I was told not to instruct you on what I thought best for Harvard. That was very good advice. Someone should give you the same advice on what I think of your opinion of Boston."[42]

In the spring of 1969, at a time when the University's town-gown relations were being mauled in the local press, the Ford Foundation announced that it wouldn't renew its support of the Joint Center for Urban Studies, product of a shotgun marriage between Harvard and MIT over which the foundation had presided a decade earlier. Pusey's response was characteristically straightforward. The place should be closed, he told John Dunlop. "My God," Dunlop exclaimed, "here we are, in the midst of all these troubles, when everyone's saying Harvard isn't alert to its urban responsibilities. . . ." Ultimately, Dunlop who became dean of Arts and Sciences that fall, was able to secure enough in private donations for the center to remain open.[43]

Pusey wasn't the only member of administrative Harvard who was out of touch. Just before the start of the 1968–69 academic year, Corporation member Hooks Burr played tennis with McGeorge Bundy, who wanted to know the biggest single issue confronting his old university. Finances, Burr told him. But what about "the student thing," Bundy pressed. Not to worry, Burr responded; that would go away before long.[44]

"We looked at Berkeley and to a lesser extent at Columbia," says John Fox, later Dean of the College, "and we concluded that what was happening there must be a result of impersonalization. People couldn't really know the institution they were attacking." Paradoxically, Fox viewed Harvard's fragmented state as a source of strength. "Because this place was so diffuse, because so much of undergraduate life was parceled out among the Houses, departments, and extra-curricular activities, we figured there was no single place to take your beef. Of course, we forgot that Mr. Bulfinch provided us with a snow-white building [University Hall] in the middle of a dark red yard."[45]

Also overlooked was the faculty's role in undermining Pusey and his administration by encouraging student agitation over the war and the University's ties to the military. ROTC in particular was a touchy issue, the most obvious and easily exploited symbol of Harvard's alleged complicity in Vietnam. "Students were looking for a target then," said economics professor Henry Rosovsky, "and they chose the easiest and safest one." Rosovsky's colleague Alan Heimert offered two shrewd pieces of advice in the closing months of 1968. "Let 'em smoke all the pot they want," he said of undergraduate drug offenders, "only keep 'em away from ROTC." Heimert's second bit of counsel was even more prophetic.

"Don't watch the players," he urged Franklin Ford. "Watch the audience." By then, the audience—in this case, the faculty of Arts and Sciences—was increasingly part of the performance, a cross between showboat melodrama and the Keystone Cops. And ROTC was the equivalent of shouting fire in a crowded theater.[46]

By now, ROTC was caught up in a complex tug-of-war between Harvard administrators and faculty members whose antipathy to the military found expression in verbal assaults on the University's own disciplinary procedures. Back in 1966, when SDS had intercepted Robert McNamara in the streets of Cambridge and forced him from his car, John Munro's denunciation of "mob violence" had been followed up by a dinner invitation to the mob's leaders. The faculty's own response had been limited to a ritualistic warning about the dangers of future disruptions. A year later, in the wake of the Dow incident, Harvard's Administrative Board placed more than seventy of the participants on academic probation. Then, in December of 1968, when a faculty meeting on ROTC in Paine Hall was disrupted by a student sit-in, fifty-two protesters were put on probation and five more, already rebuked for their part in the Dow affair, were asked by the Administrative Board to withdraw from the University. But the faculty overturned the suspensions, reasoning that any student dismissed just then would be exposed to the not so tender mercies of his local draft board.

"Faculty Saves Everyone," the *Crimson* proclaimed—everyone, that is, except the Administrative Board, which effectively was destroyed as a disciplinary agent by the reversal. Although the action was taken as a stand on the war, in effect the faculty had asserted a claim to administrative prerogatives unknown since the days of Walsh-Sweezy.

The Paine Hall sit-in set the tone for months of academic wrangling. It also completed the faculty's politicization. In the opinion of his friend and ideological ally John Dunlop, Dean of the Faculty, Franklin Ford was sabotaged that December afternoon. Faculty opposition to Ford's pro-ROTC stand was "more than passingly well organized." In response, economics professor Dunlop, along with Government Department chairman Robert McCloskey, began calling friends like Sam Beer, Oscar Handlin, and Samuel Huntington and, within days, formed what was known as the Conservative Caucus. The term was relative; the caucus was conservative only in its desire to avoid institutional positions on political issues, and in its emphasis on maintaining normal academic schedules despite the political upheaval. Later on, a liberal faction would spring up to present its own views. That winter, opposing groups of like-minded professors began meeting in Cambridge living rooms on Sunday afternoons. During the week, urgent meetings were convened so often as to devalue the word *emergency*.[47]

As tensions mounted, manners frayed. One instructor asked John Kenneth Galbraith in front of several hundred colleagues to please shut up. Another accosted Professor Laurance Wylie in a Widener Library elevator and proceeded to explain why they were no longer on speaking terms. Traditionalists declared they would boycott any gathering to which students were invited. One professor, asked on his deathbed whether he had any regrets, said he had two: his failure to complete a work in progress and his inability to take Professor X of the liberal caucus where he was going.[48]

After the sit-in at Paine Hall, an almost surreal quality stalked the faculty. "Ordinarily," says John Dunlop, "the great thing about Harvard is its civility. You can always count on someone to gently nudge a guy and let him know when he's away on Cloud Nine." Not so in the waning days of 1968. "That was a time when anyone could say anything, however ludicrous, and have it taken seriously so long as he mentioned Youth."[49]

To those who agreed with Dunlop, the chief offender was George Wald, a Nobel Prize-winner for his work on eye pigmentation, who also happened to be Harvard's most conspicuous gift to radical chic. Refused permission by black students to participate in their separate memorial service for Martin Luther King, Wald was content to sit silently at their feet. Anything but silent in faculty councils, Wald lectured colleagues on the evils of capitalism. "I think I know what is bothering the students," he said. "I think what we are up against is a generation that is by no means sure that it has a future.[50]

But Wald was moderate in comparison with Hilary Putnum, a junior member of the philosophy department who spearheaded faculty opposition to Harvard's ROTC program. "The reason ROTC is objectionable is that what the army does is objectionable," said Putnam, in particular "suppressing popular revolutions in the Third World."[51]

For those of less apocalyptic bent, there were academic standards to assail. In the fall of 1968, the University introduced Social Relations 148, "Social Change in America," which, along with its companion course Soc Rel 149, offered a harsh critique of American society, without lectures and with minimal attention paid to grading. Nine hundred undergraduates flocked to courses designed in the words of one promoter, "to produce more and better radicals." "Imperialism and the University" and "Women and Sex-Role Repression" were especially popular. One class left the classroom for the streets of Cambridge to campaign for rent control, prompting fears that unless steps were quickly taken to reassert departmental control, more political recruiting masked as instruction would emerge.[52]

Meanwhile, early in February 1969, the faculty approved a new degree program in Afro-American studies, stopping short, however, of establishing the separate independent black studies department that SDS was demanding. They also underwrote increased recruitment of black instructors and administrators, and new fellowships for postgraduate students (in the previous decade, only eight blacks had received Harvard Ph.D.'s). In addition, a social center for black students was proposed, modeled after the Jewish community's Hillel House and the Catholic Newman Center. The *New York Times* congratulated the University for defusing tensions before they could detonate as they already had at San Francisco State and other embattled campuses. Roy Wilkins and the NAACP took exception to what they perceived as a new form of racial separatism, but junior officers in the civil rights army, men like CORE's Roy Innis, repudiated Wilkins and his generation as deaf to appeals from younger blacks for a sharper sense of their own identity.

The debate was dramatized a few days later when a hundred members of Harvard Afro stormed an urban affairs course designed to help city planners and law enforcement officials with riot control. "It wants to put down riots themselves, not deal with the conditions that create them," complained the group's leader. Chants of "End racism—no riot control" provided background accompaniment for Afro's ultimatum: cancel Planning 11-3b. When the class was, in fact, dismissed, it prompted a large group of professors to register vigorous protest in the *Crimson*. Pusey seconded their gesture.[53]

If a single picture captures the incongruity of those days, it is the image of Pusey, with his legs crossed and arms folded, sitting in a leather chair while students peppered him with hostile questions about ROTC. Over the president's shoulder can be seen a blackboard, on which someone has written, "When is Harvard going to stop training people for this fucking war?" Either Pusey overlooked the obscenity or he chose to ignore it, most likely the second. If nothing else, the period reinforced the president's penchant for closing his eyes to the unpleasant.

Showered with epithets in public, spat at by undergraduates, his physical safety in question, Pusey soldiered on, sustained by faith in his own course and contempt for SDS's frontal assault on reason.

Visitors to Massachusetts Hall in the last weeks of the long New England winter of 1968–69 found the president alternately detached from events or worried about their implications for the future. Elliot

Richardson was in the president's office one afternoon when their conversation was interrupted by the telephone. To the latest installment of dismaying news, Pusey muttered softly, "Damn," then resumed the talk where it had broken off. However, to another colleague he admitted having had trouble sleeping. When Carl Pforzheimer, an old friend and classmate, warned Pusey on Washington's Birthday that his campus was on the brink of dissolution, the president didn't seem surprised. As a matter of fact, he'd spent a lot of time recently examining dossiers compiled on potential troublemakers within the student body. "You know," he concluded wearily, "we've got ourselves quite a few brickthrowers around here."[54]

A few days later, Pusey sat dumbfounded as a delegation from a group called The Conspiracy Against Harvard Education proposed a grandiose Festival of Life for Harvard Yard. The zaniness was further compounded early in March when King Collins, a former Columbia student and self-proclaimed anarchist, arrived at Harvard to terrorize professors and students alike. In one class, Collins shouted denunciation of its instructor as "totally dead . . . a desexualized being." In another lecture hall, Collins's taunts moved a group of football players in the audience to rise menacingly; for a while, the class threatend to erupt in fisticuffs. More often, Collins was a scatological prankster. One night, Eliot House master Alan Heimert was summoned to the laundry room where Collins and his entourage had taken off all their clothes. Heimert asked one of the naked visitors if he had a masculinity problem. "Fuck off," the man replied. Eventually arrested, Collins was disowned by the local branch of SDS, but was released from custody after the radical underground generated ten thousand dollars in bail money.[55]

Whatever else he was, Collins was atypical of the utterly serious men and women out to banish ROTC, which since the aborted December meeting at Paine Hall had become the nucleus of all campus dissent. McGeorge Bundy and Henry Kissinger were beyond their reach. Richard Nixon wouldn't listen to them in any event. But antiwar students could use the University as a vehicle to express their rage, and ROTC, its military apparatus, could be dealt a symbolic blow. The faculty voted to strip credit from the ROTC program the same day it approved a black studies program.

The Corporation, however, had no intention of booting army officers off campus, canceling ROTC's rent-free quarters, or replacing ROTC scholarships with University funds. It upbraided the faculty publicly for overstepping its authority by demanding such measures. By late March, with Pusey strongly committed to keeping the program, it appeared as if a compromise had been reached, with ROTC uncredited but rent-free. Yet behind the specific complaints about military training loomed the makings of a full-scale insurrection. It wasn't just the war dividing them, or the president's habitual assumption of the right to speak for Harvard. Old grievances resurfaced, everything from the decision to give honorary degrees to David Rockefeller and the Shah of Iran to Pusey's alleged anti-Semitism in the Memorial Church affair. (In fact, the president had already launched a search for the first Jewish Corporation member, one which culminated in the 1970 appointment of Yale historian John Morton Blum.)[56]

Pusey downplayed faculty discontent just as he had underestimated the seriousness of student feelings on the war. "I think it's important ROTC be kept here," he explained on March 25. "I personally feel it's terribly important for the United States of America that college people go into the military. I do think that the government in Washington remains our government. And the military arm of that government remains our arm. We should co-operate in these structures so that our influence within them remains operative."[57]

This was exactly what SDS wished to hear, particularly the group's more militant Worker-Student Alliance faction. For all its efforts to stir up student anger over Harvard's "imperialist expansion" into local neighborhoods, or the inadequacy of Harvard's response to demands for a separate department of black studies, the Maoists of WSA (known to their cohorts as The Short Hair Caucus) understood that ROTC—and only ROTC—could mobilize a broad spectrum of student opinion.

On April 7, SDS intercepted correspondence between Pusey and Franklin Ford, in which the president spelled out his hope of delaying implementation of the faculty's anti-ROTC resolutions. The next evening, a large crowd packed Lowell Lecture Hall. "Dare to Struggle. Dare to Win!" was chalked out at the front of the hall. WSA loyalists arrived with knapsacks, sleeping bags, and necessary rations. "We've built all the base we need," asserted Jarel Israel, leader of the Progressive Labor contingent. "I say fight to win! We go in tonight." Israel's supporters in the PL caucus moved three times for an immediate building seizure; three times, the idea was rejected. Scouts dispatched to case University Hall discovered police squadrons protecting the building. Temporarily frustrated in their plans, three hundred militants left the lecture hall and marched to Pusey's house, where they nailed to his front door six demands, the foremost of which were the immediate abolition of ROTC, the establishment of a full and independent black studies department, and a halt to expansion of the medical school into the surrounding residential neighborhood. Afterward, WSA members held a late-night strategy session in a nearby apartment, and stockpiled supplies, including chain saws and bullhorns.[58]

April 9 was the first springlike day in weeks. A few minutes before noon, after the police had left, a large crowd gathered outside University Hall. Inside, ironically, Franklin Ford and other deans were conferring with black students on how best to implement the new black studies program. For this reason, Ford would later recall, he refused to believe himself or his colleagues in danger.[59]

At 12:15 p.m., SDS members charged up the main staircase chanting "Fight, Fight." Among the nine deans they evicted was Archie Epps, just back from his honeymoon (whom for good measure they held responsible for killing people in Vietnam). While Epps phoned home to tell his bride he'd be late for dinner, SDS ringleaders broke into noisy debate over the presence of unfriendly journalists. "They distort everything we do," exclaimed one militant. Others rearranged the letters on the directory of the building, which they renamed Che Guevara Hall, to read "Smash Imperialism. Power to the People."[60]

After they locked the building entrances with bicycle chains, the students (among them the sons of the Secretary of the Air Force and Arthur Schlesinger Jr.) met in the second floor faculty room for a discussion of strategy. They voted against physically harming the structure, and banned the use of marijuana despite King Collins's objections. (The Occupation produced a hefty repair bill anyway, and the prohibition of pot was not about to be enforced by a group whose adherence to democratic rule did not exceed its grasp of parliamentary procedure.)

Next they issued the obligatory manifesto: "We are holding University Hall to force the Harvard Corporation to yield to our demands. We intend to stay until we win."

Outside, Steve Kelman, among SDS's most bitter foes, encountered government professor Seymour Lipset and expressed his hope that Pusey's administration would play it cool, thus enabling Harvard to become the first school to defeat the New Left. "The question is whether they will be stupid enough to call the cops," replied Lipset. At Lowell Lecture Hall, Franklin Ford attempted to refute some of the more paranoid scenarios: he insisted that there were no plans to funnel tear gas into University Hall through the building's heating system. A few hundred feet away Pusey and his deans hunkered down. Like everything else that bore the mark of rational order, their carefully prepared blueprint inspired by Columbia had gone awry. And Pusey himself, not his deans, stood at the center of the storm.[61]

The president was truly baffled by SDS's confrontation politics. "Can anyone believe the SDS demands are made seriously?" he asked. All that afternoon and into the evening, Pusey conferred with deans, house masters, and a small circle of trusted advisors. "He had more or less made up his mind to call in the police," recalled divinity school dean Krister Stendahl. The reasons why extended beyond Pusey's inelastic nature. The president had been led to believe that hordes of radical sympathizers were on their way from Berkeley and Columbia, according to Burris Young, assistant dean of freshmen. "They'd already knocked off the west coast and hit the midwest," Young later explained. "This would be the capping event. Whether it was true or not, enough believed it to justify the Bust as based on solid evidence."[62]

At around ten o'clock that night, Young called Dean of the College Fred Glimp. Young was aware of the tone within University Hall because plainclothesmen in student dress had been posted inside the building. "Let them talk themselves out. Only please don't bring in the police," said Young. Similar advice came from Derek Bok, who in the year since his installation as dean of the law school had earned a reputation among students for personal accessibility and procedural innovation. (Walking past University Hall a few minutes after its seizure, Bok was halted by an undergraduate who told him he must be glad the disturbance was occurring away from his own academic domain. "Oh, I think everyone will get his turn, don't you?" said Bok.)[63]

By nightfall, reaction to the takeover flooded into Lawrence Lowell's brick residence. Western Union deliverymen were kept busy with alumni messages. Cambridge's mayor offered to personally lead a contingent of local officers against University Hall. When Glimp asked the demonstrators to discuss their grievances, they told him that no communications were possible outside public channels. Yet even SDS respected some Harvard traditions. Asked if he intended to damage a desk used by the president, one militant replied, "Good God, no. Mr. Pusey's desk was used by Mr. Eliot."[64]

By mid-evening, there was no longer any question of whether police would be called. Robert Tonis, head of the campus security force, argued that state troopers should be used instead of local forces because they were better trained and disciplined. Tonis worried that in the highly polarized atmosphere of April 1969, the Cambridge police, who had been dealing with unruly Harvard students for years, might have difficulty reining in their own emotions. Having warned of the likelihood of bloodshed, the campus chief felt helpless to do more. "I was just part of a machine," he said afterward.[65]

Pusey felt that immediate action was necessary. He might be burned in effigy, he told his deans, and the next couple of weeks would be hellish, but allowing the takeover to drag on would divide Harvard still further. It would deny lessons learned in the previous year's disturbances at Columbia, where the effects of a prolonged occupation had been felt for months. Moreover, inside University Hall were sensitive personnel files which at any moment might compromise Pusey's faculty, just as, before the occupation, personal correspondence between the president and Dean Ford had appeared on the front pages of an underground journal called *The Old Mole*.[66]

Not far from the besieged administration building, Bok compared notes with fellow deans Krister Stendahl of the divinity school and Theodore Sizer of the education school. (Although not directly involved, Dean Roger Ebert of the medical school apparently was supportive of the group's efforts.) After discussing the matter with their own faculties during the day, the deans decided to make one last attempt to forestall violence. At 17 Quincy Street, they were informed that Pusey had retired for the night. Instead of waking him, they went to see Franklin Ford, whom they found in a decisive mood. The right decision had been made, Ford insisted. "One has to draw the line."[67]

At dawn the police were assembling near Memorial Hall. In Pusey's front yard, deans gathered. Bok, however, did not join them. April 10, he said later, was the saddest day of his life. Later, there were whispered reports that he'd offered his resignation in protest of the police action, but no evidence has been found to support this.[68]

Inside University Hall, Occupation leader Michael Ansara assured his troops that merely by holding the building they could strengthen the antiwar movement at Harvard. All around him, people typed or talked or played cards or tried to sleep. At 4:07 a.m., alarms went off in the Yard. Suspecting that a raid was imminent, students circulated wet cloths for whatever protection they might afford against tear gas.

Seventeen hours after the Occupation began, as a sound system in adjoining Weld Hall played an ear-splitting rendition of the Beatles' "Revolution," hundreds of blue-helmeted troopers from the Metropolitan District and surrounding communities swarmed into University Hall, swinging clubs and venting frustrations.

"It was the best of a lousy set of choices," contends Fred Glimp, who acknowledges, "we didn't think it through very well." Among those likely to agree was *Life Magazine*'s education editor, who suffered a three-inch gash above his left eye in the Bust. Other newsmen were hauled off to East Cambridge Criminal Court, later to be released. More than a hundred students were charged with criminal trespass and nearly fifty injuries were reported, most of them head wounds. Far more severe was the psychological violence done to an already fragile consensus.[69]

Harvard broke apart that morning. In exercising his authority, Pusey lost it. And in courting martyrdom, SDS diverted attention from its own tactics to those of a discredited administration.

Outside the Yard, not far from a movie theater whose marquee advertised Sergei Eisenstein's *Ten Days That Shook the World,* Professor Richard Herrnstein ran into a friend. "Do you approve of this?" he asked. "If it works," came the reply. "What do you mean—if it works?" "If we succeed in fomenting a political change." During the days after the raid, faculty members organized round-the-clock patrols to protect Widener Library from firebombs. Ford disputed the claim made by outraged protesters that storm troopers had invaded University Hall. "This is true," he acknowledged, "but they entered it at noon Wednesday, not dawn Thursday."[70]

"No class today, no ruling class tomorrow," someone scrawled on a blackboard in Physics 12b. The handful who showed up were informed by their instructor that the phrase constituted the day's lesson. In the philosophy department, radicals mimeographed over 75,000 broadsides to staple to the Yard's venerable elms. Beneath a heroic portrait of Lenin, self-designated "political brigades" raced up and down the stairwells of Emerson Hall en route to rap sessions in dining halls and common rooms. Visual arts majors stenciled red clenched fists and the words "On Strike" onto T-shirts and placards. Strike for the eight demands, they said.* Strike because you hate cops. Strike because your roommate was clubbed. Strike to become more human. Strike because there's no poetry in your lectures. Strike because classes are a bore. Strike for power. Strike because they are trying to squeeze the life out of you.[71]

To those moved by such slogans it was a Glorious Revolution. To Nate Pusey, his Corporation, and much of America, it was a season in Bedlam.†

* After the Bust, the students' original six demands increased to eight, including amnesty for the University Hall occupants.
† Harvard was not the only university where students took action that day. On the day of the Harvard Bust, Stanford students occupied an electronics laboratory that was engaged in secret research for the Pentagon. At Boston University, SDS members marched into the financial aid office. Student pickets blocked entrances to Cobb Hall at the University of Chicago. Twenty-seven demonstrators were arrested at Southern University in New Orleans after they tried to replace an American flag with a red, green, and black "liberation banner."

Rebels seldom make good revolutionaries.
                                    —LILLIAN HELLMAN

IN GIVING the order to terminate the occupation of University Hall before it was even a day old, Pusey had hurled himself on a sword. All night long, a race had been on to see who could seize the high ground of martyrdom. In a single stroke, Pusey squandered his lead. He also changed Harvard and redefined his office for years to come.

By noon of the next day, Pusey was judged guilty of a monumental miscalculation. Harvard was so atomized that only an extraordinary provocation could radicalize masses of students all at once, yet this was exactly what calling in the cops had achieved. While 82 percent of students polled thought the Occupation of University Hall had been unjustified, and only 15 percent wanted to cut all ties to ROTC, these same students opposed the police action by a four-to-one margin. Significantly, anti-ROTC sentiment more than doubled in the days after the Bust.

As one undergraduate, speaking for many, explained it: he woke up Wednesday morning hating SDS; Thursday morning he woke up hating Nathan Pusey. The *New York Times* said several hundred lawless students had achieved what Joe McCarthy failed to achieve—suspending the rule of reason at America's greatest university. Harvard dissolved in self-accusation. Ironically, the first faculty to denounce Pusey's decision was his beloved divinity school.[72]

Early in May, when the president appeared on *Meet the Press,* he declared the issue to be simply one of tactics—which camp's actions had been acceptable in a free university and which ones abhorrent. This view overlooked his own administration's failings, among which were the inexplicable oversight of not removing sensitive records from University Hall in the tense days before April 9, and the larger mistake of ignoring the moderate majority of students who as late as Wednesday afternoon provided a hostile cordon around the occupied administration building and who might have rallied behind Pusey had he made himself a visible, sympathetic figure.[73]

Throughout the stormy day that followed, Pusey maintained the stance he had displayed on the morning of the Bust when he defended his actions and denounced the occupying students as guilty of assaulting what he called "rational processes and accepted procedures." How could he have hoped to bargain with a bunch who had earlier ignored an adverse vote of their own adherents? It was a measure of the president's facelessness that he could turn his collar up and make his way across the Yard, overlooked by his sworn enemies. Perhaps they were too busy with their revolution to do more than rhetorical violence to the man on the throne.

On the steps of Widener Library, one angry black likened his university to Nazi Germany. "As far as I'm concerned we should all get together and make a concerted effort to fuck this place. Fuck Harvard." Picketing students carried placards with messages like "Fight the Pigs, No Expansion," and "The Corporation Is a Scab."

Two thousand students jammed Memorial Church the morning of the Bust and radical and moderate factions united in a call for a boycott of classes. Before the meeting adjourned, the law school sent word that it had mounted a sympathy strike, and the *Law Review* offered its services in documenting police brutality.

The next day, an SDS rock band provided accompaniment to the protest. "The Corporation Must Go," bannered the *Crimson*. A mass faculty meeting was neatly divided between indignation at the building's occupiers and contempt for those who had forcibly removed them. Graduate students and teaching fellows added their weight to the Strike. Afro accused the University of breaking faith over the proposed program of black studies, and something called Harvard New College promised a countercultural potpourri, complete with such courses as "Motorcycles and Sex" and "Middle-Class Suburbs in American Life."[74]

On Sunday, April 13, the Reverend Charles Price of Memorial Church told his congregation that meritocracy didn't come cheap. "There is a certain terrible sense," said Price, "in which excellence destroys community."

That afternoon, Pusey and his Corporation met with a handful of moderate students and formed a sixty-eight-member advisory board for consultation in future crises. Then the aging pillars of the Harvard establishment attempted to reopen clogged channels of communication. Francis Burr got into an argument with one protester who wanted him to transfer $300 million from the University's endowment to Roxbury's poor. Burr attempted unsuccessfully to explain that this would be illegal, a violation of existing trusts that could land him in jail. When his Corporation colleague Hugh Calkins expressed pleasure at taking part in a panel discussion attended by SDS members—for what was a university about if not rational persuasion?—one militant cut him off. "All that counts is power," he snapped. "You have it now and we intend to get it."[75]

On Monday, the first of two mass student meetings was held in Harvard Stadium. In a modern resort to Athenian democracy, students warned against any formal closing down of what they called "our university" and reiterated their long-standing demand for an end to ROTC. By a margin of just sixteen votes (out of six thousand cast), the stadium crowd extended the Strike for three more days. This gave the faculty an opening to exert its influence. One week after the Bust, with the San Francisco Mime Troup and Guerilla Theater staging its own performance outside, the faculty of Arts and Sciences overwhelmingly agreed with astronomer Owen Jay Gingerich that although military instruction had once been appropriate, "now is the time to ask ROTC to please go away . . . as soon as possible."

In the weeks to come, a flurry of meetings gave rise to a host of committees: on faculty decision-making, the House system, recruitment and retention of professors, graduate education, a merger with Radcliffe, and the governing structure of the University itself. A "Committee of Fifteen," which included five students, was established to explore the reasons behind the takeover and to recommend discipline for those involved in it. Overseers' committees poked through the rubble for themselves. Meanwhile, the two most senior members of the Corporation yielded their places to younger men, and most of Pusey's deans and personal aides took their leave.

A large bundle of papers was deposited on a law professor's doorstep, with a note that read, "Comrade, Please Return to Franklin Ford." But Ford wasn't around to receive the pilfered documents. Awaking one April morning with a weakness in his side, the dean was rushed to a hospital, victim of a stroke. In his place, Pusey named Edward Mason, whose sense of humor proved a potent weapon against the grim battalions of SDS. Warned that a large crowd was en route to University Hall hoping to stage another confrontation, Mason hurried to the building's front steps. There he was accosted by a young woman whose opening words of greeting were typical of the level of discourse of those days.

"Fuck you, Mason," she shouted.

The owlish, seventy-year-old economist didn't blink. "My dear," he told her, "I haven't had such a flattering proposal in thirty years. But where do you think we can go?"[76]

Mason was better at handling demonstrators than counting votes as he showed at a bitter meeting of the faculty on April 23. The new dean, in conjunction with economist Henry Rosovsky, expected formal ratification of Rosovsky's report calling for a black studies degree program allied to existing departments and administered through conventional channels. But Mason was in for a surprise. Largely because of the votes of natural scientists, the proposed field of concentration now became a separate department, its operations to be overseen by students and faculty members in tandem. "An academic Munich," snorted Rosovsky. "There goes the ballgame," Pusey muttered into a microphone he thought was off.[77]

The faculty decision to allow students a voice in the new department was subjected to ridicule throughout the academic world. An instructor at the University of Texas, El Paso, banned all books by Harvard pedagogues from his classroom. "We are not about to give any student group the right to hire and fire," said S. I. Hayakawa of San Francisco State College, "or the right of veto." A vice-president at the University of Wisconsin called the decision "unbelievable." Others braced for a fresh round of student demands, believing that even in retreat, Harvard would set an example for sister universities. "If Harvard, paragon of rational doers and thinkers, cannot govern and restructure itself without violence," complained *The Christian Science Monitor,* "what lies ahead for the rest of the nation?"[78]

Outside the academic community, others reacted in their own fashion to Harvard's turmoil. William Westmoreland, commander of U.S. ground forces in Vietnam, predicted future William Calleys and fresh My Lai massacres as long as Harvard shirked its obligation to train and civilize the nation's warriors. When Charlie Chaplin was asked for a bit of advice on his eightieth birthday, his response was whimsical: "Always wear a steel helmet when you're going to Harvard University."[79]

The faculty's vote, however, when combined with the Corporation's belated post-Bust agreement to strip ROTC of credit, pulled the linchpin holding together the fragile coalition of radical and moderate students. At a second mass student meeting in the stadium, held a few days after the first, the vote was two to one to end the Strike. Most students were impatient to get on with constructive reform in place of disruptive tactics. Not surprisingly, SDS was skeptical of the emerging emphasis on university restructuring. To the stalwarts of the WSA, most undergraduates had the attention span of hummingbirds. "I hate to say it," claimed one frustrated militant, "but it will take another clubbing to radicalize students. There need to be more bloody heads before anybody will really get upset."

Internal strains began to take their toll among the New Left brigades. For one thing, as one self-professed Maoist put it, "the Afros are not interested in the wider issues, which are more revolutionary than black studies." The strain was particularly evident when a crowd assembled at three o'clock one morning to burn down the Shannon Hall ROTC headquarters. Having been forewarned, Pusey stood outside his residence as the protesters passed, making threatening gestures in his direction. The

President's House was defended only by Pusey, John Dunlop, Archibald Cox, and a handful of campus cops. "Jesus, Nate," said Dunlop, "we haven't got many troops."[80]

As it turned out, they didn't need many. No sooner had the mob gathered outside the gates than they began a debate over Maoist orthodoxy. Too engrossed in dialectics to throw rocks, the militants eventually disbanded. Shannon Hall survived.

No one was surprised when the president, making his first public appearance since the Bust, received a standing ovation from business school students. But the irony must have been sweet indeed when Harvard's president was acclaimed a hero in Cambridge's working class neighborhoods, where fear of displacement by the University was outweighed by fury at those who broke laws and burned flags.

Over the next few weeks, there were more sit-ins at University Hall, bomb scares to the Faculty Club, disruptions of lectures, and angry encounters between Harvard administrators and militants, whose methods were enough to make many forget the bloody excesses of the Bust. Mary Bunting, president of Radcliffe, tried for forty-five minutes to explain to protesters the probationary status of seventeen women involved in the Paine Hall disturbance. When she was shouted down, Mrs. Bunting returned to her office followed by demonstrators chanting "Smash Rotcy, end expansion."

"Keep Harvard Open" ribbons began showing up around campus. SDS leader Jeffrey Alexander acknowledged that the group was losing support. "We have to realize that we will have to do something very militant to win our demands," he said, "something very damaging to the Corporation." Mesmerized by its own rhetoric and undercut by the faculty's conciliatory attitude, the hard left drifted off into violent irrelevance. The graduate instructor in charge of Soc Rel 149 was among those who had been arrested in the Bust. The Corporation canceled his appointment as well as his course. When the Committee of Fifteen issued its final report, it quoted Albert Camus: "If it is true that in history . . . values do not survive unless they have been fought for, the fight is not enough to justify them. The fight itself must be justified and enlightened by those values. When fighting for your truth, you must be careful not to kill it with the very weapons you are using to defend it."[81]

John Dunlop, the committee's chairman, began to assume more and more of the business of putting Harvard's badly torn community back together. The Corporation designated Archibald Cox as official crisis manager, a job that kept him busy for much of the next year and a half. As for Pusey, he was not forced out, but few doubted his lame duck status.

Embittered at the behavior of a faculty he had once revered, the president resolved to leave as soon as he felt confident no successor would face a similar ordeal.[82]

Observant passers-by noticed that the front door of Massachusetts Hall now included a peephole. The door itself was kept locked during times of tension. There was plenty of that in the months following the Bust. Not even the 1969 Commencement ceremony was immune to ideological disruption. That morning, a group of alumni and students tried to persuade the president to permit an SDS representative to formally address the crowd. Out of the question, Pusey told them. Then Charles Wyzanski, formerly head of the Overseers, conducted an informal poll of class marshals, after which he urged the president to reconsider. Pusey consulted with the Corporation, and the upshot was a decision to set aside five minutes for the organization so resolute in its opposition to the governing boards and their educational priorities.[83]

"The meeting will be in order!" the Sheriff of Middlesex County declared, to mixed cheers and raised fists. When Pusey came forward to announce the marshals' request, there was hissing in the air, which gave way to applause when he revealed his intention to grant it.

Bruce Allen, head of the SDS Labor Committee and one of sixteen students who had been required by the Committee of Fifteen to withdraw for their part in the University Hall takeover, came to the podium. Allen had a fifteen-hundred-word statement to sandwich into his brief moment in the sun. Turgid and unyielding, it denounced the Committee of Fifteen as an officially sanctioned firing squad, claimed that ROTC was a criminal conspiracy hatched by "Rockefellers and Dillons et cetera," and accused those who would expand the University of wrecking workers' homes in order to wreck their movements. Before Allen was halfway through, he was being interrupted, first with laughter, then with booing and shouts of "Throw him out!" from the audience. When he attacked Pusey as a liar, the tumult increased. Many seniors in the audience responded with a thumbs-down gesture. "Marshal," Wyzanski called out, "take that fellow off!"

Allen raced ahead with his speech.

Our seizure of University Hall [he proclaimed] is mild compared to what the people are going to do to the rulers. Every minute of this Commencement, Harvard continues to attack the people, including us as students. In the context of Harvard's training of officers, of Harvard's racism, of Harvard's expansion, this Commencement is an atrocity. It is an obscenity. Our interests as students do not lie in this tea party with these crim-

inals, these Puseys, Bennetts, and Rockefellers. It lies in fighting them, in alliance with the people! Let's get out of here![84]

Allen did, barely, leading a walkout of thirty other students from the
Yard to a counter-commencement, addressed by Hilary Putnam.

Back in the Yard, Pusey conferred degrees on eleven hundred members of the Class of 1969, 71 percent with honors, of whom a record
54 students took a summa. Amid the wreckage of the Harvard community, grades had flourished. But the morning's lesson seemed lost on
Pusey. Rather than allow the radicals to hang themselves, which happened whenever they opened their mouths, he remained anxious to turn
his own guns upon them. Others might unbend, if only for tactical advantage. Not Pusey. When four students protesting the U.S. invasion of
Cambodia in May 1970 were gunned down by National Guardsmen on
the campus of Ohio's Kent State University, members of Harvard's conservative caucus suggested that a moment of silence would be an appropriate way of opening the next faculty meeting. Pusey ruled it out of
order. A few weeks later, at ROTC's final Harvard commencement, it
was announced that the president would be unable to attend due to
continuing unrest and an overcrowded schedule. At that moment, in
walked Pusey. He couldn't stay long, he said, but he wished to say two
things: first, he congratulated those enrolled in the military studies
program. Second, he expressed his conviction that when Harvard's history was written, the recent uproar would doubtlessly be seen as the most
disgraceful period in 350 years. "He's a stubborn SOB," concluded one
junior faculty member. "But a highly principled stubborn SOB."[85]

In the meantime, there were fresh challenges from the left. When
Pusey had forecast two weeks of hell in the wake of University Hall, he
had underestimated student passions. In fact, months of unrest lay ahead.
Harvard's new disciplinary panel, the Committee on Rights and Responsibilities, would be kept busy for the next two years. While the faculty
continued to debate Vietnam, endorsing a motion calling for the war's
rapid end but rejecting formal observance of an antiwar moratorium as
politically inappropriate, student radicals continued to protest actively.
By the fall of 1969, SDS had begun to splinter. Its more extreme element, calling themselves the Weathermen, twice invaded Harvard's Center for International Affairs, roughing up some workers and smashing
windows and furniture, and the *Crimson,* fresh from endorsing Ho Chi
Minh's National Liberation Front, published arguments for the Center's
destruction. Early in 1970, demonstrators who demanded that the University set aside 20 percent of its construction jobs for "Black and Third

World" workers, trapped Ernest May, Fred Glimp's successor as Dean of the College, behind his desk.[86]

In April 1970, an offshoot of SDS organized a massive protest in Harvard Square. Demonstrators sat in the middle of Massachusetts Avenue and chanted such slogans as "Free Bobby Seale" and "Rock and Roll Is Here to Stay." When police tried to split the crowd into manageable fragments, it became unmanageable, breaking windows, setting cars afire with Molotov cocktails, looting store fronts. A four-hour battle ensued between police and some fifteen hundred rioters. Some of the protesters took refuge in the courtyards of Harvard Houses. Yet when the participants in the Trashing of Harvard Square—what state officials called one of the worst civil disturbances in Massachusetts history—were arraigned, only six were found to be Harvard students. The frightening dose of anarchy administered that evening—almost nine years to the day after the same streets resounded to chants of "Latin Si, Pusey no"—served to vaccinate the University against the romantic view that the devil could be fought with fire.[87]

Following the invasion of Cambodia and the deaths at Kent State, an intense focus on the war itself began to overshadow the radicals' demands on the University. A mass meeting turned against SDS for emphasizing issues scorned by one undergraduate as "dinky shit—the point is that people are dying in Southeast Asia."

In the midst of all this, the University moved to restore its shattered authority. Back in June 1969, on Commencement morning, Hugh Calkins of the Corporation had searched John Dunlop out of the crowd and asked him plaintively what needed to be done to get the place in order. "We worked our asses off that summer," says Dunlop of the small ad hoc committee that was formed, which eventually included two members of the Corporation plus such behind-the-scenes players as Archibald Cox and law school dean Derek Bok. Harvard announced plans to build eleven hundred units of low- and middle-income housing near the medical school in Boston. And although the University refused to join Ralph Nader's campaign against General Motors, to nearly everyone's astonishment it did endorse Cesar Chavez's boycott of California grape growers.[88]

In the fall of 1969, Dunlop succeeded Ford as dean of the faculty. Soon, his combination of protean energy, political arm-twisting, and salty irreverence had people talking of Harvard's Iron Chancellor. It was Dunlop who organized conservative forces to capture a majority of the new Faculty Council, Dunlop who paved the way for an unstuffy University of Illinois physicist to replace Keith Kane on the Corporation, Dunlop who oversaw and implemented new policies aimed at stemming the outflow of promising junior faculty, Dunlop who chaired the Committee on Governance called for in the Overseers' post-University Hall report. In the latter capacity, he was able to wield enormous influence, not only in redesigning the presidential office but in making sure it fit a candidate of his choosing.[89]

As it turned out, Dunlop had such a candidate in mind. That a new president was required seemed obvious, even to Pusey's staunchest admirers. For all the signs of progress, Harvard remained at the start of 1970 a university in suspension. Ernest May was making tentative sounds about curricular reform, and there was much talk of a merger between Harvard and Radcliffe. But all this was stalled, pending the outcome of the University's self-appraisal and the selection of a new man to carry out a new agenda.

As for the incumbent, he found solace in Thucydides, and a long view echoed by his friend and sometime-critic John Finley. While others remained glued to their own interpretation of recent turmoil, Finley preferred to place Pusey's presidency against the backdrop of an entire generation.

> *Excellence shone, our captain glittered*
> *McCarthy's foe with shield and helm,*
> *While many a shaggy warrior littered*
> *The exhausted lawn beneath an elm.*
>
> *Integrity is the hero's way,*
> *Honor's castle, friendship's bower,*
> *Fresher than LeCorbusier,*
> *Higher than Mather's airy tower,*
>
> *That will remain—that and the smile*
> *At brightest when your friends were meeting.*
> *Though you sail away while,*
> *Come back, Nate, to our ardent greeting.*[90]

Soon, it was noticed that in place of epithets, at least some Harvardians began calling their aging president by a more affectionate name—Good Old Reliable Nathan.

CHAPTER EIGHT

The Education of Derek Bok

> The larger the modern American university, the
> more it wants and the less it can afford an intel-
> lectual president. There has been a great erosion
> of authority on campus as elsewhere, and you
> need look no further than the president's office
> to understand the criteria used in choosing ex-
> ecutive officers. . . . Bok had been a labor ne-
> gotiator. He wasn't perceived as a figure of au-
> thority. He isn't A. Lawrence Lowell. Bok puts
> his feet up on the desk and calls up professors
> to talk about education.
>
> —DAVID RIESMAN
> Harvard Sociologist

> We earnestly hope that our choice, in the end,
> will send no shock waves through the com-
> munity. If it isn't met with euphoria, we hope
> it will meet at least with general acceptance.
>
> —FRANCIS "HOOKS" BURR

PUSEY announced his intention to retire in February 1970—two years
ahead of schedule. The University behaved like a dry-eyed relative of the
recently departed, anxious to get the funeral over with and get on to the
reading of the will. Speculation on a successor began immediately. In a
season of few heroes, when principled stands invited instant picket lines,

it was clear that whoever the next president would be, he would require both the ability to ration scarce resources and the political skills to re-stitch the torn fabric of Harvard's community.

The selection process which began that spring was a monument to inclusion. Over two hundred thousand letters went out from Cambridge, seeking alumni candidates. More than nine hundred names washed back, including Spiro Agnew and Abbie Hoffman. John Gardner and S. I. Hayakawa received the most mentions. Caspar Weinberger didn't do badly either. Thirty respondents nominated themselves. Alexander Heard, who as Vanderbilt's chancellor had advised President Nixon on the causes of student unrest, was urged by some. Others put forward Ramsay Clark, John Silber, McGeorge Bundy, and Elliot Richardson.[1]

Cardinal Cushing would be good for the job, one alumnus said, but, unfortunately, he was too old. Norman Mailer proposed his running mate for mayor of New York City and fellow iconoclast, Jimmy Breslin. Al Capp said that any retired brigadier general of the marines would do just fine. What Harvard undergraduates really wanted, someone sug-gested, was a nice, gray-haired Jewish mother, who would serve chicken soup to the downhearted and make sure they put on their rubbers when streets were filled with the last slush of winter.

There was one thing almost everyone agreed upon, however, and that was the need to choose a man different from the outgoing president. Invited to specify the most important qualification for his successor, Pusey responded, "A belief in God."[2]

Among the two hundred professors the Corporation solicited for advice was John Kenneth Galbraith, who relied on a winnowing process all his own. "First, I eliminated candidates on the grounds of age," he said. "Then I struck out all known adulterers, those with a tendency to alcohol, and those whose lifestyle or social life excluded them. I was then left with exactly four names." Galbraith added that he was surprised that more alumni hadn't named A. Lawrence Lowell as their favorite; perhaps they didn't know he was dead.[3]

While the public search went on, members of the Corporation went into prolonged conclave. As their "camerlingo," they chose Francis "Hooks" Burr, a Ropes and Gray lawyer with button-bright eyes, slicked-back hair, and suspenders who had a proclivity for blunt talk and a dis-arming candor. It was "a damn difficult job," said Burr, defining what kind of man would be right for a university whose own evolution re-mained murky at best. Should he be a politician or a research-oriented scholar? Internal or national in his outlook? Good administrator, or father to his people? Crisis manager or far-seeing conceptualizer? Harvard graduate or outsider untainted by the bitter divisions of recent years? Burr did not rule out an "interim pope," although he thought it was unlikely that a university embattled on so many fronts would entrust its fortunes to a caretaker.[4]

However, for all the many names discussed, and all the gestures of public debate, it was soon apparent that the Corporation had a presidential role model in mind. More precisely, it sought in one man the best qualities contained in two prominent candidates, John Dunlop and Derek Bok. One of Burr's Corporation colleagues revealed early on the drift of official thinking. "The University is going to be run by Dunbok," he told government professor James Q. Wilson. Thomas Eliot, Charles Eliot's grandson and himself a former university president, was still shrewder in predicting the race. Within days of Pusey's announcement, Eliot handicapped the contenders to succeed him. "It's Bok against the field," he said.[5]

"The best thing that happened from the past two years," Hooks Burr said at the time, "is the wind blowing through the place—of people communicating and getting to undertand a little about what the problems are." The presidency itself was something of a problem. Before a new man could fill it, the office would have to first be redefined. Was a provost required, à la Paul Buck? Or should the University institute a division of responsibilities, as had been done at neighboring MIT? How many vice-presidents were needed to replace storm windows and keep tabs on the legislature in Boston?

In keeping with Burr's 1968 prediction to his friend McGeorge Bundy, Harvard's biggest dilemma at this point was financial: in the spring of 1970 the University ran its first deficit in a quarter-century. With government aid dropping, and the uproar over University Hall contributing to a steep decline in private gifts as well, treasurer George F. Bennett was hardly exaggerating when he warned, "the crunch is coming." Without an immediate influx of at least $600,000, Dean of Admissions Chase Peterson claimed, Harvard's scholarship fund would face drastic cutbacks. On top of the money crisis, there were other pressing problems to be dealt with: curriculum reform, the Radcliffe merger, community relations, a faculty with inadequate representation by women and minorities, not to mention all the immediate causes of student unrest—the War, a fragmented community, professorial malaise, and divided loyalties.[6]

The Corporation devoted forty hours a week to refining and reducing its list of contenders. It also outlined a new kind of academic executive, a man (no one seriously believed Harvard was ready for a female president) of collegial instincts, aware that while presidents and deans come and go, tenured professors are forever. Physical and moral stamina were essential, said Burr, as were young ideas and the persuasive skills to implement them. Above all else, Harvard needed a leader more accessible than Pusey, one more inclined to mediate than mandate.[7]

The Corporation widened its net. It talked with undergraduates in dining halls and with professors at the Faculty Club. It interviewed James Bryant Conant. Even Pusey suggested names, though trying in the contest's early phase not to steer the governing board toward anyone in particular. By midsummer, Burr was persuaded to drop all nonacademic candidates from the running. Out went the Gardners and Richardsons and Weinbergers. Anything less, it was argued, would represent a stinging rebuke to academia at a time when its prestige and self-confidence were already low. Names kept on coming in—from alumni, departments, House committees. Burr and his colleague Albert Nickerson took a swing through the midwest to further the search. By the time they returned, the roster had been cut to fewer than thirty.[8]

Late that fall the Corporation's list of semifinalists was leaked to the press. Of the less than two dozen names, there were eleven Harvard faculty members, including five deans; Carl Kaysen—director of Princeton's Institute for Advanced Studies; one black—Clifton Wharton of Michigan State University; and the unlikeliest of contenders, twenty-nine-year-old Dunster House tutor Roger Rosenblatt. (Rosenblatt's inclusion was widely regarded as a pat on the back for his success as chairman of a student disciplinary committee that had ejected malcontents after University Hall.)[9]

Publication of the list galvanized the faculty's liberal caucus. "Squalid," remarked a dissenter on the left. "It shows the same clay-footed thinking that got us Pusey." Another charged that Corporation members were blacklisting contenders seen at liberal caucus meetings. The strength of this reaction emphasized how fragile was the truce between Harvard's warring camps, and how vital it was that the Corporation choose a man without enemies.

As the lobbying intensified, two names were on everyone's lips. "I got the impression pretty early that it was going to be either Dunlop or Bok," Douglas Dillon, chairman of the Overseers, said later. And however much some might fantasize about President Dunbok, there were significant differences between the dean of Arts and Sciences and his law school counterpart, differences which worked almost entirely to Bok's advantage. First of all, Dunlop, at fifty-six, was much closer to mandatory retirement than the forty-year-old Bok. Then too, while the Corporation wanted a man who knew the University from within, it was reluctant to choose too much of an insider. Dunlop, scarred from recent battles, was indelibly linked to Pusey. Nor was Dunlop the least bit squeamish about wielding power. His forcefulness and political shrewdness, which had been such assets in the aftermath of University Hall, now seemed over-powering. "The Corporation was looking for a conciliator," says one col-league, "and John would conciliate with a blackjack."[10]

Certainly, Dunlop bore little resemblance to Kingman Brewster, Yale's articulate, highly visible master of compromise who had kept his own university together during the chaos of the Sixties by forging a con-sensus of students and faculty against more conservative alumni. Brewster often had been described that summer and fall as the prototypical Ivy League president. This alone should have been a tip-off to the Corpora-tion's choice. For only one man at Harvard—Derek Bok—could boast in-timate ties to Brewster, whose law school protégé he had been, whose close friend he remained, and whose administrative record as dean closely paralleled Brewster's performance at Yale. For instance, when, early in 1969, protesting students had commandeered the law school library for an all-night gripe session over grades and curriculum, Bok didn't call the police. Instead, he sent out for coffee and doughnuts, climbed up on a table to thank the prospective lawyers for their concern, and stayed to listen to their complaints.[11]

Bok was good at listening. Then as later, he had the most durable set of eardrums this side of New Haven. Like Brewster, he combined an upper-class sense of social responsibility with a slightly shaggy charm and a keen sense of the moods and currents transmitted in dormitories and dining rooms. Lunching in the law school cafeteria one afternoon, Bok wondered out loud why it seemed impossible to make a ham-burger that didn't taste like plastic and still sold for under a dollar. Mo-ments later, the lawyer with a degree in economics was poring over numbers with the cafeteria's manager. The result of this attention to de-tail was a new, more edible burger—and an increase in sales at the deficit-plagued cafeteria.[12]

The same man was given credit—too much credit, according to some—for having updated the law school's curriculum by adding courses in poverty and criminal and environmental law to a roster heavily weighted toward corporate law, and liberalized its grading system. He was also praised for having opposed the Cambodian invasion—when it was politically timely. There were many in the law school who regarded their dean as a gifted synthesizer of ideas, a combination of skilled diplo-mat and principled politician. To detractors, however, he was as plastic as the offending burger, one whose reputation as a reformer rested on his ability to recognize and bow to the inevitable. "He glides with the tide," claimed one third-year student. "He's really a very unexceptional man," said one of Bok's professorial colleagues. "But he has the personal charm that the technocratic society deems important for leadership."[13]

From William Bentinck-Smith, Pusey's closest adviser, who was regarded by some of the president's bitterest critics as a Massachusetts Hall Rasputin, to the militant law professor Alan Dershowitz, whose outspoken reputation was earned in defense of the radical Chicago Seven, the range of Bok's support was phenomenal. Pusey himself made no secret of his admiration, their differences at the time of the University Hall affair notwithstanding. About the worst that was said of the leading contender came from a curmudgeonly colleague from outside the law school. "Bok is a small-time Kingman Brewster," he declared, "style and no principle, trendy, acquiescent."[14]

Even the rare criticisms raised against Bok had a soft, unfocused quality. Few people at Harvard claimed to know the man, despite his prominence. In the absence of such knowledge, handicappers spun their theories of succession, and the local press read such tea leaves as the cautious men of the Corporation supplied. Eighteen years earlier, it had been taken for granted that Nathan Pusey's election had much to do with his opposition to Joe McCarthy, when in fact, Pusey's political leanings held far less significance than his educational priorities and fundraising record. Now, with hundreds of campuses in turmoil and dozens of major college presidencies vacant, the same outsiders figured that Harvard's need for crisis management would outweigh her ancient tradition of promoting a graduate of the college. To such observers, it seemed almost inevitable by mid-1970 that Bok, the doughnuts-and-coffee conciliator, trained to seek consensus by his mentors Dunlop and Cox, should be selected to replace an authoritarian like Pusey.

Only later would it become clear that the Corporation had objectives more farsighted than merely quieting student protest, or that Bok himself would reject his popular image as an academic Great Compromiser. Perhaps those who complained loudest that Bok was a blank slate could have filled in some of the spaces by looking over their shoulders at his grandfather, Edward William Bok, whose governing creed of hard work and public usefulness were imparted almost by accident to the grandson he never knew.

> *Make home happy; hold loved ones first in*
> *your hearts; leave off fussing over fashionable*
> *ways of living; be natural, and you will be*
> *living the simple life though you ride in a*
> *motorcar, clean house by electricity, entertain at*
> *the country club, and have every convenience*
> *known to man. The quality of the individual is*
> *what determines the simple life, never his sur-*
> *roundings.*
>
> —EDWARD BOK

EDWARD BOK and his impoverished family arrived in Brooklyn, New York, from Holland in 1870. Throughout history, the Dutch have been known for their love of order, clarity, and industry. With an inclination to obstinacy, they have pursued commerce and culture with equal fervor, patronizing art, establishing schools, and bidding a genial welcome to rebels from every corner of Europe. From this background the young Bok brought to America a taste for practical social reform. The immigrant boy was soon editing a small church magazine by night, while working days in a local publishing firm. In due course, publisher Cyrus Curtis hired him to oversee the *Ladies' Home Journal*. During the first years of the new century, Edward Bok's emphasis on infant care and civic beautification, life in the kitchen and prayer in the church pew, coupled with the latest writings from the likes of Mark Twain and Rudyard Kipling, made the *Journal* the most widely read publication in the land.[15]

His magazine, he told George Bernard Shaw, represented the world's largest pulpit. For thirty years, he used it to promote his favorite causes: more beautiful cities, highways less pockmarked by ugly billboards, the inspection of food and drugs, and the instruction of sexual hygiene.

After he married Curtis's daughter, Mary, Bok went to live on a wooded tract outside Philadelphia where the couple raised two sons and where Bok was free to develop his Emersonian preference for plain living. "There are no nervous breakdowns in the simple life." This was the editor's declaration of war on ostentation—whether it be the bric-a-brac cluttering Victorian parlors, or wasteful attitudes toward leftovers at the dinner table. Advising readers how to live on a thousand dollars a year, Bok marketed thousands of blueprints, at five dollars a piece, for "Journal houses"—dwellings stripped bare of cupolas and balconies. He urged Americans to forsake congested urban neighborhoods, in the hope that suburban existence could counter the nervousness evident in many of the middle-class women who were his prime readers. Convinced that good morals flourished where the air was healthy, Edward Bok became a vigorous exponent of fresh-air funds and youth camps. He preached thrift, voluntarism, self-reliance, and service to others. He also joined Herbert Hoover's campaign to feed Starving Belgium, and lamented the orgy of speculation that followed World War I.

"Money is King," he complained. "Business is our God. Commerce rules." But no amount of possessions could bring permanent happiness, he maintained. True to his own advice, Bok left the *Journal* to devote himself to higher causes. He wrote seven books (including a Pulitzer Prize-winning autobiography, *The Americanization of Edward Bok*), gave generously to the Philadelphia Symphony, and established the American Peace Award. He also built "Bok Tower," a handsome carillon of pink and gray marble hovering over a Florida bird sanctuary. When he died in 1930, Edward Bok was buried at the foot of his musical monument. Inscribed on his grave were the words of his Dutch grandmother: "Make you the world a bit more beautiful and better because you have been in it."

Derek Bok was born in the year of his grandfather's death. He inherited many of the editor-philanthropist's qualities, including a preference for practical over doctrinaire liberalism, and a powerful sense of the aesthetic. (Early risers around the law school of the late Sixties could expect to find their dean directing workmen planting shrubs outside the new Roscoe Pound building. As president, Bok would rival Lawrence Lowell's attention to architectural detail, selecting the shade of brick to be used in business school housing, and picking up trash deposited in Harvard Square. Imagining a great, grassy mall in Harvard Yard—"that would be a really handsome sight"—he banned vehicular traffic and tinkered with electric carts in its place. He renovated Lowell's crumbling Houses at great cost. Less successful was his Ruritanian guardhouse, a pinkish, shingled structure whose design and construction were said to have cost the University nearly $60,000, and which the *Boston Globe* promptly dubbed one of New England's ten ugliest buildings.)[16]

Many of those asked for an assessment of Derek Bok's character, his reserve, and his obvious discomfort in the spotlight point to his early years, and especially the acrimonious divorce of his parents which occurred in 1933. The boy's father, Curtis, was a Pennsylvania jurist who dabbled in literature, authoring passionate denunciations of capital punishment and volumes drawing upon his own experiences with the law. Following their separation, Bok's mother, Margaret, left Philadelphia's Main Line for California, and henceforth none of her three children was to see their father for much more than a week or two each summer.[17]

Mrs. Bok enrolled her youngest son in a public junior high school (his classmates included Norma Jean Baker, later to become famous as Marilyn Monroe) where he distinguished himself mostly on the baseball diamond and basketball court. Next came the Harvard Military School, an Episcopal academy from which he graduated valedictorian. He found drill a boring experience, Bok said later, but at least amid such martial surroundings, he had gained a feeling for hand-to-hand combat that would stand him in good stead at the other, east coast, Harvard.[18]

At Stanford, Bok majored in political science, played a smoking clarinet in campus jazz bands, put on a Phi Beta Kappa performance in the classroom, and considered entering the Foreign Service. As a senior sponsor at Encina Hall, he counseled freshmen. (Years later, despite demands on his time as Harvard's president, Bok somehow managed to squeeze freshman advisees into his schedule.) Midway through his final year at Stanford, Bok opted for law school over the diplomatic corps. He also put aside thoughts of attending Yale, although not without trepidations.[19]

"Tales of Harvard's fierce intellectualism had been rampant on the beaches of Santa Monica," he would later explain, "and I was extremely apprehensive. My worst fears were confirmed when I passed a couple walking through the Law School courtyard. The young woman was saying to her friend, 'But Peter, you don't understand. It's an incorporeal totality quite outside of time.' Beads of sweat started from my brow."[20]

If Bok sweated over grades, his classmates weren't aware of it. One of them remembered him as someone who might have been easily hated, "except you had to like him." The same quality no doubt explains the remark from one of Bok's closest associates today: "He's the most disciplined spoiled kid I ever met." While at law school, Bok again stood out on the athletic field. He also disappeared into the library stacks for days at a time, only to surface at Saturday night gatherings of Chancery, a rowdy social club where the bar stayed open all weekend and the bridge games lasted even longer.[21]

After taking his degree magna cum laude in 1954, Bok went to Paris on a Fulbright scholarship. There he met and married Sissela Myrdal, daughter of two Nobel Prize-winners, economist Gunnar and sociologist Alva Myrdal (in a ceremony performed by former premier Pierre Mendès-France). Sissela Bok is a woman of striking good looks and retiring manner, who combines a traditional devotion to family with her own academic ambition. In fact, her reputation as an author who specializes in public and private ethics outstrips that of her husband. The Boks would have three children; perhaps because of Derek's own interrupted childhood, they would allow nothing to distract from their parenting. "There has to be something wrong with a job that interferes substantially with the lives of your wife and children," Bok remarked at the time of his election. "I'm going to be tough to move on that score."[22]

Following his marriage, Bok spent six months in a San Francisco law firm, then joined the Army, where he served as a first lieutenant in the Judge Advocate General's office in Washington. Here he helped change an Army rule allowing draftees to be classified as security risks based on membership in "subversive groups." In his spare time, he also earned a degree in economics from George Washington University. This interest shaped his subsequent teaching career at Harvard Law School, to whose faculty he was steered in 1958, largely by Kingman Brewster. Brewster had detected in Bok gifts which no grade transcript alone communicated. "He came from a prominent family," recalls Erwin Griswold, then the school's dean. "He was personable. He'd been on the *Law Review*. Unlike many graduates, who head immediately to Covington and Burley, he showed interest in the academic life. . . . His was the standard probationary period of three years. He didn't overwhelm the appointments committee. He was not brilliant, but he was more than adequately scholarly."[23]

"By purely objective criteria," said one colleague acquainted with the appointments committee and its work, "he probably would not have made it." The selection process was controlled by a small, hierarchical group, inclined to pass judgment in arbitrary fashion. Borderline candidates were expected to write something to bolster their candidacy. Bok disappeared into the stacks and emerged with a paper that a source familiar with its contents called "a blockbuster." "It established him in the school in a way that nothing else could have." And it secured his appointment to a full professorship, starting in the fall of 1961.[24]

Bok already had earned a reputation for asking questions, not all of them appreciated by his elders. Was the school all it could be? Was it doing all it might to raise morale, especially among students and junior faculty? Along with his colleague Paul Bator (later an assistant Solicitor General in the Reagan administration), Bok compared Harvard to the smaller, more familial center of legal training at Chicago. (A few years later the University of Chicago would seek him out when it was looking for a dean.) Bok also questioned some of the research being conducted at Harvard Law School, along with the school's isolation from the rest of the University.

Ironically, for one with Bok's interest in educational methods, his reputation as a classroom instructor was only middling. In a *Law Review* spoof that portrayed professors as birds, Bok was cast as the roadrunner—a tribute to his classroom pacing. "He didn't get where he was going through style," said one who knew him well. "Some men walk into a classroom like rolling off a log. They do it easily, without struggle. Derek's never related to a group well and from the start. He hardly ever looks people in the eye. He's never learned to use humor or emotion for their ends. He smothers a subject. If he can't win someone over orally he'll do it on paper. There he's in his element—more colorful, more persuasive, more urgent."[25]

Bok enhanced his academic standing in the years that followed. He also displayed a social conscience akin to his grandfather's by working on a fair housing committee established to desegregate the affluent neighborhoods of Belmont, just outside Cambridge. He became an arbitrator in labor disputes involving research labs and racetracks, consul·ed with the Labor Department in Washington and the Equal Employment Opportunity Commission. "As a professor," he was quoted as saying, "you try not to be on one side or another, but to remain neutral." (Such scruples won him plaudits from unlikely quarters. William Loeb, vitriolic publisher of the *Manchester Union-Leader,* was so impressed by Bok's impartiality in a dispute involving his paper that he urged Richard Nixon to appoint Harvard's president as special Watergate prosecutor in the summer of 1973. Bok wound up on Nixon's enemies list instead, while the prosecutor's job went, briefly, to his old friend and colleague Archibald Cox.)[26]

When Dean Griswold left Harvard in 1967 to become Lyndon Johnson's Solicitor General, many faculty members felt that Pusey should replace him with Albert Sacks, an avuncular figure to whom colleagues were inclined to go for support. But Pusey disregarded the advice and persuaded a reluctant Bok to take the job in hopes of bringing the law school into closer contact with the rest of the University. Shrewdly, Bok asked Sacks to be his associate dean, a kind of roving ambassador with special input into academic policy. The two men worked well together. Despite the pressure of outside events and a rising chorus of demands for change in curriculum and grading, Bok kept his faculty in one piece. When students invaded a faculty meeting, the dean warned of possible disciplinary action. When the protesters refused to leave, he adjourned the session. At the same time, and against stiff opposition from traditionalists, Bok permitted student representation on law school committees.[27]

As dean, Bok was highly regarded for his efforts to bolster minority and female enrollment, his campaigns to promote interdisciplinary studies with the Kennedy School of Government and the departments of history and economics, his successful completion of a $15 million fund

drive, his modernization of the curriculum and relaxation of grading requirements—even his penchant for bright-colored walls and contemporary paintings with which to adorn them. More important than any
specific actions Bok took, however, was the atmosphere of openness and
accessibility he fostered. He looked even younger than his years in his
tweed jacket and slacks, and his style of administration seemed infinitely
more sympathetic than Pusey's icy command.

Something else struck Bok's admirers, something undoubtedly noted
by Hooks Burr and the rest of the Corporation in the fall of 1970. As a
child of his age, according to one intimate, Bok is inclined to view change
favorably. "But remember, he's pre-Vietnam. He's not part of the generation that says we distrust everything and everybody, we believe only in
our own way. Bok has an excellent sense of the long run, and the kind of
changes beneficial over the long run."[28]

John Dunlop put it more succinctly. Having drunk with his friend
in bars all across America, says Dunlop, "I always thought he was a
helluva lot more conservative inside than the temper of the times suggested."[29]

Then there was the famous night of doughnuts and coffee, when
students protesting curriculum and grades, unable to boycott classes because of upcoming exams, decided to remain in the library beyond its
closing hour of eleven o'clock. They were hungry for faculty contact, remembers one faculty veteran of the period. He advised the dean to "turn
it into a lovefest." Bok did nearly that, and the contrast between his
doughnuts and Pusey's billyclubs was hard to miss. Bok's door had remained open throughout his crisis; so, it appeared, had his mind.

All this made Bok a leading contender for the presidency from the
moment Pusey announced his intention of leaving. Yet if he was without enemies, Bok also seemed to lack devoted admirers. A man with obvious abilities and not so obvious objectives—this summed up both his
appeal and his limitations. Liberals found him the most acceptable candidate likely to pass muster with the Corporation. Conservatives, on the
other hand, worried that in selecting an arbitrator over an intellectual
mandarin, Harvard was diminishing the office and surrendering to the political demands of the age.[30]

Meanwhile, Bok wasn't at all certain he wanted the job. Several
weeks before the final decision was reached, he asked a law school colleague whether he should write the Corporation a letter withdrawing his
name from the contest. He'd observed the presidential office under Pusey, he said. As dean of the law school, he could remain closer to the action and avoid being isolated from faculty and students. He could at least

hope to replace passive, casebook learning and get on with the business of reform tentatively broached in his own first months. Could he possibly have anywhere near the same impact presiding over Arts and Sciences, with its traditional distrust of outsiders from the professional schools as purveyors of expertise rather than transmitters of cultural heritage?[31]

Bok's friend advised him against the move. It would be taken as an insult, he said. The governing board would be put in an awful situation. "What if they decide they want you? They'll ignore your letter anyway. Make the decision after the fact, not before."[32]

Only half convinced, Bok agreed to wait out the selection process. His reluctance to leave a job barely begun did not diminish, however. Bok acknowledges having been "very, very ambiguous" at the time as to whether he had sufficient knowledge of what Arts and Sciences was doing and what students felt to lead the University. On a snowy night in mid-December 1970, the door of his Belmont home opened to reveal Hooks Burr. Bok poured out his reservations: he didn't like confrontations, and he thought he'd be terrible at crisis management, worse yet at fundraising. Still, he agreed to think it over and to talk at length with his friend Kingman Brewster. He promised to remain silent lest a negative decision leak out and muddy the waters for the Corporation's fallback choice. (Exactly who that was remains a secret. Almost certainly, it was not John Dunlop, whose candidacy had by then been effectively torpedoed by the liberal caucus. The liberals had sought and obtained assurances from Burr and others on the Corporation that no divisive candidate would be named. Just to make certain, the caucus had suggested an informal ban on any current member of the faculty of Arts and Sciences—and so Dunlop was out.)[33]

In the end, a mild uprising of Overseers, who alone seemed dissatisfied with the opaque picture presented them, threatened Bok's chances. Led by Clifford Alexander, whom Pusey had hired to work out minority hiring provisions, and who later served as the first black Secretary of the Army, several Overseers pushed for a full-scale interrogation of the dean. Douglas Dillon recalled a rump movement to nominate Donald Kennedy, then head of Stanford's biology department, a charismatic figure who would by 1979 be president of that west coast Harvard. Among Kennedy's qualifications was a B.A. from the nation's oldest university, something the Corporation was prepared to dispense with in its search for the right mix of firsthand knowledge and outside perspective. But the revolt fizzled and in the first week of January 1971, Burr went public.[34]

"No shock, it's Bok," the *Alumni Bulletin* proclaimed. The new president was hailed for his flexibility, judgment, and poise. To some, he seemed the candidate a computer might have selected, an amalgam of his predecessors, with Lowell's fussy attention to plant ("Only the landscaping endures," Bok has been quoted as saying, with typical modesty), Conant's aggressive egalitarianism, Pusey's aversion to the University as political player. But what Harvard really ordained at the start of 1971 was the Second Coming of Charles William Eliot. It was a prospect as theologically dubious to the new man as to his earlier model.[35]

One of the first things Bok did, after winning assurances that his young family need not reside in the President's House or his wife sacrifice her own academic career to pour tea for freshmen, was to inquire of his friend Krister Stendahl what the proper etiquette was regarding Sunday mornings. Should he, as president, attend services at Memorial Church? He hadn't done so in the past, Stendahl reminded him, so why start now? A small point, it was nonetheless revealing of a man born not with one but two silver spoons in his mouth, and along with them an ambivalent attitude toward tradition.[36]

It's a litmus paper test when you ask, what does Derek Bok stand for? He doesn't stand for very much.

—RALPH NADER
April 1979

WHILE MOST students welcomed a president in sweat shirt and sneakers who played touch football with the *Crimson* staff, the faculty was another story. "I loathe his Rotary Club, slap-on-the-back manner," one dissenting member of the English department declared. Campus gossips swapped tales of how Bok confused the Fly Club's home with the residence of Lowell House's master, how he had to ask passers-by directions to Dunster House, and told audiences his understanding of Harvard's House system derived from having lived in a Stanford dorm.[37]

Some of the older faculty members treated the new president like a schoolboy who hadn't done his homework. At his first meeting of Arts and Sciences, Bok warned against political preoccupations at the expense of academic inquiry. He also struggled to define his personal role. His ultimate function, he concluded, was to interpret the University to colleagues on different faculties. A white-haired scholar exclaimed in a stage whisper, "But, Mr. President, we *are* the university."[38]

At his austere inaugural in October 1971, Bok forgot to take his place in the seventeenth-century President's Chair. It seemed an omen. "I didn't have time to have an agenda," he recalls of the rushed interval between his election and Pusey's departure six months later. There was much improvisation about Bok's early years in Massachusetts Hall. In interviews, he talked of a three-year undergraduate degree and of reforms in educational funding. He spoke of an "overburdened" presidency (the same word employed in 1844 by Edward Everett's predecessor in the job, Jared Sparks) and sounded the alarm about "a new financial era which will force us to ration our hopes and regiment our programs according to strict priorities."[39]

Bok also outlined two principles he called paramount: that no university should make decisions with a hand to its throat, as Harvard had been forced to do in the recent past, and "that it should not tolerate or condone activities that are violent, or disruptive, or destructive of the freedom of others." When Bok said this, the windows of the president's office were still covered in thick sheets of protective plastic placed there in the tumultuous spring of 1969. But in 1971, college libraries were reporting standing room only and large circulation increases—students weren't throwing things anymore. "They have the bizarre notion," cracked government professor Stanley Hoffman about the student body, "that a university is for studying."

The question of who would be admitted to study at Harvard provided Bok with his first opportunity to recast the University. In the same month he took office, Bok announced a plan to boost ranks of Radcliffe women by 50 percent, while slightly decreasing the number of men admitted to the College, in hopes of achieving a male-female ratio of 2.5 to 1. One immediate result would be overcrowding. The long-range impact would be a different set of numbers, even more worrisome, given the fear of alumni officers that Old Girls were unlikely to contribute as generously to alma mater as their male counterparts. No one was more surprised at this sudden initiative than the admissions staffs of the two colleges. When the change was made in time for the next fall class, Bok too was astonished that his directive had so quickly been translated into official policy. He didn't doubt his influence but, in his modesty, he simply didn't identify himself as personifying the University.[40]

The lawyer with a reputation for caution spoke out again in the spring of 1972, when he told a group of alumni that Harvard's conscience would not be clear "until we manifest our willingness to enter-

tain an ROTC program compatible with our usual institutional standards." Faced with a wave of protest, Bok explained that his words had
been misinterpreted: his statement on ROTC was "a private opinion,"
one he predicted was unlikely to be carried out anytime soon. "I don't
have a decision-making power in that area," he added.[41]

Even among those who agreed with Bok's stated sentiments this oc-
casioned head-scratching. Were these gestures trial balloons or signs of
political naiveté? Could a university president—especially a Harvard president—really believe that he could express "private opinions" publicly?
Could he really expect the media to regard them as such?

Bok was also faced with frustrations concerning his faculty and
staff. Even as the Department of Health, Education, and Welfare required all federal contractors to outline plans to expand their applicant
pools of minorities and women, one of Bok's assistants published, on his
own initiative, a strongly worded report criticizing Harvard's efforts to di-
versify its teaching force. Dismayed at a drop in their numbers due to
budget cuts, graduate student teaching fellows formed a union (which
Bok refused to recognize) and staged a series of short-lived strikes. In the
fall of 1973, printers whose jobs were endangered by automation protested a $45-a-week gap in pay with unionized colleagues in Boston. The
University, fearful that police and janitors might be the next to demand
big wage boosts, held its ground. This brought complaints that Harvard
hadn't charged its attitude toward its blue-collar workforce much since
Lowell's dismissal of the scrubwomen half a century earlier.

Increasingly, the consensus president found himself contending with
many hands for the levers of power. Dissent included a petition bearing
over 2000 names in protest of Commencement's coincidence with an obscure Jewish holiday, cries for affirmative action on the *Harvard Law Review,* and persistent demonstrations calling for Harvard to divest itself of
stock in companies doing business in South Africa. Whether the subject
was a new dorm in the Yard, a new coach for the swim team, or a new
dean for his own School of Public Health, Bok's course was slowed by so
many boulders in the stream.

Having no wish to repeat Conant's noisy run-ins with the governing
boards, especially the Overseers, Bok set out to make the senior body part
of his collegial administration, to take it into his confidence, and to discard the pro-forma meetings of Pusey's day, when the Corporation jeal-
ously guarded its prerogatives, and Overseers were esteemed primarily for
their financial contacts. Now there was no one around to assist in fundraising. The early Seventies brought a wave of alumni activism, which
had left in its wake a clutch of nontraditional Overseers—four mem-

bers under thirty, seven women, three blacks, no bankers, and only a smattering of businessmen. Worse yet, the president came to resemble a man playing poker with a mirror at his back. "Any time Derek wanted to take up a sensitive matter," says one Overseer, "someone was sure to leak it to the press. After a while, he kept his own counsel."[42]

Less easily concealed was the chaotic state of Harvard's own bureaucracy. In the words of one Bok associate, "Harvard's good old days were golden at the cost of systematic administration." So slipshod was management that no one knew exactly how many worked in the comptroller's office, while the bulk of housekeeping details had been entrusted to L. Gard Wiggins, a Pusey intimate valued more for his loyalty to the president than his managerial oversight. Not surprisingly, one of the many committees formed to study University functions in the spring of 1969 recommended sweeping changes in how the place was administered. Taking his cue from its findings, Bok spent much of his first year in office mulling over résumés. He was especially anxious to hire several vice-presidents to whom he could delegate some of the responsibility, if only so he could turn his attention to education.[43]

"I didn't take this job because I enjoy administration," he remarked. But it took longer than anyone expected to implement the new governing structure, and with his chain of command missing so many vital links, everything else backed up. At one point, Bok found himself confronted by a House master who had spent two years trying to squeeze out funds to purchase new faucets for student bathrooms. Unable to locate a responsible party anywhere else in the University, the man had finally taken his complaint to Massachusetts Hall.[44]

At least in part to try to avoid such incidents, the president finally assembled a managerial team—four vice-presidents and a general counsel—which became known as the Mass Hall Whiz Kids. The University's first general counsel was Daniel Steiner, a genial veteran of liberal Democratic politics in New York, who in the spring of 1972 assumed the troubleshooter's role previously handled by Archibald Cox, and subsequently became a presidential confidant. Only one of the new vice-presidents was a Harvard man—Chase Peterson, the dean of admissions, who accepted the alumni and development portfolio, with its onerous burden of moneyraising, only because no one else wanted it.

Peterson's colleagues formed a varied assemblage of talents and styles. Hale Champion was in charge of overall finances; previously he had been an aide to Boston mayor Kevin White, and later he became Jimmy Carter's undersecretary of Health, Education, and Welfare. Stephen S. J. Hall was in charge of operations. Hall brought with him from the Sheraton Hotel chain a penchant for drawing diagrams and spouting maxims. Rome wasn't built in a day, he liked to say. " 'Course, our team didn't handle that job." Aggressive and capable, Hall roused strong emotions. Among old-timers, he offended with his corporate jargon. "If you're going to start someplace, start at the top," he told the *Crimson* in 1974. "I considered Harvard really one of the finest universities in the world as far as the product they turn out. Basically, that's what we're here for—to turn out a product."

Charles U. Daly arrived in 1971 from the U.S. Public Information Center to oversee Harvard's relations with the outside community. He boasted an impressive array of contacts assembled during successive careers in business, journalism, education, and public-interest lobbying. Having cut his teeth as a congressional liaison officer in the Kennedy White House, Daly had the clout to summon Tip O'Neill or Ted Kennedy to the phone to explain firsthand the impact on the University of affirmative action or proposed tax reforms.[45]

But Daly's tough-guy reputation was severely tarnished when Harvard unexpectedly lost the Kennedy Library to the University of Massachusetts in Boston. The library was planned as the centerpiece of Harvard's new John F. Kennedy School of Government, to be built on a twelve-acre site along the Charles River. Originally the complex had been scheduled to open in 1970, but the project was stalled, first by the lack of an alternative home for a public transit repair yard located on the site, then by neighborhood opposition to the museum portion of the complex, which was expected to draw 600,000 visitors a year to an area already heavily congested. When Bok first took office, he had committed the University to a ten-million-dollar public affairs center, which would combine, under one roof, the Kennedy School, the Center for International Affairs, and elements of the existing government and economics departments. A separate Institute of Politics would be built alongside the library, the entire complex to be designed in spectacular fashion by I. M. Pei. Pei envisioned a large, open plaza surrounded by a low brick structure and dominated by an eighty-five-foot glass pyramid. The plan also called for parking for four hundred cars, a figure city officials called grossly inadequate.[46]

No sooner had Pei's blueprint been unveiled than community groups unleashed a barrage of complaints. Leading the fight against the museum portion of the plan was Paul Lawrence, a professor at the business school. He was joined by others who lived in the big frame houses along Brattle Street, and who compared Pei's lavish vision to a kind of presidential Disneyland. A positive environmental impact statement did nothing to allay local fears, and early in 1975 the Kennedy Library Corporation abandoned its plan to build the museum in Cambridge. The prospect of continuing lawsuits was not a happy one, according to Stephen Smith, the late president's brother-in-law, who oversaw the library project. Additional delays could only escalate the costs of construction, which were already close to the ceiling of funds that had been raised for the project in the immediate aftermath of Dallas.

Belatedly, Harvard woke up to find itself competing with over a hundred other candidates for what remained of the complex. Its chief rival was the embryonic Boston campus of the University of Massachusetts, located on windswept Columbia Point. With Bok's role apparently confined to cheering on his group, Daly was left to convince the Kennedy family to split the facility in half, keeping the archives in Cambridge while constructing the museum as part of yet another corner of Boston slated for redevelopment, the old Charlestown Navy Yard. The ensuing campaign was not a model of subtlety. It included a telephoned warning from Ernest Hemingway's widow, Mary, in which she implied that if the trustees went ahead with their announced plan to site the library in "that slum" (as she designated Columbia Point), she might have to pull her husband's papers out.[47]

It didn't work. In November 1975, Harvard's last proposal was rejected. Blame for the fiasco was divided more or less evenly between Daly and Bok. Daly confessed in private that he simply had never believed the Kennedys would actually make good on their threat to take the Library elsewhere.[48]

If the president chose his Whiz Kids to serve at least partially as lightning rods, he succeeded magnificently with Steve Hall. A cost-cutting wizard, Hall endeared himself to few undergraduates when he proposed to cut down on mealtime fraud by taking the palmprints of every student, or when he actually succeeded in instituting cold breakfasts and meatless dinners on a regular basis. In an attempt to staunch the flow of red ink from the University's publishing division, the man dubbed Super Janitor issued pink slips by the bushel, until the staff of Harvard Press was reduced from 144 to 69, overhauled warehousing and shipping procedures, reduced inventory, and expanded paperback operations. Committed to publishing more than two thousand titles, half of which sold five hundred dollars' worth of copies a year—or less—the Press embarked on a vigorous pursuit of larger audiences (an effort capped in 1984 with Eudora Welty's *One Writer's Beginnings,* the first Harvard volume ever to make the *New York Times* bestseller list).

Bok himself boasted of eliminating between 150 and 200 jobs from the University payroll. Inevitably, this caused bruised feelings, especially as the impression of Mass Hall arrogance spread among the professors. (There was the alleged squash game between the Whiz Kids, who were overheard to promise one another in between volleys "to kick this faculty around . . . they're soft.")[49] Yet for all the cost-cutting and managerial shuffling, the new administration found itself losing ground on a financial treadmill. Thanks to Hall's doggedness, energy consumption was reduced by more than a fifth, but in the wake of the Arab oil embargo of 1973, costs went up anyway, by over three million dollars. Spiraling prices sent tuition rates soaring, and that plus a reduction in foundation assets meant that the share of Harvard's income derived from student revenues shot up. Meanwhile, Washington was cutting its support of higher education. Government assistance to Harvard fell from 40 percent in 1967 (the highest ever) to barely 25 percent just seven years later.

No wonder that Chase Peterson opened every Corporation meeting of the era with a briefing on long-range fundraising, sprinkled with dolorous reports on inflation's impact on faculty purchasing power, graduate teaching fellows, and the prospects of weak sisters like divinity, education, and urban affairs, each penalized under Eliot's famous dictum "Every Tub on Its Own Bottom." In the mid-Seventies a junior faculty member earned less than a New York City sanitation worker. And though Harvard managed to avoid deficits as large as Columbia's one-year record of $11,000,000, by mid-decade it was forced to reduce teaching staffs as an alternative to cutting salaries.

At the same time, some of the University's academic stars departed for greener pastures. The economics department was especially hard hit. Wassily Leontief, developer of the input-output formula by which economists gauge the impact of changes on various economic sectors, announced his intention in 1975 to leave Harvard after forty-four years. He accused his department of being too narrow and theoretical in its approach, too remote from students, and too wary of the radical perspective in the classroom. Not long after, Leontief's more conservative colleague Kenneth J. Arrow pulled up stakes and headed for Stanford.[50]

Such departures, coupled with Harvard's failure to grant tenure to such popular teachers as Doris Kearns of Government, China expert Ross Terrill, and East Asian scholar James C. Thompson, roused doubt about Harvard's once-undisputed standing as America's premier university. Presidential critics questioned Bok's utilization of Conant's old ad hoc committee for identifying peerless scholars. The process by which departments argued their case for or against a tenure candidate had been engulfed by judicial trappings, with the president serving as a kind of academic chief justice. In an attempt to make the search more rigorous, Bok added yet another layer to Conant's procedure. Blind letters listing candidates in given fields in alphabetical order were sent to hundreds of experts in that field. The notion of inviting the world's foremost scholars, for whom time was a precious commodity, to carefully rank prospective faculty members for Harvard's benefit seemed at best naive, at worst stunningly presumptuous.[51]

After a period of slow growth early in Bok's presidency, the number of tenured women spurted in the 1980s. To be sure, Harvard at mid-decade had fewer than thirty women in permanent appointments (the lack of women in significant administrative positions prompted complaints that Massachusetts Hall had the ambience of a men's locker room). Still, Bok could point to Indian specialist Diana Eck, biochemist Nancy Klecker, contemporary French literature expert Susan Suleiman, and literary critic and poet Helen Vendler. Finding qualified minority candidates was more difficult than recruiting female scholars, those around the president claimed. Fewer talented blacks or Hispanics were likely to enter academia so the argument went, when medicine, law, and public service promised more lucrative rewards. By no means everyone accepted such contentions, however, and Bok's administration remained under pressure from student activists to move more forcefully toward diversifying the faculty.

As the years slipped by, the president's energies were absorbed by fresh administrative and personnel decisions: he had to select new deans for Engineering and Applied Physics, Government, and Law, new masters for Mather and North Houses, and a new director of Buildings and Grounds. The *Crimson* once speculated that there must have been times when Bok envisioned himself being summoned to the basement of the Science Center, wrench in hand, to repair the Delta 2000 computer located there.

In the decade following the University Hall affair, Bok doubled the fourteen deans, associate deans, and assistant deans whom Pusey had relied upon to administer the College, Arts and Sciences, and graduate schools. But to the surprise of many and the disappointment of some, there was no provost to supervise purely educational functions in Bok's Harvard. While the new bureaucracy was fashioned to direct buildings and budgets, Bok reserved educational decision-making for himself. He wanted no one to come between himself and the overseeing of classroom instruction, which topped his list of personal concerns.[52]

However, as the appointments piled up and the fiscal crisis deepened, there was little time for Bok to establish himself as a forceful or widely recognized spokesman for educational reform. Not that he didn't try. Those who took the time to read Bok's initial presidential report, issued in the spring of 1971, encountered his first, tentative prodding of individual teachers and whole faculties to modernize their instructional methods and integrate their researches. He urged collaboration in public policy analysis and administration between the schools of law, public health, education, and design. He advocated continuing education, alumni colleges, films, and other technological breakthroughs geared to a society whose leisure time was growing as rapidly as the obsolescence of accepted knowledge.[53]

In his first year in office, Bok established a special fund to reward and encourage innovative college-level teachers, including those experimenting with self-paced instruction and cassette playbacks. With money from the Danforth Foundation, Harvard unveiled a Center for Teaching and Learning, at which hundreds of teaching fellows discussed the latest methods of foreign language instruction or classroom conduct.

In 1973, Bok made a historic change in the University's financial structure by overseeing Harvard's divorce from the State Street Research and Management Company, and its subsequent marriage to a new investment management firm created by and for the University. The move was the brainchild of treasurer George Putnam, bearer of a distinguished Harvard name (his grandfather had belonged to Eliot's Corporation), and a treasurer of decidedly untraditional methods. By the early 1970s, two-thirds of Harvard's endowment consisted of common stock in over 180 companies, from Avon to Xerox. To get to its current state, the University had liquidated two million dollars' worth of pork bellies, not to mention an Illinois onion farm and Palm Beach shorefront.[54]

Also in 1973, as part of Bok's campaign to rattle comfortable habits, House masters were restricted to five-year terms. This was the first of several reforms of the House system which would include appointing women masters and recruiting others who had not come from Harvard College.

In an attempt at rebuilding the atmosphere of trust on campus that had been shattered in the Sixties, Bok set aside hundreds of hours to meet with professors, attend informal lunches at the Faculty Club, write personal notes to prize-winning colleagues, and see and be seen in Houses and classrooms, at concerts; even at a Vietnam teach-in in Sanders Theater.

The president paid just as much attention to the local community, tramping Cambridge streets and presenting Al Vellucci, sometime mayor and the University's constant critic, with a Harvard chair for his City Hall office. Bok accepted Vellucci's invitation to eat spaghetti at his house, afterward putting on an apron to do the dishes. When Vellucci mentioned that his elderly mother, like many Cantabrigians of Italian descent, had never set foot inside Harvard Yard, Bok hosted the first of what became a series of annual block parties. Busloads of elderly residents came to hear the Harvard band, snack on refreshments supplied by the University, and line up to dance with the president, who managed a more or less convincing look of delight to all who stepped forward to do a two-step on a platform in the Tercentenary Theatre. "That President Bok," sighed one white-haired grandmother, "he's handsomer than Lawrence Welk."[55]

Bok was quietly building a foundation for his presidency—so quietly as to escape the notice of most observers. "Bok has to be careful about what he says," contends George Homans, veteran faculty observer of four Harvard presidents. "He has to ask himself, 'Will I have a demonstration if I say that?'" "Even success cannot be trumpeted too loudly," according to Hooks Burr, "lest a whole band of dissenters rise up." Such a cautious approach fit neatly with Bok's own preferences, but it did little to establish a sense of either his public personality or his long-range vision for Harvard. In this, he differed from his most famous predecessor. However, in other things, Derek Bok and Charles Eliot might be regarded as kindred spirits.[56]

Eliot championed the unexamined life, the here and now, practical religion, practical, useful education. "I am not interested in the past," he told a faculty member who pressed him to write his memoirs, "I am very interested in the future." Having scorned history, his shade could hardly be surprised to see it repeated a century later. Bok too cares little for the past, but dwells largely in the here and now, a gifted administrator lacking Pusey's sense of the majesty of learning for its own sake. "Derek Bok," says one colleague, "is a wonderfully fine human being, with a totally contemporary mind." For most of his presidency, that mind has grappled with the same dilemma Eliot had defined as Harvard's opportunity: how to tame a disruptive individuality perversely reasserted through group passions.[57]

Admirers conjure up dual images, of Eliot carrying home a heavy melon from the public marketplace and Bok pedaling his bicycle to James Russell Lowell's Elmwood. Eliot earned his reputation overturning the lax standards of professional schooling. Bok is no less vigorous—if less likely to be heeded—in throwing down the gauntlet to Harvard's graduate establishments of law, medicine, business, and public health. Eliot chose the first dean of Harvard College in order to escape disciplinary duties and focus his own formidable energies on educational reform. Bok surrounded himself with vice-presidents, while reserving to himself major responsibility for Harvard's intellectual agenda. Eliot fought a successful duel with classical education, and his University a century later is still fashioning replacements, as suggested by its recently adopted Core Curriculum.

Neither man can be defined exclusively by the College or the University. Like Eliot, Bok has directed his attention equally at reforming undergraduate education and at challenging the professional schools to modernize their methods. If he has not flipped Harvard over like a flapjack, he has most assuredly shaken its casual assumptions of superiority. Like Eliot, he is a man caught between cultures. As a boy in California, he idolized first athletes and then musicians. Were it not for such friends of his family as Aldous Huxley, Igor Stravinsky, and Bertrand Russell, Bok told the *Harvard Independent* in 1974, "I might have turned into a beach bum." He can still surprise friends who think of him as a legalist with appreciative summaries of a Trollope novel and a sense of humor reminiscent of Eliot at his most detached. (An associate who playfully called him to task for his habit of sending roses to Harvard's victorious women athletes wondered if this might not be interpreted as a sexist gesture. After all, would the president consider doing the same for hockey players or the football team? Given the current standing of his University's varsity squads, Bok replied, he didn't expect to confront the issue any time soon.) [58]

Eliot's competitiveness led him to row on the Charles. Henry Rosovsky, dean of Arts and Sciences, joked that in order to become a dean in Bok's Harvard, one must first take up tennis. The president's cannonball serve is locally famous. And his almost primal will to win led the Corporation to forbid him, after a fierce contest with *Crimson* editors in which he severed his Achilles tendon, to return to the basketball court. [59]

As for relations with the *Crimson*, Eliot more than once was tempted to shut the paper down. Bok endures it manfully, although the editors' habit of sending would-be reporters to his front door each Halloween to find out what the Bok family distributes to neighborhood children does little to warm their relations. [60]

Like Eliot, Bok is an emotionally reticent man. According to one close friend, "He certainly ain't a happy-go-lucky fellow." One minute, says Albert Nickerson, whose Corporation service overlapped the Pusey and Bok presidencies, "he's jolly and full of conviviality, and the next he's withdrawn into himself and you wonder where he's gone. [61]

Eliot had strong sympathies for individual students, although they were rarely revealed openly. Only those who were sick or who ran out of cash far from home were given a privileged glimpse into his ample heart. Bok says he "never knew a student that I didn't like when I had gotten to know him as an individual." As a law school instructor he went out of his way to include in Socratic give and take those at the bottom of the class. When the captain of the women's track team invited him to attend a meet with Princeton, the president was in the stands, cheering her on to victory in the 440-meter race. He was visibly concerned by her intention to compete a second time that day. He asked those around him if she should be taking such a risk. When she triumphed again in the 220, Bok was among the first to offer congratulations.[62]

On another occasion, a band of undergraduates dropped by Massachusetts Hall bearing a birthday cake for the president, only to have a squadron of secretaries prevent them from delivering it personally. The next day they opened their door to find Bok himself, a bag of homemade chocolate chip cookies in hand. After expressing his thanks, he stayed long enough to chat about the College and their impressions of it.

Bok's concern over the quality of student life has led to presidential initiatives which have bolstered the arts and resuscitated decrepit athletic facilities. In an effort to counter the Me Decade, Bok established public service programs in each of the Houses, a million-dollar fund to support student volunteerism, and a first-of-its-kind program to train instructors in ethics. (His daughter Hillary shared his concern for public service, and worked one summer in a Cambridge working-class neighborhood.)

None of this has received much attention outside the Yard, however, and for a simple reason. If Nathan Pusey appeared at times invisible, his successor has often seemed anonymous. Tennis notwithstanding, Bok's favorite pastimes—reading, gardening, and especially the writing he undertakes on post-Christmas Florida retreats—characterize his lawyer's appetite for detail and his own monkish taste for privacy. He is visibly uncomfortable in the presence of cameras. And, according to Daniel Steiner, perhaps Bok's closest confederate, the president would be happy if he never saw his name in another newspaper. "Bart Giametti talks about baseball and the Moral Majority," says one member of Bok's faculty, referring to Yale's quotable chief, "and he gets on the front page of the *New York Times*. The only way our president will get on the *Times'* front page is if someone shoots him."[63]

Tom O'Brian, who succeeded Hale Champion as financial vice-president, declares, "I've worked for him ten years, and I don't know the man." From those who think they do know him, the estimates vary wildly: "A Supreme Court justice with a touch of Milton," says one. "A pinstripe populist" claims another. To John Finley, for forty-seven years a distinguished Cambridge classicist, he is a mixture of Nathan Pusey and Gary Cooper. "God, that guy is classy," Henry Rosovsky has said of the man whom he compares to an admiral on board a ship which he, Rosovsky, has captained. Perhaps the most perceptive assessment comes from former dean of the College Fred Glimp, who would return to Massachusetts Hall in 1980 to work on alumnae relations after a ten-year absence. Bok, says Glimp, is a non-practicing Calvinist, a man who lives his work with a seriousness worthy of his Dutch forebears. Asked whether he was happy in his position, Bok ratified Glimp's view. "I associate the word 'happy' with having fun. This is not a job in which one does that, but I do think I can say two things that are more meaningful. One is that I find the job completely absorbing. The other point is that there is no other job I would rather be doing. If that's an adequate definition of 'happy,' then I am."[64]

Bok's passion for ethics, which he insists can be taught even in classrooms set aside for medical or legal training, displaces conventional theology for him just as reliance on character displaced it for Eliot. This riles traditionalists. Peter Gomes of Memorial Church says, "Mr. Bok is not antagonistic to religion, just bewildered by it. As an institution, he finds the church very peculiar. He won't harm it, he can't support it, and he certainly won't engage in it."[65]

Thirteen years after asking his friend Krister Stendahl about his church-going obligations, Bok would demonstrate that whatever else he may have learned in the intervening period, liturgical protocol was not on the list. Having suggested a welcoming reception for Boston's new Catholic prelate, a Harvard graduate named Bernard Law, on the day of the function, the president turned to Adams House master Robert Kiley for guidance. Could Kiley please tell Mr. Bok, asked the president's secretary, how one addressed an archbishop?[66]

"He thinks and thinks and thinks about things," says Albert Nickerson. However attractive this may be in the abstract, when combined with personal modesty it can lead to caution as extreme in its own way as the hubris of the Sixties. Bok says he finds it "embarrassing" to think that Harvard's Core Curriculum might set a trend in higher education. He smilingly turns aside congratulations when a member of his faculty wins a Nobel. He points out that Pusey should actually get the credit; he only hopes that his own tenured professors will do as well as those of his predecessor.[67]

The best actors, it is said, like to be surrounded by colleagues of equal talent—that way, they all look good. The same goes for Bok, who has surrounded himself with strong administrators. To David Aloian, Quincy House master and one of Bok's frequent tennis partners, the president has enough self-assurance to tolerate opposition and thrive amid ambiguity. "The cult of personality won't go around here," according to Aloian. "We have too many of them already. Success depends on people at all levels developing a respectful collegiality. There's no lofty waving of the scepter. And Derek's a master at getting talented colleagues to work together." Robert Kiley adds, "He defines leadership as the process of consultation."[68]

Bok's style of leadership—in essence, group administration—is not unique to Harvard, as the president himself points out. "There's been a change in the way people think decisions ought to be made," he explains. "It takes much longer, and you have to defend and articulate your decisions. . . . Nobody starts by having a perfect idea, and a university much more than an army depends on co-operation." This new decision-making process at the University merely mirrors that of the modern broker state—in which individual guidance and inspiration have given way to rampant participatory democracy. If there are no Bok legends, this reflects an age in which personal vividness is a tarnished coinage, hoarded mostly by journalists. "It would be easy to make flamboyant statements and please the media," Bok says. "But if you want to accomplish anything important in educational reform, you have to build a consensus."[69]

Derek Bok is a consensus seeker. To some, his vision seems cloudy, gray, and managerial, but others find rare political skills in a president who presents no stationary target and is content to operate on the margins of change. Enigmatic and intensely private, Bok suggests the Supreme Court justice he had hoped to become when he was a Stanford fraternity brother. "He feeds no fantasies, engenders no loyalties, creates no myths," says Peter Gomes, who as Preacher to the University tends the flame of seventeenth-century Harvard. But then, what other college president in the 1980s does? Even Bart Giametti, for all the admiration his Yale presidency aroused, was noticeably modest in assessing his own accomplishments when he retired. "You do what you can do," said Giametti, widely credited with restoring Yale's finances, "and you don't stay any longer than you should." In his case, that meant seven years. Having healed the gaping wounds of 1969, Bok shares with Giametti the unhappy distinction of being taken for granted in his own backyard.[70]

While Nate Pusey talked openly of a trinitarian God, Bok tries to present the other side of pre-professionalism, pleading the cause of ethics at a time when more than half the College's graduates have visions of legal or medical careers dancing in their heads. Instead of Houses and tutorials, he grapples with sex-blind admissions and the role of computers in the classroom. He did not create the bureaucratic mentality, but by most measurements, he has made it work rather well for Harvard's notoriously quarrelsome family. If he has been reluctant to make pronouncements, he has asked some penetrating questions. He has tried to practice scholarship when others prefer politics. He may yet be classed as a reformer in Eliot's tradition.

What has changed is the country itself. A century ago, Charles Eliot epitomized an age in which America's leading institutions, Harvard among them, could boldly assert a cohesive set of values in the political and social equivalent of Hobbes's state of nature. But by the time Bok became president, these same institutions were reduced to defending their own interests, often against a government requiring that they adhere to federally mandated hiring practices, budget priorities, procedural safeguards, and research limitations.

As recently as the 1930s, Bok noted, universities were not required to administer such staples of modern industrial society as unemployment compensation. Now, there were federal prohibitions on fetal experiments, incentives for dental students to train in underserved areas, and retroactive bans on student aid to any university insufficiently protective of handicapped rights. In the fall of 1984, Harvard was forced to return $4.6 million to the Department of Health and Human Services, part of a much larger claim made by the government for inflated overhead costs associated with federally sponsored research over a seven-year period.[71]

Harvard spent more than half a million dollars to install state-ordered smoke detectors. Far more costly was a seven-year standoff between the University and residents of Boston's Mission Hill neighborhood over a gigantic power plant called MAYTEP, designed to serve hospitals clustered around the medical school. From an initial price tag of $50 million, the project soared to over $250 million, while state environmental officials pondered allegations that its six diesel engines—the equivalent of 44,000 window-sized air-conditioning units—posed a cancer risk to those living in the vicinity of the plant.[72]

With the welter of government regulations and increased administrative bureaucracy, Bok gradually became the internal president Pusey had hoped to be. He defends the stance as necessary to an institution whose budget has tripled (to more than $550 million in 1984–5), and whose constantly expanding dimensions make outside crusading an unaffordable luxury. This isn't the only reason why Bok (in common with other college presidents of today) resembles more of an academic CEO than did the divinely ordained lawgivers of old. Because there is such a reliance on alumni giving, the modern university president is often seen as a man who lives in a big house and begs. This may be a reason why the average college presidency lasts just seven years.

Unlike an Eliot or a Conant, Bok appears to define his constituency like a board chairman facing the stockholders. If pressed about the larger role in challenging public thought that has traditionally been assumed by Harvard presidents, he has a ready response. "Are there no important academic issues remaining to be spoken on that I haven't addressed?" he asks. "What is my special capacity in this field to put it ahead of another? Maybe I don't love [appearing on] TV shows," he has said. "Maybe there is some shyness or modesty there. But I think it's more straightforward than that. I can see someone asking himself, who the hell is he to talk about arms control?"[73]

For those unsatisfied with the law or structural restraints as an explanation for such wariness, there is always Freudian analysis. One Cambridge witticism alludes to the intense privacy with which both Bok and his wife shroud their non-public careers: "There's nothing wrong with Derek that being married to a Norwegian instead of a Swede wouldn't cure."[74]

It took most of forty years for Charles Eliot, the founder of modern Harvard, to be accepted by Establishmentarians, something Bok hasn't forgotten. Several years ago, the president was striding across Stanford's campus at the end of a long day when suddenly he turned to his companion and indulged in a rare bit of revelation. "You know," he said, "I spent four not very happy years at this place. I've spent twenty-five very happy years at Harvard. And yet there are still people who consider me a Stanford man."[75]

Whatever else people might think of him, they could not question the depth of his commitment to Harvard, nor his desire to protect it from the centrifugal forces of an age saturated with politics. Early in his presidency, when he was looking forward to the day he could turn his undivided attention to curriculum reform and professional schooling, Bok was given a taste of what a small group of determined activists could do to disrupt the calm of the University.

In the August 1971 issue of the *Atlantic Monthly,* psychology professor Richard Herrnstein asserted that genetics played a major role in human intelligence. The article implicitly warned of the dangers of a caste system resulting from this; nowhere did Herrnstein mention race. Bok, among others, had complimented the author. A very different response came from SDS, which leafleted in the Yard, picketed Herrnstein's lectures, harassed and ultimately assaulted him before a hundred lecture students. Faced with protesters who posed a threat to his physical safety while teaching, Herrnstein appealed to the American Civil Liberties Union, of which he was a longtime member. When the ACLU disputed his contention that his constitutional rights were being violated, he quit the organization in disgust. Some fellow instructors, many of them political liberals, refused to express publicly their private words of sympathy.[76]

The president's stance was special because it represented the attitude of the University. At the same time, Bok's limited concept of presidential authority precluded him from cracking down on the protesters. Besides, the memory of April 1969 was still fresh in too many minds. Bok's personal anguish over Herrnstein's ordeal was unmistakable. He telephoned Herrnstein's wife, Susan, to ask how she was holding up, and to wonder out loud if there was anything he could do to help. Herrnstein himself could think of nothing until late in the year when, together with John Dunlop, he solicited a statement of support. Amid grumbling from some quarters that he'd waited too long, Bok complied.

"He would have stood up for principle if he had known what to do," says Herrnstein, who regards the affair as an important milestone in Bok's education, instilling in him a more realistic perception of Harvard's vulnerabilities and its president's obligation to oppose disturbers of its peace. "Bok came into office a fairly typical Massachusetts liberal," claims one who knew him well. "He thought he could talk anyone into anything. He subsequently learned that sometimes you have to be tough."[77]

"A university presupposes a certain level of decorum," Herrnstein concludes with a hint of resignation. "People who violate this underlying assumption can get away with murder—for a short time."[78]

This lesson was confirmed when, in April 1972, another crisis erupted. Afro and an ad hoc group dubbing itself the Pan-American Liberation Committee demanded that Harvard immediately sell its 680,000 shares of Gulf Oil stock. The coalition claimed that through its investments in Angola, Gulf facilitated the daily slaughter of Africans, and that by looking the other way and harvesting its dividends, Harvard was "deeply implicated" in the company's crimes. On April 19, following an all-day meeting of the Corporation, Bok announced that the stock would not be sold. Instead, the University would dispatch an observer to Angola to obtain firsthand information on Gulf's activities there. In addition, it would ask Gulf to set forth a plan to improve employment, training, and managerial opportunities for native Angolans. The militants dismissed Bok's response as "tepid sincerity and moaning liberalism."

At dawn on April 20, two dozen black students seized Massachusetts Hall. "This our turf now," said one. "Yeah, this Birth of a Nation." As the president retired to a temporary command post in Holyoke Center, Walter Leonard, a Bok assistant who was himself black, talked to the occupiers. The University obtained a restraining order forbidding the occupation, but held back from serving it. Near the end of a long day, with his student body concurrently about to strike over the continued American presence in Vietnam, and with graduate teaching fellows preparing to join them, the president's mask slipped. As he paced the tenth floor of Holyoke, Bok was asked how he would respond if alumni should exert pressure to evict the protesters inside his office. "I don't need this job," he blurted. "And alumni will not dictate how I run this University." Would he consider calling in the police to clear Massachusetts Hall? "I would never do anything to hurt a student in this University."[79]

Neither, it appeared, would he rely solely on doughnuts and coffee. Mindful of the lessons of University Hall, the president and his advisers put their faith in short attention spans instead of force. Once more, Archibald Cox was called in, and Bok left Cambridge to keep scheduled dates with Harvard alumni. This was a *ruse de guerre,* a reassuring sign to Old Boys everywhere that Harvard was not convulsed.

As Bok dined with Harvard clubs in Cleveland and Chicago, Cox put out the word that continued occupation of the building would result in a contempt-of-court citation already issued but stayed pending the administration's slowly tightening noose. Defiance of the court would result in severe penalties, particularly for law school students, whose records might be permanently stained. Meanwhile, freshmen living on the upper floors of Massachusetts Hall were moved to nearby hotels, ostensibly to escape the drums, music, and late-night speech-making. ("I'm sympathetic to their cause," said one undergraduate, "but when a band of emotionalized people scream 'Right on' at four in the morning, it doesn't increase my sympathy.") The move was also another signal to the protesters that Harvard was prepared to carry on as usual.

The *Crimson* predicted no peaceful end to the crisis unless the Corporation capitulated, even if this meant Bok's resignation. Just how wrong it was became clear on the afternoon of April 25, when the thirty-three demonstrators abruptly left the building, fists thrust upward in a defiant gesture but unable to conceal their strategic defeat. Their spokesman acknowledged that contempt-of-court charges would carry six-month jail sentences, and, "That would remove us from the

struggle. The issue is Harvard out of Gulf and not Massachusetts Hall."
While a rally heard ritual denunciations of "Pharaoh Bok," the University responded in low-key fashion, expressing pleasure that the only damage done to the building was a single broken window.

The takeover was not without impact, however. When he returned to Cambridge, Bok announced that Harvard would back two disclosure resolutions filed with General Motors and Ford. These reversed the University's historic reluctance to vote against management and gave back to the president the proxy hitherto reserved for Harvard's treasurer. In addition, Bok established the Advisory Committee on Shareholder Responsibility (ACSR), a fifteen-member panel composed of students, faculty members, and alumni which would guide yet another new committee whose membership was taken entirely from the Corporation. In mid-May, he joined other college presidents in Washington to lobby against the ongoing Vietnam war. He turned down an invitation to a Blue Room reception hosted by President Nixon, and pressed his antiwar case with Henry Kissinger in a ninety-minute meeting heavily publicized back in Cambridge.

Not long after, SDS threatened to rally hundreds outside Bok's office to demand tenure for several radical instructors in the economics department. Only eight showed up to hear Bok say he'd be glad to discuss the matter with their department chairman, Henry Rosovsky.

Few realized it at the time, but Bok was implementing Pusey's ill-starred strategy from the spring of 1969, deflecting to others the public responsibility for unpopular or difficult decisions. When professors wanted to oust a dean, Bok deferred to the Corporation. When SDS in 1972 sought permission to hold its national convention at Harvard, he said it was for the College to decide, and quietly arranged for rooms at the law school. When the question of punishment for the Massachusetts Hall demonstrators arose, Bok left the decision to Overseers and the Committee on Rights and Responsibilities, thereby permitting the occupiers to remain in college.

Bok employed a similar approach in a classical Harvard tempest several years later, when his plan to renovate the Houses spelled the end of Lowell's ivy. Much loved by sentimentalists, the plants posed a nightmare for Buildings and Grounds, which said they corroded the brick walls to the tune of $50,000 annually. Tear down the ivy, said lovers of old Harvard? One might as well melt down John Harvard's statue. Freshmen formed a "Save the Ivy" committee, and petitioned Bok to reverse the decision. The president chose to obfuscate instead, allowing only that it was an issue with "human, ethical, and ecological considerations."

Such language, when coupled with Bok's below-the-horizon profile and his technocratic advisers, inspired contempt from many student activists. Early in 1972 the *Crimson* contrasted the pragmatism of Bok's administration with Pusey's stubborn insistence that a Harvard president should have a belief in God as his motivating force. "Imagine the contempt and derision with which this was received in Langdell, Baker, Littauer, William James and the Computer Center," said the paper. "With all the important skills necessary to manipulate a great university, the godstruck old fool had cited something as intangible as a belief. For it was not only Pusey's belief in God which was pitiful and funny: it was his belief in belief of any kind. Nothing more amuses the men who run this university—and their compatriots who run our society—than men with beliefs and no power."

But the *Crimson* held a minority view. From a tactical standpoint, Bok's combination of personal charm and tireless accessibility had the desired effect. More than that, however, it bespoke a shrewd reading of changing student priorities. By February 1974, a Marine recruiter came to Harvard, and, for the first time in five years, encountered not a single demonstrator. A month later, the Chicago Seven's Jerry Rubin stood before an undergraduate audience and said he didn't want to discuss politics. "I prefer to talk about premature ejaculation." North House began holding monthly formal dances, and thirty students lined up half an hour early for interviews with the Mellon Bank and Morgan Guaranty Trust.

Bok summed up the new mood, even as he attempted to counter it by pleading the cause of public service and ethical education. "Students at Harvard don't have to worry about getting jobs when they graduate," he said in the spring of 1972, even as Massachusetts Hall was encircled by anti-Gulf demonstrators. "Now if you went to school at Ball State University in Muncie, Indiana, then you might have to worry about getting a job, but you don't have to worry here at Harvard."[80]

Whatever its source, the sudden preoccupation with grades and careers diverted students' political energies. It also smoothed the way for Bok at last to become president in more than name. Shunning media celebrity, Bok slowly dug himself out from under the administrative and ideological debris bequeathed him. As he did so, he contemplated Harvard's needs. By January 1973, he was able to tell the Overseers that undergraduate education was in dire straits, and that he was going to attempt to do something about it.

Careful as ever, Bok was quietly preparing the University for an intellectual means test of immense significance. The final missing piece in his administrative puzzle was fitted into place that May, when a battle-scarred John Dunlop responded to an invitation from Richard Nixon to chair his new panel enforcing federal price controls and the much-admired Henry Rosovsky took his place as dean of Arts and Sciences. In Rosovsky the master delegator had the perfect delegate, and a fresh start to a presidency hitherto caught in the net of administrative housekeeping.

CHAPTER NINE

In Search of Coherence

Universities are designed to achieve particular purposes. Their special mission is the discovery and transmission of knowledge. In performing these functions, they may receive support from many sources in society. Their members may have a wide variety of relationships with public and private organizations. Their professors may affect many areas of society through teaching and research. Nevertheless, unlike other organizations, such as political parties, environmental associations, or civil rights groups, their institutional goal is not to reform society in specific ways. Universities have neither the mandate nor the competence to administer foreign policy, set our social and economic priorities, enforce standards of conduct in the society, or carry out other social functions apart from learning and discovery.

—DEREK BOK
March 1979

IT TAKES five years for a Harvard president to learn his job, Nathan Pusey said; only in the following decade can he really begin to make his impact felt. As if to disprove the theory, by the fall of 1976 Derek Bok could point to administrative overhaul, diversification of the student body, restructuring of University finances, a fresh community outreach, and, perhaps most important, a reduction in his faculty's emotional temperature. All these contributed to Bok's ongoing efforts to knit his university back together, but a binding sense of institutional purpose was still lacking. In a larger sense, Harvard's confusion mirrored the country's own crisis of confidence. Battered by Vietnam and Watergate, drained by inflation, adrift under commonplace leadership, Americans turned inward in the Seventies. So did Harvard.

Granted, Bok told reporters early in his presidency, a man in his position should speak up on matters of educational impact, including the draft and other policies affecting students. But "if it comes to speaking out on a number of social issues that his position does not prepare him to speak on, I don't think anybody is going to listen very long."[1]

Notorious for reading everything that goes into Massachusetts Hall, and for responding personally to every letter that crosses his desk, Bok has justified, or rationalized, his reluctance to take the national stage by pointing to the excessive demands on his time sure to follow. On those rare occasions when he has thrust his views before a wider audience, it has not been to comment on the decline of humanistic values in a throwaway culture, let alone abortion or Grenada. Rather, Bok has confined himself primarily to criticisms of federal actions which might have negative implications for Harvard: CIA recruiting on campus, Reagan Administration budget cuts, Congress's inclination to pass legislation requiring universities to behave in certain socially desirable ways regardless of increased costs and diminished autonomy.[2]

Over time, the president devised methods of communication that reflected his background in labor negotiation. Chief among them were his Open Letters, which he began issuing in the late Seventies, addressing a broad range of academic, social, and political questions. Closely reasoned and matter-of-fact in style, Bok's encyclicals attracted more praise outside Cambridge than within the Harvard community, which largely dismissed them as restatements of the obvious. But this, too, didn't seem to faze the president. Worried that the debate over moral issues was being reduced to slogans, chants, and picket signs, Bok said, "I write the letters not so much to persuade as to establish a level of discourse." In speaking *to* his institution, he did not presume to speak *for* it. "In most cases my role is not to decide academic issues but to see that the most important questions are identified and carefully considered."[3]

Bok's concerns point to the newly defined limits of academic influence. Since the Second World War, the university had become a prime instrument of national development. In the Sixties, it had joined the policymaking process in ways unimagined in Conant's generation. Now, in the aftermath of disillusionment, its options were narrowed, its vocabulary in need of refurbishing. Any man in Bok's place must formulate new definitions of academic freedom. Did it extend to a laboratory producing genetic breakthroughs or engaged in laser-beam research? In an age when universities through the admissions process served as gatekeeper to the American Dream, how was their autonomy to be supervised? Could they remain strictly neutral in the affairs of corporations in which they held substantial investments? As they safeguarded timeless values, could they serve the immediate needs of society?[4]

Bok argued that universities should be more adventurous and energetic in tackling outside problems than most traditionalists allowed, but he was unwilling to go as far as some activists toward making Harvard "a kind of collective political and economic force." Rather than trying to influence public affairs actively, Bok felt that the University should foster ethical standards in its curricula. He spelled out his position in an Open Letter:

> Academic programs have great social value, although their fruits are often intangible and long-term in nature. Before we jeopardize these programs, we should also recognize that very rarely will the institutional acts of a single university—or even universities as a group—have any substantial possibility of putting an end to the misfortunes that exist in society. Individual scholars will occasionally have an influence through the persuasive power of their knowledge and ideas. The name of Harvard may succeed in attracting public attention, if only briefly. But we should not confuse the power to obtain publicity with the power to determine events. . . . There comes a point where symbolism must give way to real threats to academic freedom, real financial losses, and real administrative burdens. If we do not acknowledge this point, we will merely succeed in damaging important functions of the University without doing anything to alleviate the sufferings of others.[5]

Bok's belief in Harvard's ethical responsibility to society would influence the development of its new Core Curriculum, first unveiled in 1977. In the meantime, however, his ideas did not stop other Harvard figures from becoming directly involved in the public's business. Bok's former dean of the faculty, John Dunlop, went from supervising wage and price controls for Richard Nixon to serving as Gerald Ford's Secretary of Labor. Before South Vietnam collapsed in the spring of 1975, economist Arthur Smithies had been retained by its government to help stabilize the economy. "No Goddamn Harvard men, you understand," Nixon warned, over the prospect of Cantabrigians on his White House staff, only to relent for Dunlop, Henry Kissinger, and Daniel Patrick Moynihan.

What historian Ernest May called "action intellectuals" flocked to join Jimmy Carter's administration in 1977. Law school professor Philip Heyman helped direct the FBI's Abscam investigation. Samuel Huntington took a leave from the Center for International Affairs to advise the National Security Council on the MX missile and Iran. Government professor Joseph Nye devised a compromise plan clearing the way for sale of nuclear fuel to India, while Nye's faculty colleague Robert Bowie held a top post at the CIA.

In September of 1980, Roger Fisher of the Harvard Negotiation Project set out with a graduate student on a diplomatic mission to Teheran, the Iranian capital, in which fifty-two Americans were being held hostage by student militants sworn to the radical Islamic doctrines of Ayatollah Khomeini. The State Department had supplied Fisher with street maps of the city, and rooms were reserved in a hotel one block from the occupied U.S. embassy. But on arriving at the Iranian's Paris outpost, where they had expected to pick up visas, the negotiating team from Harvard was disappointed. No visas awaited them, there or in Bonn, where they flew next in hopes of persuading Khomeini's diplomats there to grant them entry, so they were forced to return home.[6]

While his faculty engaged in such derring-do, Bok labored manfully in Cambridge's often thorny vineyards. Although a flattering profile in *Penthouse* magazine applauded his strict new guidelines for CIA recruiting on campus, the president was more often the object of attacks. Student activists were dismayed by his refusal to boycott corporations such as Nestlés and J. P. Stevens; law school students demanded a say in selecting a new dean to replace Albert Sacks; and blacks were angered over his rejection of their demand for a Third World Center. A protest was touched off when a dining hall worker was suspended for overcooking cauliflower.

Plans for a complete merger with Radcliffe were shelved in 1977, after Radcliffe president Matina S. Horner persuaded trustees and alumni that it was no time to allow the separate college to wither away while women and their scholarly aspirations were at last beginning to be recognized. Under the terms of a "non-merger merger," all housing was to be co-educational and there would be a joint admissions program and full access to all libraries and athletic facilities. But Radcliffe's administrative structure survived intact, as did its fundraising apparatus. To some observers, it appeared that Bok had been snookered, first in the original selection of Horner, later in negotiations falling short of a genuine merger. Others faulted Harvard's administration for failing to achieve instant parity between the sexes.[7]

Throughout his presidency, Bok has been vexed by pleas for divestiture of Harvard's stock in firms doing business in South Africa. Each year, spring would signal new student protestations. Corporation meetings were picketed, rallies addressed, petitions circulated. In April 1973, demonstrators forced the president from his office and into the yellow clapboard house which Conant had used as a wartime residence. Six months later, protesters only grudgingly allowed Bok to complete his remarks dedicating the new home of the long-awaited John F. Kennedy School of Government. Bok was not pleased when his fellow orator of the day, Senator Edward Kennedy, hushed the crowd so that a dissident spokesman could make the case against naming the school's library after an industrialist whose fortunes derived in part from South African operations. Critics seized upon Bok's apparent insensitivity to the South Africa issue as the latest proof of a devotion to institutional prosperity over moral authority. Tainted money fueled modern Harvard, they claimed. The official response recalled Booker T. Washington's to a similar allegation made earlier in the century against his Tuskegee Institute: "T'ain't enough."[8]

Back in 1963, claimed psychologist David McClelland, Harvard peers had disdained his idea of marketing theories about human motivation to government agencies and corporations. "In the Sixties, if you said *business,* people spat on you. Now I'm a hero." In between, McClelland had sold his private firm for $3.2 million. "When I got to Harvard I thought the rewards here were not in teaching," he explained. "Everyone here was kind of interested in getting out of it." If not everyone, surely a great many of McClelland's faculty colleagues have been able to parlay their own talents, plus the Harvard name, into lucrative sidelines. The University itself maintains over eighty centers, projects, programs, and institutes, each hustling for outside funding. For $5000 and up, corporations could get first crack at the business school's brainiest applicants. For $50,000, a sponsor could see his name emblazoned on a Kennedy School classroom. For $650,000, the Carnegie Corporation funded a brand-new Institute for the Study of Smoking Behavior and Policy.

Critics called it checkbook scholarship, but Harvard pleaded financial necessity when the West German pharmaceutical firm Hoechst offered to sign a multi-year research contract worth fifty million dollars.

On a smaller scale, DuPont ponied up six million dollars over a five-year period. In both cases, Harvard guaranteed to these contributors exclusive rights to any discoveries in biomedical research. While President Bok extolled the glories of adult education, his school of business reaped as much in tuition from thirteen midcareer programs as was taken in from all those enrolled in conventional graduate instruction.

"Can you imagine if Harvard had invested in Eastman Kodak when it was inventing the camera?" inquired Bok's general counsel Dan Steiner. "All our problems would be solved."

Unfortunately for Harvard and her president, such attitudes led to problems of another sort. A 1980 controversy revolved around Bok's stated desire to back Professor Mark Ptashne in a bioengineering venture. No sooner had Bok spoken than some members of his faculty rose up to protest what they saw as Science for Profit, and its disturbing effects on institutional priorities and individual advancement. Ptashne needn't have worried; he secured venture capital from CBS chairman William Paley and the Rockefeller family, among others. Within four years, his Cambridge-based Genetics Institute was engaged in a race with a California competitor over patent rights to a blood-clotting agent called Factor 8—and a worldwide market estimated to be worth $250 million annually.[9]

In the meantime, Bok threw in the towel, persuaded, he said, that this particular investment in technology transfer might be inconsistent with academic values. No such scruples prevented him from accepting $1.2 million from South Korean businessmen wishing to fund a chair at Harvard promoting studies in their country's economic miracle, however. As part of a general belt-tightening, the president halted the separate mailing of his annual report, and was prepared to block a $16.5 million addition to the Fogg Art Museum, only to reverse himself a few weeks later when donors made up a $300,000 shortfall. "We have been burnt many times before," asserted the Corporation's Hooks Burr, in justifying Bok's cautious approach, "and it has cost a lot of money."

Burr didn't mention it, but what was seared into every administrator's memory was the fiasco of MAYTEP, the alternative energy plant designed to service the University's medical school complex in the Mission Hill section of Boston. Originally sold to Bok in the early Seventies as a fifty-million-dollar investment in energy independence, the project multiplied fivefold in cost, until the irreverent suggested that a $350 million fund drive launched in the late Seventies might appropriately be called the MAYTEP Campaign.

As Bok presided over an institution struggling to cope with double-digit inflation, oil stoppages, bad investments, and MAYTEP, conspiracy theorists took it for granted that his primary assignment from the Corporation was to keep the political lid on Harvard while the fundraisers performed their specialty. Some even alleged that Harvard's new Core Curriculum represented little more than Conant's General Education program dressed in new fittings to be sold to alumni givers as an educational innovation worthy of their contributions.[10]

It's a cynical hypothesis, overlooking not only Bok's long-expressed interest in reforming undergraduate education, but also the widely shared institutional fear that Harvard, in common with the rest of American higher education, lacked a sense of priorities and standards. Moreover, the theory ignores the fiscal realities of a decade in which academic purchasing power was dramatically reduced, Harvard faced pressure from competing institutions out to raid its brightest stars, and its run-down physical plant, much of it dating to Lowell's era, put off scientists and athletes alike. In truth, it was less economics than politics that accounted for the Core.

> *An educated man should be able to form a fair offhand judgment as to the goodness or badness of the method used by a professor in his exposition. To be educated is in fact to be able to do this.*
>
> —ARISTOTLE

> *We're living in an age when the United States is becoming smaller and smaller by any index. That doesn't mean she is declining, only that others are growing. . . . None of us realized that the American Century would only last fifteen or twenty years.*
>
> —HENRY ROSOVSKY

HARVARD AMBLED along in the mid-Seventies, its search for educational values poised as ever between equity and quality. The press duly reported a number of changes, more or less imposed by what the *Crimson* continued to call the Real World. In the spring of 1976, Arts and Sciences voted to permit cross-registration for ROTC courses at nearby MIT. That fall, the University Health Services began paying for nontherapeutic abortions. The DU Club chose a black president, the first in Harvard history. Undergraduate humorists fired off a message to UN Secretary General Kurt Waldheim demanding admission to the world body for the newly independent state of Lampoon. As part of the organization's centennial observance, Poonies carried signs in UN Plaza reading "Register Surprise, Not Guns."[11]

Of all the changes that had come to Harvard since 1876, none could compare with the diversity of enrollment. By mid-decade, more than a tenth of Harvard's students came from abroad, and observers were struck by the growing number of Asian and Spanish descent. While over sixty languages were taught in Cambridge, a stream of urban planners and economic specialists from Harvard centers and from the Institute for International Development went to work in the Third World and nurtured the University's global reputation.

In the modern world, Bok wrote in the spring of 1977, events were far beyond the control of a few superpowers. America must henceforth be prepared to achieve her objectives through negotiation and accommodation. She must take into account competing interests, and acknowledge the death of her own once undisputed leadership. Already, Sweden and Switzerland enjoyed richer per-capita living standards. Other countries had higher rates of economic growth. How Americans reacted to the evolution in their status carried with it profound implications. Would they grow insular and defensive, he asked, or would they accept interdependence by becoming more sensitive to the needs and contributions of others?[12]

At the same time that he asked America to accept a diminishing world role, Bok could defend his own institution against those who questioned its traditional claim to superiority. William Lipscomb received a 1976 Nobel Prize in chemistry for his twenty-year exploration of boranes, work which led directly to a new treatment for cancer. A year later, another Nobel in physics went to John Van Vleck, whose research in quantum mechanics paved the way for laser development. In spite of some newsworthy departures, Harvard's faculty was still rated preeminent in seven of nineteen academic departments. In its ranks were such acknowledged leaders as Konrad Bloch in biology, biographer Jackson Bate and playwright William Alfred in English, zoologist E. O. Wilson, sociologists Daniel Bell and David Riesman. Up-and-coming stars included libertarian philosopher Robert Nozick, economist Martin Feldstein, geologist Stephen Gould, and astronomer Riccardo Giacconi. Merely reciting their names and fields of endeavor conveyed the scope of modern Harvard's reach and internationalism.[13]

So much variety, however dazzling, exacted a price. More than ever, departments tended to make their own decisions instead of relying on centralized guidance. Great researchers were as disinclined to waste time in the classroom as in making the acquaintance of experts who spoke a different academic language. In an effort to foster institutional loyalty, the faculty moved to correct its own most blatant abuses, and voted a 20 percent ceiling on the amount of time professors could devote to outside consulting. And yet Harvard seemed to its president like some ill-prepared Mulligan's Stew, larger and less cohesive than at any time since the late Fifties, when he had first arrived at the law school with heady expectations.

"I looked forward to luncheon conversations with lively archeologists just back from digging in some exotic land or perhaps astronomers brimming with theories of life on other planets," he recalled. But nothing could have been more remote from Harvard Law School in 1958. Bok's hopes had again been raised when a young historian had invited him and several colleagues to join in a weekly poker game. "But after two disastrous weeks, I was forced to conclude that I simply could not afford to communicate with the rest of the University via the gaming table."[14]

Since that time, of course, Bok's contacts with the Harvard faculty had expanded to a scale he could have hardly imagined. In between choosing a dean of education and superintendent of buildings and grounds, passing on the appointment of physicists and sociobiologists, and allocating resources between botany and preventive medicine, he had been able to observe a lot. In the process, the educational reformer merged with the social tinkerer to conceive a master plan. Harvard, Bok decided, would now undertake to define its intellectual mission for the last years of the twentieth century. Simultaneously, it would attempt to forge a sense of common purpose.

Lacking both inclination and clout to impose a personal vision, Bok sought an ally who shared his outlook and who could avoid polarizing factions while gaining respect for his own fairness and intellectual substance. So it was that in the fall of 1973 he settled on Henry Rosovsky, one of the "White Berkeleyites" who had taken refuge in the East following the campus disorders of the mid-Sixties, to succeed John Dunlop as dean of Arts and Sciences. As a participant in Harvard's own brush with chaos during that time, Rosovsky had chaired the committee that designed a new black studies program, only to quit when faculty colleagues yielded control to student activists. Having taken a prominent role in the agony of Pusey's final months, he had nonetheless retained the friendship of many associates who agreed on little else.

Long before 1973, the dean's job had been raised to immense prestige by men like Paul Buck and McGeorge Bundy. Rosovsky proved their equal. He was rated by friends as a vastly self-assured, powerful thinker who was also a gifted tactician. Rosovsky had earned his nickname, "Ironpants." "Henry has a marvelous ability to sit for hours and listen to anything that's said and not look bored to death," said Franklin Ford. He also had a better natural grasp of politics than Bok, who once excused himself from a prospective meeting with a Massachusetts pol on the grounds that the powerbroker from Beacon Hill was "evil." According to a government professor, "A meeting with Henry makes you realize what a session with Lyndon Johnson must have been like."[15]

At the time of his selection, Rosovsky's near-universal acceptance said much about ebbing faculty passions. No less important, the new dean complemented Bok's emphasis on ordered change and global outlook. In part because of his own sensitivity to foreign cultures, in part because of his ability to achieve incremental reform through seemingly endless rounds of bargaining and negotiation, Rosovsky is a pivotal figure in the history of modern Harvard. But he is hardly a typical one. His divergence from the norm only begins with an undergraduate degree from William and Mary.

The son of Russian Jews—his grandmother liked to tell stories of Napoleon's retreat from Moscow and his father was a judge in the short-lived regime of Alexander Kerensky—Rosovsky was born in September 1927 in Danzig (now Gdansk), Poland. To avoid Nazi persecution, the family moved first to Brussels, then to France. In May 1940, the Rosovskys walked down a gangplank in Hoboken, New Jersey. Within two years, Henry was playing touch football at the Cherry Lawn School in Darien, Connecticut. Next came William and Mary, followed by a stint in the Army's Counter Intelligence Corps, G.I. Bill graduate schooling in economics at Harvard, and military service in Korea. In 1952, Rosovsky returned to Harvard, where he was elected to membership in Lowell's Society of Fellows.

After his 1956 marriage, Rosovsky went to Tokyo to study Japan's economic recovery and Asia in general. He was a full professor of economics at Berkeley in the mid-Sixties when the student rebellion erupted there, and he had no trouble accepting an offer from Harvard when his west coast colleagues seemed willing to abandon academic principles,

principles extremely important to the mind of a global wanderer descended from the White Russian village of Rosovo and endowed with memories of Fascist persecution.[16]

Within a year of his appointment as dean of Arts and Sciences, Rosovsky submitted a balanced budget, the faculty's first since 1970. Shortly thereafter, he released a twenty-two page letter summarizing the dismal state of undergraduate education at Harvard and soliciting ideas for its renovation. Reminding his colleagues of the tremendous growth that had occurred since 1945, he drew a picture of liberty become license. Since the early Fifties, he noted, the number of faculty members had multiplied seven times as fast as had Harvard undergraduates. But the proportion of courses with undergraduate enrollment had been reduced by more than one-fourth. Graduate students were taking the place of senior faculty in large lecture courses and tutorials alike.[17]

The real crisis, Rosovsky said, was a malaise among educators who didn't know their own fundamental beliefs about general education. "At the moment," he wrote, "to be an educated man or woman doesn't mean anything." This was hardly an exaggeration, given Harvard's Chinese menu of 2600 course offerings, and slackened standards that permitted credit for students evaluating the nutritional content of their own diets (not to mention "Auto Mechanics," "Scuba Diving," and "Photo Essay on Mexico"). In the late Seventies, a minor scandal ensued from the revelation that Harvard had given academic standing to twenty-two students studying the multiflex offense as taught by its football quarterback.[18]

Rosovsky's appeal to his colleagues encouraged other colleges, including Amherst, Middlebury, Cornell, and Stanford, where administrators were likewise trying to redefine the meaning of undergraduate education. In the words of Johns Hopkins president Steven Miller, "We're turning out highly technical, highly skilled people who are literally barbarians."[19]

By the time Rosovsky began his attempts at reform, Yale and Princeton were already embarked on ill-fated efforts to revamp undergraduate curricula. Determined to avoid their mistake of entrusting the process to small, blue-ribbon panels, Rosovsky, with a shrewd grasp of faculty politics, aimed to involve as many of his colleagues as possible. In the spring of 1975, he established seven separate task forces and distributed among them responsibility for everything from admissions policy to the quality of life in the Houses. It quickly became apparent, however, that the heart of Rosovsky's effort was in an eleven-member group chaired by government professor James Q. Wilson and charged with curricular reform.

In his own pursuit of academic essentials, Rosovsky forsook the pattern of Conant's search thirty years earlier for a coherent national culture. In contrast to Paul Buck's wartime committee, with its preponderance of historians and humanists, Wilson's panel included relatively few of either, while it boasted two undergraduates. In another major departure from Conant's pattern, the panel did not deal with the University's overall mission or its historic role as America's educational trendsetter. In fact, at the outset, it couldn't even agree on a statement of principles. Some urged an early focus on goals, to be followed by the means to achieve them. Wilson advised his colleagues to reverse the process, and to let others infer Harvard's educational objectives from the changes it made. With memories of April 1969 still fresh, "any statement regarding Harvard's responsibility to the world would have so divided us that we would never have gotten to the main issue at hand," Wilson said. So, he and his colleagues embarked on a search to identify the several kinds of learning which ought to be the property of a Harvard man or woman. If these methods, or modes of inquiry, could be isolated, then the next step—designing courses to inculcate them—would follow.[20]

Phyllis Keller, an associate dean who served as the administration's representative on the Wilson task force, summed up the underlying change of outlook surrounding Harvard's latest attempt at threshing intellectual straw in her book *Getting at the Core:*

> The social and intellectual atmosphere of the 1970s fostered a concern not with survival but with the quality of life in a democratic society. Rosovsky was part of a self-confident postwar generation of scholars who took the durability of democratic institutions for granted. They had found ample opportunity to develop their talents, had been tested by meritocratic standards, and had won recognition almost beyond their expectations. What they feared was not the loss of democracy but its tendency to slide to a lowest common denominator. In a sense, Rosovsky wanted to build quality control into the system of education. Thus his emphasis was on the cultivation of the individual more than on the needs of society.[21]

The initial report of Wilson's group condemned the proliferation of undergraduate courses, while at the same time warning that "if the requirements [of the new curriculum] are too precise and the courses that meet these requirements too few, it becomes difficult to recruit faculty to teach the essential courses." If an alternative to the old-fashioned survey course that had evolved under Conant's General Education could be found, Wilson would embrace it. As for course content, "The substantive problems addressed might be narrowly chosen as long as the meth-

ods employed were fully elaborated." Fittingly, a professor of government
was overseeing a highly political process.

In defining common requirements, everything depended on how the
question was phrased. If asked which bodies of knowledge were more or
less important, the faculty almost surely would split.

> There are simply too many facts, too many theories, too many
> subjects, too many specializations [Wilson's report noted] to
> permit arranging all knowledge into an acceptable hierarchy.
> But if the faculty is asked instead what intellectual skills, what
> distinctive ways of thinking, are identifiable and important, it
> is not clear that either the "knowledge explosion" or the size of
> the faculty has made that question unanswerable.[22]

Here lay the core of the Core, with its emphasis on analysis to the
exclusion of synthesis, and its embrace of specialization and methods common to graduate instruction. To Conant's contemporaries, talk of a
knowledge explosion was a smokescreen for the intellectual equivalent
of junk mail. Among the basic Redbook courses was Samuel Beer's
"Western Thought and Institutions." When Beer retired in 1978, no one
stepped forward to continue his review of Anglo-Saxon society, the Puritan Revolution, Bismarckian Germany, and philosophy from Aquinas to
Marx. Instead, the new Core offered "Nationalism, Religion and Politics
in Central Eurasia," "Black Literary Movements of the Early 20th Century," and "Moral Reasoning 19," "a careful analysis of . . . the writings of Moses Maimonides, influential twelfth century Jewish philosopher."[23]

Academic politicians, it seemed, were as wedded to the pork barrel
as their counterparts in Washington. As a result, the process by which the
faculty accepted the Core was compared to the route a rivers-and-harbor
bill follows through Congress. First, Wilson's report was amended by
historian Bernard Bailyn, who reduced its eight proposed areas of concentration to five, forestalled a humanists' revolt over inadequate commitment to foreign languages, and placated natural scientists who were
upset over what they deemed a "public policy" bias built into the program by political scientist Wilson. Then it was Bailyn's turn to be attacked for overemphasizing the historical perspective. Nevertheless, Rosovsky got the go-ahead he wanted when the faculty, in May 1977,
approved curriculum reform in principle, and directed its dean to proceed.[24]

At this point an unforeseen factor entered the debate. Late in 1977,
rumors, later verified, circulated that Rosovsky had been offered the pres-

idency of Yale and had rejected it in order to complete what he had started with the Core. Sociologist George Goethels, who calls the final curriculum "a farce," speaks for many of his colleagues: "It got through the faculty of Arts and Sciences because everyone loves Henry." This view was seconded by another professor, who credited the dean's refusal to leave Cambridge as a turning point in the faculty's consideration of the reform. "We felt we owed him something," he explained.[25]

And what of the president's role during all this academic logrolling? "I put him on a couple of committees," said Rosovsky afterward, "and he performed very valiantly." In fact, participants recall Bok attending meetings, taking notes in the back of the room, contributing mostly by his presence—and his implicit support for what Rosovsky was trying to do. The two men held similar views about the educational process, dating back to a series of long conversations before Bok's inauguration. Now, as senior faculty members put their finishing touches on Wilson's outline, the president and the dean prepared to reap a harvest of goodwill.[26]

Contrary to those who thought of him as Rosovsky's silent partner, Bok was moving to put his own imprint on the emerging program. Never before had society been pressed by so many moral dilemmas, the president told an alumni audience in 1976. Never before had traditional moral arbiters and guides like faith, family, and cultural norms been so lacking in influence. Whether or not ethical standards had declined in the modern world, "most people seem to think that they have, and this belief in itself can erode trust and spread suspicion in ways that sap the willingness to behave morally toward others."[27]

The Wilson task force had proposed that one of the Core's clusters revolve around moral and political philosophy. By the time the plan was presented for final faculty review in the spring of 1978, under Bok's quiet influence this had become Social Analysis and Moral Reasoning, one of five general areas of knowledge which together would comprise eight of the undergraduate's thirty-two courses. (The others were science and mathematics, history, literature and the arts, and foreign languages and cultures.)

Before the Core's final outlines were shaped, Rosovsky again made sure to solidify his political base by inviting over eighty colleagues to assist. In January 1978, the entire faculty received a thirty-five-page summation, accompanied by a letter from the dean promising full debate at two upcoming meetings. Allowing four years in which to phase in the new courses, Rosovsky promised further opportunities for review once they became fully operational in the fall of 1982.

By the time the final proposal was brought to the faculty that

March, interest was running high. Rosovsky said he hadn't seen such a crowd since the time of troubles a decade before. In his opening argument, the dean described the Core as "a modest proposal." Critics thought otherwise. Mathematician William Bossert attacked the proposal as old wine—vinegar, perhaps—in new bottles, a host of nondepartmental courses lacking the rigor of departmental offerings. To Bossert, the curriculum offered a superficial pursuit of educational breadth. Others disputed the need for restrictions on student choice, or questioned the existence of any such thing as an essential core of required knowledge. To many, the very process by which the Core had emerged undermined the case of its proponents. Wilson's eight study areas had shrunk to Bailyn's five. Language requirements had been tossed aside, only to be retrieved. Natural sciences had ridden a roller coaster all their own as had other components. A scent of political expedience could be detected. As Professor Anthony Oettinger noted, "This motion . . . cannot fail to pass; it has become totally content-free."[28]

Early in May 1978, by a vote of 182 to 65, Arts and Sciences voted to replace General Education with the Core Curriculum. Instead of broad survey courses, Harvard would now rely on highly specific replacements in areas as diverse as abstraction in modern art and microbial and molecular biology. In place of Natural Science I and Central Themes in American History, incoming students would opt for "Politics, Mythology, and Art in Bronze Age China" and "Tuberculosis in the 19th Century." Old warhorses gave way to modern hobbyhorses.

The 80-to-100 new courses originally spoken of eventually ballooned to 122. At first the press was slow to grasp what this meant. In the wake of the faculty vote, the *New York Times* described the Core as "a radical departure from established methods of undergraduate education." "Not since 1945," chimed the *Washington Post,* "had the academic world dared to devise a new formula for developing the educated man." To the *Saturday Review,* the Core represented "a quiet revolution."[29]

What it really represented, however, was ratification of the expanding intellectual universe, and the admission that methodology had become the dominant force in a community unable to agree on the relative value of course content. Size alone had dictated many of the changes. When the Redbook was adopted in 1947, Harvard's population included 340 professors in 28 departments. By May 1978, that figure had grown to 733 professors in 54 departments. Those who hoped for greater interdisciplinary studies, and who took heart from broad Core areas like Literature and Arts or Foreign Languages and Cultures, overlooked the fact that the essentially artificial joining of subjects had been done for political reasons, namely, the faculty's belief that five areas of concentration would be less unwieldy than Wilson's original eight.

In determining what was essential to an American citizen in the closing years of the twentieth century, only a minority of the faculty was inclined to look beyond the four walls of its own laboratory or library carrel. In his final report to the faculty, Rosovsky interpreted this from a positive angle. "Broadly stated," he wrote, "the goal of the Core is to encourage a critical appreciation of the major *approaches* to knowledge, so that students may acquire an understanding of what *kinds* of knowledge exist in certain important areas, how such knowledge is *created,* how it is *used,* and *what it might mean* to them personally." (This was a modern variation of what Lawrence Lowell had called "an ability to use information rather than a memory stacked with facts.")

The dean was less frank in some of his public explanations of the new program. In September 1978, he told *People Magazine* that

> There has been a revolution in American society since the Second World War. We have opened up our best schools on a merit basis. . . . The American system does not slam the door on a young person, regardless of class lines. But we face the serious problem of transmitting shared values to students of such varied backgrounds. What's at stake is the restoration of common discourse in which all students can share.[30]

Yet common discourse and shared values were exactly what was missing from the Core. Even the name was a misnomer. Unlike Columbia's venerable program in Contemporary Civilization, or Stanford's much more recent excursion into Western Society, the new Harvard curriculum contained no single course required of every undergraduate. The new course catalog referred to "particular modes of apprehending and articulating experience," but this was unlikely to fuse the splinters of academia, nor would it instill more than passing appreciation for the subject at hand. Proliferation of esoteric courses might keep the faculty happy, because everyone could be content that no one else's specialty was deemed more important than his own. But the deliberate exclusion of broad-based courses like "Introduction to the History of Art" gave the lie to Rosovsky's claims in the mass media that the new Core was meant to forge a latter-day version of Conant's coherent national culture. The Core had evicted the Redbook for the Yellow Pages.

"I don't really think it's crucial for anyone to know anything about Brazilian Indians," declares veteran professor George Homans of the resulting emphasis on esoterica, "even though I've studied Brazilian Indians." On the other hand, "it is very important to be grounded in the Anglo-Saxon constitutional tradition." No less worrisome to Homans, whose Harvard career began as an undergraduate in the fall of 1928, was the tendency to romanticize Third World cultures at the expense of greater powers.[31]

Rosovsky was kept busy denying press accounts that the Core was a Back to Basics movement. He was in danger of becoming a hero to Neanderthals, he remarked at one point. "A liberal education should provide a common core of intellectual experience for all students," the dean told *The New Yorker*. "I'd rather have a doctor who understands pain and love and suffering than a doctor who knows only about the latest drug to come on the market."[32]

Taking Rosovsky at his word, it's still hard to see how his non-core Core would instill the sensitivity of which he speaks. And it's highly questionable if the central idea behind the Core, with its stated ambition to expose students to different kinds of academic methodology, can succeed in the short amount of time allowed each undergraduate. Can a non-scientist gain more than the slightest familiarity with scientific techniques in a single course or two? Can a historian in one semester instruct undergraduates in how to assess the very methods he is teaching? Above all, how much perspective or context exists in courses devoted to Asian monuments or Urdu poetry?

To those encouraged by Harvard's experiment, Rosovsky and Bok had won a major victory over institutional inertia. More than that, they had encouraged the teaching of courses outside one's specialty and had banished flabby distribution requirements which had made undergraduate education the equivalent of filling in a Green Stamp book. Rosovsky himself detected a new sense of excitement in undergraduate classrooms, while Bok pointed to ninety new courses taught by senior faculty. Throughout the University, the president claimed, professors were throwing away their yellow course outlines and starting afresh. Then there was the Core's moral reasoning component, which for Bok was an imaginative answer to the age-old quandary of how a college should approach the instruction of values and moral choice. After initial grumbling, student enthusiasm grew rapidly. Before long, overflow crowds filled Sanders Theater for Moral Reasoning 21. Lotteries were required in such oversubscribed courses as "The American Century" and "Art and Politics in Europe 1660–1820."[33]

Most revealing, however, was Bok's declaration that the process by which the Core was formulated was nearly as important to Harvard as the final product that resulted. It got people thinking seriously about undergraduate education, said Bok, after more than a quarter-century's emphasis on graduate or similarly specialized training. And it infused new energy into a faculty and a university at last breaking away from what one dean called "the touchy-feely school of the Sixties."[34]

Following Harvard's example, other schools moved to reform their curricula. Some, such as the University of North Carolina at Chapel Hill, adopted Harvard's "modes of inquiry" approach. After twenty years of national conflict and confrontation, educators shared the popular desire for reaffirmation of structure and cohesion. In a very real sense, Harvard had made it safe to experiment with this, even if the outcome had as much to do with a reassertion of faculty authority as it did with intellectual advance.[35]

But Bok was the last person to pronounce Harvard's reforms either revolutionary or necessarily applicable elsewhere. "There are no completely new curricula around," he has said. What's more, he believes that the *New York Times* and other media outlets overstressed the impact of the Core on the rest of higher education. "It's hard to find a first-rate college where you don't have the faculty understanding what it's doing and agreeing with it." Citing the fact that 83 percent of his Core courses are taught by tenured faculty is the closest Bok comes to a boast.[36]

It is revealing of Harvard's changed outlook, about itself and its place in the larger scheme of American education, that the Core was fashioned in hopes of achieving institutional coherence, not national. If others wished to profit by the experience, they must do so by observance. There would be no Redbook for them to consult. Nor would there be any single educational spokesman to fill Conant's role in addressing the entire community of scholars. Even if Bok had been so inclined, he did not have the time. In fact, the ink had barely dried on the new course catalogs than Harvard's president was on the road raising money, a third of a billion dollars needed to refurbish the physical side of a university that had just come through the academic equivalent of a heart bypass operation.

*The real power of universities stems from the
force of individual ideas and not from the use
of their portfolios or their purchasing offices.*
                                              —DEREK BOK
                                              May 1979

FEW NOTED IT at the time, but the debate over the Core crystalized Bok's
deepest concerns. It also set the stage for a series of changes in graduate
education. In a 1979 address to Harvard alumni, the president set forth
an agenda. From his own experience and observations, he said, it seemed
clear that the tradition of American pluralism was under serious strain.
The country no longer seemed diverse, just divided. "We read daily of
gray power, gay power, red power, black power; sunbelt and frostbelt;
environmentalists and hard-hats; industry groups, professional groups,
educational groups—all more conscious of their rights; all more aware of
their claims on the rest of society; all more sensitive to the impact of
other groups on their special interests."

The politics of activism, warned Bok, could become the politics of
immobility. What could universities do to combat such trends? A quarter-century earlier, they had supplied specialists in science and engineering, medicine and international affairs. Yet pluralistic America required
leaders, not just experts in their chosen field; it needed those capable of
forging a more harmonious society, and those who would "find better ways
of resolving differences without the constant resort to government assistance."

Before the term was fashionable, Bok declared himself a neocon-
servative. What he was really after, however, was the cohesion that had
been fractured by interest-group politics and the modern broker state. To
this end, he called for academic instruction grounded in ethics, because
ethical choice involved, more than anything else, "an effort to plan out
actions with a careful regard for the legitimate interests of others."
Courses such as economics that involved social analysis encouraged students to perceive connections between different parts of society and to
understand their impact on one another. Foreign cultures were examined
in hopes of detecting historical and social patterns as well as revealing
more clearly the pathway toward social organization and humane values
here at home.

Ideally, ethical instruction would involve interdisciplinary cooperation. For instance, medical students require more than classroom competence to minister to the sick, Bok argued in another context. They must

take into account the social equation involving abortion, euthanasia, and human experimentation. They must also be grounded in the economics of health care, in order to better evaluate the costs and benefits of new technologies and procedures.

More than half a century before Lawrence Lowell had emphasized the need for broad-based education. "But Lowell looked upon breadth and depth as prerequisites for a full life," Bok said. "We see them now as essential ways of reintegrating society so that its separate parts can function more harmoniously together."[37]

These were ambitious plans, even though couched with reservations about the limits imposed on a single institution to carry them out. Harvard's new Kennedy School of Government, which moved into its permanent home in 1978, was in a sense Bok's monument to the concept.

The study of public policy is nearly as old as Harvard. As Thomas Hollis, one of the college's earliest benefactors, wrote in the first years of the eighteenth century, "More books, especially on government, are going for New England. Should these go safe, no principal books on that first subject will be wanting in Harvard College from the days of Moses to these times." Charles Eliot proposed a school of public service in 1907, and had devoted much of his energies to promoting a class of professional experts to guide the nation through its industrial and social coming of age.

In 1966, Harvard had decided to honor John F. Kennedy with a full-fledged school of government. The school would offer master's degrees in public administration and public policy, mid-career programs building upon the work of Conant's Littauer Center, and an Institute of Politics, designed to expose students at all levels to practical politicians as well as academic theorists. Although by the late Seventies 150 public-policy programs were offered by American universities, the Kennedy School represented the most ambitious effort yet to establish public policy as a new professional discipline, on a par with law, business, or medicine.[38]

Influenced by the disappointments of the Sixties, struggling to cope with government's expanded role in the wake of the Great Society, the Kennedy School sought to involve the whole range of Harvard expertise. Utilizing land-use planners from the school of design, health care economists from the medical school, lawyers equipped to deal with administrative law and its impact on public policy, divinity school faculty whose focus was ethics, JFK made up in experimental verve what it lacked in structural discipline. Its Center for Business and Government, which opened in September 1982, focused on public-private partnerships, exposing government executives to managerial techniques successfully applied in the corporate sector.

Critics assumed that Harvard had learned nothing since the Sixties, desiring only to produce a generation of public servants still brighter and better than their predecessors. The Kennedy School was an easy target, with its heavy concentration of analytical courses emphasizing statistics, econometrics, and microeconomics. Jonathan Alter described the school in the March 1983 *Washington Monthly* as quantifying the unquantifiable. Alter found it ironic that *Essence of Decision,* the bible of public-policy education written by the school's dean Graham Allison, was a seminal interpretation of the Cuban missile crisis in which major stress was placed on human behavior instead of scientific models.[39]

Alter's point would be well taken if the Kennedy School featured little more than academic navel-staring. But there was more, enough so that the school soon became an object of open hostility from other faculties. No effort was made to conceal the resentment felt toward Bok himself, whose fundraising pitches invariably stressed JFK at the expense of more established parts of his realm. One senior professor was quoted as saying, "He'll [Bok] start the John F. Kennedy School of Religion next, if somebody doesn't stop him."[40]

Made sensitive to such charges, Bok seemed deliberately to avoid the place. When he did make an appearance at the school, it was not to discuss government policy or JFK's status in Harvard's fractious family, but his own campaign to reform college athletics. His hand was evident anyway, particularly when he transferred the City and Regional Planning program from an already struggling graduate school of design to JFK. Later, Bok created joint professorships between the two schools, an indication of the close ties he hoped to establish among public-policy components throughout the University.

If Bok seemed unusually preoccupied with the Kennedy School, perhaps it was because here as nowhere else at Harvard could he hope to pursue his commitment to ethical instruction and intellectual cross-pollination. No amount of research, whatever its quality, could alone overcome such national problems as cancer, crime, or unemployment. Yet, said Bok, it was hard to imagine any of them being solved without new knowledge. "And since universities are the prime source in our society for advanced training, research, and highly specialized knowledge, they have not only an opportunity but an obligation to devote part of their energies to this task." This was not, as some critics alleged, Harvard telling America yet again how to conduct its affairs. Rather, as alumnus Lansing Lamont said in a 1979 profile of Bok, it was a modern-day version of the seventeenth-century institution's commitment to a learned clergy. Lamont concluded that Bok wanted more than competent specialists; he hoped to produce "an elite of catholically educated public servants."[41]

From a continent away, Clark Kerr overheard rumors that were swirling around the Harvard community in the mid-Seventies, to the effect that Bok wasn't enjoying his job, and hoped to leave it soon. With adoption of the Core in 1978, there was less talk of an impending resignation. "Along about the seventh or eighth year," Bok's friend David Aloian said, "I sensed he was less awed by the office, more confident in his ability to handle it well and provide leadership. He was beginning to know alumni. He was well received in his travels. The Kennedy School took off. He made some good appointments, and then there was Henry and the faculty coming together around the Core. All of these were healing, positive things."[42]

Initially surprised at how much power a Harvard president had, Bok became accustomed to passing on tenured faculty and selecting deans without the provosts or search committees common to other universities. What's more, he remarked, "Harvard has a way of absolutely enveloping you in its affairs, its problems as well as its successes." He had finally put down roots, finding a home which he had every intention of defending against those who believed it politically or intellectually timid. The cosmopolite who preferred soccer to football had become a Saturday afternoon regular at Harvard Stadium and a dutiful participant in each year's varsity dinner, a four-hour marathon.[43]

Swallowing his distaste for academic panhandling, Bok took to the road after 1978 to raise $350 million, having first declared that the proceeds would buttress existing departments, rather than fostering physical expansion. Strengthening the silos, some called it, instead of building new missile defenses. The man who had once doubted his fundraising gifts proved an intrepid salesman, winning appreciative laughter by contrasting arch-rivals Harvard and Texas. The latter's endowment might for the moment be number one, Bok said, but for reasons unlikely to endure. "While theirs rests on oil," he explained, "ours rests on hard work."[44]

But with this newfound confidence came fresh whispers that the president didn't listen as much as he once had. In the spring of 1978, Bok was again confronted by student demonstrators upset over Harvard's refusal to divest stocks in firms doing business in South Africa. A thousand protesters surrounded the president and some followed him to his car. Bok remained mute, a tight-lipped smile on his face, until he spotted a reporter. "It's just another day in the life of a university president," he quipped. But it wasn't only protesting students who voiced frustration over the president's growing taste for centralized decision-making. "A lot of things don't reach the Overseers," complained one member of that body, "until they get in the *New York Times*."[45]

Early in 1978, the *Times* along with other journals devoted extensive coverage to Bok's annual report, a document widely, if facilely, interpreted as a stiff challenge to the prevailing methods of education at his own university's business school. The B School occupied a curious place at Harvard. Its huge endowment was insufficient to mask an intellectual inferiority complex as old as the idea that commerce could be taught on a par with the drama of Molière or Benthamite utilitarianism. For many north of the Charles River, it remained a trade school. In December 1977, *MBA Magazine* had taken a poll of some eighty-five business school deans, the results of which did nothing to bolster confidence in Cambridge: Stanford ranked first, with Harvard and Chicago in a virtual dead heat for second. Add to this a clash of personalities involving Bok and outgoing dean Lawrence Fouraker, and one can readily understand the seismic shock set off by the president's questioning of the school's heavy reliance on the case method of instruction.

Implicit in Bok's criticism was the idea that there was too little attention being paid to moral reasoning as a valid component of corporate planning. This was like calling the Vatican's theology heretical, or faulting the Pentagon as a center of neutralism. Each year, a significant portion of the school's faculty was engaged in developing cases, a fifteen-million-dollar research effort liberally backed by corporate America. The resulting case library (some six thousand strong, which was constantly augmented and updated) formed the core of Harvard's business instruction. It also provided a lucrative sideline because dozens of other schools were willing to pay handsomely to obtain cases with so prestigious a stamp upon them.[46]

While all this raised doubts as to the purity of academic research being conducted there, still more sweeping were Bok's assertions that case instruction itself was hardly suited to teaching sophisticated concepts and analytic techniques. Such defects mattered little, wrote the president, "in an age when the knowledge applicable to business decisions was rudimentary. As the corporate world grows more complex, however, the problem becomes more serious." In writing this, Bok took note of the more eclectic methods being pursued at Stanford, Chicago, Carnegie-Mellon, and MIT.

Others defended the case method as appropriate for a group of students expecting to render managerial judgments at the highest echelon of corporate America. Alumni urged adherence to Harvard's traditional purpose of preparing general managers for senior executive positions—19 percent of the top three executives in Fortune 500 firms were Harvard Business School graduates—and held its methodology far superior to the numbers crunching practiced at Chicago and other schools.

Bok was accused by disgruntled instructors of practicing what one called "a certain amount of intellectual snobbery." Critics of the report, including Dean Fouraker, questioned whether the president had actually visited any business school classes to see the case study method in action.

By the fall of 1980, Fouraker was gone, replaced by a taciturn Canadian named John H. MacArthur. In large part because of his predecessor's fundraising abilities, MacArthur had a solid financial footing from which to tinker with the curriculum. The one thing he would not dispense with was the case method. "The solution," said MacArthur, "is to manage it, not abandon it."

Ironically, the dean of Yale's new School of Management, whose doors had opened at the same time Bok's report was issued, credited Bok's findings with influencing New Haven's course design. Though Bok's credentials as prophet were less apparent in his own backyard, still, by 1980 a number of changes in the business school were underway. These included cuts in the student workload, which had reached nearly ten thousand pages of reading a year, and significant bolstering of ethical instruction. Some things, however, were constant: far more students enrolled in a course called "Power and Influence" than in "Ethical Aspects of Corporate Policy."[47]

While Bok's confrontation with his faculty at the business school smoldered, his relations with the school of public health burst into conflagration. In June 1978, half of the school's professors petitioned the president to remove its dean, Howard Hiatt, a hard-charging, often abrasive reformer whose field of expertise was not in public health issues but in cancer research. The resulting fracas presented a classic battle between Bok and a faculty afflicted with what Hiatt himself called a "yellow fever mentality."

The dean had been chosen by Bok to bring Public Health into closer cooperation with the medical school, while increasing the amount of attention paid to health economics and systems management. Hiatt had also forged links with other fields, including law, economics, business, and environmental sciences. He had shared faculty with the business school, and developed fellowships for journalists and government officials.

None of this pleased researchers devoted primarily to the study and conquest of disease. Their dissatisfaction led to a tense encounter in August 1978. In a style belying his public image as soft-spoken consensus-seeker, Bok admonished Hiatt's critics:

> Whether you happen to agree or not, your dean is widely applauded for making a determined effort to carry out reforms of great promise and significance. . . . Whether you choose to admit it or not, the resignation of the dean will be interpreted by many, many people as a victory for those who oppose substantial reform and a signal that continued change will be exceedingly difficult if not impossible. . . . The most probable result will be the appointment of a safe, comfortable dean with scant prospects for distinguished leadership.[48]

Bok's firm stand had kept Hiatt's job out of immediate jeopardy. But it did nothing to allay faculty discontent. With a forty-million-dollar fund drive imperiled, Bok's interest in medicine outlasted Hiatt's deanship. So did his willingness to challenge the white-coated Old Guard, as the medical school would discover for itself.

Even as the fight at Public Health confirmed the president's growing mastery, other incidents seemed to justify John Dunlop's claim that his friend lacked "that internal New England hardness" possessed by Conant and Pusey. If Hiatt was criticized for dictating too much, Bok's law school dean, James Vorenburg, was faulted for his tolerance of open warfare within his faculty and student body. Vorenburg's nickname was "Sleepy Jim." At his law school, legal instructors first approved and then rejected changes in grading methods which would allow them to count classroom participation in arriving at a final mark. Other controversies revolved around the lack of minority instructors (just two out of seventy in 1982) and the number of outside commitments which diverted professional time that might otherwise be spent with aspiring lawyers.[49]

Law school radicals belonging to a school of thought dubbed "Critical Legal Studies," and headed by a flamboyant instructor named Duncan Kennedy, vowed, in Kennedy's words, to "flatten hierarchies" and expose law students to Marxist thought. For his part, Kennedy proposed sweeping changes at the school, among them admission by lottery and equal pay for academic and nonacademic staff members. Some reforms were launched, following an in-house report minimizing the case study method enshrined at the law school since Christopher Columbus Langdell had introduced it in the 1870s. Vorenburg also took steps toward more interdisciplinary reliance and a greater use of computers.[50]

In the fall of 1982, the school was back in the news when black students denounced a course on race and legal issues being taught in part by a white civil rights lawyer. According to the Black Law Student Association and the Third World Coalition, the instructor, Jack Greenberg, should not teach the course because of his color and his refusal to resign as director of the NAACP Legal Defense and Education Fund. The *New York Times* declared, "There is little point to pride if its price is ignorance." Columnist Carl Rowan, himself black, denounced what he called "racist, anti-intellectual, anti-civil-rights behavior from youngsters who would not be at Harvard except that millions of Americans of all races fought courageously for generations against racism, know-nothing politics and the elitists who argued that educational and constitutional safeguards should go only to a privileged few." Black professor of government Martin Kilson claimed that the law school deserved better than "the banal ethnocentrism rampant among members of the Harvard Black Law Students Association."[51]

Over the next two years unrest continued at the law school. Students demanded input into admissions and faculty appointments. They reiterated complaints about professors who were more engaged by outside consulting than by classroom instruction. In the spring of 1984, there was a building takeover, and a polarized faculty found itself the object of widespread public scrutiny and more than a little ridicule. As one of Bok's associates said, "Derek must be going through the tortures of the damned." Yet the president steadfastly refused to impose any solution, or to publicly characterize the turmoil engulfing his former bailiwick. As Bok saw it, there was an important difference between the Public Health controversy and the one at the law school. The former, which was a formal challenge to his dean, demanded an unequivocal show of support, while the latter revolved primarily around internal faculty relationships.[52]

Bok was less inclined to adopt a hands-off attitude when it came to other parts of his realm. In the spring of 1980, a dispute arose over the prospective appointment of University of Chicago economist Arnold Harberger as head of the Harvard Institute for International Development. Harberger became an object of student and faculty resentment because of his earlier work with the Central Bank of Chile. "Oh, you mean the Beast of Patagonia," Harberger cracked when asked about his Chilean connection. Bok considered it no laughing matter, but rather an issue of academic freedom.[53]

Bok's Open Letter that followed constituted Harvard's first full discussion of the topic since the McCarthy era. Disqualifying candidates because of politics or past behavior, Bok said, would surely deny the University able scholars. "Brilliant and creative people are sometimes eccentric or even irresponsible." Yet these traits were easily outweighed by potential contributions in publishing and teaching. Moreover, Bok wrote, it had taken years of effort to persuade the public that ideological judgments had no place in academia. Neither Marxists nor foes of abortion nor proponents of intelligence heritability should be excluded on political grounds.

Of course, he acknowledged, there might be extreme cases such as a proponent of religious bigotry who also happened to be a first-rate literary critic or an apologist for terrorism who was also a world-famous nuclear physicist. But unlikely as they were, such instances ought not be used to bar from the community those whose presence was merely distasteful. "Surely members of a university should be willing on occasion to tolerate the presence of someone whose opinions they abhor," Bok concluded, "rather than run the risk of excluding able professors, arousing bitter controversies, weakening our most precious bulwarks against outside political interference, and making ideological or doctrinal judgments that could eventually prove to be neither principled nor wise."[54] As it turned out, Harberger decided not to take the job.

Another Bok stand that same year paid off more immediately. A committee chaired by Memorial Church's Peter Gomes proposed that instead of a separate Third World Center the University establish a foundation to expand social interaction and to provide a regular forum for students and faculty members of all races to attack campus divisions. This followed a study of race relations at Harvard by Archie Epps, now Dean of Students, which endorsed the popular view that minority undergraduates were "separatist in orientation and . . . isolated from the college mainstream."[55] Bok wrote an Open Letter promising support for the foundation and reiterating his endorsement of affirmative action. Although Gomes's recommendations were not widely popular in Harvard's black community, and the preacher had long been a thorn in the president's side, he stood firm for the Harvard Foundation, which gradually gathered momentum and a constituency during the five years that followed.[56]

In 1982 the president devised another fresh approach to the issue of institutional leadership. At that year's Commencement, he quoted a column by James Reston on the nuclear debate and then invited five of Harvard's experts to prepare what he called "an objective account of the basic facts about nuclear arms control." The result, *Living With Nuclear Weapons*, was neither as neutral nor as purely analytical as the president may have intended. Although the book came out against the B-1 bomber, it also opposed both a full nuclear freeze and George Kennan's idea of a 50 percent reduction in the U.S. missile stockpile. Not surprisingly for a document produced by committee, the final text struck some as—in the words of co-author Stanley Hoffman—"wishy-washy." Yet it was unequivocal in assuming a world balanced by mutual deterrence.[52]

By the time Harvard published *Living With Nuclear Weapons* in the spring of 1983, Bok had written a book of his own, entitled *Beyond the Ivory Tower: Social Responsibilities of the Modern University*. The author's defense of institutional autonomy was generally well received, as was his warning against the Sixties' reflexive celebration of the academic service center, the multiversity. Bok's cautious approach to technological innovation and the social responsibilities of researchers moved Robert Wood, his old antagonist in the Kennedy Library controversy from the University of Massachusetts, to quote McGeorge Bundy: "Gray is the color of the truth."

Others questioned Bok's broader vision of the University and the leadership responsibilities assigned to its president. Pleased by the diversity found among America's three thousand institutions of higher learning, Bok was willing to accept what he called "genial anarchy" as the inevitable price of departmental rule. Presidents, he declared, have "an important but distinctly limited role" to play. As Wood said, Bok dealt with the outside world as he might with a purple elephant—very carefully.[58]

In August 1983, Bok tackled the Solomon Amendment, Congress's insistence that young men who had failed to register for the draft not receive federal student aid funds. After first expressing doubts about the constitutionality of such a ban, and questioning its fairness on economic grounds, Bok decided not to compensate for lost federal assistance with scholarship funds or to subsidize loans and employment. Instead, he invited students who were defying the statute to apply for campus jobs outside the range of federal work-study funds, and offered them loans at regular rates of interest.

The president explained his decision by pointing out that there were a variety of reasons why students might choose to refuse federal aid, "such as a belief that government grants are the tainted fruit of an unjust system of taxation." If the University considered the merits of every such claim, it would be embroiled in an endless round of political position-taking, alienating both students and alumni opposed to the use of tuition and donations to support principles with which they took exception.

In addressing the argument that the restriction on aid unfairly penalized needy students, Bok wrote, "It is hardly clear that because the government does not subsidize everyone, it cannot refuse to subsidize those who disobey its laws." In the next breath, he softened this with some carefully weighed words. A university had a certain relationship to its students, he said. "They may not be family members, but they are not strangers either." Although he and other officials might not approve of the choices they made, he was not willing to eject them or deny them the means with which to pursue their studies. "Those who fail to register will pay a price for their convictions. But they are still our students. We may not agree with them in resisting the law nor wish to shield them from the consequences of their acts. But we surely have an interest in enabling them to finish the education for which they came to us in the first place." This was vintage Bok: a gesture and an offering for everyone, conveyed in the sensitive, almost tormented words of a man who saw many sides of an issue.[59]

He showed these qualities again when Secretary of Defense Caspar Weinberger was nearly shouted down at a law school appearance in November 1983. Bok said at the next meeting of his faculty council that something had to be done. Others agreed that discipline should be meted out by an authority with greater credibility than the Administrative Board. But two council members disagreed. Just because Weinberger was the object of a fusillade of eggs, tomatoes, ketchup, and epithets from members of the Spartacus Youth League, they said, there was no justification for expulsion or even a public statement of outrage.[60]

A year passed before Bok expressed an official reaction to the Weinberger affair. In general, "temporary booing or cheering at a public speech is not considered an infringement of free speech. Sustained noise does represent an interference if it lasts long enough or is repeated often enough to interfere with the orderly expression of ideas or to prevent a significant segment of the audience from hearing the speaker." Free speech as a principle, it would appear, could be tested by stopwatch or decibel level.[61]

"People in my position," Bok has said, "especially those who have been in office for some time, have a responsibility to speak as cogently and effectively as we can. Whether anyone is listening, we have no way of knowing." But what of the president's reluctance to use the Harvard pulpit? "It's not Derek worrying about the personal risk," an intimate revealed, "but he doesn't want to be the person who causes Harvard trouble."[62]

As a highly contemporary theory of leadership, Bok's approach suggests how much frustration Eliot or Conant might feel in today's world. Would either man have responded as Bok did to a June 1984 column in which Ann Landers noted that the University of Colorado's regents had voted to permit professional note-takers at the discretion of individual instructors to sell classroom notes? Landers sought the opinion of leading educators and printed responses from Duke's Terry Sanford ("totally unacceptable"), Williams's John W. Chandler ("a travesty on the true nature of education"), Notre Dame's Reverend Theodore Hesburgh ("part of the current nuttiness and lack of standards that dilutes higher education to the point of idiocy"), and the president of Harvard. Bok's reply: "Without knowing more of the facts, I would have thought that the proper course would be to ban professional note-taking. It is conceivable that there are special considerations not mentioned in the brief article. Having often been criticized by trigger-happy people who did not know all the facts, I would not wish to pass judgment on this situation."[63]

Bok has been more outspoken in prodding his own institution to stay ahead of intellectual trends. Instead of Pusey's line-item annual reports, his are sweeping overviews of individual schools and disciplines. Bok's 1983 assessment of his own profession was typical. "The blunt, inexcusable fact is that this nation, which prides itself on efficiency and justice, has developed a legal system that is the most expensive in the world, yet cannot manage to protect the rights of most of its citizens."[64]

The former law school dean did not hesitate to point a finger of blame at his fellow legal educators who, he claimed, were encouraging law students to place the interests of clients ahead of those of society. At the same time, the profession itself was siphoning off too many of the best minds, at the expense of teaching, business, and engineering. The law was guilty, he wrote, of "a massive diversion of exceptional talent into pursuits that often add little to the growth of the economy, the pursuit of culture or the enhancement of the human spirit."

Predictably, Bok's assault generated widespread media attention. The University's news office was swamped with requests for interviews from the New York Times, the MacNeil-Lehrer Report, the Boston Globe, and others. Bok refused them all, and denied that his critique was a national document at all. He insisted that it was strictly an internal report. No one who knew Bok well could have been surprised. As dean of the law school, he had once read two hundred of G. Harrold Carswell's judicial opinions before publicly opposing Richard Nixon's unsuccessful Supreme Court nominee. Much later, in preparing a presidential report on the state of American medicine, he delved into a formidable stack of medical books and articles. Such meticulous attention to detail inspired John Dunlop to comment that Bok worked harder at his job than almost any other university president around. But it also provided ammunition to

those who professed ignorance as to what larger goals the president had
in mind. And it reinforced his popular image as an intellectual bricklayer
rather than an architect in the mold of Charles Eliot or James Conant.[65]

Visitors to the president's office in the early Eighties found a relaxed, confident man who sometimes liked to remove his shoes and throw
one leg over the arm of his chair while chatting informally. His relations
with the *Crimson* remained frosty, and he was as exasperated as ever
when, in the words of one student reporter, "you try to get the conversation to stupid things" like John Harvard's birthday or the subject matter
of the president's dreams.[66]

With those less inclined to probe his psyche, Bok could lower his
guard. After dinner in Lowell's old mansion at 17 Quincy Street, he was
apt to put his feet up on a Chippendale bench and swap stories. He was
a vastly more comfortable figure in the summer of 1984 than when the
author first interviewed him nine years earlier. This time, no News Office
official sat in on the discussion. Bok roamed widely across his own Harvard experiences, detouring from time to time to put an especially candid
statement off the record. When told at the close of one conversation how
dramatically changed the mood in his corner office appeared, Bok smiled
and remarked that after fourteen years, he had undoubtedly made sufficient mistakes so as not to worry about one or two more.[67]

He would never enjoy the spotlight. Yet Bok had become willing
to appear in it, at least occasionally, to promote worthy causes. In the
spring of 1984, he wrote a strong argument on behalf of affirmative action for *The New Republic*. A few weeks later, he appeared on a network newscast to give his support for dramatic reform of college athletics.
With basketball scandals at Tulane and elsewhere, Bok and other college
presidents began to make headway in their campaign to take the admissions process back from athletic directors, and to raise the minimum standards for college entrance and graduation.

After more than ten years on the job, Bok had achieved substantial
progress toward his educational objectives, and his financial goals as
well. The $250 million Harvard Campaign became a $350 million one,
and the University's endowment flirted with the two billion dollar figure.
Bok himself was increasingly recognized as an educational statesman. In
a 1985 *U.S. News and World Report* survey of influential Americans,
he ranked twentieth among non-public officeholders, behind Michael
Jackson and Roone Arledge but ahead of every other college president.

Bok's school of education has come through rocky times and developed a new curriculum to train academic administrators at the state

and municipal level. Medicine and Public Health are focusing attention on the staggering costs of health care, and strengthening their own preventive efforts in toxicology, nutrition, and environmental health. There is the New Pathway program for aspiring doctors, under which a small group of students pursue unconventional studies by means of problem-based learning methods rather than in traditional lectures. The law school is moving to broaden student exposure to a world beyond the corporate firm by providing financial support for those considering internships and careers in public service, and arranging lectures and discussions on civil rights and racially motivated violence through its Center for Criminal Justice.

Throughout the University, Bok has brought about a heightened awareness of public policy and ethics. "By the time he's through," says A. Michael Spence, the forty-year-old economist who in June 1984 succeeded Rosovsky as dean of the faculty, "he will have gotten moral reasoning into every school at Harvard." Given this achievement, it is ironic that for much of the public, and more of the press, Bok may be remembered as the president who blocked divestiture of Harvard stock in firms doing business in South Africa.[68]

The seeds of University policy on the divestiture issue were planted in the Austin Report, drawn up in January 1971 at Nathan Pusey's request. "Before anything else," it declared, a university was a "center of free inquiry" and not an institution for social change. It must remain neutral, except in those extraordinary instances "where there is no longer room for argument among people who accept our basic socio-economic-political system." In his book *Beyond the Ivory Tower,* Bok approvingly quoted the late Fritz Machlup, the Princetonian who had insisted that "The institution or its faculty as a body has no brain and no heart, and should have no mouth either. . . ."

Yet for those enraged by the apartheid system in South Africa and the 350 American firms doing business in that country, the institution could hardly exist without a conscience. Bok acknowledged as much with his own attempt at constructive engagement. In August 1979, he summoned presidents from seven eastern colleges and proposed an intercollegiate scholarship program for black Africans—this just weeks after bestowing an honorary degree on Bishop Desmond Tutu, secretary-general of the South African Council of Churches and the most prominent opponent of the Pretoria government's officially sponsored racism.

But Bok and the Corporation were unalterably opposed to divesting Harvard's stock holdings in South African firms, assets whose value fluctuated between $400 million and nearly $600 million. They argued that in settling for divestiture the University would be trading away its leverage on companies employing South Africans, in return for a temporary emotional lift. An inappropriate use of resources entrusted to academic purposes, such a gesture would also break down the University's insulation from outside pressures to conform.[69]

Bok put forth this argument in greater detail in one of his Open Letters in the spring of 1979. He distinguished between fresh investment in companies doing business primarily in South Africa and those firms incidentally engaged there. Because American holdings in South Africa amounted to barely one percent of U.S. direct investment abroad and universities exercised even less influence in corporate councils, Bok questioned whether so drastic an action as total divestiture would help or hurt South African blacks. He quoted black leaders on both sides of the issue to strengthen his case that divestiture would produce hardships far greater than the moral satisfaction likely to accrue to Americans washing their hands of a dirty business.[70]

Repeatedly, Bok has expressed his willingness to enter the debate over South Africa. Yet for student activists whose chosen forum is the streets—or the grassy strip surrounding Massachusetts Hall—the president's lawyerly briefs have not sufficed. At a law school forum called to discuss changes in legal education, the president was bearded by forty protesters demanding that he schedule another public discussion of University policy toward the Pretoria regime. "There are a great many injustices in the world," Bok responded, "and picking among them is not easy."

When Brandeis and Boston Universities decided to selectively divest their holdings, Bok repeated his stand. "We're not going to make decisions on moral issues simply to avoid arguments and picket lines." Clearly uncomfortable with the issue, when confronted by it at faculty meetings in 1979 and again in 1982 Bok was thrown off balance. The man who proposed to communicate his own moral intensity through the written word was unprepared when Stanley Hoffman asked to know whether there were *any* circumstances under which Harvard might rid itself of South African stock.[71]

Along with others who share his views, Bok has preferred to talk about Harvard's support of the Sullivan Principles, guidelines for U.S. investment drawn up by a black Philadelphia minister in 1977 and since approved by more than one hundred firms who promised to desegregate their South African workplaces, provide equal pay for equal work, enhance job training opportunities, increase the number of nonwhite managers, and improve housing and schooling for the black majority.

Late in 1984, with interest in the issue again building, the private sector began promising to actively influence other companies in South Africa to support an end to apartheid laws and to promote greater mobility for black workers. By then, nearly fifty universities had sold their holdings in U.S. firms engaged in South African operations. Massachusetts and other state governments had done so, as had numerous cities and pension funds. Harvard students established an alternative Endowment for Divestiture that would siphon off money graduating seniors might otherwise donate to the regular class gift.

Bok tried to demonstrate other ways in which his University opposed apartheid. Harvard made grants to nonwhite South Africans to pursue graduate studies in Cambridge. (The president himself chaired a national program bringing eighty to ninety such students to the United States each fall.) Harvard urged numerous companies in which it held stock to comply with the Sullivan Principles. And when Baker International, a California producer of mining and drilling equipment, refused to supply information regarding its South African activities, Harvard divested its 60,000 shares of Baker stock. Still, Bok viewed this as but a single failure of persuasion, not a change in basic policy.

Meanwhile, pressure continued to mount: the Harvard Board of Ministry and a group of law school professors joined Bok's own Advisory Committee on Shareholder Responsibility which, in May 1984, for the first time called on the University to divest. The Corporation, unsurprisingly, rejected the counsel.

A *Crimson* poll in the spring of 1985 turned up contradictory evidence of student opinion. Even as thousands crowded the Yard to hear the Reverend Jesse Jackson excoriate the president, 14 percent said that Harvard should not sell any of its South African stock, 34 percent replied it should sell some (based on ethical or other considerations), and 19 percent responded "don't know." Thus, for all the sound and fury, just one-third of the students interviewed by the *Crimson*—itself staunchly pro-divestiture—supported Jackson's demand that Harvard immediately sever all commercial ties with the government in Pretoria.[72]

This did not diminish the size of the crowd assembled to hear Jackson denounce those who "preach moralism by day and get economic gratification by night." Nor did it prevent demonstrators from blockading Massachusetts Hall (forcing Bok once again to take shelter, this time at the Kennedy School), or from staging a one-day occupation of the Corporation's headquarters at 17 Quincy Street, or from holding a South African diplomat invited to address the Conservative Club prisoner at Lowell House—the first such breach of decorum since Dow Chemical's recruiter was entrapped at the height of the Vietnam War.[73]

From an office ringed by picketers, Bok tried to defuse the issue. He wrote a letter endorsing proposed economic sanctions against the white minority government, and later testified in Washington in support of a bill embodying such measures that had been introduced by Senator Edward Kennedy. But Bok added that his views were strictly his own; Harvard would continue to refrain from taking institutional positions. It would also hold on to its stock.[74]

What demonstrators hoped to achieve was largely undercut when the ACSR reversed its earlier stand, refused to hold an open meeting on the issue, and all but threw in the towel before an immovable president and Corporation. In Washington, Bok called the Reagan Administration's policy of constructive engagement inadequate. He criticized official policy as contributing to repression and human suffering, yet still made no mention of plans by his own University to divest any of its holdings.

Bok may well be right in arguing for institutional neutrality as the necessary price of academic freedom. Still, his reluctance to carry his cause beyond official pronouncements and occasional forced confrontations seemed to confirm his stance as one whose conscience was held hostage to economic considerations. The *Crimson* chose its words carefully when it labeled the president a first-rate lawyer—"and a third-rate leader."[75]

In a 1983 interview with *U.S. News and World Report,* Bok had acknowledged that any effort to teach students about ethical values would produce more cynicism than enlightenment, "if the institutions themselves are perceived to be ethically careless or insensitive." At the same time, he reiterated his longstanding opposition to taking institutional positions on public questions of the day. He explained that to bridge the gap, Harvard and other universities should "take the time to explain to students our attitudes on these questions. And when we disagree with the students, we should explain the grounds of disagreement with sufficient care so that any sensible person would recognize that moral questions have not been cavalierly tossed aside, ignored or subordinated to the selfish interests of the university."[76]

Bok felt that he had met that test. Having pondered the issue from all angles and hammered out a position consistent with his personal values, the president held to his case with an obstinacy—or courage—reminiscent of Nathan Pusey.

With the passage of time, Bok and Pusey seemed to have more in common, a convergence dramatized in the spring of 1979 when they occupied the same platform at the dedication of Harvard's newest library, a flat, largely underground structure as austere and understated as the man it honored. The Pusey Library, said Bok, symbolized his predecessor's personal willingness to "sacrifice grandeur and visibility" if it would advance the University's cause. The same words might be applied to Bok himself.

As Harvard approached her 350th anniversary, a favorite guessing game revolved around Bok's future. It was a form of parlor entertainment, complicated by Henry Rosovsky's appointment in October 1985 to the Corporation, the first Harvard professor to join the governing board in more than a century. This move could be interpreted as foreshadowing Bok's own departure (on the theory that Rosovsky, of all people, would not have to be educated as to the University's needs or the presidential candidates best equipped to satisfy them). A more Machiavellian school of thought held that with Rosovsky at his side, Bok just might decide to stay on longer, or that it might all be part of an effort to elevate Rosovsky himself to the presidency, his age (fifty-seven) notwithstanding. Although it was widely assumed that Bok might choose to depart in a blaze of glory, having stashed away $358 million as Harvard's birthday present to itself, it was difficult to know just where else he would be happy. A foundation job would almost certainly bore him. The Supreme Court seat he was said to desire was all but ruled out by Ronald Reagan's 1984 reelection. More likely, when he leaves, he will return to the law school, where he retains a tenured professorship and where he might supplement his teaching with writing, and the reflections of a not-so-elder statesman.[77]

Trying to assess a sitting president's performance is a little like examining Mars through a microscope. In Bok's case, it's made harder still because of the jealous privacy with which the man surrounds himself and his decisions. Yet in guarding his true self from public scrutiny, he may have succeeded too well. For there are few in Bok's Harvard, despite their personal admiration for this immensely civilized figure, who profess to see a theme to his presidency. I think otherwise. I think that Harvard in 1986 can celebrate a return to institutional integration—as much as any such institution can integrate its purposes—and a restoration of standards that were all but washed away in the convulsive Sixties. The ground will have been laid for another, different kind of leader, a man (is Harvard yet ready for a woman?) more willing to share his views with an America more inclined to listen.

Until then, the oldest university in the land can thank its twenty-fifth president for the most systematic questioning of graduate education since Charles Eliot virtually reinvented professional schooling a century ago. It can take lessons from the political process by which the Core Curriculum emerged. It can appreciate the period of reconstruction and relative calm, much as Americans today are belatedly thankful for Dwight Eisenhower's reassuring interlude.

When asked his intentions about life after Massachusetts Hall, Bok is characteristically unrevealing. "You'll wake up one day and I'll be gone." As a man of his word, he no doubt means it. History, however, is unlikely to let him off the hook so easily.[78]

Source Notes
and Acknowledgments

Of all literary artists, historians and biographers should be most anxious to cultivate humility. For they, far more than any novelist, playwright, or poet, must rely on other sources to supply them with facts and sharpen their judgments. I have been especially fortunate in this regard. From Derek Bok and Nathan Pusey, to the last six men who have served Harvard as dean of her faculty of Arts and Sciences, to dozens of Corporation members, Overseers, House masters, deans, professors, student leaders, and journalists, virtually everyone whom I have asked to speak with has readily complied. Many were generous with their time as well as their recollections of life in Cambridge dating back to the early years of this century.

This is particularly important since the University's strict fifty-year rule precludes usage of any recent documentary materials contained in Harvard's voluminous archives. To overcome that obstacle, I set off to track down and interview as many participants in the last half-century of Harvard's development as I could find. Ultimately, they numbered more than one hundred, and their memories comprise an invaluable part of the resulting manuscript.

I did not stop there. Besides those papers closed to public scrutiny under the fifty-year rule, the Harvard University Archives contain a vast amount of material which is open. Thanks to Harley P. Holden and his staff, I was able to wade through a fair amount, including collections dealing with Charles Eliot and Lawrence Lowell, alumni publications dating to Eliot's presidency, several decades' worth of the *Harvard Crimson,* and large files compiled during the tumultuous years of the late 1960s, when Harvard in common with other American universities went through a time of severe internal testing.

In addition, I was able to ferret several thousand pages of useful material out of the Library of Congress, and other collections at the John F. Kennedy Library in Boston and the Columbia Oral History Collection in New York. I am grateful to the staffs of all these institutions, and to countless other individuals who have, over the years, taken an interest in my work and contributed fragments for inclusion in it.

Observing the workings of modern Harvard is a bit like watching an octopus performing a highwire act. From the start, the challenge I confronted was to find a structure and narrative technique which would explain the institution for those who had never set foot in Cambridge without so broadening the focus as to lose the attention of the roughly quarter-million Harvard alumni.

This same balancing act extends to the identification of sources. Some of those with whom I spoke requested that they not be identified by name. Wherever possible, I have identified my sources within the text itself, thus cutting back on the need for notes in an already lengthy work. While it is impossible to mention everyone who provided assistance, several persons deserve to be singled out. The most important include President Derek Bok, who took time from an overcrowded schedule to grant two extensive interviews; his predecessor Nathan Pusey; deans Henry Rosovsky, John Dunlop, Franklin Ford, McGeorge Bundy, Edward Mason, and the incumbent dean of Arts and Sciences, A. Michael Spence; legendary figures from recent Harvard history such as John Finley, Thomas Perkins, George Homans, and Mason Hammond; and members of the Harvard Corporation going back to William Marbury (whose intimate knowledge of Harvard affairs is rooted in conversations with his own predecessors from Lawrence Lowell's governing boards).

This book could not have achieved any of its objectives without the warm support of James Conant's family, specifically his widow Grace, son Theodore, and daughter-in-law Helen. They made it possible for me to see Conant's personal papers and diaries, with their revealing and sometimes surprising accounts of campus life in the historic years before, during, and just after the Second World War.

While I may appear to have adopted a rather bemused attitude toward some of the editorial judgments made by the *Harvard Crimson* in years gone by, I should also make plain my debt to several generations of *Crimson* reporters and editors. Their publication, arguably the finest college newspaper in the country, is an indispensable source for chroniclers of twentieth-century Harvard. The same is true of *Harvard Magazine* under its perceptive and thoughtful editor, John T. Bethell, and its various forerunners which have informed or angered alumni since the time of President Eliot.

The Harvard University News Office, under Deane Lord and Dave Rosen, was especially helpful in enabling me to trace the pattern of Derek Bok's presidency as it has unfolded in numerous accounts by journalists inside and outside of Cambridge. Cathy Abrahamson devoted much time and energy toward finding and copying virtually every article concerning Harvard and its presidents to have appeared in American periodicals since 1930. Kay Luther did an expert job of typing the manuscript through its many permutations.

It is customary for any author at this point to express gratitude toward his editors. In my own case, the feeling is much more than ritualistic. There is hardly a page which does not in some way bear the stamp of Alice Mayhew and her colleagues Henry Ferris and Veronica Johnson. As a result of their work, the final text is far closer to the concision and simplicity which any writer should strive for, and which any New Englander will readily recognize as the region's stylistic calling card. My literary agent, Rafe Sagalyn, has proved once again both friend and counsel. And during those inevitable moments when I despaired of explaining General Education to my own satisfaction, or understanding the five remarkable captains who have guided Harvard along the river of time which begins in the headwaters of the Civil War, I was blessed with the support and encouragement of friends like Steve and Fern Chapman, Ed and Jane Chefey, Michael and Kay Epperson, Bob and Cathy Rapp. The same goes for my associates in Senator Pete Wilson's office, above all, Bob White, Otto Bos, Lynda Royster, Desrie Haacke, and Curt Erixon.

The words on my dedication page bear witness to, without fully conveying, the contribution of two extraordinary persons, without whose friendship this book could never have been undertaken nor completed. No words can fully discharge the debt I owe them, or measure the positive impact of their collaboration on my life.

INTERVIEWS

David Aloian, Joseph Alsop, David Bailey, Letitia Baldridge, W. Jackson Bate, Tom Baughman, Samuel Beer, William Bentinck-Smith, John T. Bethell, John Morton Blum, Derek Bok, Mr. and Mrs. William Bossert, Mrs. Paul Buck, McGeorge Bundy, Francis Burr, Paul Cabot, Hale Champion, Grace Conant, Helen Conant, Theodore Richards Conant, Tom Cook, T. Jefferson Coolidge, Thomas E. L. Dewey, C. Douglas Dillon, Burton Drebben, John Dunlop, Thomas Eliot, Archie C. Epps III, James Fallows, Daniel Fenn Senior, Daniel Fenn Junior, John Finley, Franklin Ford, John Fox, John Kenneth Galbraith, Andrew Gleason, Fred Glimp, Peter Gomes, George Goethels, Albert Gordon, Erwin Griswold, Mason Hammond, Alan Heimert, Andrew Heiskell, Richard Herrnstein, George Homans, Matina Horner, Fred Jewett, Greg Johnson, Amanda Kane, Phyllis Keller, Stephen Kelman, Francis Keppel, Clark Kerr, Robert Kiley, Oie Kistner, Spencer Klaw, Winthrop Knowlton, Corliss Lamont, Lansing Lamont, Martin Linsky, John L. Loeb, Polly Logan, Deane Lord.

Jay MacLeod, John Marquand, Leo Marx, Harvey Mansfield, William Marbury, Edward Mason, Nina McCain, John J. McCloy, Jonathan Moore, Albert Nickerson, Thomas O'Brian, Eliot Perkins, Carl Pforzheimer, Gerard

Piel, Don K. Price, Nathan Pusey, George Putnam, Nancy Randolph, John Reardon, Thomas Reardon, James Reynolds, Lowell Richards, Elliot Richardson, David Rosen, Henry Rosovsky, Albert Sacks, Arthur Schlesinger Junior, Jacob Schlesinger, Robert Shenton, A. Michael Spence, Daniel Steiner, Krister Stendahl, Adam Ullam, Al Vellucci, Sidney Verba, Raymond Vernon, F. Skiddy von Stade, Warren Wacker, Kevin White, Dean K. Whitla, James Q. Wilson, Charles Wyzanski, John Womack, Burris Young.

Interviews from the Columbia Oral History Collection, by permission of the Trustees of Columbia University in the City of New York:
Roger Baldwin, Paul Buck, Mary P. Bunting, James B. Conant, William Cowley, W. E. B. Du Bois, William Laurence, Ralph Lowell, Arthur Page, Norman Ramsay.

John F. Kennedy Presidential Library Oral History Collection: Felix Frankfurter, A. Chester Hanford, Arthur Krock, Nathan Pusey, Payson Wild.

In addition, I have benefited from conversations or correspondence with the following: Barry Bingham Senior, Harry Blackmun, Ben Bradlee, James Carroll, Milton Eisenhower, Elizabeth Fainsod, John K. Fairbank, Paul Freund, Michael L. C. Henderson, David Ives, Harry Levin, Christopher Lydon, A. Theodore Lyman, Donald Massey, John McAleer, James Miller, Leonard Nash, Paul Nitze, Harold B. Sedgwick, Muriel Snowden, Caspar Weinberger.

CHAPTER NOTES

In an attempt to make these notes inclusive, without allowing them to become intrusive, I have restricted them as much as possible to primary sources. This is particularly so in later chapters where the relative paucity of treatment accorded by others to the Pusey and Bok years heightens the importance accorded to such firsthand information as can be obtained through interviews, correspondence, diaries, memoirs, and other first-person accounts. I hope the reader will accept this, recognizing that the very mass of data presented might otherwise result in a cluttered, needlessly distracting approach.

PROLOGUE
The Country and the College

1. Enrique Hank Lopez, *The Harvard Mystique* (New York, 1979), p. 11.

2. Doris Kearns, in her revealing book *Lyndon Johnson and the American Dream* (New York, 1976), describes her first meeting with Johnson, a White House dance at which the towering Texan literally swept her off her feet. "Do your men ever dance at Harvard?" he inquired teasingly. "Of course they do," she replied. "Bull," he told her. "I know what goes on up there. And I bet they can't dance like I'm dancing right now."

The story of Nixon's unconcealed resentment of the college responsible for the likes of Daniel Ellsberg and other leaders of the antiwar movement comes from an interview with Elliot Richardson, one of the Cabinet members forced to listen while the president disparaged their alma mater.

3. Interview with Nathan M. Pusey, John F. Kennedy Presidential Library Oral History Project (hereafter referred to as JFK-OHP).

INTRODUCTION
Thinkers and Doers

1. No one who writes about Harvard can be unaware of his debt to Samuel Eliot Morison. I cheerfully acknowledge my own, which is especially great in chronicling the college's earliest days. My main source for much of this account is Morison's *Three Centuries of Harvard, 1636-1936,* published by the Harvard University Press in Cambridge in 1936. It is a compendium, painstakingly researched and stylishly written, of Morison's previous volumes, *The Founding of Harvard College* (Cambridge, 1930) and *Harvard College in the Seventeenth Century* (Cambridge, 1935), and it is peerless in supplying general readers with what they need to know about pre-Eliot Harvard.

2. For an alternative to Morison's view of Harvard's origins, see Winthrop S. Hudson, "The Morison Myth Concerning the Founding of Harvard College," *Church History,* vol. 8, 1939.

3. Morison's essay on Harvard's religious unorthodoxy, keynote address of the tercentenary celebration in 1936, is reproduced in *The Harvard Book, Selections from Three Centuries,* edited by William Bentinck-Smith (Cambridge, Mass., 1982), pp. 4–10. Bentinck-Smith's service to the student of Harvard history is, in its way, scarcely less than Morison's own. His mélange of historical tidbits and timeless arguments is stuffed with useful information, as can be seen in my own references (hereafter listed as HB).

4. Byron R. Bentley, "Colonial Harvard: Its Progressive and Liberal Spirit," *Harvard Graduates' Magazine* (hereafter referred to as HGM), June 1930.

5. Kenneth Silverman, *The Life and Times of Cotton Mather* (New York, 1984), p. 160.

6. *Ibid.,* pp. 396–98.

7. Morison, *Three Centuries,* p. 61.

8. Jack Shepherd, *Cannibals of the Heart* (New York, 1980), p. 34; additional information about the sixth president's Harvard years can be found in Paul Nagel's *Descent From Glory* (New York, 1983), pp. 41–43.

9. Among works useful to understanding Federalist Harvard: Samuel Eliot Morison, *Harrison Gray Otis* (Boston, 1969); Benjamin Labaree, *Patriots and Partisans* (Cambridge, 1962); and Van Wyck Brooks, *The Flowering of New England, 1815–1865* (New York, 1936).

10. For a delightful account of Harvard as experienced by Emerson, see Gay Wilson Allen, *Waldo Emerson, A Biography* (New York, 1981), pp. 41–59.

11. HB, pp. 443–45.

12. James MacGregor Burns, *The Vineyard of Liberty* (New York, 1982), p. 338.

13. Everett's lament, echoed by others who held his office in the days before Eliot, is reported in Samuel Eliot Morison's "The Harvard Presidency," *New England Quarterly,* December 1958; and "The President's Chair," *American Heritage,* December 1971.

14. Henry Adams, *The Education of Henry Adams* (Boston, 1961), pp. 54–55. Lawrence Lowell, incidentally, did not find Adams to his liking. The same man who, on the day of his wife's funeral, threw his head back while striding across the Weeks Bridge and declared, "I must remake my life," was unsympathetic to the refugee from Harvard's history department, with his preference for immersion in the past to active involvement in the present.

15. *Ibid.,* p. 60.

16. HB, pp. 446–49.

17. James MacGregor Burns, *The Workshop of Democracy* (New York, 1985), p. 24.

CHAPTER ONE

The Soil and the Seed

1. Hugh Hawkins, *Between Harvard and America: The Educational Leadership of Charles William Eliot* (New York, 1972), p. 154.

2. Edward H. Cotton, *The Life of Charles W. Eliot* (Boston, 1927), p. 201.

3. Alexander Eliot, "Eliot of Harvard," *American Heritage,* August 1974.

4. Cleveland Amory, *The Proper Bostonians* (Boston, 1948), p. 105; Henry James, *Charles W. Eliot* (Boston, 1930), Vol. I, p. 176.

5. The best account of Eliot's singular youth is contained in James, *Charles W. Eliot;* additional details and interpretation can be found in Cotton, *The Life of Charles W. Eliot;* Hugh Hawkins, *Between Harvard*

and America, "President Eliot's Own Story," an autobiographical summary which appeared in the December 1926 edition of HGM; and A. Eliot, "Eliot of Harvard."

6. George Herbert Palmer, *The Autobiography of a Philosopher* (New York, 1930), pp. 10–11.

7. James, *Charles W. Eliot,* Vol. I, p. 209.

8. Eliot's college years and his subsequent unspectacular career in the classroom are recounted at length in James, *Charles W. Eliot;* Hawkins, *Between Harvard and America;* and Cotton, *The Life of Charles W. Eliot.* Some of their significance in laying the groundwork for Eliot's New Education is suggested in Frederick Rudolph, *The American College and University* (New York, 1962); V. T. Thayer, *Formative Ideas in American Education* (New York, 1965); and Laurence Veysey, *The Emergence of the American University* (Chicago, 1965).

9. James, *Charles W. Eliot,* Vol. I, pp. 73–74.

10. Some of Eliot's harsher views are recounted in Francis Greenwood Peabody's "Charles W. Eliot" which, along with a wealth of other anecdotal information, is to be found in the December 1926 HGM. Equally revealing is Dean LeBaron Briggs's memoir, "President Eliot, As Seen by a Disciple," in the November 1929 edition of *The Atlantic Monthly.*

11. Charles W. Eliot, "The New Education," *The Atlantic Monthly,* April 1869.

12. Daniel J. Boorstin, *The Democratic Experience* (New York, 1974), pp. 382–83, 483.

13. Van Wyck Brooks, *Scenes and Portraits* (New York, 1954), p. 123; HB, p. 21.

14. Eliot's early years in office, and the whirlwind of reform they contained, are described in James, *Charles W. Eliot;* and "President Eliot's Own Story." Hawkins, *Between Harvard and America.* Also useful are "President Eliot's Administration," HGM, June 1894, and Merle E. Curti, *The Social Ideas of American Education* (Paterson, N.J., 1959).

15. A. Eliot, "Eliot of Harvard"; James, *Charles W. Eliot,* Vol. I, pp. 200–01.

16. Samuel Eliot Morison, ed., *The Development of Harvard University Since the Inauguration of President Eliot, 1869–1929,* pp. 288, 461–62.

17. *Ibid.,* pp. 557–58. Eliot wasn't taking any chances. After all, Daniel Coit Gilman, Johns Hopkins' founding father, walked away from his job as Yale's librarian when trustees denied him the services of a janitor to light a stove on frigid winter mornings. Abraham Flexner, *The American College* (New York, 1970), p. 47.

18. Elizabeth Drinker Bowen, *Yankee From Olympus* (New York, 1943), pp. 286–87.

19. George Santayana, *Persons and Places* (New York, 1963), pp. 156–60; John Jay Chapman readily acknowledged his infatuation with all

things British. "It required years of experience and hard thinking," he wrote near the end of his life, "for me to throw off my impressions of the English as a race of supermen." Not surprisingly, such views colored his attitude toward Eliot's distinctly American college; Page Smith, *The Rise of Industrial America* (New York, 1984), p. 829.

20. Interview with George Putnam; Rollo W. Brown, *Harvard Yard in the Golden Age* (New York, 1948), p. 27.

21. Rudolph, *The American College and University,* p. 293; Phyllis Keller, *Getting at the Core* (Cambridge, Mass., 1982), p. 5; Hawkins, *Between Harvard and America,* p. 105.

22. Hawkins, *Between Harvard and America,* p. 113; Jerome D. Greene, "Harvard in the Nineties," in *College in a Yard,* edited by Brooks Atkinson (Cambridge, Mass., 1957).

23. Edward D. Page, "Yale College—The Results of Twenty Years of Conservative Administration," *The Nation,* February 18, 1886.

24. Hawkins, *Between Harvard and America,* p. 54; interview with the Reverend Daniel Fenn Senior.

25. Nicholas Murray Butler, *Across the Busy Years* (New York, 1935), p. 205; Fenn interview.

26. Hawkins, *Between Harvard and America,* p. 114; Eliot once went so far as to laud a gallant goal line stand by Yale—before a mob of his own college's students celebrating their victory over New Haven. Another amusing account of his attitude toward the game is contained in Charles Hopkinson, "Briggs Yelled With Yale," in *College in a Yard,* pp. 99–101.

27. Hawkins, *Between Harvard and America,* p. 115; interview with Thomas E. Eliot.

28. Insights into Roosevelt's sometimes strained relations with his alma mater are to be found in Marian L. Peabody, "Theodore Roosevelt Visits Cambridge," *Harvard Alumni Bulletin,* May 3, 1958; "Theodore Roosevelt," HGM, March 1919; an identically titled piece in the same publication for June 1919, by TR's classmate Charles G. Washburn; Barbara Tuchman, *The Proud Tower* (New York, 1962), pp. 146–47. A view from the Yard toward Harvard's most famous living graduate is that of Barrett Wendell, the celebrated drama instructor who turned against Roosevelt following the latter's 1912 break with the GOP. "Astute but not profound," judged Wendell after a February 1912 visit with Roosevelt, who was at least inclined to second his old friend's judgment of Cambridge itself as "the most densely local place—in point of ideas—this side of Paradise." *Barrett Wendell and His Letters,* edited by M. A. DeWolfe Howe (Boston, 1924), pp. 242–44.

29. James, *Charles W. Eliot,* Vol. II, p. 159.

30. Bliss Perry, *And Gladly Teach* (Boston, 1935), pp. 227–29.

31. Interview with W. E. B. Du Bois, Columbia Oral History Collection (hereafter referred to as COHC), pp. 69, 88, 91; interview with Arthur W. Page, COHC, pp. 6–9.

32. Perry, *And Gladly Teach*, p. 170.

33. Additional description of the prevailing milieu of Harvard and Boston during this period can be found in Ellery Sedgwick, *The Happy Profession* (Boston, 1946); Van Wyck Brooks, *Scenes and Portraits* (New York, 1954); Rollo W. Brown, *Harvard Yard in the Golden Age;* Santayana, *Persons and Places;* Atkinson, ed., *College in a Yard.*

34. David McCullough, *Mornings on Horseback* (New York, 1981), p. 201.

35. *Harvard Crimson,* September 30, 1875.

36. John Marquand, "New Bottle, Old Wine," in Atkinson, ed., *College in a Yard.*

37. FDR's Harvard years receive extensive treatment in several fine biographies, including Frank Friedel, *The Apprenticeship* (Boston, 1952); James MacGregor Burns, *The Lion and the Fox* (New York, 1956); Geoffrey Ward, *Before the Trumpet* (New York, 1985); Ted Morgan, *FDR: A Biography* (New York, 1985).

38. Interview with Roger Baldwin, COHC, p. 14; Paul Buck, *Social Sciences at Harvard, 1860–1920* (Cambridge, Mass., 1965), pp. 85–96.

39. For additional background on student activism during this period, see W. Reed Bigelow, "Harvard's Better Self," *New England Magazine,* December 1890; Amory, *The Proper Bostonians,* p. 173.

40. The tale of Harvard's participation in the Chicago fair is told in HGM, September 1893.

41. Charles F. Thwing, "President Eliot's Message," HGM, March 1909; Hawkins, *Between Harvard and America,* p. 152.

42. Hawkins, *Between Harvard and America,* p. 153.

43. Richard B. Hovey, John Jay Chapman, *An American Mind* (New York, 1959), pp. 147–48.

44. Harvard's role in the controversy surrounding U.S. expansionism is portrayed in Hawkins, *Between Harvard and America;* Tuchman, *The Proud Tower;* James, *Charles W. Eliot;* Charles Eliot Norton quoted Franklin: "There never was a good war. . . . America has been compelled against the will of all her wisest and best to enter into a path of darkness and peril. Against their will she has been forced to turn back from the way of civilization to the way of barbarism, to renounce for the time her own ideals. With grief, with anxiety, must the lover of his country regard the present aspect and the future prospect of the nation's life." *Letters of Charles Eliot Norton,* edited by Sara Norton and M. A. DeWolfe Howe (Boston, 1913), pp. 264–69.

45. James, *Charles W. Eliot,* vol. II, p. 169.

46. Thwing, "President Eliot's Message."

47. Hawkins, *Between Harvard and America,* pp. 270–71.

48. Lincoln Steffens, *The Autobiography of Lincoln Steffens* (New York, 1920), p. 608.

49. James, *Charles W. Eliot,* Vol. II, pp. 201–2.

50. *Ibid.,* pp. 287–304.

51. *New York Times,* August 23, 1926; James, *Charles W. Eliot,* Vol. II, p. 300.

52. James, *Charles W. Eliot,* Vol. II, pp. 305–6.

53. *Ibid.,* pp. 16, 330–32.

CHAPTER TWO
The Great Assimilator

1. Clippings describing the reaction to Eliot's retirement and the subsequent electioneering that led up to Lowell's victory are contained in a series of scrapbooks, part of the A. Lawrence Lowell Collection at the Harvard University Archives in Cambridge (hereafter referred to as LL-PP).

2. Bill Adler, *Presidential Wit, from Washington to Johnson* (New York, 1966), p. 90; "The New President of Harvard," *The Congregationalist,* October 2, 1909.

3. There is a wealth of Lowelliana to be found in the Harvard Archives. Some of the more useful include a tribute at the time of Lowell's death, which appeared along with a number of personal anecdotes in the January 1943 issue of the *Harvard Alumni Bulletin* (hereafter referred to as HAB); Louis M. Lyons's article in the *Boston Globe,* January 6, 1943; a collection of "Lowellisms" assembled by John E. Pember in the *Boston Herald,* November 27, 1932; Mark A. DeWolfe Howe's recollections of his old friend in the *Boston Globe,* January 10, 1943; "Bob Washburn Says," in the same paper for December 13, 1937; Harland Ratcliffe's "Alma Mater: Ave atque vale to President Lowell," *University Club News,* January 1933; and Charles Angoff's "Lowell of Harvard," *The American Mercury,* August 1933.

In addition, I was fortunate to speak with a number of old men who in their youth knew Lowell as a friend and colleague. Among the most helpful were Eliot Perkins, Mason Hammond, George Homans, the Reverend Daniel Fenn Senior, and Carl Pforzheimer. In a special category is Nathan Pusey, whose graceful tribute, "Lawrence Lowell and His Academic Revolution," was published by the Harvard University Press in 1980.

4. Hawkins, *Between Harvard and America,* p. 271.

5. Interview with Ralph Lowell, COHC, p. 26.

6. The best biographical work on Lowell is Harvard's own, Henry Aaron Yeomans, *Abbott Lawrence Lowell, 1856–1943* (Cambridge, Mass., 1948). It contains considerable information on the Lowell dynasty, as does Ferris Grenslet's *The Lowells and Their Seven Worlds* (New York, 1948). No less helpful to the student of Lowell and his presidency is the 1980 thesis by James A. MacDougal of New York University, "A. Lawrence Lowell, Educator and Innovator."

7. Horace Gregory, *Amy Lowell, Portrait of the Poet in Her Time*

(Freeport, N.Y., 1958), is good on the Lowell milieu; the quote about Boston's sad decline comes from an interview with Professor Mason Hammond.

8. Interview with Arthur M. Schlesinger Junior.

9. Amory, *The Proper Bostonians*, pp. 33–34, 87–89.

10. Geoffrey Ward, *Before the Trumpet*, p. 232.

11. *Boston Globe*, January 14, 1909.

12. Fenn interview.

13. I have taken my quotes from Lowell's many public addresses primarily from the published editions which Lowell himself oversaw during his lifetime. The most important include *A. Lawrence Lowell, At War with Academic Tradition in America* (Cambridge, Mass., 1934); *Facts and Visions: Twenty-four Baccalaureate Sermons* (Cambridge, Mass., 1944); "The Spirit of the University," HGM, June 25, 1925; *Conflicts of Principle* (Cambridge, Mass., 1932); and *What a University President Has Learned* (New York, 1938). In addition to these collections, the Harvard University Archives has assembled numerous other Lowell speeches, never published.

14. John Reed, "Almost Thirty," *The New Republic*, April 29, 1936.

15. Seymour Martin Lipset and David Riesman, *Education and Politics at Harvard* (New York, 1975), pp. 129–31; Lyman Beecher Stowe, "From Horses to Sailboats," *Outlook and Independent*, May 28, 1930.

16. Lowell's innovations are described at length in Yeomans, *Abbott Lawrence Lowell;* two other useful sources are Angoff, "Lowell of Harvard," and Frederick P. Keppel's profile, "President Lowell and His Influence," *The Atlantic Monthly*, June 1933.

17. *Harvard Crimson*, April 16, 1917.

18. Lowell's Annual Report for 1916–17, Harvard University Archives.

19. A lively account of the disillusioning sequel to World War I is contained in Geoffrey Perrett's *America in the Twenties* (New York, 1982), chapters 1 through 4.

20. Robert Dickson Weston, "Reconstruction," HGM, December 1919.

21. Interview with C. Douglas Dillon. I should also mention an invaluable source of undergraduate recollections in each year's Commencement edition of the *Harvard Crimson*, preceded by several days' coverage of alumni reunions. These are gold mines of oral history.

22. DeWolfe Howe, "Recollections."

23. Michael E. Parrish, *Felix Frankfurter and His Times, The Reform Years* (New York, 1982), pp. 121–22; Frankfurter himself recalled Lowell's telling the committee that he would resign were Chafee dismissed, and Chafee quoted the president to the effect that "the teaching at Harvard could not be controlled from Wall Street"; Leonard Baker, *Brandeis and Frankfurter, A Dual Biography* (New York, 1984), p. 256.

24. Bruce Kuklick, *The Rise of American Philosophy, Cambridge, Massachusetts, 1860–1930* (New Haven, 1977), pp. 407–13.

25. Interview with John Marquand.

26. Interview with Francis Burr. Burr's story is seconded by Charles Wyzanski.

27. Interview with McGeorge Bundy; A. Lawrence Lowell to Helen F. Keefe, March 9, 1922, Folder 1007, LL-PP.

28. Yeomans, *Abbott Lawrence Lowell*, p. 345.

29. In a letter to Edward W. Frost dated January 23, 1922, and contained in Folder 981, LL-PP, the president was even more blunt in explaining his attitude toward blacks. He believed it impossible, wrote Lowell, to compel southern and western men to live and dine alongside Negro students. To do so would risk losing them entirely, and with them, Harvard's claim to national influence. All this, "for the sake of applying a fallacious principle of social equality in favor of two or three negroes a year."

30. Interview with Eliot Perkins.

31. Confidential source; A. Lawrence Lowell to Rufus S. Tucker, May 20, 1922, Folder 1056, LL-PP; Langdon P. Marvin to A. Lawrence Lowell, June 12, 1922, "Jews" Folder, LL-PP; Donald A. Ritchie, James M. Landis, *Dean of Regulators* (Cambridge, Mass., 1980), p. 33.

32. Martin I. Marty, *Pilgrims in Their Own Land: 500 Years of Religion in America* (Boston, 1984), p. 291.

33. Perkins interview.

34. Letter to author from Paul Freund; interview with Edward Mason.

35. Interview with David Aloian.

36. The scrubwomen controversy is covered in Gardner Jackson's article, "Harvard Explains," *The Nation*, February 19, 1930. Lowell's own explanation of his decision can be found in a letter to Gale Seaman, February 27, 1930, "Scrubwomen" folder, LL-PP. The resentments bred by such arrogance spilled over into bitter appraisals, like Heywood Broun's "Why I Won't Send My Boy to Harvard," undated.

37. LeBaron Russell Briggs to A. Lawrence Lowell, December 6, 1924, LL-PP.

38. Letter from Harold B. Sedgwick to author.

39. Interview with Carl Pforzheimer.

40. Perkins interview.

41. Interview with Claude Fuess, COHC, p. 267.

42. Hammond interview.

43. Richardson interview; HAB, January 1943.

44. Sedgwick to author.

45. *New York Times*, December 9, 1923.

46. A. Lawrence Lowell to James Byrne, February 13, 1929, Folder 352, LL-PP.

47. Interview with David Riesman; Perkins interview.

48. "A Fifth Year Report," Class of 1928, Harvard University Archives.

49. A. Lawrence Lowell to Grenville Clark, December 14, 1931, Clark folder, LL-PP.

50. Interview with Albert H. Gordon.

51. A. Lawrence Lowell to Lee Tire and Rubber Company, June 27, 1932, LL-PP.

52. Mark Muro, "The Best Club in the World," *Harvard Magazine,* September–October 1983.

53. Interview with William Marbury.

54. *Boston Globe,* November 22, 1932; Yeomans, pp. 389–93.

55. Perkins interview.

56. Amory, *The Proper Bostonians,* p. 373.

57. Yeomans, *Abbott Lawrence Lowell,* p. 406.

CHAPTER THREE

A Dorchester Mr. Chips

1. Conant's own account of his election is to be found in his memoir, *My Several Lives* (New York, 1970), hereafter referred to as MSL. First-hand recollections of the politicking that led up to his election over Murdock came in interviews with Eliot Perkins, George Homans, and John Finley.

2. Confidential sources—more than one, and all in a position to know for themselves of the reasons behind Murdock's failure to win the presidency.

3. Confidential sources.

4. Among the finest sources for information about Conant is a Ph.D. dissertation written with Conant's cooperation by William McCullough Tuttle of the University of Wisconsin, entitled "James B. Conant, Pressure Groups, and the National Defense, 1933–45." The work is much more than its title reveals, and draws heavily on Conant's personal papers and memories he shared in several interviews with Tuttle.

5. James Bryant Conant to Mrs. Harold Brown, May 17, 1933, in his personal papers at the Harvard University Archives (hereafter referred to as JBC-PP).

6. Interview with Theodore Conant. There are a number of articles which shed light on the seemingly unemotional Conant. I benefited most from John R. Tunis, "John Harvard's Biggest Boy," *American Magazine,* October 1933, a six-part biographical series about the new president which appeared in the *Boston Herald* in May 1933; "Conant States His Creed for Harvard," *New York Times Magazine,* March 18, 1934; Kermit Roosevelt, "Harvard's Prize Kibitzer," *Saturday Evening Post,* April 23, 30, 1947. In addition, Conant was the subject of frequent coverage by such magazines as *Time* and *Newsweek.* His remarks popped up regularly in educational journals like *School and Society.* Conant's annual reports, available at the Harvard University Archives, are another invaluable source for any student of his presidency.

7. Additional profiles of use include Lester Velie, "Conant of Harvard," *Coronet,* January 1946; Merle Borrowman, "Conant the Man," *Satur-*

day Review of Literature, September 21, 1963; and "Conant's Triple Life," *New York Times Magazine*, July 20, 1941. Finally, there is the Conant file contained in Harvard's Quinquennial Catalog in the Harvard University Archives. Not surprisingly, given the range of his activities and the prominence with which he pursued them, it is the largest single entry in the Catalog, three cartons stuffed with articles by and about the president.

8. Millicent Bell, *Marquand, An American Life* (Boston, 1979), pp. 57–62.

9. JBC Diary, Harvard University Archives, January 8, February 12, January 5, 1912.

10. *Ibid.*, July 5, 1912.

11. Paul F. Douglass, *Six Upon the World* (Boston, 1954), pp. 337–38.

12. MSL, p. 3; interview with Spencer Klaw.

13. Mason interview.

14. Perkins interview.

15. Interview with F. Skiddy von Stade; interview with Francis Keppel; interview with Fred L. Glimp.

16. Interview with Peter Gomes; interview with Theodore Conant; interview with David Bailey.

17. Lawrance Thompson and R. H. Winnick, *Robert Frost*, edited by Edward Connery Lathem (New York, 1981), p. 360.

18. Paul Douglass, "Conant's Concept of Higher Education Administration," *The Journal of Higher Education*, February 1954, p. 61.

19. *New York Times*, February 17, 1978.

20. Fifth Year Report, Harvard Class of 1928, Harvard University Archives.

21. Interview with Samuel Beer.

22. Interview with John Kenneth Galbraith.

23. T. Conant interview; letter to author from T. Conant.

24. John Toland, *Adolf Hitler* (New York, 1974), p. 133.

25. The story of Conant's visit to the Signet is an authentic Harvard legend, lovingly recounted by John Finley, among others.

26. Letter from Paul Freund to author.

27. Letter from Charles Wyzanski to author.

28. Interview with William L. Laurence, COHC, pp. 239–40.

29. "Highbrows at Harvard," *Time*, September 14, 1936; Joseph Barnes, "The Greatest Scholars View a Darkened Universe," *Current History*, November 1936, pp. 73–76.

30. In addition to extensive coverage of the tercentenary in the daily press (my own account relies heavily on the *New York Times* and several Boston papers, among them the *Globe*), there are a host of thoughtful articles written at the time, in an effort to assess Harvard's institutional health and future role in national affairs. Among the best: Stewart Mitchell, "Harvard After Three Centuries," *New England Quarterly*, March 1937; Alfred

North Whitehead, "Harvard: The Future," *The Atlantic Monthly*, September 1936; John R. Tunis, "Men of Harvard—25 Years Later," *The Reader's Digest*, December 1936; Bernard De Voto, "A Puritan Tercentenary," *Harper's Magazine*, September 1936; William M. Houghton, "Farewell to Harvard?," *American Mercury*, September 1936; and Raymond Walters, "The Harvard Tercentenary Days," *School and Society*, September 26, 1936. *Time* and *Newsweek* also provided extensive coverage of the anniversary.

31. JBC Diary, January 25, 1935.

32. Walter Lippmann, "The Harvard Anniversary," *New York Herald Tribune*, May 26, 1936.

33. *Harvard Crimson*, January 6, 1933.

34. A. Lawrence Lowell to FDR, February 20, 1936; FDR reply, March 6, 1936; FDR to Felix Frankfurter, April 16, 1936; A. Lawrence Lowell to FDR, April 14, 1936; FDR to Felix Frankfurter, April 16, 1936— all in the FDR Library, Hyde Park, New York.

35. "The University Tradition in America—Yesterday and Tomorrow," *School and Society*, September 26, 1936.

CHAPTER FOUR
Mr. Conant Goes to War

1. Letter from Paul Freund to author.

2. MSL, pp. 157–60.

3. Among the most useful articles published at the time of Walsh-Sweezy, there are critical accounts of Conant's behavior in Rolf Kaltenborn, "Why Men Leave Harvard: A Study in Social Science," *The Student Advocate*, May 1937; "The Case of Dr. Conant," *The New Republic*, June 15, 1938; Marshall H. Stone, "Crisis at Harvard," *The Nation*, December 2, 1939; "To Save Harvard," *Time*, October 16, 1939; "Harvard's Liberalism: Myth or Reality," *American Teacher*, May–June 1937; and "The Harvard Firing Line," *The New Republic*, November 29, 1939.

Making the case on behalf of Conant's administration is Irwin Ross, "The Tempest at Harvard," *The Atlantic Monthly*, October 1940; and Ward Henry, "Education at the Crossroads," *Harvard Guardian*, November 1939. I should also point out a well-argued view from inside which takes exception to my own conclusion about the whole affair, and specifically to the widely held view that neither Walsh nor Sweezy quite lived up to their early promise: John K. Fairbanks's memoir, *Chinabound* (New York, 1982), pp. 151–52. As Fairbanks put it, "I have always thought the resulting system [Conant's ad hoc committee] should be known as the Alan R. Sweezy Memorial Appointment Procedure."

4. Lewis S. Finer to JBC–PP, December 18, 1975. Conant did not have access to the information contained in Finer's letter when he wrote his mem-

oirs. Consequently, it has not appeared in print until now. Owing to his innate reticence—Conant readily acknowledged pulling his punches in the final manuscript—it is also entirely possible that he would have shied away from writing anything which might reflect adversely on his onetime friend and later rival, Kenneth Murdock, in any case.

5. The Boston papers were filled with accounts of Harvard's turmoil; Conant himself recounted the squabble in detail, MSL, pp. 161–70; Finley interview; Perkins interview.

6. Interview with Francis Keppel.

7. Perkins interview.

8. "Humanity's Experiment with Free Institutions," *Vital Speeches*, September 26, 1939.

9. The *Harvard Alumni Bulletin* is a superb source for much of the era's ambience, as is the *Harvard Crimson*. "Who Runs Harvard," by Leo Marx (*The Harvard Progressive*, December 1939) suggests some of the resentments harbored by left-wing elements against the governing boards, with their heavy concentration of personal wealth and social status.

10. Klaw interview.

11. Only weeks before the Nazi invasion of France, Heinrich Bruning told Conant that the German dictator had lost a golden opportunity to wrap up the conflict the previous autumn, when he had failed to invade Holland; JBC Diary, April 10, May 9, 1940.

12. *Ibid.*, May 17, 1940.

13. MSL, p. 212; JBC Diary, June 1, 1940. Conant estimated the overall ratio of supportive over critical letters at two and a half to one.

14. JBC Diary, June 11, 1940.

15. MSL, pp. 216–17.

16. *Christian Science Monitor*, May 25, 1940.

17. In a conversation with Harold Dodds, Conant summed up his position as follows: "Expressed my views as USA armed to the teeth, belligerent and running the world. A Pax Americana like the Pax Britannica of the 19th Century"; JBC Diary, June 29, July 4, 1940.

18. His own pro-war activities, some of them skirting the line between legal and illegal conduct, reminded Conant of the old saying, "It is easy to get money but hard to stay out of jail." JBC Diary, August 26, 1940; *Ibid.*, September 4, July 9, 1940. As for Claflin, Conant dismissed his defeatist views, and decided there was nothing that could be done to change them pending all-out air assaults against England. He sounded an almost relieved note once the attacks began, and the British proved themselves capable of throwing off the Luftwaffe.

19. Unless otherwise noted, quotes from Conant's public remarks are taken from JBC-PP.

20. JBC Diary, October 8, 16, 1940; Perkins interview.

21. JBC Diary, November 3, 5, 1940. In common with other observers,

Conant underestimated the dimensions of FDR's triumph over Willkie. His own prediction was for a margin of between 40 and 60 electoral votes. In fact, the president was reelected, 449 to 82.

22. MSL, p. 222; JBC Diary, November 21, 1940.

23. In response to the appeal of one close friend that he not risk his life by going to London at the height of German air attacks on the city, Conant was adamant. "In the long run, no one is indispensable, least of all to a university. . . . I believe that actions speak louder than words. I have been quite active as a private citizen in urging a more belligerent policy for the United States. I think it has some value for a man who has taken such a position to show that he is willing to take risks." JBC to Frank B. Jewett, December 27, 1940; JBC Diary, February 3, 1941, JBC-PP.

24. Perkins interview; Mason interview.

25. MSL, p. 252.

26. *Ibid.,* pp. 253–57; JBC to Grace R. Conant, March 8, 1941, JBC-PP. Anyone doubting the strong emotions flowing beneath Conant's deceptively chilly exterior need only read the wartime correspondence to his wife, signed with "Much, much love, from your adoring Jim."

27. MSL, pp. 262–63.

28. MSL, pp. 268–69.

29. *Ibid.,* pp. 275–77. For another account of Conant's initial skepticism, see Peter Goodchild, *J. Robert Oppenheimer, Shatterer of Worlds* (Boston, 1981), pp. 45–46.

30. "Conant's Triple Life," *New York Times Magazine,* July 20, 1941.

31. *Boston Globe,* December 9, 1941.

32. Especially helpful in reconstructing a sense of the mood on campus during those years leading up to and following Pearl Harbor, is the *Harvard Alumni Bulletin's* regular feature "The Undergraduate Week."

33. Grace R. Conant, "A Hostess Remembers Mr. Churchill," *Harvard Magazine,* September–October 1983.

34. Symptomatic of Conant's continuing interest in his educational responsibilities at a time when the war effort might have consumed his total energies, is his article on postwar schooling, "No Retreat for the Liberal Arts," which appeared in the February 21, 1943, *New York Times Magazine. Time's* August 31, 1942, issue includes "Conant's Arsenal," detailing some of the changes overtaking Harvard in the months since Pearl Harbor.

35. A number of persons recalled Paul Buck for me, including his widow and such associates as John Finley, Eliot Perkins, and Samuel Beer.

36. *Boston Globe,* June 14, 1942.

37. *Harvard Magazine's* July–August 1985 issue contains recollections of those involved in the Manhattan Project.

38. Laurence interview, COHC, pp. 300–01.

39. Letter from Paul Nitze to author.

40. Interview with W. Jackson Bate.

41. *Boston Globe,* January 11, 1943.

CHAPTER FIVE
Redbook, Red Scare

1. Interview with William H. Cowley, COHC, pp. 644–47; Finley interview.

2. For some interesting background on the parameters of the debate, see Byron S. Hollinshead, "General Education at Harvard," *Journal of General Education,* October 1946; "Now, the Harvard Plan," *Newsweek,* August 6, 1945; "Report of the Harvard Committee," *Senior Scholastic,* December 10, 1945; and "American Education Must Roll with the Punch," *Saturday Evening Post,* August 18, 1945. Anticipating Conant's own contribution to the discussion is his October 1939 address before the *New York Herald Tribune* Forum, "A Free Classless Society," with its strong endorsement of education as an agent for social mobility and national bonding.

3. *General Education in a Free Society* (Cambridge, Mass., 1945); Finley interview; see also the chapter in MSL devoted to "The Harvard Report," pp. 363–73. Conant's assessment of the Buck Committee was contained in a letter to his friend and administrative ally in June 1945, in which he praised the committee for having broadened its focus beyond any single institution, and accepted the task "of making education serve the continuance of a free society on this continent *in the twentieth century.*"

4. Carl G. Miller, "Applause for the Harvard Report," *Education,* October 1945; Harry Hansen, "Harvard's Sixteen Courses," *Survey Graphic,* September 1945.

5. Keppel interview.

6. Rachel H. King, "Harvard Versus Christianity," *The Christian Century,* January 23, 1946. For a very different critique, see F. O. Matthiessen, "Harvard Wants to Join America," *The New Republic,* August 20, 1945; and Leon Mones, "Harvard Report: A Socially Impotent Education?" *The Clearinghouse,* January 1946.

7. Jacques Barzun, "Harvard Takes Stock," *The Atlantic Monthly,* October 1945; Arthur B. Moehlman, "Education in a Free Society," *Nation's Schools,* October 1945; Franklin J. Keller, "A Democratic Philosophy of American Education—The Harvard Report," *High Points,* December 1945.

8. Kermit Roosevelt, "Harvard's Prize Kibitzer"; "Ambassador to the Cosmos," *The Saturday Review,* December 6, 1947; Wyzanski interview; T. Conant interview.

9. T. Conant interview.

10. T. Conant interview; interview with Gerard Piel; MSL, pp. 493–99.

11. Interview with Matina Horner.

12. Putnam interview.

13. Interview with William Bentinck-Smith; Perkins interview.

14. Aloian interview.

15. For an interesting treatment of the G.I. Bill and its nationwide ramifications, see "Books and Bonuses," in Joseph C. Goulden, *The Best Years, 1945–50* (New York, 1976), pp. 66–84.

16. Far too little has been written about Wilbur J. Bender, a transplanted Ohioan whose impact on postwar Harvard was second only to Conant's. A revealing account of the demographic overhaul the two men achieved is Richard O. Ellis's "You Can't Tell a Harvard Man," *The Christian Science Monitor*, May 1, 1948.

17. The origins of the Russian Research Center are covered in depth in Paul Buck's interview with COHC, pp. 17–21; the decision to inform FBI agents of book purchases from an ideologically suspect bookstore is revealed in the same interview (p. 38), as is Conant's fear of anything such as a permanent Center (p. 54). Interview with Adam Ullam.

18. Keppel interview.

19. James B. Conant, "Our College System: A Re-Evaluation," *New York Times Magazine*, June 4, 1950; "Chemist of Ideas," *Time*, September 23, 1946. For another interesting view of Conant, the modern Renaissance man, there is "The Common Sense of Mr. Conant," an address delivered by his friend Gerard Piel in October 1967, and generously shared with me.

20. T. Conant interview.

21. Keppel interview.

22. Marbury interview.

23. Wyzanski interview.

24. *Ibid.*

25. MSL, pp. 437–44; Galbraith interview.

26. Wyzanski interview.

27. *Ibid.*

28. Much has been written about the 1947 Commencement. At the time, however, few in the audience—Conant included—grasped the enormity of what Marshall was proposing. Similarly, the common reaction to Aleksandr Solzhenitsyn's landmark address berating the West as an exhausted volcano some thirty years later was, to quote one member of the Harvard community on the platform that day, "monumental boredom—compounded by curiosity as to just how much longer the thing would drag on."

29. Interview with Leo Marx. An invaluable source of information on Matthiessen, especially the sad final months of his life, is the October 1950 issue of *Monthly Review*, a tribute composed by friends and colleagues. I am also grateful to Professor Harry Levin for providing me with a copy of "Matty at Harvard," yet another reminiscence issued in conjunction with the renaming of rooms in Eliot House in the late scholar's memory.

30. Beer interview.

31. *Monthly Review,* October 1950.

32. Interview with Amanda Kane.

33. Marbury interview.

34. Douglass, *Six Upon the World.*

35. MSL, pp. 454–57. For additional background on Conant's evolving views of the Soviet threat and Harvard's responsibility in meeting it, see his articles, "Freedom and the University," *NEA Journal,* November 1950; "The University and the State," *Journal of Higher Education,* June 1947; "Education in an Armed Truce," *The Atlantic Monthly,* October 1948; and "Challenge of the Times, A National Philosophy," *Vital Speeches,* August 15, 1948.

36. Buck interview, COHC, p. 41.

37. An excellent account of these troubled times is to be found in Diane Ravitch's *The Troubled Crusade* (New York, 1983), pp. 93–99.

38. Eliot interview.

39. Once again, I am indebted to the *Harvard Crimson* and its superb pre-Commencement issues, with their recollections by alumni of life on campus as they experienced it. One should especially note the stories told at twenty-fifth and fiftieth class reunions.

40. JBC Diary, September 29, 1951, For a good summary of Clark, one can turn to Elliot Richardson in *The Creative Balance* (New York, 1976), p. 343.

41. "The Private School Controversy," *The Saturday Review,* May 3, 1952, sets forth the positions argued by Conant and Cushing. Another useful source is *Newsweek*'s September 22, 1952, profile, "Dr. Conant: In Science Pure, In Education Controversial."

42. Interview with Nathan Pusey.

43. Marbury interview; JBC Diary, December 23, 1952.

44. JBC Diary, January 1, 1953; Bundy interview.

45. Perkins interview; interview with Andrew Gleason.

46. MSL, p. 544.

47. Letter from William F. Buckley to author.

48. JBC Diary, June 11, 1953; Keppel interview.

49. Foreshadowing Conant's post-Harvard career, see Charles D. Biebel's 1971 University of Wisconsin thesis, "Politics, Pedagogues, and Statesmanship: James Bryant Conant and the Public Schools, 1933–47," and also a thick sheaf of Conant's writings on public education and a classless society housed at the Harvard University Archives.

50. Borrowman, "Conant the Man."

51. T. Conant interview.

52. Pusey interview; interview with Helen Conant.

53. T. Conant interview; Riesman interview.

54. Conant's antipathy to funerals was so pronounced that he hadn't intended to return to Cambridge for that of his mother—not, at least, until he was virtually shamed into doing so by Dean Williard Sperry of his

divinity school. In fact, according to friends, he carried with him written instructions forbidding such a service in the event of his own sudden death.

55. Transcript of Memorial Service for James Bryant Conant, April 11, 1978. Transcript available from Harvard University Archives.

CHAPTER SIX

The Bishop from Appleton

1. Ravitch, *The Troubled Crusade,* pp. 98–102. One poll of social science teachers conducted in the year 1955—well *after* McCarthy's humiliation at the hands of congressional investigators and Army lawyers—showed that while 35 percent of those questioned would allow a known Communist to teach, 45 percent would not.

2. The cases of Wendell Furry, Leon Kamin, and Helen Deane Markham are covered in great detail in a number of publications, including the *Harvard Alumni Bulletin,* as well as newspapers in Boston, New York, and elsewhere. Of particular interest is Harold Lord Varney's "Harvard Betrays Its Heritage," *American Mercury,* September 1957, along with publications issued by the fiercely anti-Communist Veritas Group.

My own account relies in part on a detailed memorandum of the events of those days by William Marbury ("Harvard and the Cold War"), never published and now locked away in the University's archives under terms of its strict fifty-year rule. Fortunately, during the course of a visit with Marbury in the spring of 1984, I was able to hear portions of the document read aloud, at which time I took notes of the chronology and various roles assumed by a number of Marbury's associates on the Corporation and throughout official Harvard. I also benefited from interviews with Paul Cabot, Joseph Alsop, and others identified in the text.

3. Interview with Paul Cabot; Alsop interview; Marbury interview.

4. Alsop interview; unpublished Marbury memo.

5. *Ibid.*

6. *Ibid.*

7. Interview with Erwin Griswold.

8. Griswold interview; Wyzanski interview.

9. Ronald Steel, *Walter Lippmann and the American Century* (New York, 1980), p. 524. Even now, those who were close to the selection process are reluctant to discuss it publicly. Some useful background can be gleaned from a series of profiles of Pusey that ran in the *Boston Globe* in June 1952. The fact that he was less obscure than popularly believed is confirmed by Amanda Kane, widow of Corporation member and Pusey intimate Keith Kane, who, as a trustee of Smith College, had heard the Iowan speculated about as a potential president for that women's school; Bailey interview; Gordon interview.

10. Unless otherwise noted, quotes from Pusey speeches are taken from Pusey's Quinquennial Catalog file in the Harvard University Archives.

11. Pusey was the subject of numerous profiles at the time of his selection and shortly thereafter, including the *Globe* series mentioned in Note 9. The *Harvard Alumni Bulletin* is an invaluable source, both in 1953 and eighteen years later, when it published a long retrospective of the Pusey years, dated June 14, 1971. *Time* and *Newsweek* chimed in with articles of their own, especially in the mid-Fifties, when Pusey's active involvement in the religious revival at Harvard earned him widespread attention from the national media. Also useful is Archie C. Epps, *A Short History of Harvard College* (Cambridge, Mass., 1983), and Gilbert Bailey, "Pusey of Harvard," New York Times Magazine, September 27, 1953.

12. *Globe* series, June 1953.

13. Bailey interview; Gordon interview.

14. Pusey interview.

15. *Boston Herald,* June 1, 1928; confidential source.

16. Cabot interview; *Time,* March 1, 1954. For biographical background, see HAB, June 6, 1953.

17. Alsop interview.

18. Gomes interview.

19. Confidential source; Beer interview. I should also point out, however, that the view held by Beer and others is by no means unanimous. George Goethels, for one, believes that Pusey was not patronized, at least during his early days on campus, and that the mood did not really begin to change until after the so-called Battle Over Memorial Church.

20. Glimp interview.

21. Pusey interview.

22. Pusey's courtship of John D. Rockefeller was in fact quite accidental. Spending the first weekend after his selection with the multimillionaire, the new president attended church and engaged in far-ranging conversations with his host, following which, without prompting, Rockefeller decided to contribute a million dollars toward carrying out Pusey's dream of a revived divinity school. Kane interview; Bailey interview. For additional information on Pusey and the divinity school, see "Building the Kingdom," *Time,* October 18, 1954.

23. Pusey interview.

24. Pusey's address was reproduced in many forums. It can be found in its entirety in Pusey's volume of speeches, *The Age of the Scholar* (Cambridge, 1963), pp. 1–8.

25. Bailey interview; Griswold interview.

26. Pusey interview.

27. The strange tale of McCarthy's taping of his arch-rival from Appleton is to be found in an interview with Norman Ramsay, COHC, pp. 261–62.

28. More pointed still was Pusey's declaration to his first Harvard class,

reported in the *Boston Globe* for September 25, 1953, that people in Cambridge were more interested in reading books than burning them. See also Mary Hanely, "Pusey Raps Politics, Inroads Hit," *Christian Science Monitor,* September 26, 1953.

29. The Bundy-Diamond-Bellah dispute originated in *The New York Review of Books* in July 1977; my own account relies on *The Chronicle of Higher Education,* August 1, 1977.

30. This was by no means the only time that Harvard was accused of compiling information regarding the private lives of its faculty. According to at least one highly respected senior professor, one reason why the Harvard administration was so anxious to retrieve files from University Hall, following the student takeover of April 1969, was the presence there of highly confidential files dealing with, among other things, professorial sex lives.

31. Conant's son, Theodore, believes his father may well have been approached by FBI agents, only to refuse any surveillance of nonpolitical activities, or any surveillance at all which could not be justified according to rigid tests of national security. The exact amount of FBI involvement on campus will not be known until the fifty-year rule is breached or the archival statute of limitations runs out. Ironically enough, as reported by the *Harvard Crimson* in 1985, Conant himself was the object of FBI snooping, a fact revealed to the paper through the Freedom of Information Act.

32. Interview with John Dunlop.

33. For a highly critical account of events leading up to the Memorial Church fracas, see William W. Bartley's attack in the *Harvard Crimson,* March 28, 1958, as well as Leonard Silk's *The American Establishment* (New York, 1980), pp. 44–48. Pusey's own justification of the church as a predominantly Christian one appears in the April 9, 1958, *Crimson.*

34. Gomes interview; Bentinck-Smith interview.

35. Silk, pp. 45–47; Pusey interview.

36. Mason interview; interview with Archibald Cox.

37. Interview with James Reynolds; Pusey interview.

38. Pusey interview.

39. Wyzanski interview.

40. Interview with Raymond Vernon.

41. David Halberstam, *The Best and the Brightest* (New York, 1969), pp. 61–74; Bundy interview; Bate interview.

42. Halberstam, p. 72.

43. *Ibid.,* p. 73.

44. Gordon interview; confidential source.

45. Interview with Francis Burr; confidential source.

46. Bundy interview; Bate interview.

47. Perkins interview; Pusey interview; Griswold interview.

48. Interview with William Bossert.

49. Interview with L. Fred Jewett.

50. Bailey interview.

51. Perkins interview; Keppel interview.

52. Bundy interview.

53. *Harvard Crimson,* September 30, 1961. Unfortunately, Bender's prescription was transformed in the Sixties, until his class of gifted freshmen, widely varied in their skills and ambitions, was redefined to perceive itself as what David Halberstam memorably described as America's best and brightest.

54. Andrew Holleran, in *Our Harvard* (hereafter referred to as OH), edited by Jeffrey L. Lant (New York, 1982), p. 246.

55. Pusey examined the internationalization of Harvard in "The Exploding World of Education," *Fortune,* September 1955, and in numerous later interviews with the Boston and New York press. It was also a favorite theme of his book *The Age of the Scholar.*

56. I am indebted to Professor Don Price for the loan of "Harvard and the Federal Government," the September 1961 report which galvanized other schools to reexamine their own relations with Washington.

57. *Ibid.,* p. 27; Clark Kerr, *The Uses of the University* (Cambridge, 1963), pp. 57–60.

58. Especially useful in understanding the changed nature of the modern university is a series of three long articles published in *The New Yorker* in April and May 1969 under the umbrella title "Center of a New World." Marcus Cunliffe's "Harvard," part of *Encounter Magazine*'s series on Universities in Mid-Century (undated), is also helpful.

59. Nathan Pusey, *The Age of the Scholar,* pp. 51–52.

60. See Chapter Five, "Politics," of James Ridgeway's *The Closed Corporation, American Universities in Crisis* (New York, 1968).

61. *Ibid.*

62. *New York Herald Tribune,* November 3, 1963.

63. Interview with Richard Herrnstein.

64. Background on the Kennedy-Harvard connection can be found in the *Harvard Crimson*'s retrospective, "Kennedy and Harvard: A Complicated Tie," November 26, 1963, and in Lawrence Loder's "Jack Kennedy at Harvard," JFK Quinquennial Catalog, Harvard University Archives, as well as in several of the standard Kennedy biographies. The University News Office compiled a special report entitled "Kennedy and Harvard," which included a number of press and other comments about the New Frontier's Harvard associations. For another view, see Will Oursler in the April 23, 1961, issue of *American Weekly,* along with "What Is It That Makes Harvard Important Now?" *Business Week,* March 11, 1961.

65. Pusey interview.

66. Pusey interview; letter from Ben Bradlee to author; Cabot interview.

67. Pusey interview; Pusey interview, JFK-OHP.

68. Interview with John L. Loeb; interview with Letitia Baldridge.

69. Cabot interview.

70. Fifth report, Class of 1940, Harvard University Archives.

71. See "The Changing Face of Harvard College," *Saturday Review,* October 19, 1963. Written by Humphrey Doermann, Bender's successor as dean of admissions, this is an especially authoritative look at the changes instituted under Conant and accelerated by Pusey. McGeorge Bundy, "Were Those the Days?" *Daedalus,* Summer 1970.

72. Perkins interview.

73. *Ibid.*

74. Finley interview; interview with Burris Young.

75. Herrnstein interview. Kerr's seminal analysis of the modern university—a view that he to this day protests was misinterpreted as unduly favorable—is contained in his *The Uses of the University.*

CHAPTER SEVEN

Children of the Storm

1. J. Anthony Lukas, "A Fairly Old Grad Looks at Harvard," *New York Times Magazine,* June 8, 1969.

2. Pusey interview; Burr interview.

3. In fact, this was but the latest *Crimson* broadside against the president, forerunner of a series of critical editorials that would win the newspaper the highest award given for college editorializing in 1962. However much he may have smarted under the paper's attacks, Pusey never displayed resentment, but went on meeting editors on a regularly scheduled basis—a practice only stopped by his successor, Derek Bok, who felt it suggested journalistic favoritism.

4. Ravitch, *The Troubled Crusade,* pp. 187–90.

5. A helpful source for anyone seeking to understand the forces building toward the student upheaval of the late Sixties is *The University Crisis Reader,* vols. I and II, edited by Immanuel Wallerstein and Paul Starr (New York, 1971). Other useful sources, culled from a vast amount of material printed at the time and since: Roger Rappoport and Laurence J. Kirshbaum, *Is the Library Burning?* (New York, 1969); Milton Viorst, *Fire in the Streets: America in the 1960s* (New York, 1979); Allen J. Matusow, *The Unraveling of America: A History of Liberalism in the 1960s* (New York, 1984); *The Embattled University,* edited by Stephen R. Graubard and Geno A. Ballotti (New York, 1970), and Henry Steele Commager, The Commonwealth of Learning (New York, 1968), as well as such general histories of the era as William Manchester's *The Glory and the Dream: A Social History of America, 1932–72* (New York, 1974).

Of special relevance to the Harvard situation are Eli Ginzberg's article in the *Journal of College Placement*, December 1969–January, 1970; John T. Bethell, "The University on Trial," *Harvard Magazine*, March–April 1979; Marshall W. Meyer, "Harvard Students in the Midst of Crisis," *Sociology of Education*, Summer 1971; Stephen H. Armstrong, "Why Harvard Fails," HAB, September 30, 1968; Nathan Glazer, "The Six Roots of Campus Trouble," HAB, September 21, 1970; Adam B. Ullam, "The University Should Mind Its Own Business," HAB, September 15, 1969. A particularly useful secondary source is Christopher Jencks and David Riesman, *The Academic Revolution* (New York, 1969). Joel R. Kramer's "The Undergraduate" column in HAB, March 17, 1969, says much about the atomization of modern Harvard, where little besides the blue exam book served to unite a terribly fragmented student body—and its professors.

6. A superb essay on those days is Faye Levine's "When the Bright Colors Faded," contained in *My Harvard, My Yale,* edited by Diana Dubois (New York, 1982). No less informative is the chapter "The Sixties and Beyond," in Seymour Martin Lipset and David Riesman, *Education and Politics at Harvard* (New York, 1975).

7. The single finest account I have been able to find of the whole tormented string of events which led up to University Hall is Dan Swanson's "A History of the Strike," *Harvard Crimson*, April 10, 1974. It is exhaustive in its reporting of the roots of Harvard's anguish.

8. Interview with Albert L. Nickerson.

9. Nelson Aldrich, "Harvard on the Way Down," *Harper's Magazine*, July 1976; HAB, July 14, 1971.

10. "Center of a New World," *New Yorker* series, April–May 1969.

11. *New York Times,* December 11, 1962.

12. *New York Times,* May 29, 1963; Michael Barone, OH; Jesse Kornbluth, "O Harberg, My Harberg," in *My Harvard, My Yale.*

13. Irving Howe, "New Styles in Liberalism," *Dissent Magazine,* Summer 1965.

14. Wyzanski interview.

15. Wyzanski interview; interview with Mary Bunting, COHC, pp. 230–31; 140, 161–62, 234.

16. The battle over parietals is covered in detail in the *Harvard Alumni Bulletin,* as well as in the *Harvard Crimson* and local newspapers.

17. Thompson and Winnick, *Robert Frost,* pp. 514–15. Presumably, Kennedy would have been less complimentary had he known of Frost's private definition of "a liberal" as a man who wouldn't take his own side in a fight. But then, perhaps revisionist historians are correct in saying that Kennedy himself was no liberal.

18. Levine, "When the Bright Colors Faded," pp. 104–05.

19. Nathan M. Pusey, "Student Protest and Commitment," *School and Society,* December 11, 1965.

20. Jacques Barzun, *The American University* (New York, 1968), pp.

70–71. Barzun's analysis of the causes of student disaffection is among the most penetrating I have encountered.

21. *New York Times,* October 22, 1967.

22. Perkins interview.

23. Sylvester Monroe, "Guest in a Strange House," *Saturday Review of Education,* February 1973.

24. *New York Times,* April 13, 1969.

25. Interview with Archie C. Epps III. Also useful for historical background on recent black history and Harvard: Marya Mannes, "Nessfeness at Harvard," *The Reporter,* May 31, 1956; Marcia G. Synott, "The Admission and Assimilation of Minority Students at Harvard, Yale, and Princeton, 1900–1970," *History of Education,* Fall 1979 (which in turn formed the basis for her book *The Half-Opened Door,* Westport, Conn., 1981); and two articles by Martin Kilson, "The Black Experience at Harvard," *New York Times Magazine,* September 2, 1973, and "Blacks at Harvard: Crisis and Change," HAB, April 1973.

26. Young interview; Lukas, "A Fairly Old Grad Looks at Harvard."

27. Confidential source; Epps interview.

28. Kornbluth, "O Harberg, My Harberg," pp. 123–25; *New York Times,* November 8, 1966. The McNamara incident also received extensive coverage from newsweeklies.

29. Kornbluth, p. 126.

30. Young interview.

31. Kelman's book, *Push Comes to Shove* (New York, 1970), is as indispensable to an understanding of Harvard in the Sixties as Morison's volumes are to the student of the colonial institution. The reader might also turn to Kelman's essay in OH, pp. 289–304.

32. Rudd's own account of the Columbia strike of 1968 can be found in *The University Crisis Reader,* vol. II, *Confrontation and Counterattack* (New York, 1971), pp. 177–94; also see Kelman, *Push Comes to Shove.*

33. Cox interview.

34. Swanson, "A History of the Strike."

35. E. J. Kahn, *Harvard Through Change and Through Storm* (New York, 1969), pp. 150–51.

36. Dunlop interview.

37. Cox interview; Pusey interview; Bentinck-Smith interview.

38. Bentinck-Smith interview; Pusey interview.

39. President's Report, 1967–68, Harvard University Archives. In April 1968, Pusey told an audience at Rice University—at the height of Columbia's turmoil—"I think the students themselves are beginning to question some of the techniques being used in expressing their dissatisfaction." *Boston Globe,* April 26, 1968; Lukas, "A Fairly Old Grad Looks at Harvard."

40. Pusey reiterated his opposition to the university as a political player in numerous forums, including press conferences, formal addresses, and pri-

vate conversations. See *Chronicle of Higher Education,* March 11, 1968. The story of McNamara and the proposed electronic barrier cutting off North Vietnamese infiltration into the South is told in Halberstam, pp. 765–66. A very different use of Harvard expertise came in a September 1966 appeal by twenty-two leading scientists to President Johnson to halt the use of anti-personnel and chemical weapons in Vietnam. The appeal was spearheaded by Harvard chemists, biochemists, and bacteriologists.

41. Perkins interview.

42. Confidential source; interview with Kevin H. White.

43. Dunlop interview.

44. Burr interview.

45. Interview with John Fox.

46. Interview with Henry Rosovsky; Heimert interview.

47. Dunlop interview; interview with Andrew Gleason; Beer interview.

48. Confidential source; interview with Harvey Mansfield.

49. Dunlop interview.

50. Kahn, *Harvard Through Change and Through Storm,* p. 119. Wald did not lack a sense of humor. Not long after the Dow Chemical incident, he found himself lecturing students on the polarization of light. To illustrate his argument, Wald held up a piece of cellophane, then remarked good-naturedly, "I wouldn't dare come before this class with Saran Wrap."

51. The remarks attributed to Putnam, like most of my account of those frenetic days, is based on an amalgam of sources, including the *Harvard Crimson* and the *Harvard Alumni Bulletin.* The latter was consistently outstanding in its coverage: fair, unbiased, as diverse as the alumni body to which it reported.

52. Kelman includes significant coverage of the two Soc Rel courses and their impact on student opinion in *Push Comes to Shove;* see also HAB, February 24, 1969.

53. See HAB issues for February, 1969.

54. Richardson interview; Pforzheimer interview.

55. Interview with James Fallows; interview with Greg Johnson; Heimert interview.

56. Confidential sources.

57. Of particular help in reporting on events leading up to University Hall and the Bust that followed are the *Harvard Crimson* issues not only from the time, but retrospectives of the era, published on the fifth and tenth anniversaries of the takeover. I have relied heavily on these, along with HAB's coverage, itself remarkably thorough and objective. See also "The Occupation, The Bust, The Strike, The Aftermath," HAB, April 28, 1969; Katherine Greenberg and Michael Ryan, "Busted! The Harvard Strike Ten Years After," *Boston Magazine,* April 1979; Ralph Maloney, "The War Was Two Years Ago," *The Atlantic Monthly,* March 1970.

58. Kelman, pp. 254–65; confidential source.

59. Interview with Franklin L. Ford; Kahn, *Harvard Through Change and Through Storm*, p. 19.

60. Epps interview. At the University Archives in Cambridge is a voluminous collection of materials relating to the takeover and subsequent events, perhaps the best source of primary information available.

61. Kelman interview; Ford interview.

62. Interview with Krister Stendahl; Young interview.

63. Young interview; confidential sources; *Harvard Crimson*, 1981 Commencement issue.

64. Young interview; Glimp interview; Kahn, *Harvard Through Change and Through Storm*, p. 80.

65. Interview with Warren Wacker; *Harvard Crimson*, April 10, 1979. Pusey himself in the same issue recalled his surprise at what was happening. Berkeley and Columbia notwithstanding, said the former president, "I thought our people were so sophisticated that they wouldn't get caught up in that sort of thing. . . . Well, it was almost a disease. It just exploded in a way. The idea of students attacking Harvard was absurd, nonsensical. Harvard was not the evil kind of organization they were trying to portray it."

66. Pusey interview; Epps interview; interview with Don Price.

67. Stendahl interview; Bentinck-Smith interview; Glimp interview.

68. The report of Bok's threatened resignation, carried in the *Boston Globe* at the time of his election to succeed Pusey, is almost certainly untrue. It goes against everything we know of the man's style, and close friends attest to this.

69. Glimp interview.

70. Herrnstein interview. In addition to the *Harvard Crimson* and HAB, there is *Time*'s April 25, 1969, edition, "Campus in a Cruel Month."

71. *Time*, April 25, 1969. Also see "Harvard: The Voice of a Non-Striker," *Wall Street Journal*, May 6, 1969, for a good view of the other side of the political fence.

72. *New York Times*, April 11, 1969.

73. To this day, it remains obscure exactly why admittedly sensitive records were never removed from University Hall before the Occupation—or precisely what made the documents so sensitive. Many theories have been argued. The simplest is probably the closest to the truth, namely that neither Ford nor Pusey, for all their subsequent denials, really believed that Harvard students would forcibly take over a Harvard building. Pusey said as much in his interview with the *Harvard Crimson* a decade after the tumult had died down. And Ford, in telling me that he felt himself protected because of his meeting with black undergraduates on April 9, conveyed a belief that the right tactics on his part and that of other administrators might permanently forestall any action by radicals.

74. See Kelman. *Newsweek*'s April 23, 1969, issue reports in detail on the Strike, as do the *New York Times* and *Boston Globe* for the period.

75. Burr interview; according to Francis Keppel, real authority—that is, *perceived* authority—passed from the Corporation to the Overseers, who, following considerable debate, decided to issue a statement broadly endorsing the president's actions, at the same time choosing to avoid the mistake of their Cornell counterparts, who went public with a divided and feeble statement of support for their embattled president, thus weakening his position.

76. Mason interview.

77. Confidential source.

78. *Christian Science Monitor,* April 25, 1969.

79. Bundy interview; HAB, April 28, 1969.

80. Dunlop interview; Pusey interview.

81. Report of the Committee of Fifteen, Harvard University Archives.

82. Pusey interview.

83. Wyzanski interview.

84. HAB, July 1, 1969.

85. Bailey interview; Gordon interview; confidential source.

86. *New York Times,* October 8, 1969; "Harvard: Faculty Organized in Response to Crisis," *Science,* July 4, 1969.

87. "Bringing It All Back Home," HAB, May 4, 1970.

88. Dunlop interview; HAB, October 6, 1969. See also HAB, October 26, November 17, December 8, 1969.

89. Wacker interview; Dunlop interview; Beer interview; Ford interview.

90. HAB, June 14, 1971.

CHAPTER EIGHT
The Education of Derek Bok

1. Especially useful as background to the presidential search are two articles published in the *Harvard Alumni Bulletin:* Roger Rosenblatt, "The University in Suspension," April 13, 1970, and John T. Bethell, "Harvard, 1970: A New Awakening," January 5, 1970. The actual search process was described in numerous publications at the time, including the *Harvard Alumni Bulletin,* the *Harvard Crimson,* and others.

2. Bailey interview.

3. Galbraith interview.

4. Burr interview.

5. Interview with James Q. Wilson; Perkins interview.

6. Long before University Hall, Harvard had begun worrying about retaining its most promising faculty. See "Poor Harvard," *Newsweek,* June 10, 1968; and "Harvard Faculty: How Can You Keep 'Em After They've Seen California?" *Science,* May 31, 1968. The upshot of all this was a concerted drive to build new housing, boost salaries, and make junior positions more

attractive in terms of promotional opportunities, secretarial assistance, office space—all of which only added to the University's financial woes.

7. Burr interview; Nickerson interview.

8. Confidential source.

9. Rosenblatt left Harvard not long after, for a distinguished career with *Time* Magazine, and as an essayist on PBS's *MacNeil-Lehrer Report.*

10. Dillon interview; confidential source. One member of the Corporation stoutly denies that he or his colleagues were looking for a conciliator at all. If so, it suggests once again just how easy it is for those not privy to the body's inner councils to place their own interpretation on its thinking.

11. Al Larkin, "The Cautious Presidency of Derek Bok," *Boston Globe New England Magazine,* June 4, 1978.

12. "Flexible President of Harvard," *New York Times,* January 13, 1971.

13. *Ibid.; Harvard Law Review,* February 1, 1968.

14. Putnam interview; Bentinck-Smith interview. One of the first bits of advice offered Bok concerned Bentinck-Smith, and the wish many had to see him once and for all eliminated from the Harvard administration. In fact, he was given a position as a kind of writer-in-residence, from which to prepare several in-house historical publications, including an official updating of Morison's history. *New York Times,* January 13, 1971.

15. My account of Edward Bok's life and career comes from the Bok chapter contained in David Shi, *The Simple Life* (New York, 1984).

16. An excellent biographical profile of the new president is "The Compleat Bok," written with its subject's full cooperation by John T. Bethell, and appearing in the February 8, 1971, *Harvard Alumni Bulletin.* Also see Peter J. Howe, "Bok's Past—and Future," *Harvard Crimson,* November 18, 1984. As for Bok's meticulous attention to architectural and esthetic details, there are several sources, including Corporation member George Putnam, various *Crimson* pieces over the years, and more than one associate who prefers anonymity. Aside from denying the reported cost of his guardhouse project, Bok is understandably reluctant to discuss it in much detail.

17. Confidential sources.

18. "The Compleat Bok"; Bok File of press clippings, presidential reports, and transcripts of speeches in the Harvard University News Office (hereafter referred to as HBF).

19. Interview with Thomas Reardon.

20. Terry Anzar, "Derek C. Bok: A Stanford Man at Harvard," *Stanford Magazine,* undated, HBF.

21. "Compleat Bok"; HBF; confidential source.

22. "Compleat Bok." In fact, Bok and his family have maintained their privacy to a striking degree. By all accounts, the children are as unspoiled by public attention and as genuinely interested in public service as their parents.

23. Griswold interview.

24. Confidential source.

25. *Ibid.*

26. HBF; Larkin, "The Cautious Presidency."

27. Confidential source; Larkin; "Compleat Bok."

28. Confidential source.

29. Dunlop interview.

30. Confidential source.

31. Confidential source; interview with Derek Bok.

32. Confidential source.

33. Bok interview; Burr interview.

34. Dillon interview. Clifford Alexander was among the handful of those who did not acknowledge my written request for an interview.

35. Aloian interview.

36. Burr interview; Stendahl interview.

37. "New Leader's Vigor Calms Harvard," *New York Times,* November 29, 1971; interview with Robert Kiley; Gomes interview; confidential source.

38. Confidential sources.

39. Bok interview; "The Harvardization of Derek Bok," *Time,* January 18, 1971; "Harvard Picks a President," *Newsweek,* January 18, 1971.

40. Historian and former director of the Harvard library system Oscar Handlin has remarked that he would resolve the admission problem quite easily—by simply selling one hundred places in each freshman class to the highest bidder, and then permitting sex-blind admissions for the rest of the class.

41. Ten years later, Bok was still protesting that candid remarks of his were being misinterpreted, this time following his declaration that grades should be a factor in determining who received federal scholarship and other aid. Coming at a time of widespread cuts by the Reagan Administration, the president's remark was seized upon by critics as one more sign that he was trimming his sails and positioning Harvard to curry favor with Washington.

42. Burr interview; interview with Thomas Jefferson Coolidge; Nickerson interview.

43. Interview with Hale Champion.

44. Bok interview. The *Harvard Crimson* took special pleasure in reporting the president's trials and tribulations in staffing his administration.

45. In the same Commencement issue, the paper carried profiles of Bok's four vice-presidents, and of Daniel Steiner. In the course of researching a profile of the Bok administration for *The Real Paper* late in 1975, I had occasion to interview all but Steiner (whom I subsequently spoke with as part of researching this work). Those interviews, combined with fresh material derived from subsequent conversations with the colleagues and successors of the five, form the basis of my current assessment.

46. The Kennedy Library controversy was heavily covered in the Boston and New York papers, as well as the *Harvard Crimson*. At the JFK Library in Boston is a substantial file on the matter, which I also consulted.

47. Confidential source.

48. Confidential source.

49. Rick Smith, "Technocrat in the Pulpit," *The Real Paper*, January 21, 1976.

50. More than a few around Cambridge speculate that Leontief's decision to leave Harvard was not unrelated to the University's mandatory retirement age. The professor politely but firmly declined my request for an interview.

51. Bate interview; confidential source.

52. Interview with Daniel Steiner.

53. President's Report, 1970–71, Harvard University Archives.

54. Putnam interview.

55. Interview with Al Vellucci.

56. Homans interview; Burr interview.

57. Wyzanski interview.

58. "Stalking the Wild Derebok," *Harvard Independent,* May 14, 1974; Aloian interview.

59. Putnam interview.

60. Even Bok has not had to put up with quite the degree of journalistic irreverence as his immediate predecessor, whose churchgoing ways encouraged a streak of playful—or cruel—patronization. After Pusey made clear his opposition to a new building that threatened to overshadow his own carefully designed skyline, the editors of the *Crimson* promptly published a front page headline proclaiming, "Pusey Fights Erection in Harvard Square."

61. Confidential source; Nickerson interview.

62. Bok interview; Aloian interview.

63. Steiner interview; confidential source.

64. Interview with Tom O'Brian; confidential sources; Finley interview; Glimp interview; "Stalking the Wild Derebok."

65. Gomes interview.

66. Kiley interview.

67. Nickerson interview; Bok interview; Aloian interview.

68. Aloian interview; Kiley interview.

69. Bok interview.

70. Interview with Bruce Belfiore; Finley interview; Gomes interview; *New York Times,* April 23, 1985.

71. See Chapter Two, "Institutional Autonomy and the Demands of the State," in Bok's *Beyond the Ivory Tower: Social Responsibilities of the Modern University* (Cambridge, 1982).

72. The MAYTEP fracas has consumed a good many column inches in the *Harvard Crimson* and other papers over the years. For additional back-

ground, I am indebted to Mayor Kevin H. White and members of his administration, especially Lowell Richards.

73. Bok interview.

74. Confidential source.

75. Confidential source.

76. Herrnstein interview.

77. *Ibid.*

78. *Ibid.*

79. The *Harvard Crimson* provided extensive coverage of the Mass Hall takeover, in issues throughout mid and late April 1972. Bok's testy affirmation of his own authority has become something of a Harvard legend, repeated whenever the early days of his presidency are discussed.

80. *Harvard Crimson,* February 23, 1974. Much of my account of Bok's early years is taken from stories and interpretations carried in the *Crimson.* To list every issue consulted would result in a manuscript of unmanageable length.

CHAPTER NINE

In Search of Coherence

1. Unless otherwise noted, quotes from Bok's public remarks are taken from the Bok File kept in the University News Office (HBF).

2. See "Bok Blasts Aid Cuts in New Budget," *Harvard Crimson,* April 24, 1985. Along with his reluctance to speak out on issues peripheral to education went a personal distaste for journalistic invasion of his privacy. As Al Larkin reported in his *Globe* profile, "The Cautious Presidency of Derek Bok," Bok's home phone number was listed in the Boston directory, which didn't prevent the president from passing word on to news organizations of his displeasure when a reporter took advantage of the fact to call him up.

3. Bok interview.

4. "The University and the Public Beyond Its Walls," an interview with Derek Bok, *Kettering Review,* Winter 1985.

5. "Reflections on the Ethical Responsibilities of the University in Society: An Open Letter to the Harvard Community," Derek Bok, March 9, 1979 (hereafter Bok's open letters are referred to as OL).

6. The story of Fisher's aborted negotiation, as well as other Harvard contributions to the public-policy arena, is contained in the *Harvard Crimson*'s 1984 Commencement issue.

7. Horner interview.

8. Gomes interview.

9. Connie Page, "Alas, Poor Harvard," *New England Monthly,* May 1985, pp. 69–76. See also "Harvard Marches Uphill and Down Again," *Science,* December 5, 1980; *Harvard Crimson* 1981 Commencement issue;

"Harvard and Technology Transfer," *Washington Post,* June 28, 1982. The technology-transfer issue is also addressed in Bok, *Beyond the Ivory Tower,* Chapter Six; and "Academic Science and the Quest for Technological Innovation," *New York Times,* May 22, 1983.

10. Confidential source.

11. *Harvard Magazine,* July–August 1977.

12. President's Report, 1976–77, Harvard University Archives.

13. "The Harvard Campaign" (1978), a thick, very glossy promotional brochure issued in conjunction with the University's massive fund drive in the late Seventies, contains a useful historical time line, complete with most of Harvard's Nobel Prize–winners.

14. President's Report, 1974–75, Harvard University Archives.

15. *Harvard Magazine,* September–October 1983; Ford interview; confidential source.

16. One of the best biographical pieces on Rosovsky is "An Educated Person," *The New Yorker,* December 4, 1978.

17. Phyllis Keller, *Getting at the Core* (Cambridge, 1982), pp. 36–39.

18. Among the many articles that purport to describe the origins of Harvard's drive for curriculum reform, I benefited especially from Fred Hechinger, "Searching for the Ideal College Curriculum: Does Harvard Have the Answer?" *Today's Education,* November–December 1978; Peter Engel, "Harvard's Soft Core," *The Washington Monthly,* January 1980; and James Q. Wilson, "Harvard's Core Curriculum: A View from the Inside," *Change,* November 1978. Keller's book is invaluable, albeit clearly friendly to Rosovsky and the final product which he shepherded through the faculty.

19. "Five Ways to Wisdom," *Time,* September 27, 1982.

20. Wilson interview.

21. Keller, *Getting at the Core,* pp. 43–44.

22. *Ibid.,* p. 52.

23. Engel, "Harvard's Soft Core."

24. Heimert interview; Keller, *Getting at the Core,* pp. 70–74.

25. Goethels interview; confidential source.

26. In fact, says Rosovsky, it took him less than twenty-four hours to accept Bok's offer of the deanship, in large part because he knew the president, his priorities, and his personal methods of achieving them. Most of all, he knew how important curriculum reform was to Bok, and assumed it would be his own primary objective once in office.

27. HBF.

28. *Harvard Magazine,* May–June 1978, contains a full account of the faculty debate preceding adoption of Rosovsky's Core; Oettinger's memorable quote is contained in an essay on the nationalizing impact of education and politics, written by and graciously supplied to me by Professor Samuel Beer.

29. Engel, "Harvard's Soft Core."

30. *People Magazine,* September 25, 1978. Other articles at the time also stressed Rosovsky's arguments, including *Time,* March 27, 1978, and *Newsweek,* May 15, 1978.

31. Homans interview.

32. "An Educated Person," *The New Yorker.*

33. Bok interview.

34. *Ibid.*; confidential source.

35. Edward B. Fiske, "Wave of Curriculum Change Sweeping American Colleges," *New York Times,* March 10, 1985.

36. Bok interview.

37. Alumni Exercises, June 7, 1979, HBF.

38. "Learning to Lead," *Newsweek,* May 16, 1977; "Careers," *New York Times,* March 16, 1977.

39. Jonathan Alter, "Harvard Versus Democracy," *The Washington Monthly,* March 1983.

40. Michael Ryan, "Harvard on the Skids," *Boston Magazine,* December 1978.

41. Christopher Reed, "Harvard Dedicates a New School for Public Servants," *Harvard Magazine,* January–February 1979; Lansing Lamont, "The College Restored," *Harvard Magazine,* November–December 1979.

42. Kerr interview; Aloian interview.

43. Bok interview.

44. Reardon interview; HBF. Bok himself admitted to enjoying the fund-raising ritual more than he had expected, in part, no doubt, because he was good at it, in part because it afforded him a chance to come in contact with a wide range of people, fodder for a curious mind.

45. Confidential source.

46. For my account of the uproar over the business school, I have relied on the following: Thomas C. Hayes, "Harvard's Business School Is Scrutinized," *New York Times,* March 18, 1980; Larry Kramer, "Harvards Fight Fiercely Over the Business School," *Washington Post,* June 8, 1979; Walter Kiechel III, "Harvard Business School Restudies Itself," *Fortune,* June 1979; Susan Heller Anderson, "Business Dean Sets New Harvard Style," *New York Times,* October 6, 1980; Thomas C. Hayes, "A Vote for Harvard Business Method," *New York Times,* January 28, 1980; interviews with Albert H. Gordon, Winthrop Knowlton, and John Dunlop, and profiles of John Fouraker and John MacArthur in *MacLean's,* July 16, 1979, and May 12, 1980, respectively.

47. "Harvard Business School Shuns Change," *New York Times,* March 5, 1984.

48. For background on the Hiatt controversy, see Ryan, "Harvard on the Skids," and a lengthy review of the facts in the case compiled for release by the University News Office on August 24, 1978. In addition, I have had

conversations with individuals close to the case who, not surprisingly, wish to remain anonymous.

49. Dunlop interview; confidential source.

50. See the *Harvard Crimson* for May 3 and 4, 1984, as well as an in-depth profile of Duncan Kennedy in the same publication, "Radicalism and the Law," April 18, 1985.

51. *New York Times,* August 9, 11, 1982.

52. Confidential source; *The Chronicle of Higher Education,* June 2, 1982; Bok interview.

53. *Boston Globe,* February 24, 1980.

54. Bok OL, "Reflections on Academic Freedom," April 11, 1980.

55. *New York Times,* February 1, 1981; "For a Firm Foundation," *Harvard Crimson,* February 9, 1981; Gomes interview; Epps interview.

56. Bok OL, "On Issues of Race at Harvard," February 27, 1981.

57. Andrew Kopkind, "Living With the Bomb at Harvard," *The Nation,* June 4, 1983; "Bok Asks Five Experts for Nuclear Arms Study," *Harvard Crimson,* undated (HBF).

58. Robert Wood, "Steady As She Goes," *Harvard Magazine,* undated (HBF).

59. Derek Bok, "Statement to the Harvard Community," August 12, 1983.

60. Herrnstein interview.

61. Bok OL, "Reflections on Free Speech," September 21, 1984. It was not long after this Open Letter was released that one Bok intimate tried through third parties to persuade him to stop issuing what he called "those damned papal encyclicals." The president was not persuaded. As for Weinberger, he made it clear that he had no intention of staying away from his alma mater. "I suppose you can take it as the ultimate compliment," he told the *Harvard Crimson* seventeen months later, "that the great bulk of the [protesters] at Harvard were trying to prevent what was being said from being heard." His strongest epithet for those who tried to shout him down? "Immature."

62. HBF; confidential source.

63. *Washington Post,* June 11, 1984.

64. President's Report, 1982–83, Harvard University Archives.

65. Confidential source; "Easy-Going Bok Likes to Chat," *Boston Herald-American,* January 15, 1977; Bok interview; Dunlop interview.

66. Interview with John Baughman; Andrew S. Doctoroff, "Beyond the Mass Hall Mystique," *Harvard Crimson,* January 10, 1985.

67. Interview with Andrew W. Heiskell; Bok interview.

68. Interview with A. Michael Spence.

69. The debate over South Africa has been carried on in many forums, including the *Harvard Crimson, Harvard Magazine,* other publications, student discussions, and faculty debates. I have synthesized my own account

from all these, as well as from conversations with a number of participants in what remains an ongoing contest of ideas.

70. Bok OL, "Reflections on the Ethical Responsibilities of the University in Society," March 9, 1979.

71. *Harvard Crimson,* March 13, 1984; confidential source.

72. *Harvard Crimson,* April 4, 5, 1985.

73. *Harvard Crimson,* April 25, May 3, 1985.

74. *Harvard Crimson,* April 3, 1985; *Washington Post,* May 25, 1985.

75. *Harvard Crimson,* April 30, 1985.

76. *U.S. News & World Report,* February 24, 1983; see also Derek C. Bok, "Can Ethics Be Taught?" *Change,* undated.

77. Confidential source.

78. *Harvard Crimson,* 1981 Commencement issue.

Index